S0-BNC-069

Cambridge Studies in Criminology

Edited by
Alfred Blumstein, *H. John Heinz School of Public Policy and Management, Carnegie Mellon University*
David P. Farrington, *Institute of Criminology, University of Cambridge*

The Cambridge Studies in Criminology series aims to publish the highest quality research on criminology and criminal justice topics. Typical volumes report major quantitative, qualitative, and ethnographic research, or make a substantial theoretical contribution. There is a particular emphasis on research monographs, but edited collections may also be published if they make an unusually distinctive offering to the literature. All relevant areas of criminology and criminal justice are included; for example, the causes of offending, juvenile justice, the development of offenders, measurement and analysis of crime, victimization research, policing, crime prevention, sentencing, imprisonment, probation, and parole. The series is global in outlook, with an emphasis on work that is comparative or holds significant implications for theory or policy.

Other books in the series

Life in the Gang: Family, Friends, and Violence, by Scott H. Decker and Barrik Van Winkle
Delinquency and Crime: Current Theories, edited by J. David Hawkins
Recriminalizing Delinquency: Violent Juvenile Crime and Juvenile Justice Reform, by Simon I. Singer
Mean Streets: Youth Crime and Homelessness, by John Hagan and Bill McCarthy
The Framework of Judicial Sentencing: A Study in Legal Decision Making, by Austin Lovegrove
The Criminal Recidivism Process, by Edward Zamble and Vernon L. Quinsey
Violence and Childhood in the Inner City, by Joan McCord
Judicial Policy Making and the Modern State: How the Courts Reformed America's Prisons, by Malcolm M. Feeley and Edward L. Rubin
Schools and Delinquency, by Denise C. Gottfredson
The Crime Drop in America, edited by Alfred Blumstein and Joel Wallman
Delinquent-Prone Communities, by Don Weatherburn and Bronwyn Lind
White-Collar Crime and Criminal Careers, by David Weisburd and Elin Waring, with Ellen F. Chayet
Sex Differences in Antisocial Behaviour: Conduct Disorder, Delinquency, and Violence in the Dunedin Longitudinal Study, by Terrie Moffitt, Avshalom Caspi, Michael Rutter, and Phil A. Silva
Delinquent Networks: Youth Co-Offending in Stockholm, by Jerzy Sarnecki
Criminality and Violence among the Mentally Disordered: The Stockholm Metropolitan Project, by Sheilagh Hodgins and Carl-Gunnar Janson
Why Corporations Obey the Law: Assessing Criminalization and Cooperative Models of Crime Control, by Sally S. Simpson

Police Innovation

Over the last three decades American policing has gone through a period of significant change and innovation. In what is a relatively short historical time frame the police began to reconsider their fundamental mission, the nature of the core strategies of policing, and the character of their relationships with the communities that they serve. This volume brings together leading police scholars to examine eight major innovations which emerged during this period: community policing, broken windows policing, problem oriented policing, pulling levers policing, third party policing, hot spots policing, Compstat and evidence-based policing. Including advocates and critics of each of the eight police innovations, this comprehensive book assesses the evidence on impacts of police innovation on crime and public safety, the extent of the implementation of these new approaches in police departments, and the dilemmas these approaches have created for police management. This book will appeal to students, scholars and researchers.

DAVID WEISBURD is Walter E. Mayer Professor of Law and Criminal Justice at the Hebrew University Law School in Jerusalem, and Professor of Criminology and Criminal Justice at the University of Maryland, College Park. He is the author or editor of eleven books and more than sixty scientific articles that cover a wide range of criminal justice topics.

ANTHONY A. BRAGA is Senior Research Associate in the Program in Criminal Justice Policy and Management at Harvard University's John F. Kennedy School of Government. His research focuses on working with criminal justice agencies to develop crime prevention strategies to deal with gang violence, illegal firearms markets, and violent crime hot spots.

Police Innovation
Contrasting Perspectives

Edited by

David Weisburd and Anthony A. Braga

CAMBRIDGE
UNIVERSITY PRESS

CAMBRIDGE UNIVERSITY PRESS
Cambridge, New York, Melbourne, Madrid, Cape Town, Singapore, São Paulo

Cambridge University Press
The Edinburgh Building, Cambridge CB2 2RU, UK

Published in the United States of America by Cambridge University Press, New York

www.cambridge.org
Information on this title: www.cambridge.org/9780521544832

© Cambridge University Press 2006

This book is in copyright. Subject to statutory exception
and to the provisions of relevant collective licensing agreements,
no reproduction of any part may take place without
the written permission of Cambridge University Press.

First published 2006

Printed in the United Kingdom at the University Press, Cambridge

A catalogue record for this book is available from the British Library

ISBN-13 978-0-521-83628-9 hardback
ISBN-10 0-521-83628-X hardback

ISBN-13 978-0-521-54483-2 paperback
ISBN-10 0-521-54483-1 paperback

Cambridge University Press has no responsibility for the persistence or accuracy of
URLs for external or third-party internet websites referred to in this book, and does not
guarantee that any content on such websites is, or will remain, accurate or appropriate.

David Weisburd: For Ariel Yehuda, who achieves whatever he sets his mind to, yet always finds time for the needs of others.

Anthony A. Braga: To Cassie, my friend and companion

Contents

Figures

Tables

Notes on contributors

ANTHONY A. BRAGA is Senior Research Associate in the Program in Criminal Justice Policy and Management of the Malcolm Wiener Center for Social Policy at Harvard University's John F. Kennedy School of Government. He received his MPA from Harvard University and Ph.D. in Criminal Justice from Rutgers University. His research focuses on working with criminal justice agencies to develop crime prevention strategies to deal with urban problems such as firearms violence, street-level drug markets, and violent crime hot spots. He has served as a consultant on these issues to the Rand Corporation; National Academy of Sciences; US Department of Justice; US Department of the Treasury; Bureau of Alcohol, Tobacco, and Firearms; Boston Police Department; New York Police Department; and other state and local law enforcement agencies.

JOHN ECK is a Professor in the Division of Criminal Justice at the University of Cincinnati where he teaches graduate courses on research methods, police effectiveness, crime prevention, and criminal justice policy. Dr. Eck is internationally known for his studies on problem-oriented policing, the prevention of crime at places, the analysis and mapping of crime hot spots, drug dealing and trafficking control, and criminal investigations. He was a member of the National Academy of Sciences Committee on Police Policy and Research, and a former Director of Research for the Police Executive Research Forum, where he helped pioneer the development and testing of problem-oriented policing. Dr. Eck is an Individual Affiliate of the Center for Problem-Oriented Policing and a judge for the British Home Office's Tilley Award for Excellence in Problem Solving. He earned his Ph.D. in criminology from the University of Maryland and his bachelors and masters degrees from the University of Michigan.

GEORGE L. KELLING, Ph.D., is a professor in the School of Criminal Justice, Rutgers University, Newark, faculty chair of the Police Institute at Rutgers University, Newark, and a Senior Fellow at the Manhattan

Institute. In 1972, he began work at the Police Foundation and conducted several large-scale experiments in policing, most notably the Kansas City Preventive Patrol Experiment and the Newark Foot Patrol Experiment. The latter was the source of his contribution to his most familiar publication in the *Atlantic*, "Broken Windows," with James Q. Wilson. During the late 1980s, Dr. Kelling developed the order maintenance policies in the New York City subway that ultimately led to radical crime reductions. His areas of special interest are the police, the relationships among fear, crime, and disorder, community crime control, and the evolution of policing strategies and tactics. He consults with numerous major police departments in the United States, along with Australian, British, and Canadian police departments and oversight agencies.

DAVID M. KENNEDY joined the faculty of the John Jay College of Criminal Justice at the beginning of 2005. From 1991 to 2004, he was a senior researcher at the Program in Criminal Justice Policy and Management, Kennedy School of Government, Harvard University. He has written and consulted extensively in the areas of community and problem-solving policing, police corruption, and neighborhood revitalization. He has performed field work in police departments and troubled communities in many American cities, London, Sydney, and Puerto Rico. He is the co-author of a seminal work on community policing, *Beyond 911: A New Era for Policing*, and numerous articles on police management, illicit drug markets, illicit firearms markets, youth violence, and deterrence theory, including editorials in the *New York Times*, *Washington Post*, and elsewhere. He has advised the Justice Department, the Department of the Treasury, the Bureau of Alcohol, Tobacco, and Firearms, the Office of National Drug Control Policy, and the White House on these issues.

STEPHEN D. MASTROFSKI is Professor of Public and International Affairs at George Mason University, where he directs the Administration of Justice Program and the Center for Justice Leadership and Management. Research interests include measuring police performance and assessing police reforms. He has received the Academy of Criminal Justice Science's O. W. Wilson Award for outstanding contributions to police education, research, and practice.

LORRAINE MAZEROLLE is an Associate Professor in the Department of Criminology and Criminal Justice at Griffith University. She received her Ph.D. from Rutgers University, New Jersey in 1993 and spent an additional seven years as an academic in the USA (at Northeastern

University and the University of Cincinnati). She is the recipient of numerous US and Australian research grants on topics such as problem-oriented policing, police technologies (e.g., crime mapping, gunshot detection systems, 3-1-1 call systems), community crime control, civil remedies, street-level drug enforcement, and policing public housing sites. In 2003, Associate Professor Mazerolle was admitted as a member to the Academy of Experimental Criminologists and now serves as the Vice President of the Academy. She also serves on the Board of Studies for the Australian Institute for Police Management, on the Capital Cities Lord Mayors Drug Advisory Board and as an Associate Editor of the *Journal of Experimental Criminology*. Associate Professor Mazerolle is the author of *Policing Places with Drug Problems* and a co-editor, with Jan Roehl, of *Civil Remedies and Crime Prevention*. She has written many scholarly articles on policing, drug law enforcement, displacement of crime, and crime prevention.

TRACEY MEARES is Max Pam Professor of Law and Director, Center for Studies in Criminal Justice at the University of Chicago. She received her B.S. in General Engineering from the University of Illinois, and her J.D. from the University of Chicago Law School. She joined the University of Chicago faculty in 1994 after serving as an Honors Program Trial Attorney in the Antitrust Division of the United States Department of Justice. Prior to serving as a Department of Justice prosecutor, Ms. Meares clerked for Judge Harlington Wood, Jr. of the US Court of Appeals for the Seventh Circuit. Ms Meares's teaching and research interests center on criminal procedure and criminal law policy, with a particular emphasis on empirical investigation of these subjects. In addition to teaching at the Law School, Ms Meares has an appointment as a Research Fellow at the American Bar Foundation. She is also a faculty member of the University of Chicago Center for the Study of Race, Politics, and Culture and an executive committee member of the Northwestern/University of Chicago Joint Center for Poverty Research.

MARK H. MOORE is the Guggenheim Professor of Criminal Justice Policy and Management at Harvard's Kennedy School of Government. He has written extensively in the fields of criminal justice, public management, and the voluntary sector. In the field of policing, his significant publications include *Beyond 911: A New Era for Policing?*, *Recognizing Value in Public Policing: The Challenge of Measuring Police Performance*, *What Citizens Should Value (and Measure!) in Police Department Performance*. He was also one of the principal authors of the Urban

Institute's evaluation of the Federal Government's COPS Program responsible for the section of the report that used detailed case studies of twelve different police agencies to determine whether and how the grants they received from the COPS program helped them make the transition to a new strategy of policing. He was also a member of the National Academy of Sciences Panel on Policing that produced the report entitled: *Fairness and Effectiveness in Policing*.

JANET RANSLEY is a Senior Lecturer in the School of Criminology and Criminal Justice, Griffith University. Her areas of interest include policing and governance, white-collar crime, forensic mental health, and commissions of inquiry. Recent publications include: *Third Party Policing*, Cambridge University Press, forthcoming; and "Miscarriages of Justice" in T. Prenzler and J. Ransley (eds.) *Police Reform: Building Integrity* (2002). She is currently researching a book on government inquiries, and a project on counter-terrorist policing.

DENNIS P. ROSENBAUM is Professor of Criminal Justice and Director of the Center for Research in Law and Justice at the University of Illinois at Chicago. Previously, he served as Director of Graduate Studies, Department Head, and Dean. His primary areas of interest include the evaluation of police, community, school, and multiagency initiatives to prevent crime and delinquency. In the absence of a real hobby, he is working with the Chicago Police Department to develop geo-based Internet surveys that will "measure what matters" to community residents with respect to neighborhood problems, police performance, community performance, police–community relations, and related topics. He has written various books and articles on community crime prevention and community policing, and teaches graduate courses in policing, research methods, program evaluation, and community processes.

ELI B. SILVERMAN, Ph.D., is Professor Emeritus at John Jay College of Criminal Justice and the Graduate Center of City University of New York. He has previously served with the US Department of Justice and the National Academy of Public Administration in Washington, DC and was a Visiting Exchange Professor at the Police Staff College in Bramshill, England. He has served as an expert witness, consultant to, and trainer with numerous criminal justice agencies. His areas of interest include: community policing, crime analysis and information systems, police management, training, operations, use of force, integrity control, comparative policing, policy analysis,

Compstat, and crime mapping. His recent publications include: "Compstat" in *Encyclopedia of Law Enforcement* (2005); "Policing a Diverse Community: A Case Study," in *Policing and Minority Communities*, Dolores Jones-Brown and Karen Terry (eds.) (2003); "Zero Tolerance," in *Encyclopedia of Crime and Punishment*, David Levinson, (ed.) (2002).

WESLEY G. SKOGAN is Professor of Political Science and a member of the research faculty at the University's Institute for Policy Research. His research focuses on public encounters with the institutions of justice, including the police, crime prevention projects, and community-oriented policing. His most recent books on policing are *Community Policing: Can it Work?* (2004), *On the Beat: Police and Community Problem Solving* (1999) and *Community Policing, Chicago Style* (1997). Professor Skogan chaired the National Research Council's Committee to Review Research on Police Policy and Practices. The Committee's report, *Fairness and Effectiveness in Policing: The Evidence*, was published in 2004.

WILLIAM H. SOUSA is an Assistant Professor in the Department of Criminal Justice at the University of Nevada Las Vegas. He received his Ph.D. from Rutgers University (2003) and his M.S. in Criminal Justice from Northeastern University (1995). From 2000 to 2004, he was the Director of Evaluation for the Police Institute at Rutgers-Newark where he participated in studies related to violence and disorder in New Jersey neighborhoods. His current research projects involve police order-maintenance practices, police management, and community crime prevention.

RALPH TAYLOR received his Ph.D. in social psychology at Johns Hopkins University in 1977. He has previously held positions at Virginia Tech (1977–1979), and Johns Hopkins University (1978–1985). He was a Visiting fellow at the National Institute of Justice in 1997. He currently teaches and researches in the Department of Criminal Justice at Temple University where he has been since 1984. He served as department chair from July 2000 through July 2004. He edited *Urban Neighborhoods* (1986) and authored *Human Territorial Functioning* (1988), *Research Methods in Criminal Justice* (1994) and *Breaking Away from Broken Windows* (2000). His most recent refereed publications include Robinson, Lawton, Taylor, and Perkins (2003), "Multilevel Longitudinal Impacts of Incivilities"; Taylor, Anderson, and McConnell (2003), "Competencies and interest in a problem-focused undergraduate research methods criminal justice course"; and Taylor (2002), "Fear of crime, local social ties, and collective efficacy: Maybe masquerading measurement, maybe déjà vu all over again." His research has been funded by the National Science Foundation, the National Institute of Mental Health, the National Institute of Justice, and the National Institute of Corrections.

DAVID WEISBURD is the Walter E. Meyer Professor of Law and Criminal Justice at the Hebrew University Law School in Jerusalem and Professor of Criminology and Criminal Justice at the University of Maryland, College Park. Professor Weisburd also serves as a Senior Fellow at the Police Foundation, and Chair of its Research Advisory Committee. He was a member of the National Research Council working group on Evaluating Anti-Crime Programs and its panel on Police Practices and Policies. Professor Weisburd is author or editor of 11 books and more than 60 scientific articles, and is founding editor of the *Journal of Experimental Criminology*. He received his Ph.D. from Yale University.

BRANDON C. WELSH, Ph.D., is an Associate Professor in the Department of Criminal Justice, University of Massachusetts Lowell. His research interests include the prevention of delinquency and crime and economic analysis of prevention programs. Funded research has included studies on the monetary costs of juvenile offending in urban areas and the role of public health in the prevention of juvenile criminal violence. Dr. Welsh is an author or editor of six works, including *Evidence-Based Crime Prevention* (2002, with Lawrence Sherman, David Farrington, and Doris MacKenzie). Recent articles have appeared in *Criminology & Public Policy, Justice Quarterly, Crime and Justice: A Review of Research*, and *Annals of the American Academy of Political and Social Science*. He was a member of OJJDP's Study Group on Very Young Offenders and a contributing author to its volume, and has been a consultant to the United Nations Office on Drugs and Crime and the British Home Office.

CHRISTOPHER WINSHIP is the Norman Tishman and Charles M. Diker Professor of Sociology in the Faculty of Arts and Sciences and a Fellow of the Hauser Center for Nonprofit Organizations. Prior to coming to Harvard in 1992, he was Professor of Sociology, Statistics, and Economics at Northwestern University and a senior faculty research associate in the Institute for Policy Research there. He is the author of a variety of articles on various statistical issues – the analysis of qualitative dependent variables, selection bias, and counterfactual causal analysis. His research has also focused on changes in the social and economic status of African-Americans during the twentieth century. In particular, he has examined changes in youth unemployment, marital behavior, and prison incarceration. For the past eight years he has been working with and studying a group of black inner city ministers known as the Ten Point Coalition. He holds a Ph.D. in Sociology from Harvard.

1 Introduction: understanding police innovation

David Weisburd and Anthony A. Braga

Introduction

Over the last three decades American policing has gone through a period of significant change and innovation. In what is a relatively short historical time frame the police began to reconsider their fundamental mission, the nature of the core strategies of policing, and the character of their relationships with the communities that they serve. Innovations in policing in this period were not insular and restricted to police professionals and scholars, but were often seen on the front pages of America's newspapers and magazines, and spoken about in the electronic media. Some approaches, like broken windows policing – termed by some as zero tolerance policing – became the subject of heated political debate. Community policing, one of the most important police programs that emerged in this period, was even to give its name to a large federal agency – The Office of Community Oriented Policing Services – created by the Violent Crime Control and Law Enforcement Act of 1994.

Some have described this period of change as the most dramatic in the history of policing (e.g., see Bayley 1994). This claim does not perhaps do justice to the radical reforms that led to the creation of modern police forces in the nineteenth century, or even the wide-scale innovations in tactics or approaches to policing that emerged after the Second World War. However, observers of the police today are inevitably struck by the pace and variety of innovation in the last few decades. Whether this period of change is greater than those of previous generations is difficult to know since systematic observation of police practices is a relatively modern phenomenon. But there is broad consensus among police scholars that the last three decades have "witnessed a remarkable degree of innovation in policing" (Committee to Review Research 2004: 82).

In this volume we bring together leading police scholars to examine the major innovations in policing that emerged during the last decades of the twentieth century. We focus on eight innovations that are concerned with change in police strategies and practices: community policing,

1

broken windows policing, problem-oriented policing, pulling levers policing, third-party policing, hot spots policing, Compstat and evidence-
based policing. This is of course not an exhaustive list of innovation in
policing during this period. For example, we do not examine technological innovations such as advances in computerized crime mapping or the
use of DNA in criminal investigations. We also do not examine innovations in tactics and strategies that affected only specialized units or were
applied to very specific types of crimes. Our approach was to identify
innovations that had influence on the broad array of police tasks and on
the practices and strategies that broadly affected the policing of American
communities.

We title the chapters examining each police innovation reviewed in this
volume under the heading "Advocate" and "Critic." In this context our
book seeks to clarify police innovation in the context of chapters written by those who have played important roles in developing innovation,
and those who have stood as critics of such innovation. Nonetheless, we
do not take a debate format in our book. Authors did not respond to
each other's papers, but rather sought to present a perspective that would
clarify the benefits of the innovation examined, or the potential problems
that the innovation raises for policing. The critics often identify promising
elements of innovation while pointing out the difficulties that have been
encountered in the applications of innovation in the field. The advocates
often note the drawbacks of particular strategies, while arguing that they
should be widely adopted. Accordingly, our chapters represent serious
scholarly examination of innovations in policing, recognizing that established scholars may disagree about the directions that policing should
take while drawing from the same empirical evidence.

By design the essays in this volume take a "micro" approach to the problem of police innovation, focusing on the specific components, goals, and
outcomes associated with a specific program or practice. In this introductory chapter, we would like to take a "macro" approach to the problem
of police innovation that allows us to see how innovation more generally emerged and developed during this period. We do not think that the
dramatic surge in police innovation of the last few decades occurred as a
matter of chance. Our approach is to see the development of innovation
in policing as a response to a common set of problems and dilemmas.
This approach can also help us to understand the broad trends of police
innovation that we observe.

Understanding innovation and policing

Many scholars seem to take for granted what strikes us as a central
problem in understanding the broader phenomenon that our volume

examines. Why did we observe a period of significant innovation in policing in the last decades of the twentieth century? One simple answer to
this question would be to note that institutions change, and that when
faced with new ideas that have potential to improve their functioning
they will naturally choose what is innovative. However, those who have
studied the diffusion of innovation have been led to a very different view
of the processes that underlie the adoption of new products, programs,
or practices. Everett Rogers, who pioneered the scientific study of diffusion of innovation, argues, for example, that "more than just a beneficial
innovation is necessary" to explain its widespread diffusion and adoption
(1995: 8). Indeed, there are many examples of innovations that represent
clear improvements over prior practice, yet fail to be widely adopted.

Rogers brings the example of the "Dvorak Keyboard" named after
a University of Washington researcher, who sought to improve on
the "Qwerty" keyboard in use since the late nineteenth century. The
"Qwerty" keyboard was engineered to slow down typists in the nineteenth century in order to prevent jamming of keys that was common
in the manual typewriters in that period. However, as the engineering
of typewriters improved in the twentieth century, there was no longer a
need for a keyboard engineered to slow typists down. Indeed, it seemed
natural that a better arrangement of the keyboard would be developed
that would allow for quicker typing that would cause less fatigue. Dvorak
developed such a keyboard in 1932 basing his arrangement of the keys on
time and motion studies. Dvorak's keyboard was clearly an improvement
on the Qwerty keyboard. It allowed for more efficient and faster typing,
and led to less fatigue on the part of typists. But today more than seventy
years after Dvorak's development of a better and more efficient keyboard,
the Qwerty keyboard remains the dominant method. Indeed, Dvorak's
keyboard is merely an interesting historical curiosity.

The diffusion of innovation requires that there be a "perceived need"
for change in the social system in which an innovation emerges (Rogers
1995: 11). That need can be created by industries or interest groups, for
example through advertisements that lead consumers to believe that they
must have a particular new product or service. Often in social systems,
the recognition that something must change is brought about by a period
of crisis or challenge to existing programs or practices (see e.g., Rogers
1995; Altschuler and Behn 1997). In this context, we think that the key to
understanding the emergence of a period of rapid innovation in policing
in the last decades of the twentieth century lies in a crisis in policing that
emerged in the late 1960s. Identifying that period of crisis can help us
to understand not only why we observe so much police innovation in
recent decades, but also why that innovation follows particular patterns
of change.

The crisis of confidence in American policing

The decade of the 1970s began with a host of challenges to the police as well as the criminal justice system more generally (LaFree 1998). This was the case in part because of the tremendous social unrest that characterized the end of the previous decade. Race riots in American cities, and growing opposition, especially among younger Americans, to the Vietnam War, often placed the police in conflict with the young and with minorities. But American fears of a failing criminal justice system were also to play a role in a growing sense of crisis for American policing. In 1967, a presidential commission report on the Challenge of Crime in a Free Society reinforced doubts about the effectiveness of criminal justice in combating crime in the United States:

In sum, America's system of criminal justice is overcrowded and overworked, undermanned, underfinanced, and very often misunderstood. It needs more information and more knowledge. It needs more technical resources. It needs more coordination among its many parts. It needs more public support. It needs the help of community programs and institutions in dealing with offenders and potential offenders. It needs, above all, the willingness to reexamine old ways of doing things, to reform itself, to experiment, to run risks, to dare. It needs vision. (President's Commission 1967, 80–81)

Shortly after the presidential report on the Challenge of Crime in a Free Society, the Kerner Commission on Civil Disorders published a report which was also to raise significant questions about the nature of criminal justice in the United States, and the organization of American policing. However, in this case it was the question of race and the relationship between police and minority communities that was to have center stage. The challenges to patterns of American discrimination against African Americans were not focused primarily on the police, but the police, in addition to other criminal justice agencies, were seen as "part of the problem" and not necessarily working to help in producing a solution to difficult social issues:

In Newark, Detroit, Watts and Harlem, in practically every city that has experienced racial disruption since the summer of 1964, abrasive relationships between police and Negroes and other minority groups have been a major source of grievance, tension and ultimately disorder. (Kerner Commission 1968: 157)

The concerns of the commission reports in the 1960s and the sense of growing alienation between the police and the public in the latter half of that decade led policymakers, the police, and scholars to question the nature of American policing, and in particular the strategies that were dominant in policing since World War II. A recent National Research Council Committee to Review Research on Police Policy and Practices has termed these approaches as the "standard model of policing" (Committee to Review Research 2004; see also Weisburd and Eck 2004):

This model relies generally on a "one size fits all" application of reactive strategies to suppress crime, and continues to be the dominant form of police practices in the United States. The standard model is based on the assumption that generic strategies for crime reduction can be applied throughout a jurisdiction regardless of the level of crime, the nature of crime, or other variations. Such strategies as increasing the size of police agencies, random patrol across all parts of the community, rapid response to calls for service, generally applied follow-up investigations, and generally applied intensive enforcement and arrest policies are all examples of this standard model of policing. (Weisburd and Eck 2004: 44)

A number of important questions about the standard model of policing had been raised in the 1960s. Nonetheless, there was little serious academic inquiry into the impact of policing strategies on crime or on public attitudes. The need for such research was apparent, and in the 1970s serious research attention was to begin. One important impetus for such studies of the police came from the federal government. With the Omnibus Crime Control and Safe Streets Act of 1968 a research arm of the Department of Justice was established, eventually to become the National Institute of Justice, which was to invest significant resources in research on police and other components of the criminal justice system. But important funding for research on policing was also to come from private foundations. Perhaps the most important contribution to policing was made by the Ford Foundation in 1970 when it established the Police Development Fund. The Fund and the Police Foundation which it established, was to foster a series of large-scale studies on American policing. McGeorge Bundy, then president of the Ford Foundation, argued in announcing the establishment of a Police Development Fund in 1970:

The need for reinforcement and change in police work has become more urgent than ever in the last decade because of rising rates of crime, increased resort to violence and rising tension, in many communities, between disaffected or angry groups and the police. (Bundy 1970)

With the establishment of the Police Foundation and the newly established federal support for research on the criminal justice system, the activities of the police began to come under systematic scrutiny by researchers. Until this time, there had been a general assumption that policing in the post-World War II era represented an important advance over previous decades and was effective in controlling crime.

For example, perhaps the dominant policing strategy in the post-World War II period was routine preventive patrol in police cars. It was drawn from a long history of faith in the idea of "police patrol" that had become a standard dogma of policing for generations. As George Kelling and his colleagues wrote in their introduction to the Kansas City Preventive Patrol Experiment, a study conducted by the Police Foundation:

Ever since the creation of a patrolling force in 13th century Hangchow, preventive patrol by uniformed personnel has been a primary function of policing. In 20th century America, about $2 billion is spent each year for the maintenance and operation of uniformed and often superbly equipped patrol forces. Police themselves, the general public, and elected officials have always believed that the presence or potential presence of police offices on patrol severely inhibits criminal activity. (Kelling, Pate, Dieckman, and Brown 1974: 1)

Preventive patrol in police cars was the main staple of police crime prevention efforts at the beginning of the decade of the 1970s. As Kelling and colleagues noted in the Police Foundation report on the Kansas City study, "(t)oday's police recruits, like virtually all those before them, learn from both teacher and textbook that patrol is the 'backbone' of police work" (Kelling *et al.* 1974: 1). The Police Foundation study sought to establish whether empirical evidence actually supported the broadly accepted assumptions regarding preventive patrol. The fact that questions were raised about routine preventive patrol suggests that the concerns about the police voiced in the decade before had begun to impact the confidence of police managers. As Kansas City Police Chief Clarence M. Kelley, later to become director of the Federal Bureau of Investigation (FBI), said in explaining the need for the Kansas City experiment: "Many of us in the department had the feeling we were training, equipping, and deploying men to do a job neither we, nor anyone else, knew much about" (Murphy 1974: v).

To understand the impact of the Kansas City study on police managers and researchers, it is important to recognize not only that the study examined a core police practice but that its methodological approach represented a radical departure from the small-scale evaluations of police practices that had come earlier. The Kansas City Preventive Patrol Experiment was a social experiment in policing on a grand scale, and it was conducted in a new Foundation that had significant resources and was backed by the well-established and respected Ford Foundation. Patrick Murphy, the distinguished police manager, and president of the Police Foundation at the time, suggests just how much the Foundation itself saw the experiment as a radical and important change in the quality of police research.[1]

This is a summary report of the findings of an experiment in policing that ranks among the few major social experiments ever to be completed. The experiment was unique in that never before had there been an attempt to determine through such extensive scientific evaluation the value of visible police patrol. (Murphy 1974: v)

This context, both in terms of the centrality of the strategy examined, the scale of the research, and the prestige of the institutions that supported the study, including the Kansas City Police Department and its chief, Clarence Kelley, were to give the findings of the study an impact that is in retrospect out of proportion to the actual findings. One study in one jurisdiction, no matter how systematic, cannot provide a comprehensive portrait of the effects of a strategy as broad as routine preventive patrol. Moreover, the study design was to come under significant academic criticism in later years (Minneapolis Medical Research Foundation 1976; Larson and Cahn 1985; Sherman and Weisburd 1995). Nonetheless, in the context of the decade in which it was conducted, this study was to have a critical impact upon the police and police researchers. This was especially the case since the research findings were to be consistent with a series of other studies of core police practices.

Kelling and his colleagues, in cooperation with the Kansas City Police Department, took fifteen police beats and divided them up into three groups. In five of these, called "reactive" beats, "routine preventive patrol was eliminated and officers were instructed to respond only to calls for service" (Kelling et al. 1974: 3). In five others, defined as "control" beats, "routine preventive patrol was maintained at its usual level of one car per beat" (ibid.: 3). In the remaining five beats, termed "proactive" beats, "routine preventive patrol was intensified by two to three times its usual level through the assignment of additional patrol cars" (Kelling et al. 1974: 3). When Kelling and his colleagues published the results of their study in 1974 it shattered one of the bedrock assumptions of police practitioners – that preventive patrol was an effective way to prevent crime and increase citizens' feelings of safety. They concluded simply that increasing or decreasing the intensity of routine preventive patrol in police cars did not affect either crime, service delivery to citizens, or citizens' feelings of security.

Another large-scale study conducted by William Spelman and Dale Brown and published in 1984 was also to challenge a core police assumption of that period – that improvement in rapid response to calls for service would lead to improvements in crime fighting. This study was developed in good part because of the findings of a prior investigation in Kansas City that found little support for the crime control effectiveness of rapid response to calls for service (Kansas City Police Department 1977).

With support from the National Institute of Justice, Spelman and Brown interviewed 4000 victims, witnesses, and bystanders in some 3300 serious crimes in four American cities. This was another major study in terms of the resources brought to bear and the methods used. Again it examined a strategy that was aided by technological advances in the twentieth century and that was a central dogma of police administrators – that police must get to the scene of a crime quickly if they are to apprehend criminal offenders. Spelman and Brown explained:

> For at least half a century, police have considered it important to cut to a minimum their response times to crime calls. The faster the response, they have reasoned, the better the chances of catching a criminal at or near the scene of the crime. (Spelman and Brown 1984: xxi)

Based on the data they collected, however, Spelman and Brown provided a very different portrait of the crime control effectiveness of rapid response to calls for service:

> Rapid police response may be unnecessary for three out of every four serious crimes reported to police. The traditional practice of immediate response to all reports of serious crimes currently leads to on-scene arrests in only 29 of every 1,000 cases. By implementing innovative programs, police may be able to increase this response-related arrest rate to 50 or even 60 per 1000, but there is little hope that further increases can be generated. (Spelman and Brown 1984: xix)

These findings based on a host of systematic data sources from multiple jurisdictions provided little support for the strategy of rapid response as a police practice to do something about crime. Indeed, Spelman and Brown found that citizen reporting time, not police response time, most influenced the possibility of on-scene arrest. Marginal improvement in police response times was predicted to have no real impact on the apprehension or arrest of offenders.

The Kansas City Preventive Patrol Experiment and the National Institute of Justice study of police response time were not the only studies to "debunk" existing police practices. James Levine, for example, analyzed national crime data on the effectiveness of increasing the number of police in an article published in 1975. His title sums up his findings: "The Ineffectiveness of Adding Police to Prevent Crime." Despite the fact that this effort and many others that challenged conventional police practices did not represent the kind of systematic data collection or analysis of the Police Foundation and National Institute of Justice studies, they followed a similar "narrative" which became increasingly common as the 1990s approached. Levine, for example, begins by noting the broad consensus for the principle that adding more police will make cities safer. He then goes on to note that "(s)ensible as intensified policing may sound on the surface, its effectiveness in combating crime has yet to be demonstrated" (Levine 1975: 523). Finally, drawing upon simple tabular data on police strength and crime rates over time, he concludes:

It is tempting for politicians and government leaders to add more police: it is an intuitively sensible and symbolically satisfying solution to the unrelenting problem of criminal violence . . . The sad fact is, however, that they receive a false sense of security; in most situations they are just as vulnerable with these extra police as without them. (Levine 1975: 544)

Follow-up investigations were also the subject of critical empirical research during this period. The standard model of policing had assumed that general improvements in methods of police investigations would lead to crime control gains both because more active offenders would be imprisoned and thus unable to commit crime, and because potential offenders would be deterred by the prospect of discovery and arrest (Committee to Review Research 2004). But a series of studies in the 1970s and early 1980s suggested that investigations had little impact upon crime (Greenwood *et al.* 1975; Greenwood, Petersilia, and Chaiken 1977; Skogan and Antunes 1979; Eck 1983). This was the case in good part because many crimes, especially property crimes, were found to be unlikely to be solved by police investigations. These studies consistently showed that if citizens did not provide information about suspects to first responding officers, follow-up investigations were unlikely to lead to successful outcomes.

In retrospect, many of these studies overstated what could be learned about standard police practices from the findings gained (Weisburd and Eck 2004). And, in practice, there were evaluations in this period that produced more promising findings regarding standard police practices such as routine preventive patrol (e.g., see Press 1971; Schnelle, Kirchner *et al.* 1977; Chaiken 1978). Nonetheless, as the United States entered the decade of the 1990s there appeared to be a general consensus that traditional police practices did not work in preventing or controlling crime. As Michael Gottfredson and Travis Hirschi wrote in their classic book *A General Theory of Crime* in 1990: "No evidence exists that augmentation of patrol forces or equipment, differential patrol strategies, or differential intensities of surveillance have an effect on crime rates" (Gottfredson and Hirschi 1990: 270).

David Bayley wrote even more strongly in 1994:

The police do not prevent crime. This is one of the best kept secrets of modern life. Experts know it, the police know it, but the public does not know it. Yet the police pretend that they are society's best defense against crime . . . This

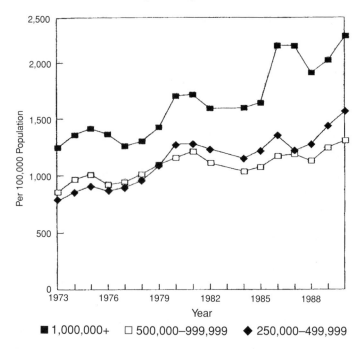

Figure 1.1 Total violent crime (trends in violent crime rates by city size)
Source: Reiss and Roth, 1993

is a myth. First, repeated analysis has consistently failed to find any connection between the number of police officers and crime rates. Secondly, the primary strategies adopted by modern police have been shown to have little or no effect on crime. (Bayley 1994: 3)

This view of the ineffectiveness of policing strategies was reinforced by official crime statistics. These statistics, widely available to the public, suggested that the police were losing the "war on crime." In particular, in America's largest cities, with their well-established professional police forces, crime rates and especially violent crime rates were rising at alarming rates. Between 1973 and 1990 violent crime doubled (Reiss and Roth 1993). It did not take a statistician to understand that the trends were dramatic. For example, in Figure 1.1 we report the trends in violent crime rates by city size per 100,000 population. Clearly crime was on the rise, and the trend had been fairly consistent over a long period. Thus, not only were scholars showing that police strategies did little to impact upon crime, but the overall crime statistics commonly used by the government and community to define police effectiveness were providing a similar message.

Crisis and change in American policing

It is against this backdrop that the innovations that we examine in this volume develop. Our view is that the challenges to police effectiveness, rising crime rates, and concerns about the legitimacy of police actions that developed in the late 1960s created a perceived need for change in what some have described as the industry of American policing (Ostrom, Whitaker, and Parks 1978; Committee to Review Research 2004). Unfortunately, there is no hard empirical evidence that would allow us to make this link directly, since the study of the adoption of innovation has only recently become a subject of interest for police scholars (e.g., see Weiss 1997; Klinger 2003; Weisburd, Mastrofski, McNally et al. 2003). Accordingly, there have been few systematic studies of these processes and scholars were generally not concerned about the emergence of innovation as a research problem when these innovations were being developed.

Nonetheless, we think it reasonable to make a connection between the perceived failures of the standard model of American police practices and the experimentation with innovation, and openness to the adoption of innovation that occurred in the last decades of the twentieth century. Certainly, such a link is made by many of those who fostered innovation in policing. For example, in his proposal for a problem-oriented policing in 1979, Herman Goldstein referred directly to the growing evidence of the failures of traditional police practices:

Recently completed research questions the value of two major aspects of police operations – preventive patrol and investigations conducted by detectives. Some police administrators have challenged the findings; others are awaiting the results of replication. But those who concur with the results have begun to search for alternatives, aware of the need to measure the effectiveness of a new response before making a substantial investment in it. (1979: 240)

William Bratton (1998a) in describing the emergence of Compstat in New York City, also refers to the failures of traditional approaches, and the need for innovation that would allow the police to be more effective in doing something about crime problems:

The effects of rapidly responding to crimes were muted because research showed it took people almost 10 minutes to decide to call the police in the first place. And police riding in air-conditioned squad cars, rapidly going from call to call, did not make people feel safer. In fact, it further separated the police from the public, the consumers of police services.

Fortunately, the researchers and practitioners did not stop their work at finding what was not working, but began to look at how to think differently about crime and disorder and develop strategies that would work. (1998: 31)

More generally, the turn of the last century was a period of tremendous change in police practices. This is perhaps most evident in the development of community-oriented policing, which was aided by financial support from the Office of Community Oriented Policing Services established in 1994. As Wesley Skogan reports in this volume, community policing in some form has been adopted by most police agencies in the United States. In a Police Foundation survey conducted in 1997, 85 percent of surveyed police agencies reported they had adopted community policing or were in the process of doing so (Skogan forthcoming). A Bureau of Justice Statistics survey (2003) conducted at the turn of the century found that more than 90 percent of departments in cities over 250,000 in population reported having full-time, trained community policing officers in the field (Bureau of Justice Statistics 2003).

The openness of police agencies to innovation is perhaps even more strongly illustrated by the sudden rise of Compstat as a police practice. Compstat was only developed as a programmatic entity in 1994 and was not encouraged financially by federally funded programs. Nonetheless by the turn of the century more than a third of larger police agencies had claimed to have implemented the program and a quarter of police agencies claimed that they were planning to adopt a Compstat program (Weisburd *et al.* 2003).

A number of police scholars have suggested that the changes that such surveys observe are more cosmetic than substantive. Some studies have documented the "shallow" implementation of police innovations, and have suggested that in the end the police tend to fall back on traditional methods of conducting police work (e.g., see Clarke 1998; Eck 2000). For example, even in police agencies that have adopted innovations in problem-oriented policing, careful analysis of the activities of the police suggest that they are more likely to follow traditional police practices than to choose innovative approaches (Braga and Weisburd in this volume). Moreover, the main practices of the standard model of policing continue to dominate the work of most police agencies (Committee to Review Research 2004).

While the depth of innovation over the last few decades remains a matter of debate, it is certainly the case that police agencies have become open to the idea of innovation, and that new programs and practices have been experimented with and adopted at a rapid pace over the last few decades. We think this openness can be traced to the crisis in police legitimacy and effectiveness that we have described.

Understanding the form and character of police innovation

Recognizing the importance of the challenges to policing that began to emerge in the late 1960s can help us to understand not only the cause for a period of rapid innovation, but also the form and character of the innovations that we observe in this period and which are the focus of our volume. The innovations we study here represent different forms of adaptation to similar problems. Overall, they seek to find a solution to a set of challenges to the effectiveness and legitimacy of policing we have reviewed.

Community policing, which is examined in the next section of our volume, is one of the first new approaches to policing to emerge in this modern period of police innovation. Community policing programs were already being implemented and advocated in the 1980s (e.g., Trojanowicz 1982; Goldstein 1987; Cordner 1988; Green and Mastrofski 1988; Weisburd and McElroy 1988; Trojanowicz 1989), and by the 1990s, as we have already noted, the idea of community policing had affected most American police agencies. Police practices associated with community policing have been diverse and have often changed over time. Foot patrol, for example, was considered an important element of community policing in the 1980s, but has not been a core component of more recent community policing programs. Community policing has often been implemented in combination with other programs, such as problem-oriented policing, thus making it difficult to distinguish the core components of community policing from those of other innovations that developed during this period.

Nonetheless, community policing represented a radical departure from the professional model of policing that was dominant in the post-World War II period. For decades the police had assumed that the main task of policing was to fight crime, and that the police, like other professionals, could successfully carry out their task with little help and preferably with little interference from the public. The police were the experts in defining the nature of crime problems and the nature of the solutions that could be brought to do something about them. The community in this context did not have a central role in the police function, and the responsibility for crime problems lay squarely in the hands of the policing industry.

One core element of the community policing movement was that the community should play a central role in defining the problems the police address, and that these problems should extend much beyond conventional law enforcement. As Kelling and Moore (1988: 4) argue, "during the 1950s and 1960s, police thought they were law enforcement agencies primarily fighting crime." In the "community era" or community policing era, the police function broadens and includes "order maintenance, conflict resolution, provision of services through problem solving, as well as other activities" (Kelling and Moore 1988: 2). The justification for these new activities was drawn either from a claim that historically the police had indeed carried out such functions, or that the community from which the police gained legitimacy saw these as important functions of the police.

David Bayley notes that this approach "creates a new role for police with new criteria for performance":

If police can not reduce crime and apprehend more offenders, they can at least decrease fear of crime, make the public feel less powerless, lessen distrust between minority groups and the police, mediate quarrels, overcome the isolation of marginal groups, organize social services, and generally assist in developing "community." These are certainly worthwhile objectives. But are they what the police should be doing? They are a far cry from what the police were originally created to do. (Bayley 1988: 228)

One way to understand the early development of community policing is to recognize that it responds to the question: What is the justification for the police if they cannot prevent crime? While crime fighting has increasingly become a central concern in community policing over the last decade, an important contribution of community policing to police innovation was its recognition that there were many critical community problems that the police could address that were not traditionally defined as crime problems. The expansion of the police function was to become an important part of many of the innovations that are discussed in this volume. This definition of new tasks for policing can be seen in part as a response to the failure of police to achieve the crime control goals of the professional model of policing.

Other innovations in policing in this period also looked to redefine the role of the police in one way or another. Broken windows policing, the subject of Part II of our volume, also seeks to direct the police to problems that had often been ignored in standard police practices. The idea of broken windows policing developed out of a Police Foundation study, the Newark Foot Patrol Experiment, published in 1981. From that study James Q. Wilson and George Kelling (1982) identified a link between social disorder and crime which suggested the importance of police paying attention to many problems that were seen in earlier decades as peripheral to the police function. Wilson and Kelling were impressed by the activities of the police officers who walked patrol in the Police Foundation study, and thought that what might be seen in traditional policing as inappropriate behavior actually held the key to public safety and crime reduction. Kelling and Coles (1996: 18) write:

Most New Jersey police chiefs were dismayed when they learned from program evaluators what (anonymous) officers, who were supposed to be "fighting crime," were actually doing while on foot patrol. For example, after being called a second time during the same evening to end brawls in the same bar, one foot patrol officer had had enough: although the "bar time" was some hours away, he ordered the bar closed for business as usual. The bartender grumbled, closed up, and opened the next day for business as usual. When this incident was recounted to the chief of the department in which it occurred . . . he responded, "that wouldn't happen in my department, the officer would be fired."

Wilson and Kelling argued that concern with disorder was an essential ingredient for doing something about crime problems. Indeed, the broken windows thesis was that serious crime developed because the police and citizens did not work together to prevent urban decay and social disorder:

(A)t the community level, disorder and crime are usually inextricably linked, in a kind of developmental sequence. Social psychologists and police officers tend to agree that if a window in a building is broken *and is left unrepaired*, all of the rest of the windows will soon be broken. (Wilson and Kelling 1982: 31)

In the context of crime, Wilson and Kelling argued "that 'untended' behavior also leads to the breakdown of community controls":

A stable neighborhood of families who care for their homes, mind each other's children, and confidently frown on unwanted intruders can change in a few years or even a few months, to an inhospitable and frightening jungle. A piece of property is abandoned, weeds grow up, a window is smashed. Adults stop scolding rowdy children; the children emboldened, become more rowdy. Families move out, unattached adults move in . . . Such an area is vulnerable to criminal invasion. Though it is not inevitable, it is more likely here, rather than in places where people are confident they can regulate public behavior by informal controls . . . (Wilson and Kelling 1982: 31)

Broken windows policing encourages the police to be concerned with problems of disorder, and moves crime itself to a secondary, or at least second-stage goal of the police. From the perspective of the crisis of policing we have described, broken windows policing again responds to the crisis of police effectiveness by expanding the police function. Both in community policing and broken windows policing the failures of crime fighting became less important, because the police function was seen to lie in good part in other activities.

Problem-oriented policing, the subject of Part III of our volume, also sought to broaden the problems that police approached. In Herman Goldstein's original formulation of problem-oriented policing in 1979 he argued that the "police job requires that they deal with a wide range of behavioral problems that arise in the community" (1979: 242). However, in this case, the solution for the crisis of policing was not found in the definition of new tasks for the police, bur rather in a critique of traditional police practice. Goldstein assumed that the police could impact crime and other problems if they took a different approach, in this case, the problem-oriented policing approach. Accordingly, a second response to the crisis we have described is not to accept, as some academic criminologists had, that the police could not do something about crime and thus to search to define other important police functions as central (Gottfredson and Hirschi 1990; Bayley 1994) but to argue that the strategies of the standard policing model were flawed and that new more effective models could be developed.

Problem-oriented policing sought to redefine the way in which the police did their job. Goldstein argued that the police had "lost sight" of their primary task which was to do something about crime and other problems, and instead had become focused on the "means" of allocating police resources. He identified this pathology as a common one in large organizations, and sought through the model of problem solving to develop a more successful method of ameliorating crime and other community problems.

Other innovations in policing that emerged fully only in the 1990s also take the approach that the police can be effective in doing something about crime if they adopt innovative police practices. Pulling levers policing discussed in Part IV, adopts a problem-oriented approach, but provides a broader and more comprehensive combination of strategies than more traditional problem-oriented policing programs. Pioneered in Boston to deal with an "epidemic" of youth violence (Kennedy, Piehl, and Braga 1996), the pulling levers approach begins by drawing upon a collection of law enforcement practitioners to analyze crime problems and develop innovative solutions. It seeks to develop a variety of "levers" to stop offenders from continuing criminal behavior that include not only criminal justice interventions, but also social services and community resources.

Third-party policing discussed in Part V, offers another solution to the failures of the standard policing model. It follows suggestions made by Herman Goldstein (1979) that the "tool box" of police strategies be expanded. In this case, however, the resources of the police are expanded to "third parties" that are believed to offer significant new resources for doing something about crime and disorder.[2] The opportunity for a third-party policing approach developed in part from more general trends in the relationship between civil and criminal law (Mann 1992; Mazerolle and Ransley in this volume). The expansion of the civil law and its use in other legal contexts as a method of dealing with problems that were once considered to be the exclusive province of criminal statutes created important new tools for the police. Third-party policing asserts that the police cannot successfully deal with many problems on their own, and thus that the failures of traditional policing models may be found in the limits of police powers. Using civil ordinances and civil courts, or the resources of private agencies, third-party policing recognizes that much social control is exercised by institutions other than the police and that crime can be managed through agencies other than the criminal law.

Hot spots policing discussed in Part VI, was first examined in the Minneapolis Hot Spots Experiment (Sherman and Weisburd 1995). The Minneapolis study was developed as a direct response to the findings of the Kansas City Preventive Patrol Experiment. Drawing upon empirical evidence that crime was clustered in discrete hot spots (e.g., see Pierce, Spaar, and Briggs 1986; Sherman, Gartin, and Buerger 1989; Weisburd, Maher, and Sherman 1992), Sherman and Weisburd argued that preventive patrol might be effective if it was more tightly focused. If "only 3 percent of the addresses in a city produce more than half of all the requests for police response, if no police are dispatched to 40 percent of the addresses and intersections in a city over one year, and, if among the 60 percent with any requests the majority register only one request a year, then concentrating police in a few locations makes more sense than spreading them evenly through a beat" (Sherman and Weisburd 1995: 629). Hot spots policing does not demand that the police change their strategies, but requires that they focus them more carefully at places where crime is clustered.

Compstat, discussed in Part VII, also responds to the failures of the standard model of policing by critiquing the ways in which the police carry out their task. However, in the case of Compstat the focus is less on the specific strategies that the police are involved in and more on the nature of police organization itself. Herman Goldstein noted in 1979 that the failures of the standard model of policing could be explained by the fact that police organizations were poorly organized to do something about crime. Compstat was designed to overcome that limitation. It sought to empower the police command structure to do something about crime problems. William Bratton, the New York City police chief who coined the term and developed the program wrote:

We created a system in which the police commissioner, with his executive core, first empowers and then interrogates the precinct commander, forcing him or her to come up with a plan to attack crime. But it should not stop there. At the next level down, it should be the precinct commander, taking the same role as the commissioner, empowering and interrogating the platoon commander. Then, at the third level, the platoon commander should be asking his sergeants . . . all the way down until everyone in the entire organization is empowered and motivated, active and assessed and successful. It works in all organizations, whether it's 38,000 New York cops or Mayberry, R. F. D. (Bratton 1998b: 239)

Evidence-based policing, discussed in Part VIII also traces the failures of traditional policing practices to the ways in which the police carry out their tasks. It draws from a much wider set of public policy concerns, and a broader policy movement than other police innovations examined in this volume. There is a growing consensus among scholars, practitioners, and policymakers that crime control practices and policies should be rooted as much as possible in scientific research (Sherman 1988; Cullen and Gendreau 2000; MacKenzie 2000; Sherman *et al.* 2002). Over the last decade there has been a steady growth in interest in the evaluation of criminal justice programs and practices reflected in part by the growth in criminal justice funding for research during this period (Visher and Weisburd 1998; http://www.crimereduction.gov.uk/crimered.htm). Increasing support for research and evaluation in criminal justice may be seen as part of a more general trend toward utilization of scientific research for establishing rational and effective practices and policies. This trend is perhaps most prominent in the health professions where the idea of "evidence-based medicine" has gained strong government and professional support (Millenson 1997; Zuger 1997), though the evidence-based paradigm is also developing in other fields (e.g., see Nutley and Davies 1999; Davies, Nutley, and Smith 2000). The evidence-based approach does not necessarily assume that the police can be more effective, but it argues that a reliance on evidence in the police industry is a prerequisite for the development of effective policing practices (Sherman 1988).

Conclusion

In our Introduction we have traced the wide diffusion of innovations in the last decades of the twentieth century to a crisis of police practices that had begun to develop in the late 1960s. We have argued that it is not accidental that so much innovation was brought to American policing during this period. Indeed, such innovation can be understood in the context of a series of challenges to American policing that created a perceived need for change among the police, scholars, and the public. We have also argued that the paths of police innovation can be understood in the context of the critiques that developed of standard policing models. In some cases, the innovations minimized the importance of crime fighting, which had been the main focus of earlier policing models. Such innovations responded to the crisis of policing by defining a broader or new set of tasks which the police could perform more effectively. Other innovations, however, started with a critique of the methods used in the traditional policing models. These innovations assumed that the police could be more effective, even in preventing or controlling crime, if the tactics used were changed.

In the following chapters prominent police scholars examine each of the innovations that we have discussed. The format of advocates and critiques provides a broad framework for assessing these innovations and allows us to identify the major advantages and disadvantages of these approaches. In our conclusions we try to draw more general lessons from these contributions, and discuss the possible directions that police innovation will take in the coming decades.

NOTES

We would like to thank our colleagues John Eck, David Klinger, Cynthia Lum, Lorraine Mazerolle, and Stephen Mastrofski for their thoughtful comments on an earlier draft of this introductory chapter. Helpful comments were also provided by Kristen Miggans, a graduate student at the University of Maryland, who also assisted us in preparing the manuscript for publication.

1. It is important to note that a number of large social experiments were conducted during this period (e.g., see Bell *et al.* 1980; Struyk and Bendick 1981) and thus the Kansas City Preventive Patrol experiment can be seen as part of a larger effort to subject social programs to systematic empirical study.
2. It is important to note that the impetus for third-party policing does not necessarily come from the police. Mazerolle and Ransley (2006) argues that a variety of external demands have imposed third-party policing on the police industry.

REFERENCES

Altschuler, A. A. and Behn, R. D. (eds.) (1997). *Innovation in American government: Challenges, opportunities, and dilemmas.* Washington, DC: The Brookings Institution.

Bayley, D. H. (1988). Community policing: A report from the devil's advocate. In J. R. Greene and S. D. Mastrofski (eds.), *Community policing: Rhetoric or reality?* (pp. 225–238). New York: Praeger.

(1994). *Police for the future.* New York: Oxford University Press.

Bell, J. G., Robins, P. K., Spiegelman, R. G., and Weiner, S. (eds.) (1980). *A guaranteed annual income: Evidence from a social experiment.* New York: Academic Press.

Bratton, W. J. (1998a). Crime is down in New York City: Blame the police. In W. J. Bratton and N. Dennis (eds.), *Zero tolerance: Policing a free society.* London: Institute of Economic Affairs Health and Welfare Unit.

Bratton, W. J. with Knobler, P. (1998b). *Turnaround: How America's top cop reversed the crime epidemic.* New York: Random House.

Bundy, McGeorge. (1970, July). Press Conference. Presented in New York City, NY.

Bureau of Justice Statistics. (2003). *Local police departments 2000.* Washington, DC: Bureau of Justice Statistics, US Department of Justice.

Chaiken, J. (1978). What is known about deterrent effects of police activities. In J. Cromer (ed.), *Preventing crime* (pp. 109–136). Beverly Hills, CA: Sage Publications.

Clarke, R. (1998). Defining police strategies: Problem solving, problem-oriented policing and community-oriented policing. In T. O'Connor Shelley and A. C. Grant (eds.), *Problem-oriented policing: Crime-specific problems, critical issues, and making POP work.* Washington, DC: Police Executive Research Forum.

Committee to Review Research on Police Policy and Practices. (2004). *Fairness and effectiveness in policing: The evidence.* Washington, DC: The National Academies Press.

Cordner, G. (1988). A problem-oriented approach to community-oriented policing. In J. Greene and S. Mastrofski (eds.), *Community policing: Rhetoric or reality?* New York: Praeger.

Cullen, F. and Gendreau, P. (2000). Assessing correctional rehabilitation: Policy, practice, and prospects. In J. Horney (ed.), *Policies, processes, and decisions of the criminal justice system: Criminal justice 3.* Washington, DC: US Department of Justice, National Institute of Justice.

Davies, H. T. O., Nutley, S., and Smith, P. (2000). *What works: Evidence-based policy and practice in public services.* London: Policy Press.

Eck, J. E. (1983). *Solving crime: A study of the investigation of burglary and robbery.* Washington, DC: Police Executive Research Forum.

    (2000). Problem-oriented policing and it's problems: The means over ends syndrome strikes back and the return of the problem-solver. Unpublished manuscript. Cincinnati, OH: University of Cincinnati.

Goldstein, H. (1979). Improving policing: A problem oriented approach. *Crime and Delinquency,* 24, 236–258.

    (1987). Toward community-oriented policing: Potential, basic requirements, and threshold questions. *Crime and Delinquency,* 25, 236–258.

Gottfredson, M. and Hirschi, T. (1990). *A general theory of crime.* Palo Alto, CA: Stanford University Press.

Greene, J. and Mastrofski, S. (eds.) (1988). *Community policing: Rhetoric or reality?* New York: Praeger.

Greenwood, P. W., Chaiken, J., Petersilia, M., and Prusoff, L. (1975). *Criminal investigation process, III: Observations and analysis.* Santa Monica, CA: Rand Corporation.

Greenwood, P. W., Petersilia, J., and Chaiken, J. (1977). *The criminal investigation process*. Lexington, MA: D.C. Heath.

Kansas City Police Department. (1977). *Response time analysis*. Kansas City, MO: Kansas City Police Department.

Kelling, G. L. and Coles, C. M. (1996). *Fixing broken windows: Restoring order and reducing crime in our communities*. New York: The Free Press.

Kelling, G. L. and Moore, M. H. (1988). From political to reform to community: The evolving strategy of police. In J. R. Greene and S. D. Mastrofski (eds.), *Community policing: Rhetoric or reality?* New York: Praeger Publishers.

Kelling, G. L., Pate, A., Dieckman, D., and Brown, C. E. (1974). *The Kansas City preventative patrol experiment: Technical report*. Washington, DC: Police Foundation.

Kelling, G. L., Pate, A., Ferrera, A., Utne, M., and Brown, C. E. (1981). *Newark foot patrol experiment*. Washington, DC: The Police Foundation.

Kennedy, D., Piehl, A., and Braga, A. (1996). Youth violence in Boston: Gun markets, serious offenders, and a use-reduction strategy. *Law and Contemporary Problems*, 59, 147–196.

Kerner Commission. (1968). *National advisory commission on civil disorder*. Washington, DC: US Government Printing Office.

Klinger, D. A. (2003). Spreading diffusion in criminology. *Criminology and Public Policy*, 2(3), 461–468.

LaFree, G. (1998). *Losing legitimacy: Street crime and the decline of social institutions in America*. Boulder, CO: Westview Press.

Larson, R. C. and Cahn, M. F. (1985). *Synthesizing and extending the results of police patrols*. Washington, DC: US Government Printing Office.

Levine, J. P. (1975). Ineffectiveness of adding police to prevent crime. *Public Policy*, 23, 523–545.

MacKenzie, D. (2000). Evidence-based corrections: Identifying what works. *Crime and Delinquency*, 46, 457–471.

Mann, K. (1992). Punitive civil sanctions: The middleground between criminal and civil law. *Yale Law Journal*, 101(8), 1795–1873.

Mazerolle, L. G. and Ransley, J. (2006). *Third-party policing*. Cambridge: Cambridge University Press.

Millenson, M. L. (1997). *Demanding medical excellence: Doctors and accountability in the information age*. Chicago: University of Chicago Press.

Minneapolis Medical Research Foundation, Inc. (1976). Critiques and commentaries on evaluation research activities – Russell Sage reports. *Evaluation*, 3(1–2), 115–138.

Murphy, P. V. (1974). Foreword. In G. L. Kelling, T. Pate, D. Dieckman, and C. E. Brown, *The Kansas City preventative patrol experiment: Technical report*. Washington, DC: Police Foundation.

Nutley, S. and Davies, H. T. O. (1999). The fall and rise of evidence in criminal justice. *Public Money and Management*, 19, 47–54.

Ostrom, E., Whitaker, G., and Parks, R. (1978). Policing: Is there a system? In J. May and A. Wildavsky (eds.), *The policy cycle*. New York: Russell Sage Foundation.

Pierce, G., Spaar, S., and Briggs, L. R. (1986). *The character of police work: Strategic and tactical implications*. Boston, MA: Center for Applied Social Research, Northeastern University.

President's Commission on Law Enforcement and Administration of Justice. (1967). *The crime commission report: The challenge of crime in a free society*. Washington, DC: US Government Printing Office.

Press, S. J. (1971). *Some effects of an increase in police manpower in the 20th precinct of New York City*. New York: New York City Rand Institute.

Reiss, A. J., Jr. and Roth, J. A. (eds.) (1993). *Understanding and preventing violence: Panel on the understanding and control of violent behavior*. Washington DC: National Academy Press.

Rogers, E. M. (1995). *Diffusion of innovations* (4th ed.). New York: Free Press.

Schnelle, J. F., Kirchner, R. E., Jr., Casey, J. D., Uselton, P. H., Jr., and McNees, M. P. (1977). Patrol evaluation research: A multiple-baseline analysis of saturation police patrolling during day and night hours. *Journal of Applied Behavior Analysis*, *10*, 33–40.

Sherman, L. W. (1998). *Evidence-based policing. Ideas in American policing series*. Washington, DC: The Police Foundation.

Sherman, L. W. and Weisburd, D. (1995). General deterrent effects of police patrol in crime "hot-spots": A randomized controlled trial. *Justice Quarterly*, *12*, 626–648.

Sherman, L. W., Gartin, P. R., and Buerger, M. E. (1989). Hot spots of predatory crime: Routine activities and the criminology of place. *Criminology*, *27*, 27–56.

Sherman, L. W., Farrington, D., Welsh, B., and MacKenzie, D. (eds.) (2002). *Evidence based crime prevention*. New York: Routledge.

Skogan, W. G. (in Press). Impediments to community policing. In L. Fridell and M. A. Wycoff (eds.), *The future of community policing*. Washington, DC: Police Executive Research Forum.

Skogan, W. G. and Antunes, G. E. (1979). Information, apprehension, and deterrence: Exploring the limits of police productivity. *Journal of Criminal Justice*, *7*, 217–241.

Spelman, W. and Brown, D. K. (1984). *Calling the police: Citizen reporting of serious crime*. Washington: US Government Printing Office.

Struyk, R. J. and Bendick, M., Jr. (eds.) (1981). *Housing vouchers for the poor: Lessons from a national experiment*. Washington, DC: The Urban Institute Press.

Trojanowicz, R. (1982). *An evaluation of the neighborhood foot patrol program in Flint, Michigan*. East Lansing, MI: National Neighborhood Foot Patrol Center, Michigan State University.

   (1989). *Preventing civil disturbances: A community policing approach*. East Lansing, MI: Michigan State University, National Center for Community Policing.

Visher, C. and Weisburd, D. (1998). Identifying what works: Recent trends in crime prevention strategies. *Crime, Law and Social Change*, *28*, 223–242.

Weisburd, D. and Eck, J. E. (2004). What can police do to reduce crime, disorder, and fear? *Annals of the American Academy of Political and Social Science*, *593*, 42–65.

Weisburd, D. and Lum, C. (2005). The diffusion of computerized crime mapping policing: Linking research and practice. *Police Practice and Research*, 6(5), 433–448.

Weisburd, D. and McElroy, J. E. (1988). Enacting the CPO (Community Patrol Officer) role: Findings from the New York City pilot program in community policing. In J. R. Greene and S. D. Mastrofski (eds.), *Community policing: Rhetoric or reality?* New York: Praeger Publishers.

Weisburd, D., Maher, L., and Sherman, L. W. (1992). Contrasting crime general and crime specific theory: The case of hot-spots of crime. *Advances in Criminological Theory*, 4, 45–70.

Weisburd, D., Mastrofski, S. D., McNally, A. M., Greenspan, R., and Willis, J. J. (2003). Reforming to preserve: Compstat and strategic problem solving in American policing. *Criminology and Public Policy*, 2(3), 421–456.

Weiss, A. (1997). The communication of innovation in American policing. *Policing*, 20, 292–310.

Wilson, J. Q. and Kelling, G. L. (1982). Broken windows: The police and neighborhood safety. *The Atlantic Monthly*, March, 29–38.

Zuger, A. (1997). New way of doctoring: By the book. *The New York Times*. December 16.

Part I

Community policing

2 *Advocate*
The promise of community policing

Wesley G. Skogan

Community policing is very popular. So popular is the concept with politicians, city managers, and the general public, that few police chiefs want to be caught without some program they can call community policing. In a 1997 survey of police departments conducted by the Police Foundation, 85 percent reported they had adopted community policing or were in the process of doing so (Skogan 2004). The biggest reason for not doing so was that community policing was "impractical" for their community, and my own tabulations of the data found these replies were mostly from small departments with only a few officers. Bigger cities included in the survey (those with populations greater than 100,000) all claimed in the 1997 survey to have adopted community policing – half by 1991 and the other half between 1992 and 1997. By 2000, a federal survey with a much larger sample found that more than 90 percent of departments in cities over 250,000 in population reported having full-time, trained community policing officers in the field (Bureau of Justice Statistics 2003).

What do cities that claim they are "doing community policing" actually do? They describe a long list of projects. Under the rubric of community policing, officers patrol on foot (in the 1997 survey, 75 percent listed this), or perhaps on horses, bicycles, or segways. Departments variously train civilians in citizen police academies, open small neighborhood storefront offices, conduct surveys to measure community satisfaction, canvass door-to-door to identify local problems, publish newsletters, conduct drug education projects, and work with municipal agencies to enforce health and safety regulations.

However, community policing is not defined by these kinds of activities. Projects, programs, and tactics come and go, and they should as conditions change. Communities with different problems and varied resources to bring to bear against them should try different things. Community policing is not a set of specific programs. Rather, it involves changing decisionmaking processes and creating new cultures within police departments. It is an *organizational strategy* that leaves setting priorities and the means of achieving them largely to residents and the police who serve in their neighborhoods. Community policing is a process rather than a product. It has three core elements: citizen involvement, problem solving, and decentralization. In practice, these three dimensions turn out to be densely interrelated, and departments that shortchange one or more of them will not field a very effective program.

This chapter sets the stage for a discussion of community policing. It reviews the three core concepts that define community policing, describes how they have been turned into concrete community policing programs, and reports some of what we know about their effectiveness. It draws heavily on my experience evaluating community programs in a number of cities, as well as on what others have reported. It summarizes some of the claims made for community policing, and some of the realities of achieving them in the real world.

Community involvement

Community policing is defined in part by efforts to develop partner-ships with community members and the civic organizations that represent many of them collectively. It requires that police engage with the public as they set priorities and develop their tactics. Effective community policing requires responsiveness to citizen input concerning both the needs of the community and the best ways by which the police can help meet those needs. It takes seriously the public's definition of its own problems. This is one reason why community policing is an organizational strategy but not a set of specific programs – how it looks in practice *should* vary con-siderably from place to place, in response to unique local situations and circumstances. Listening to the community can produce new policing priorities. Officers involved in neighborhood policing quickly learn that many residents are deeply concerned about problems that previously did not come to police attention. To a certain extent they define things differ-ently. The public often focus on threatening and fear-provoking *conditions* rather than discrete and legally defined *incidents*. They can be more con-cerned about casual social disorder and the physical decay of their com-munity than they are about traditionally defined "serious crimes." They worry about graffiti, public drinking, and the litter and parking problems created by nearby commercial strips. The public sometimes define their problem as people who need to be taught a lesson. In Chicago, a well-known social type is the "gangbanger (gang member)," and people want them off the street. The police, however, are trained to recognize and organized to respond to crime incidents, and they have to know what people do, not just who they are. Given these differences, community residents are unsure if they can (or even should) rely on the police to help them deal with these problems. Many of these concerns thus do not generate complaints or calls for service, and as a result, the police know surprisingly little about them. The routines of traditional police work ensure that officers will largely interact with citizens who are in distress because they have just been victimized, or with suspects and troublemakers. Accordingly, community policing requires that departments develop new channels for learning about neighborhood problems. And, when they learn about them, they have to have systems in place to respond effectively.

Civic engagement usually extends to involving the public in some way in efforts to enhance community safety. Community policing promises to strengthen the capacity of communities to fight and prevent crime on their own. The idea that the police and the public are "co-producers" of safety, and that they cannot claim a monopoly over fighting crime, predates the community policing era. In fact, the community crime prevention movement of the 1970s was an important precursor to community policing. It promoted the idea that crime was not solely the responsibility of the police. The police were quick to endorse the claim that they could not solve crime problems without community support and assistance, for it helped share the blame for crime rates that were rising at the time (cf. Skogan, Hartnett, DuBois *et al.* 1999). Now police find that they are expected to lead community efforts. They are being called upon to take responsibility for mobilizing individuals and organizations around crime prevention. These efforts include neighborhood watch, citizen patrols, and education programs stressing household target-hardening and the rapid reporting of crime. Residents are asked to assist the police by reporting crimes promptly when they occur and cooperating as witnesses. Community policing often involves increases in "transparency" in how departments respond to demands for more information about what they do and how effective they are. A federal survey of police agencies found that by 1999 more than 90 percent of departments serving cities of 50,000 or more were giving residents access to crime statistics or even crime maps (Bureau of Justice Statistics 2001). Even where efforts to involve the community were already well established, moving them to center stage as part of a larger strategic plan showcasing the commitment of the police to community policing.

All of this needs to be supported by new organizational structures and training for police officers. Departments need to reorganize in order to provide opportunities for citizens to come into contact with their officers under circumstances that encourage these exchanges. There has to be a significant amount of informal "face time" between police and residents, so that trust and cooperation can develop between the prospective partners. To this end, many departments hold community meetings and form advisory committees, establish store front offices, survey the public, and create informational web sites. In Chicago they hold about 250 small police–public meetings every month. They began doing so in 1995, and by mid-2003 residents had shown up on more than half a million occasions to attend almost 25,000 community meetings (Skogan and Steiner 2004). In some places, police share information with residents through educational programs or by enrolling them in citizen–police academies that give them in-depth knowledge of law enforcement. By 1999, almost 70 percent of all police departments – and virtually every department serving cities of 50,000 or more – reported regularly holding meetings with citizen groups (Bureau of Justice Statistics 2001).

What are the presumed benefits of citizen involvement? Community policing aims at rebuilding trust in the community and ensuring support for the police among taxpayers. Opinion polls document the fact that Americans have given up thinking that politicians and government adequately represent them; for example, Moy and Pfau (2000: 13) note that there is "a profound and consistent lack of confidence in the executive branch of the federal government," and document that the proportion of Americans who believe that "the government in Washington" can be trusted "to do what is right" dropped from 76 percent in 1964 to just 14 percent in 1994. Police come off better than most government institutions, when Americans are asked how much confidence they have in them. My own review of public opinion polls indicates that during the 1990s police did better than the presidency and the Supreme Court, and Americans had much more confidence in the police than they had in the Congress. In May 2004, Americans were most confident in their military (85 percent had "a great deal" or "quite a lot" of confidence in them), but police came next, at 64 percent. Less than half of Americans had that much confidence in the Supreme Court, and only 30 percent in the Congress.

However, community policing is especially about recapturing the legitimacy that police have in large measure lost in many of America's minority communities. The same opinion polls show that African Americans and recent immigrants have dramatically less confidence in the police, and are much more likely to believe that they are brutal and corrupt (Skogan and Steiner 2004). They are the only growing part of the population in a surprisingly large number of American cities, and civic leaders know that they have to find ways to incorporate them into the system. Police take on community policing in part because they hope that building a reservoir of public support may help them get through bad times (see the discussion of "nasty misconduct" below) when they occur. Community policing might help police be more effective. It could encourage witnesses and bystanders to step forward in neighborhoods where they too often do not, for example. More indirectly, it might help rebuild the social and organizational fabric of neighborhoods that previously had been given up for lost, enabling residents to contribute to maintaining order in their community (Sampson, Raudenbush, and Earls 1997).

However, I do not know of a single police department that adopted community policing because they thought that it was a *direct* route to getting the crime rate down. Efforts to evaluate it need to focus as well on the important community and governance processes that it is intended to set in motion, because they represent potentially important "wins" on their own. The extent of the public's trust and confidence in the police is an obvious first issue. For example, after eight years of citywide community policing, Chicagoans' views of their police improved by 10–15 percentage points on measures of their effectiveness, responsiveness, and demeanor. Latinos, African Americans and whites all shared in these improvements (Skogan and Steiner 2004). Evaluators also should look into the "mobilizing" effects of programs, including the extent of parallel community self-help efforts and extending even to the possible development of organizational and leadership capabilities among newly activated residents. Sociological research indicates that "collective efficacy" (a combination of trust among neighborhood residents and the expectation that neighbors will intervene when things go wrong) plays an important role in inhibiting urban crime. However, the same work indicates that it is mostly white, home-owning neighborhoods that currently have it, and researchers have yet to document how neighborhoods that do *not* have collective efficacy can generate it for themselves (Sampson, Raudenbush, and Earls 1997). Although its effects on collective efficacy are undocumented, the rhetoric of community policing and its accomplishments in turning out residents point in this direction, and this should be an important focus of evaluation in this area.

An important spin-off of civic engagement is that the adoption of community policing almost inevitably leads to an expansion of the police mandate, and this further expands the list of points on which it should be evaluated. Controlling serious crime by enforcing the criminal law remains the primary job of the police. But instead of seeing the police exclusively in these terms, and viewing activities that depart from direct efforts to deter crime as a distraction from their fundamental mission, advocates of community policing argue that the police have additional functions to perform and different ways to conduct their traditional business. As a practical matter, when police meet with neighborhood residents in park buildings and church basements to discuss neighborhood problems, the civilians present are going to bring up all manner of problems. If the police who are present put them off, or have no way of responding to their concerns, they will not come back the next month. Community policing takes seriously the public's definition of its own problems, and this inevitably includes issues that lie outside the traditional competence of the police. Officers can learn at a public meeting that loose garbage and rats in an alley are big issues for residents, but some other agency is going to have to deliver the solution to that problem. When police meet with residents in Chicago, much of the discussion focuses on neighborhood dilapidation (including problems with abandoned buildings and graffiti) and on public drinking, teen loitering, curfew and truancy problems, and disorder in schools. There is much more talk about parking and traffic than about personal and property crime, although discussion of drug-related issues comes up quite often (Skogan, Steiner, Hartnett *et al.* 2003). The broad range of issues that concern the public requires in turn that police form partnerships with other public and private agencies that can join them in responding to residents' priorities. They could include the schools and agencies responsible for health, housing, trash pickup, car tows, and graffiti cleanups.

In practice, community involvement is not easy to achieve. Ironically, it can be difficult to sustain in areas that need it the most. Research on participation in community crime prevention programs during the 1970s and 1980s found that poor and high-crime areas often were not well endowed with an infrastructure of organizations that were ready to get involved, and that turnout for police-sponsored events was higher in places honeycombed with block clubs and community organizations (Skogan 1988). In high-crime areas people tend to be suspicious of their neighbors, and especially of their neighbors' children. Fear of retaliation by gangs and drug dealers can undermine public involvement as well (Grinc 1994). In Chicago, a 1998 study of hundreds of community meetings found that residents expressed concern about retaliation for attending or working with the police in 22 percent of the city's beats (Skogan and Steiner 2004). In addition, police and residents may not have a history of getting along in poor neighborhoods. Residents are as likely to think of the police as one of their problems as they are to see them as a solution to their problems. It probably will not be the first instinct of organizations representing the interests of poor communities to cooperate with police. Instead, they are more likely to press for an end to police misconduct. They will call for new resources from the outside to address community problems, for no organization can blame its own constituents for their plight (cf. Skogan 1988). There may be no reason for residents of crime-ridden neighborhoods to think that community policing will turn out to be anything but another broken promise; they are accustomed to seeing programs come and go, without much effect (Sadd and Grinc 1994). They certainly will have to be trained in their new roles. Community policing involves a new set of jargon as well as assumptions about the new responsibilities that both police and citizens are to adopt. The 2000 survey of police departments by the federal government found that "training citizens for community policing" was common in big cities; in cities of more than 500,000, 70 percent reported doing so (Bureau of Justice Statistics 2003).

In addition, community policing runs the risk of inequitable outcomes. In an evaluation of one of the very first programs, in Houston, Texas, I found that whites and middle-class residents received most of the benefits of the program. They found it easy to cooperate with the police, and shared with the police a common view of who the troublemakers were in the community. Blue-collar blacks and Latinos remained uninvolved, on the other hand, and they saw no visible change in their lives (Skogan 1990). Finally, the investment that police make in community policing is always at risk. Nasty episodes of police misconduct can undermine those efforts. When excessive force or killings by police become a public issue, years of progress in police–community relations can disappear. The same is true when there are revelations of widespread corruption.

On the police side there may be resistance in the ranks. Public officials' and community activists' enthusiasm for neighborhood-oriented policing encourages its detractors within the police to dismiss it as "just politics," or another passing civilian fad. Officers who get involved can become known as "empty holster guys," and what they do gets labeled "social work." Police officers prefer to stick to crime fighting. (For a case study in New York City of how this happens, see Pate and Shtull 1994.) My first survey of Chicago police, conducted before that city's community policing program began, found that two-thirds of them disavowed any interest in addressing "non-crime problems" on their beat. More than 70 percent of the 7500 police officers surveyed thought community policing "would bring a greater burden on police to solve all community problems," and also "more unreasonable demands on police by community groups" (Skogan and Hartnett 1997). Police are often skeptical about programs invented by civilians, who they are convinced cannot possibly understand their job. They are particularly hostile to programs that threaten to involve civilians in setting standards or evaluating their performance, and they do not like civilians influencing their operational priorities. Police can easily find ways to justify their aloofness from the community; as one officer told me, "You can't be the friend of the people and do your job."

On the other hand, some studies point to positive changes in officers' views once they become involved in community policing. Lurigio and Rosenbaum (1994) summarized twelve studies of this, and found many positive findings with respect to job satisfaction, perceptions of improved relations with the community, and expectations about community involvement in problem solving. Skogan and Hartnett (1997) found growing support for community policing among officers involved in Chicago's experimental police districts, in comparison to those who continued to work in districts featuring policing as usual.

Problem solving

Community policing also involves a shift from reliance on reactive patrol and investigations toward a problem-solving orientation. In brief (for it is discussed in detail in other chapters of this book) problem-oriented policing is an approach to developing crime reduction strategies. Problem solving involves training officers in methods of identifying and analyzing problems. It highlights the importance of discovering the situations that *produce* calls for police assistance, identifying the causes which lie behind them, and designing tactics to deal with these causes. Problem solving is a counterpoint to the traditional model of police work, which usually entails responding sequentially to individual events as they are phoned in by victims. Too often this style of policing is reduced to driving fast to crime scenes in order to fill out pieces of paper reporting what happened. Problem solving, on the other hand, calls for examining patterns of incidents to reveal their causes and to help plan how to deal with them proactively. This is facilitated by the computer analyses of "hot spots" that concentrate large volumes of complaints and calls for service. Problem-oriented policing also recognizes that the solutions to those patterns may involve other agencies and may be "non-police" in character; in traditional departments, this would be cause for ignoring them. The best programs encourage officers to respond creatively to the problems they encounter, or to refer them appropriately to other agencies (Eck 2004).

Problem-solving policing can proceed without a commitment to community policing. A key difference between problem solving and community policing is that the latter stresses civic engagement in identifying and prioritizing a broad range of neighborhood problems, while the former frequently focuses on patterns of traditionally defined crimes that are identified using police data systems. Problem-oriented policing sometimes involves community members or organizations in order to address particular issues, but more often it is conducted solely by specialized units within the police department. On the other hand, community policing involves neighborhood residents as an end in itself, and in evaluation terms it is important to count this as a "process success." The problem with relying on the data that is already in police computers is that when residents are involved they often press for a focus on issues that are not well documented by department information systems, such as graffiti, public drinking, and building abandonment. Effective programs must have systems in place to respond to a broad range of problems, through partnerships with other agencies. The 2000 survey found that in cities of more than 250,000 residents, more than 50 percent of departments reported they had formed problem-solving partnerships with community groups and local agencies (Bureau of Justice Statistics 2003).

Is this easy to do? It is at least as hard as involving the community, for bureaucracies are involved, and interagency cooperation can easily fail. For a long list of familiar bureaucratic and political reasons, other city and state agencies usually think that community policing is the police department's program, not theirs. They resist bending their own professional and budget-constrained priorities to accommodate police officers who call on them for help. Making this kind of interorganizational cooperation work turns out to be one of the most difficult problems facing innovative departments. When the chief of an East Coast city was new, he told me that he could handle things in his department; his biggest fear was that his mayor might not handle the city's other agencies, and that they would not provide the kind of support that community policing requires. If community policing is the police department's program, it may fail. Community policing must be the city's program.

It is also hard to involve police officers in problem solving. Cordner and Biebel (2005) did an in-depth study of problem-solving practice in a major American city. Although the department had been deeply committed to problem solving for more than fifteen years, they found that street officers typically defined problems very narrowly (e.g., one address, or one suspected repeat offender); their analysis of it consisted of making personal observations from their car; they crafted solutions from their own experience; and two-thirds of the time their proposed solution did not go past arresting someone. The study concluded that, after fifteen years of practice, this department's "glass" was only "half full." What observers would classify as "full-scale" problem solving was rarely encountered. Even the advocates of problem solving (you will hear from them in later chapters) admit that it requires a great deal of training, close supervision, and relentless follow-up evaluation to make it work. However, one important organizational function that often gets shortchanged is training. Training is expensive and officers have to be removed from the line – or paid overtime – to attend. And few departments are adequately staffed with supervisors who themselves were full-fledged problem solvers (Eck 2004).

Community policing has also revived interest in systematically addressing the task of crime prevention. In the traditional model of policing, crime prevention was deterrence based. To threaten arrest, police patrol the streets looking for crimes (engaging in random and directed patrol), they respond quickly to emergency crime calls from witnesses and victims, and detectives then take over the task of locating offenders. Concerned residents, on the other hand, do not want the crime that drives these efforts to happen in the first place. Their instinct is to press for true prevention. Police-sponsored prevention projects are in place throughout the country. Problem solving has brought crime prevention theories to the table, leading police to tackle the routine activities of victims and the crucial roles played by "place managers" such as landlords or shopkeepers, and not just offenders (Eck and Wartell 1998; Braga, Weisburd, Waring *et al.* 1999). When community policing came to Chicago, one of the first actions of a new district commander was to convince a bank to open an ATM machine in his police station, so residents had a safe place to go to transact business. An emphasis on "target hardening" has gotten police involved in conducting home security surveys and teaching self-defense classes. But when communities talk about prevention they mostly talk about their children, and ways of intervening earlier with youths who seem on a trajectory toward serious offending. Much of the work preventing the development of criminal careers lies with agencies besides the police, including family courts, children's protection agencies, parents, peer networks, and schools. To their efforts the police add involvement in athletic and after school programs, DARE (Drug Awareness and Resistance Education) presentations in schools, special efforts to reduce violence in families, and initiatives that focus attention on the recruitment of youths into gangs.

Decentralization

Decentralization is an organizational strategy that is closely linked to the implementation of community policing. Decentralization can be pursued at two levels. Typically, more responsibility for identifying and responding to chronic crime and disorder problems is delegated to mid-level commanders in charge of the geographical districts or precincts that make up a city. Departments have had to experiment with how to structure and manage a decentralization plan that gives mid-level managers real responsibility, and how to hold them accountable for measures of their success. Here community policing intersects with another movement in policing (and the subject of another pair of chapters in this book), the emergence of a culture of systematic performance measurement and managerial accountability.

The idea is to devolve authority and responsibility further down the organizational hierarchy. Departments do this in order to encourage the development of local solutions to locally defined problems, and to facilitate decisionmaking that responds rapidly to local conditions. The police are not independent of the rest of society, where large organizations in both the public and private sectors have learned that decentralization can create flexibility in decisionmaking at the customer contact level. There may be moves to flatten the structure of the organization by compressing the rank structure, and to shed layers of bureaucracy within the police organization to speed communication and decisionmaking. In Chicago, most of the department's elite units – including detectives, narcotics investigators, special tactical teams, and even the organized crime unit – are required to share information and more closely coordinate their work with the geographical districts. The department's management accountability process calls them on the carpet when they fail to serve as "support units" for uniformed patrol officers (Skogan *et al.* 2003). To flatten the organization, Chicago abolished the civil service rank of captain, leaving the department with just three civil service ranks (Skogan and Hartnett 1997).

At the same time, more responsibility for identifying and responding to community problems may be delegated to individual patrol officers and their sergeants, who are in turn encouraged to take the initiative in finding ways to deal with a broad range of problems specific to the communities they serve. Structurally, community policing leads departments to assign officers to fixed geographical areas, and to keep them there during the course of their day. This is known as adopting a "turf orientation." Decentralization is intended to encourage communication between officers and neighborhood residents, and to build an awareness of local problems among working officers. They are expected to work more autonomously at investigating situations, resolving problems, and educating the public. They are being asked to discover and set their own goals, and sometimes to manage their work schedule. This is also the level at which collaborative projects involving both police and residents can emerge. By 1999, a national survey of police departments found that assigning officers geographically was virtually the norm in cities over 250,000 (Bureau of Justice Statistics 2001).

This pattern of dual decentralization is adopted not only so that police can become more proactive and more preventive, but also so that they can respond efficiently to problems of different magnitude and complexity. Under the professional model, marching orders for the police traditionally come from two sources: 911 calls from the public concerning individual problems, and initiatives or programs originating at police headquarters or even City Hall. Every experienced officer can tell stories of the crazy things officers sometimes have to do because "downtown" announced a citywide initiative that was irrelevant for their district. A Chicago commander once described to me how he was punished (he lost a day's pay) because – as a district commander – he assigned two officers to identifying abandoned cars and getting them towed, rather than the maximum of one officer that the rule book mandated. He used this story to good effect whenever officers complained in a meeting that the department was getting away from its traditional practices because of community policing.

Decentralization, paired with a commitment to consultation and engagement with local communities, also allows the police to respond to local problems that are important to particular communities. Police were not organized to respond to the organized groups and community institutions that make up "civil society." Now surveys of departments indicate that, as part of a community policing initiative, virtually all larger departments now consult local advisory boards representing specific communities.

Is decentralization easy to pull off? It is at least as hard as problem solving, and politically risky to boot. For all of the adoption of specific programs, researchers who track trends in police organization are skeptical that there has been much fundamental "flattening" of police hierarchies – which is, after all, about their jobs (Greene 2004). Resistance to reform does not just come from the bottom of the organization. Junior executives at police headquarters may resist authority being taken from them and pushed to lower levels in the organization. Managers at this level are in a position to act as a filter between the chief and operational units, censoring the flow of decisions and information up and down the command hierarchy (for a case study of how this can undermine community policing initiatives, see Capowich 2005). This is one reason why special community policing units are often run from the chief's office, or housed in a special new bureau – this enables the department to get neighborhood officers on the street while bypassing the barons who dominate key positions at headquarters. Too often they are command-and-control oriented and feel most comfortable when everything is done by the book. Discussions of community policing often feature management buzz words like "empowerment" and "trust," and this makes them nervous because they also worry about inefficiency and corruption.

And, of course, these concerns are real. One of the dilemmas of community policing is that calling for more operational and street-level discretion runs counter to another trend in policing, which is to tighten the management screws tighter and create an increasingly rule-bound environment in order to control police corruption and violence. Ironically, *many* of the recent innovations discussed in this book go the other way; they recognize, widen, and celebrate the operational independence of individual officers. Community policing recognizes that problems vary tremendously from place to place, and that their causes and solutions are highly contextual. We expect police to use "good judgment" rather than somehow enforce "the letter of the law." Decentralizing, reducing hierarchy, and granting officers more independence, and trusting in their professionalism are the organizational reforms of choice today, not tightening things up to constrain officer discretion. But police do misuse this discretion, and they do take bribes.

It may be difficult to pull off decentralization to the turf level because it takes too many people. Community policing is labor-intensive, and may require more officers. Police managers and city leaders will have to find the officers required to staff the program. Finding the money to hire more officers to staff community policing assignments is hard, so departments may try to downsize existing projects. This can bring conflict with powerful unit commanders and allied politicians who support current arrangements. Police departments also face "the 911 problem." Their commitment to respond to 911 calls as quickly as possible dominates how resources are deployed in every department. Community policing has encountered heavy political resistance when the perception arose (encouraged to be sure by its opponents) that resources previously devoted to responding to emergency calls were being diverted to this "social experiment."

Decentralization is also difficult to manage because evaluation of the effectiveness of many community policing initiatives is difficult. The management environment in policing today stresses "accountability for results" (Weisburd, Mastrofski, McNally *et al.* 2003). Units are not rewarded for their activities, however well meaning, but for declining crime. However, the public often wants action on things that department information systems do not account for at all. In decentralized departments, residents of different neighborhoods make different demands on police operations. They value the time officers spend meeting with them, and they like to see officers on foot rather than driving past on the way to a crime scene. As a result, both individual and unit performance is harder to assess in community policing departments (Mastrofski 1998).

Prospects

An unanswered question about community policing is whether it can survive the withdrawal of federal financial support and attention. Under the 1994 Violent Crime and Law Enforcement Act, the federal government spent billions of dollars to support community policing. Federal agencies sponsored demonstration projects designed to spur innovation and promote the effectiveness of community policing, and they promoted it heavily through national conferences and publications. The Act specified that one of the roles of these new officers should be "to foster problem solving and interaction with communities by police officers." Innovations such as community policing highlight the importance of training for officers, and the 1994 crime act also funded the creation of regional community policing centers around the country. By 1999, 88 percent of all new recruits and 85 percent of serving officers worked in departments that were providing some community policing training (Bureau of Justice Statistics 2001).

The issue is whether police departments will continue to staff their community policing components. Federal financial support for community policing certainly is on the wane. Now crime is down, a new team is in the White House, and federal largesse toward local law enforcement is being redirected to post-September 11 concerns. Even where commitment to community policing is strong, maintaining an effective program can be difficult in the face of competing demands for resources. For example, between 1995 and 2003, the city of Cleveland received $34 million in federal assistance for hiring police officers, but for 2004 that figure shrank to $489,000, and the city expected to receive even less in 2005. To handle the shortfall they cut 250 officers from the payroll and closed the neighborhood mini-stations that were created as part of the city's community policing effort (Butterfield 2004). There is also pressure from the federal government to involve local police extensively in enforcing immigration laws. This is being stoutly resisted by many chiefs of police, who claim that it would be a great setback to their community involvement and trust-building projects. We shall see if they can continue to resist.

A second issue is whether community policing can survive accountability management. This is another new thing in policing, and many of its features push in the opposite direction. Community policing continues to ask officers to think and act in new and unaccustomed ways, and many of its presumed benefits do not show up in police information systems. To a significant extent, in this new management environment what gets measured is what matters. Top managers decide what is a success, and hold mid-level managers to their standards. The accountability process is about harnessing the hierarchy to achieve top management's objectives, which are in turn driven by the data they have at hand, and those data say little about community priorities. The thrust of New York City's Compstat and similar management initiatives all over the country is that measured accomplishments get attention and unmeasured accomplishments do not. As a result, there is a risk that the focus of departments will shift away from community policing, back to the activities that better fit a recentralizing management structure driven by data on recorded crime.

Community policing also stresses the importance of developing the general purpose skills of line officers through education and training, and it frequently features talk about empowering rank-and-file employees and encouraging them to act autonomously. It stresses that workers at the very bottom of the organization are closest to the customer, and are to use their best judgment about how to serve the neighborhoods where they are assigned. However, these are at best low priorities for Compstat-style accountability management. Community policing is an attack on the traditional hierarchical structure of police departments. It calls for the bottom-up definition of problems. Police researchers attribute many of the problems of contemporary policing to the mismatch between the formal hierarchical structure of police organizations and the true nature of their work, which is extremely decentralized, not amenable to "cookie cutter" solutions, dependent on the skills and motivation of the individual officers handling it, and mostly driven externally by 911 calls rather than management strategies. Perhaps the accountability process has ridden to the rescue of the traditional hierarchical structure, trying again to impose that hierarchy on work that does not fit its demands. Is the accountability process the last refuge of the command-and-control mentality of the past, and can community policing survive it?

The final question is whether community policing can live up to its promises. Like many new programs, its adoption in many instances preceded careful evaluation of its consequences. The effectiveness of community policing has been the subject of some research, ranging from its impact on crime to how openly it is embraced by the officers charged with carrying it out. There has not been enough research to definitively address the effectiveness question. As this chapter has documented, implementing a serious community policing program is risky and hard, and departments can fail at it.

REFERENCES

Braga, A. A., Weisburd, D. L., Waring, E. J., Mazerolle, L. G., Spelman, W., and Gajewski, F. (1999). Problem-oriented policing in violent crime places: A randomized controlled experiment. *Criminology, 37*, 541–580.

Bureau of Justice Statistics. (2001). *Community policing in local police departments 1997 and 1999.* Washington, DC: Bureau of Justice Statistics, US Department of Justice.

(2003). *Local police departments 2000.* Washington, DC: Bureau of Justice Statistics, US Department of Justice.

Butterfield, F. (2004). As cities struggle, police get by with less. *New York Times,* July 27.

Capowich, G. E. (2005). A case study of community policing implementation: Contrasting success and failure. In K. R. Kerley (ed.), *Policing and program evaluation.* Upper Saddle River, NJ: Prentice Hall.

Cordner, G. and Biebel, E. (2005). Problem-oriented policing in practice. *Criminology and Public Policy, 4*, 155–180.

Eck, J. E. (2004). Why don't problems get solved? In W. G. Skogan (ed.), *Community policing: Can it work?* Belmont, CA: Wadsworth.

Eck, J. E. and Wartell, J. (1998). Improving the management of rental properties with drug problems: A randomized experiment. In L. G. Mazerolle and J. Roehl (eds.), *Civil remedies and crime prevention, 9* (pp. 161–183). Monsey, NY: Criminal Justice Press.

Greene, J. R. (2004). Community policing and organization change. In Wesley G. Skogan (ed.), *Community policing: Can it work?* (pp. 30–53). Belmont, CA: Wadsworth.

Grinc, R. M. (1994). "Angles in marble": Problems in stimulating community involvement in community policing. *Crime and Delinquency, 40,* 437–468.

Lurigio, A. and Rosenbaum, D. (1994). The impact of community policing on police personnel. In D. P. Rosenbaum (ed.), *The challenge of community policing: Testing the promises.* Thousand Oaks, CA: Sage Publications.

Mastrofski, S. D. (1998). Community policing and police organization structure. In J. Brodeur (ed.), *Community policing and the evaluation of police service delivery* (pp. 161–189). Thousand Oaks, CA: Sage Publications.

Moy, P. and Pfau, M. (2000). *With malice toward all? The media and public confidence in democratic institutions.* Westport, CT: Praeger Publishing.

Pate, A. M. and Shtull, P. (1994). Community policing grows in Brooklyn: An inside view of the New York Police Department's model precinct. *Crime and Delinquency, 40,* 384–410.

Sadd, S. and Grinc, R. (1994). Innovative neighborhood oriented policing: An evaluation of community policing programs in eight cities. In D. P. Rosenbaum (ed.), *The challenge of community policing: Testing the promises* (pp. 27–52). Thousand Oaks, CA: Sage Publications.

Sampson, R. J., Raudenbush, S., and Earls, F. (1997). Neighborhoods and violent crime: A multilevel study of collective efficacy. *Science, 277,* 918–924.

Skogan, W. G. (1988). Community organizations and crime. In M. Tonry and N. Morris (eds.), *Crime and justice: An annual review, 10*. Chicago: University of Chicago Press.

(1990). *Disorder and decline: Crime and the spiral of decay in American cities*. New York: The Free Press.

(2004). Community policing: Common impediments to success. In L. Fridell and M. A. Wycoff (eds.), *Community policing: the past, present, and future*. Washington, DC: The Annie E. Casey Foundation and the Police Executive Research Forum, 159–168.

Skogan, W. G. and Hartnett, S. (1997). *Community policing, Chicago style*. New York: Oxford University Press.

Skogan, W. G. and Steiner, L. (2004). *Community policing in Chicago, year ten*. Chicago: Illinois Criminal Justice Information Authority.

Skogan, W. G., Hartnett, S., DuBois, J., Comey, J., Kaiser, M., and Lovig, J. (1999). *On the beat: Police and community problem solving*. Boulder, CO: Westview Press.

Skogan, W. G., Steiner, L., Hartnett, S., DuBois, J., Bennis, J., Rottinghaus, B., Kim, S., Van, K., and Rosenbaum, D. (2003). *Community policing in Chicago, years eight and nine*. Chicago: Illinois Criminal Justice Information Authority.

Weisburd, D., Mastrofski, S., McNally, A. M., Greenspan, R., and Willis, J. (2003). Reforming to preserve: Compstat and strategic problem solving in American policing. *Criminology and Public Policy, 2*, 421–456.

3 *Critic*
Community policing: a skeptical view

Stephen Mastrofski

About two decades ago a few American police leaders caught the wave of community policing reform, and now just about everybody's going surfing. Early interest in this reform can be attributed to police anxieties about skyrocketing crime and urban violence, unmet rising expectations from the civil rights movement, and middle-class alienation from government authority (Fogelson 1977: ch. 11). Like a "perfect storm" these forces converged in the 1960s, stimulating intense criticism from blue ribbon commissions and a daily drumbeat of negative press for police. Calls for change were issued, some of them radical: community control of policing, deprofessionalization, and reassignment of some core police tasks to other government agencies and the private sector. Alarmed and intent on ending this crisis of legitimacy (LaFree 1998), progressive police and scholars began to experiment with ways to make American police both more effective and more democratic without losing many of the advances made in policing in the previous half century. The resulting "community policing" reforms were influenced by fashions in organization development intended to make them less bureaucratic, more responsive to the "customer," and more results-oriented (Mastrofski 1998; Mastrofski and Ritti 2000).

Unlike some reforms that narrow their focus over time, community policing has remained multifaceted and diverse. Some departments emphasize broken windows policing, others feature problem-oriented policing and still others stress policing that establishes stronger police–public partnerships (Mastrofski, Worden, and Snipes 1995: 540–541). Much of the reform literature suggests that all of these are desirable and compatible. Whether or not that is so, it is clear that different elements of community policing appeal to different audiences, and it has led to fruitless debates over what community policing "really" means. In fact, it is this ambiguity and flexibility that gives community policing its all-things-to-all-people character and has contributed to its political viability over two decades, embraced by public leaders across the political spectrum. However, this diversity makes it difficult to conduct a rigorous inquiry into the merits of community policing, a finding noted by the panel on police policies and practices organized by the National Research Council to assess, among other things, this reform (Committee to Review Research 2004: 232–233). It concluded that community policing was simply too amorphous a concept to submit to empirical evaluation and recommended that researchers evaluate it by breaking it down into more specific components.

The editors of this volume seem to have taken the NRC panel's recommendation; they have organized chapters around a number of specific reforms that have in fact been widely construed as important elements of community policing: problem-oriented policing, broken windows policing, third-party policing, offender-focused policing, and hot spots policing. Therefore, I will limit my discussion of community policing to those efforts that seek to link the police more closely to the community in "partnership" arrangements: joint activities to coproduce services and desired outcomes, giving the community a greater say in what the police do, or simply engaging with each other to produce a greater sense of police–community compatibility.

I will fulfill my role as community policing critic by offering a skeptical view. The skeptic is a thoughtful doubter; doubting is a methodology, not a conclusion. To the extent that community policing is a good thing, it should withstand the careful scrutiny of thoughtful doubters. I will ask four questions about community policing in the United States. How has the community policing reform movement changed what the public expects of its police? How has the community policing movement changed the way that policing is organized and performed? How, if at all, has community policing produced beneficial public outcomes – less crime and disorder, more or better service, more social capital, and more equitable service delivery? What impact has community policing had on police legitimacy?

The public's expectations of the police

Reform movements are built on promises that may stimulate expectations not previously held widely. They can fuel change because "Nothing happens unless first a dream" (Sandburg 1970). Community policing begins with a distinct advantage, for its advocates promise to deliver what the public has long dreamed of but received only in middle-class suburbs: client-oriented, "service-style" policing (Wilson 1968). So it seems unlikely that community policing has changed what folks *want*, but it may well have altered that to which a good many feel *entitled*, especially those segments of society that were heretofore least likely to enjoy it, the economically and socially disadvantaged. The majority of Americans are probably aware in a general way of community policing and its promises (Harris Poll 1999), but most probably cannot articulate the finer points of community policing programs. Nonetheless, it appeals to powerful political and cultural themes of our time that have to do with a blend of both communitarian and good-government ideals (Manning 1984; Crank 1994; Lyons 1999: 18–25).

There has been virtually no research on what citizens expect of their police that would enable us to draw conclusions about the impact of community policing. Here we must rely upon a bit of indirect evidence and a great deal of speculation. The promises of community policing reform have steadily rained down on the American public over the last decade, leaving us with a reasonable, if untested, assumption that they have had at least some impact. Community policing has been a significant presence in many local news outlets around the nation, and in virtually all of them the picture of community policing has been unremittingly positive (Mastrofski and Ritti 1999; Chermak and Weiss 2002). The most frequently mentioned theme in community policing stories is the police–community partnership dimension (Mastrofski and Ritti 1999), followed by bringing more resources to the local police, and producing tangible results. This provides some fuel for speculation about the "field of dreams" that community policing advocates are building in the minds of the American public. It has two basic elements: police responsiveness and results. Community policing promises greater police responsiveness that takes the form of accessibility, the police knowing and appreciating what citizens want, and better prospects in the competition for police services. Deeply embedded in responsiveness is also an expectation of civility and caring, concerns that were front and center in the legitimacy crisis of the 1960s (Reiss 1971). Under results I include safer, easier to live in communities and a stronger "community" through shared values and collective action. If asked to articulate what they expect from community policing, citizens would give these themes dominance. They have been nicely summarized as a yearning to "get back to Mayberry" (Lyons 1999: 163).

If the public has come to embrace community policing's promises as entitlements, what does that mean for the future of community policing? Pre-existing expectations do significantly color how citizens evaluate the policing they receive (Reisig and Chandek 2001), but as Shakespeare noted, "Oft expectation fails and most oft there where most it promises." Community policing reformers have encouraged the public to expect so much more, which makes it all the more imperative for police organizations to demonstrate results.

The organization and practice of policing

Community policing has been well marketed, but to what extent has it transformed the nature of policing in a nation where local influences predominate? I will consider three ways in which police organizations might be transformed: the adoption of new programs and altered structures, changes in the philosophy and culture of the rank-and-file, and changes in how the police practice their work at the street level.

Community policing programs and structures

We expect two kinds of programmatic and structural changes from community policing. First, it should broaden police organization goals because it should increase responsiveness to the much wider range of services citizens presumably want from their police compared to the much narrower confines imposed by the "professional" model. Second, it should alter the way police are organized to accomplish their goals.

If we were to measure changes in organization goals by observing police departments' mission statements and strategic plans, we would undoubtedly conclude that community policing has had a major transformative effect. By 2000 more than 80 percent of large police departments and more than 60 percent of small ones reported that they had incorporated community policing values in their mission statements (Roth, Roehl, and Johnson 2004: 20). However, mission statements and plans by themselves tell us little about the goals that the organization really enacts. We learn more about the organization's commitment to the community-oriented mission by examining such things as how the organization routinely evaluates itself, how it evaluates and rewards its officers, and how it prepares them to answer the demands of community policing. What little we know about the transformation of police organizations in these domains is not particularly encouraging. The vast majority of departments still expend most of their energies tracking traditional crime and enforcement statistics, rather than developing performance systems that track neighborhood quality of life and problem-solving (Weisel and Eck 1994: 66; Skogan and Hartnett 1997: 241; Greene 2004: 39). Perhaps most telling, recruit training has not been substantially revised to promote community policing.[1]

Despite reformers' admonition that community policing cannot be defined solely as a set of programs, program implementation has been a common strategy for accomplishing its goals. Neighborhood Watch, citizen police academies, citizen surveys, and the establishment of community policing units are some examples of programs that are often appended to the existing organization (Roth *et al.* 2004: 8). In addition, a department may adopt certain structures thought to *facilitate* police–community partnerships, such as drawing beat boundaries to coincide with neighborhood boundaries, permanent assignment of officers to beats, and delegating decisionmaking to the lowest level to enable a more fine-tuned degree of responsiveness to community preferences and needs (Roth *et al.* 2004: 18–21). The adoption of such programs has been variable by type of program, but nonetheless widespread across the American landscape (Maguire and Mastrofski 2000; Roth, Ryan, Gaffigan *et al.* 2000; Maguire and Katz 2002). Most importantly, in a relatively short time the number of police agencies adopting such programs has grown significantly (Roth *et al.* 2004). However, these types of studies tend to indicate that the *partnership* aspects of community policing are the most weakly implemented (Maguire and Katz 2002; Maguire and King 2004; Roth *et al.* 2004).

The above evidence is based exclusively on police agency self-reports to the Office of Community Oriented Policing Services (COPS) and from mail surveys. Questions about the validity of such data naturally arise. The popularity of community policing creates a strong incentive to skew the department's self-presentation in favor of program adoption, especially since 1994, when large federal grants from COPS became available to departments willing to show a commitment to implementing community policing (Maguire 2002: 52–53; Maguire and Katz 2002: 513). And even if a program has been adopted, there is the question of "dosage," how extensive and intensive the program is over time and space (Maguire and Mastrofski 2000; Roth *et al.* 2004: 4). These claims about community policing adoption, measured from a distance, through the eyes of interested parties, and without much precision or independent validation, should be interpreted as an indication of the *desirability* of community partnership programs and structures, or the desirability of the *appearance* of these programs.

We might have greater faith in indirect measures of structural change in police organizations, debureaucratizing changes thought instrumental to the accomplishment of community policing, but based on measures arguably less susceptible to the reactivity of the desirability of reform (Maguire 1997; Mastrofski 1998; Mastrofski and Ritti 2000; Greene 2004). The most comprehensive analysis found mixed results between 1987 and 1998 (Maguire, Shin, Zhao, and Hassell 2003). Large municipal police agencies moved significantly toward the community policing ideals of decentralization, lower administrative intensity, and greater civilianization. Some aspects of spatial differentiation did increase (more police stations and mini-stations), but the number of beats did not. On the other hand, hierarchical flattening did not occur, nor did hierarchical segmentation, and vertical differentiation continued to increase. Police agencies also failed to become less formalized and less functionally differentiated. This hardly constitutes evidence of a revolution in the structure of policing.

A more valid approach to measuring community policing program implementation is on-site observation, but here we lack a sufficiently large, representative sample of organizations monitored over time. What we have instead are a small collection of in-depth case studies and cross-sectional comparisons of departments, most of which were selected because they were thought to exemplify good community policing implementation. Some of these have claimed successes in implementing community policing (Roth *et al.* 2000: ch. 7), but a substantial number have also documented failures and disappointments (Greene, Bergman, and McLaughlin 1994; Sadd and Grinc 1994; Tien and Rich 1994; Rosenbaum and Wilkinson 2004).

Skeptics should be prepared to accept that some departments have made changes in programs and structures, moving them closer to the ideals of community policing reformers. But there is reason to think that many, and probably most, American police departments fall far short of those few leaders. Some have understood this sort of phenomenon from the perspective of "institutional" organization theory (Meyer and Rowan 1977; DiMaggio and Powell 1983). One version of this theory distinguishes early adopters of a reform from later adopters (Tolbert and Zucker 1983). Early adopters are driven to undertake new structures and programs to meet the demands of their technical environment (e.g., high or rising crime rates). These pioneers experiment and are willing to take risks by innovating to improve their technical performance in such domains as reducing crime and improving the quality of life. But for industries such as policing, that do not use validated technologies that are well proven to produce the desired results, the further diffusion of these innovations among the vast majority of police organizations depends primarily upon their becoming accepted as the "right" thing to do – entirely independent of the quantity and quality of empirical evidence on their ability to accomplish desired goals (Scott 1992). Once important leaders in policing begin to adopt community policing as the "right" way to do things, and once political leaders embrace it, rigorous scientific evidence regarding its performance becomes irrelevant as organizations scramble to adopt the programs and structures of the early adopters. This may account for the success of programs such as DARE, which flourished before any evidence was available on its ability to prevent illicit drug use and which continues to flourish in the face of evidence that it provides no prevention benefits (Rosenbaum and Hanson 1998; Gottfredson, Wilson, and Najaka 2002). In fact, it accounts for the phenomenon that strikes some researchers as curious: that billions of dollars have been spent on community policing reforms and millions on research on community policing, but there is so little rigorous evidence on its effects on crime and disorder (Weisburd and Eck 2004).

Some researchers have applied institutional theory to policing (see Crank 2003 for a review), but there is relatively little evidence on the early-versus-late-adopter diffusion model. Ritti and Mastrofski (2002) found evidence consistent with that model in their examination of articles on community policing in professional police journals. Based on a nationally representative mail survey, Moon (2004) examined the extent to which community policing programs were adopted in the late 1990s, comparing the influence of technical and institutional pressures on early and late adopters. While not a complete confirmation of institutional theory's application to the diffusion of community policing, his research strongly supported the greater power of institutional over technical influences as the driving force behind community policing adoption at this stage.

Community policing philosophy and culture

"Community policing is a philosophy, not a program" (Roth *et al.* 2000: 183) is a popular phrase among academics and practitioners. From this I infer that community policing is implemented only when police officers in large numbers adopt an appropriate set of values; whether or not community policing has been externalized into programs and structures, it has not been implemented until police officers have internalized it. Depending on how one defines "philosophy," this can be a very low standard or a very high one. If a philosophy means what one thinks, feels, or avers (Sparrow, Moore, and Kennedy 1990: ch. 5), then the implementation standard is rather low. It is well established in social psychology and the study of police that values or philosophies measured in these ways are weak predictors of actual practice (Ajzen 1987; Worden 1989; Mastrofski and Parks 1990; Snipes and Mastrofski 1990; Terrill and Mastrofski 2004). Nonetheless, police attitudes about community policing in general, and specifically the partnership aspects of community policing are by some accounts overwhelmingly positive (e.g., Weisburd, Greenspan, Hamilton *et al.* 2001: 25–26). Such surveys ask officers to assess community policing principles in the abstract, but it is the particulars of officers' experiences in their departments that have the greatest meaning for how they act, and here the level of rank-and-file skepticism is much higher

(Sadd and Grinc 1994; Zhao, He, and Lovrich 1999; Schafer 2001: ch. 9; Rosenbaum and Wilkinson 2004).

If we take the philosophy-not-a-program (PNAP) perspective to mean that community policing must not only be embraced, but that it must guide practice, then we set a much higher standard. Some evidence suggests that officers who claim to embrace community policing values also behave differently from those who do not (Mastrofski *et al.* 1995; Mastrofski, Snipes, Parks, and Maxwell 2000; Terrill, Paoline, and Manning 2003), but we note that far more powerful are the structural and programmatic elements (e.g., whether the officer has been given a community policing assignment). On the whole, a pro-community policing attitude does not appear to be a powerful predictor of officer behavior.

"Probably the biggest obstacle facing anyone who would implement a new strategy of policing is the difficulty of changing the ongoing culture of policing" (Moore 1992: 150). A skeptic should wonder about the validity of this claim, a fellow traveler to PNAP, because it may have the causal mechanism of behavioral change backwards. It is like blaming the patient's heart attack on his failing heart, rather than his diet, exercise, and genes. In the same way, changes in the occupational police culture may be less the *cause* of community policing practices than the *consequence* of structural changes, focusing on occupational culture as the change directs attention away from what might shape practice.

There is some evidence to suggest that a *monolithic* police subculture opposed to the principles of community policing may have never existed (Muir 1977; Worden 1995) and even if it once did, it is now splintered into many different subgroups with varying degrees of support and opposition to community policing (Cochran and Bromley 2003; Wood, Davis, and Rouse 2004). Over the last three decades hiring practices have changed, increasing the proportion of officers who are female, minority, and college educated (Committee to Review Research 2004: 79). These sorts of people may be more receptive to community policing (Weisburd *et al.* 2001: 31; Cochran and Bromley 2003: 102), but most research also shows that police socialization processes exert far more influence over officers' behavior than hiring practices (Committee to Review Research 2004: ch. 4).

What are the structural determinants of police culture, and to what extent have they been transformed to produce the expected changes in police practice? The principal management tool for shaping police practices is training, and, unfortunately, we have little rigorous evidence on the impact of police training in general, much less that of community policing training (Committee to Review Research 2004: 141–147). Of the handful of studies that look at the effects of training relevant to community policing, some indicate that it does yield more community policing practices and about an equal number indicate that it has no effect. Critics of the usual community policing training have argued that it wrong-headedly seeks to change officers' values and beliefs rather than giving them skills they can use to promote values they already possess (Buerger 1998; Haar 2001). Perhaps a more fundamental problem with community policing training is that many departments may use it as the sole or principal mode of changing police culture, and when its message is not reinforced by supervisors, managers, and policies that determine how performance is measured, monitored, and rewarded, there can be little hope that any fruit born of the training will but die on the vine. Indeed, police departments seem to invest more energy into converting the rank-and-file to a community policing philosophy than they do motivating supervisors and managers to promote community policing and giving them the skills and resources needed to do it. Large-scale studies are not available to document the scope of this problem, but this is a theme of case studies reporting disappointing results in the implementation of community policing (Schafer 2001; Rosenbaum and Wilkinson 2004). Even the experiences of Chicago suggest that getting the training right is no easy matter, and getting the hierarchy capable and on board is challenging too (Skogan and Hartnett 1997). Creating the proper structural environment for community policing is then no slam dunk, and there is good reason to suspect that large numbers of departments are not even getting close to the basket.

Police reformers have long emphasized the role of the top executive in shaping the culture and ultimately the practices of the police agency (Goldstein 1990; Sparrow *et al.* 1990; Moore and Stephens 1991). I have elsewhere expressed skepticism about the capacity of the police chief to transform the organization in this sort of way (Mastrofski 2002), but we lack objective and rigorous empirical tests of this proposition. We are not without autobiographical accounts of leadership success (Bratton 1998; Kerik 2001), albeit to create organizational cultures that tried to undo the brand of community-partnership policing that is the focus of this chapter, but these accounts are clearly not the product of disinterested, rigorous evaluation.

Community policing at the street level

The greatest discretion in the delivery of police services rests with the lowest-ranking officers, so the ultimate test of the reform's impact will be observed at the street level. This section is organized according to different types of practices that community policing, as construed in this chapter, is supposed to promote. I consider whether officers who receive or show some form of community policing "dosage" (e.g., community policing specialist assignment, training, positive attitude toward community policing) to a greater extent than others engage in more of the desired practice.

Engaging the community. One of the great attractions of community policing is its promise to bring officers face-to-face with the public – to learn more about people and their problems, solve them, or at least comfort them when they cannot be solved. Permanent beat assignments, foot and bike patrol, mini-stations, and park-and-walk tactics are designed to increase "face time" between officers and their clientele. The philosophy of community policing highly values these interactions. Systematic observations of community policing present disappointing results. The data from a handful of departments suggest that the daily routine of both patrol generalists and specialists does not involve heavy engagement with the public, especially those in the neighborhoods to which officers are assigned.[2]

Many expect that community policing will produce a decline in the use of arrest and physical coercion. Some systematic field research shows that the style of community policing embraced by management may influence the use of verbal and physical coercion (Terrill and Mastrofski 2004: 127), and another study suggests that officers who embrace community policing make fewer arrests (Mastrofski *et al.* 1995: 552), but in the first case the researchers were unable to illuminate the mechanisms by which management achieved these results,[3] and in the second they were unable to determine whether making fewer arrests was a good thing (Mastrofski 2004). A study of situations where officers were seeking citizen compliance showed that officers positively disposed to community policing were not statistically distinguishable from negatively disposed officers in their resort to coercion (Mastrofski, Snipes, and Supina 1996: 291). The limited evidence suggests that community policing has not had profound effects on the use of coercion.

Aside from improving the quantity and quality of police–citizen encounters on the street, many departments employ programs to increase police–citizen interaction in settings that focus on the discussion of priorities, exchanging information and ideas, and planning for joint citizen–police problem-solving ventures. Perhaps the most earnest and sustained effort of this sort, and certainly the most studied, is Chicago's (Skogan, Steiner, Benitez *et al.* 2004). Chicago's police-sponsored "beat meetings" offer neighborhood residents an opportunity to influence police priorities, participate in problem-solving, and evaluate and discuss the quality of police service in the neighborhood. Researchers report that the extent to which these things are achieved varies greatly, but that on the whole, public involvement has improved over the last decade. Large numbers of residents show up, citizens actively discuss neighborhood problems, police provide information, solutions are proposed, and over time this has become as likely in disadvantaged neighborhoods as in those that are better off. By 2002 over half of the observed beat meetings involved equal police–citizen participation (Skogan *et al.* 2004: 19–23). However, despite intensive efforts, the meetings have had much less success in mobilizing citizens to engage in collective self-help behavior. It seems that large numbers of those who go to the trouble to participate tend to view the meetings as places to lobby for service delivery, not participate in its coproduction.

Seattle's neighborhood partnership efforts emerged from community groups organizing on their own to influence police and policing, but an in-depth study there yielded a less positive assessment than in Chicago (Lyons 1999). Despite some early advances in advancing democratic mechanisms for interaction, problem-solving, and accountability (both among different citizen groups and between citizens and local government), these were observed to atrophy, and instead Seattle's community groups served as a device to secure community conformance to police structures and priorities.

Providing services. Community policing advocates expect that officers will be more inclined to serve the public in ways that appeal to those who desire direct benefits. Community policing specialists do not appear to be more inclined than generalists to engage in such activities as: controlling problem citizens, being nice to citizens, spending time on citizens' problems (Mastrofski *et al.* 2000; Snipes 2002), or using an informal, order maintenance solution (Novak, Hartman, Holsinger, and Turner 1999). Some studies do show that training and officer attitudes are associated with an increased proclivity to deliver services, but even here the results are mixed (Committee to Review Research 2004: 142–145). Some (including a randomized experiment) show the expected relationship, but others (also including a randomized experiment) do not. One study found that officers having both training and a pro-community policing attitude were more inclined to grant citizens' requests to control people who were bothering them (Mastrofski *et al.* 2000), but another found that officers more positively oriented to community policing spent less time on their encounters with citizens (Snipes 2002). At best, the capacity of community policing to enhance service-style practices is contingent on currently unspecified conditions, making the prediction of improvements a river boat gamble.

Process-oriented policing. Many community policing reformers want officers to attend to the processes of police–citizen interaction so that citizens feel good about those interactions – regardless of what the police do to or for the citizen. That is, the public should accept these actions as legitimate. Legitimacy requires officers to show respect to citizens, listen to their complaints and viewpoints, show concern for their well-being through inquiry and demonstrations of understanding, and demonstrate procedural fairness (Mastrofski 1999; Tyler 2004). While there is a growing body of evidence indicating that when police behave in these ways, police legitimacy is increased and concomitantly citizen compliance and law abidingness also increase (Sherman 1997b; Committee to Review Research 2004; Tyler 2004), there is very little evidence about the extent to which *community policing* efforts are responsible for officers engaging in these actions. Of the two studies testing this, one found that officers who regarded community policing positively were more likely to get citizens to comply with their requests to stop or avoid misbehavior, but this analysis also showed that pro-community policing officers were generally not more likely to resort to legitimacy-enhancing procedural methods (Mastrofski *et al.* 1996: 290; McCluskey, Mastrofski, and Parks 1999). The researchers hypothesized that officers who embraced community policing were perhaps more skilled at fitting the most effective compliance strategy to the particular circumstances. Another study of adherence to constitutional standards of search and seizure found that those officers who were most strongly committed to community policing were also those who committed the largest share of constitutional violations, perhaps because they were more committed to ridding the community of troublemakers than adhering to procedural requirements (Gould and Mastrofski 2004). Thus, we cannot say with any confidence that community policing has really contributed to a more procedurally sensitive style of policing in America.

The outcomes of policing

Reformers claim that community policing will lessen crime, disorder, and fear of crime. They also expect that it will render more and better service to the public and increase the social capital in our communities. Some expect that it will produce a more equitable distribution of services – giving more to those who have less. And, ultimately, community policing perhaps above all, is expected to produce more support for the public police, a greater degree of legitimacy. What does the evidence show?

Crime, disorder, and fear of crime

The National Academies have recently published a volume that includes a review of research on the impact of community policing. I draw liberally upon its findings here, and those of a somewhat modified version of its report published by the two researchers who chaired this part of the National Academy of Science (NAS) review (Committee to Review Research 2004: ch. 6; Weisburd and Eck 2004). Both of these reports concluded that the available research shows that foot patrol, storefront offices, newsletters, and community meetings do not reduce crime, although some may influence perceptions of disorder, a pattern consistent with earlier reviews of the literature (Rosenbaum 1988; Sherman 1997b). Community policing programs designed to increase police–community interaction or make police more visible and accessible were found to reduce fear of crime and perceptions of disorder, but only one strategy, police officers making routine, door-to-door contact with residents, was shown to reduce crime. Finally, they noted a growing body of research that finds with consistency that when police undertake acts perceived as enhancing procedural fairness, citizens are more likely to comply with police requests and more likely to obey the law in the future (see McCluskey 2003; Tyler 2004).

The experts' review of community policing's effectiveness in reducing crime, fear, and disorder seem equivocal at best and pessimistic at worst. The National Academies committee concluded:

Some community policing strategies appear to reduce crime, disorder, or fear of crime. Many others have not been found to be effective when evaluated. (Committee to Review Research 2004: 246)

Nonetheless, the research available suggests that when the police partner more generally with the public, levels of citizen fear will decline. Moreover, when the police are able to gain wider legitimacy among citizens and offenders, nonexperimental evidence suggests that the likelihood of offending will be reduced. (Committee to Review Research 2004: 250–251)

Weisburd and Eck (2004: 59) were somewhat more cautious:

Yet in reviewing existing studies, we could find no consistent research agenda that would allow us to assess with strong confidence the effectiveness of community policing. Given the importance of community policing, we were surprised that more systematic study was not available.

The skeptic's perspective on this body of research subscribes to the following points. First, the claim that community policing at least reduces fear of crime and perceptions of disorder deserves closer scrutiny. Even the experimental evaluations failed to control for the possibility that reductions in people's cognitions of crime and victimization risk were due to a sort of Hawthorne effect. That is, it may be that what produced these results was the perception that citizens were receiving more or better attention; the control groups did not include programs that ensured comparable levels of service of a different sort, nor did they attempt to create a comparable sense of "specialness" enjoyed by the community policing treatment groups.

Second, we should not place too much weight on the small number of studies that have shown that door-to-door home visits reduce crime. Even though these were based on experimental evaluations, the theory that links an infrequent home visit to neighborhood crime reduction requires considerable elaboration. How is it that so mild an intervention could yield a significant reduction in crime? Did this cause neighbors to mobilize more effectively to prevent crime, and if so, how does that square with so many other studies that show that such citizen mobilizations show no crime reduction effects? Did these visits render better information for police to identify and arrest criminals? To take preventive action?

Third, nearly *all* community partnership programs suffer from a similar set of theoretical and practical challenges that make success problematic. Their failure may be due to weak implementation, which I have already indicated is likely widespread (see also Rosenbaum 1988). But it seems just as likely that even where the programs have been thoroughly and vigorously implemented, success will be haphazard at best. Stronger police–community partnerships, at least as implemented, do not appear to add much to a community's capacity to control crime and disorder. That is because police organizations (a) have not done much to develop better relations with those who have the best information about crime and disorder, and (b) police have not developed systems that can sift through and process information that will really help them develop effective strategies to reduce crime and disorder. There can be little doubt that effective policing depends upon a cooperative citizenry, but the value added by community policing programs, which focus on citizens predisposed to work with the police, has been marginal. Even special programs designed to make youths feel good about the police (DARE, police athletic leagues), in the hope that they will later provide useful information about crime and other community problems, are very weak interventions when compared with the day-to-day experiences those youths and their acquaintances have with the police. The public is more cooperative when they perceive the police to be considerate and fair (Tyler and Huo 2002), but this has not been a well-developed aspect of community policing programs (see next paragraph). Those most likely to have the best information about crime are the very ones who also report the worst experiences with the police. And it is not at all clear that police departments have figured out how to use effectively the information that does flow to them from the public. Crime analysis units still comprise a very small part of police departments, and recent reports about their limitations are not very reassuring (O'Shea and Nicholls 2003), nor are reports that departmental communications about community-based problem solving are too poorly written to facilitate departmental monitoring (Skogan *et al.* 2004: 154).

Fourth, despite the undeniable appeal of a kinder, fairer police also being more effective in reducing crime, the relevance of these studies to community policing must be questioned. Community policing promises to deliver this style of policing, and the question for us is whether *community policing* interventions have done so and can therefore be linked to those desirable outcomes. As mentioned earlier, research has not linked community policing to this tendency to engage in procedural fairness. Further, we know nothing of the effects of community policing training and other strategies to promote this style of policing. The evidence suggests that when officers engage in procedural fairness, citizens are more compliant and law-abiding, but the real trick appears to be in finding ways to get officers to adopt those approaches, and here the very limited evidence available on community policing is not too promising.

Building social capital

Some research offers a beacon of hope to community policing advocates. Researchers are finding that collective efficacy (social cohesion among neighbors and a willingness to act toward the common good) is associated with lower levels of violence and disorder, and that this may be causal in nature (Sampson and Groves 1989; Sampson, Raudenbush, and Earls 1997; Sampson and Raudenbush 1999; Reisig and Parks 2004). Neighborhoods are socially efficacious when members monitor the behavior of children, intervene to prevent socially disruptive practices (e.g., truancy, prostitution, drug dealing), and to secure resources from public and private institutions that can benefit the neighborhood. Through these mechanisms the neighborhood's capacity to prevent and react to threats to safety and order are enhanced. Although there is much still to be learned about the effects of social efficacy on crime and disorder, these findings are encouraging. The key question is whether community policing promotes social efficacy. Unfortunately, the answer seems to be that most community policing programs are not well suited to promote this purpose.

The most obvious problem with the popular community partnership programs is that they simply do not focus on developing the skills and habits among the public (or the police) that build collective efficacy. Neighborhood Watch does little to build social cohesion where it does not already exist. DARE tries to produce individuals with a drug-free lifestyle, but does little to develop the civic virtues of persons engaged in collective enterprises for the common good. Citizen–police academies teach a great deal about how police organizations operate, but that seems useful mostly for getting citizens to fit in with the department's organizational structures and routines, not for taking the initiative in one's own neighborhood. The problem with most community policing partnership programs is that they focus too much on how to conform to police expectations rather than how members of the community can be given the will, skill, and resources to themselves engage in behaviors that contribute to less crime and a higher quality of life in the community. Whether the police are even the best instrument or should take the lead to promote collective efficacy is debatable. While the evidence on community-based efforts is not especially heartening (Sherman 1997a), there is some encouraging evidence about certain school-based programs (Gottfredson 1997). Wherever such efforts are sponsored, they are hard work, especially in those neighborhoods that are most disadvantaged, because the limitations of distrust, lack of resources, and inexperience in organizing present great challenges.

To be sure, some departments attempt to address the challenge of building collective efficacy by coming to grips with how to foster civic habits in citizens and sharing decisionmaking power in police. The best known of these is Chicago's. But as already indicated, despite impressive levels of participation in beat meetings (following a "re-engineering" of the city's original model), Chicago has not enjoyed much success in mobilizing residents to *act*, and the police department has a high turnover rate in officers attending the meetings, which undermines the establishment of stronger police-community relations (Skogan *et al.* 2004: 154). The picture of Chicago's "district advisory committees," operating at a more strategic level, is far less positive, lacking a clear purpose and getting more advice from police than they give to them. Thus, while Chicago's community policing may have made significant advances in developing the bases for social capital, it has a long way to go.

More equitable distribution of policing's benefits

Liberals are attracted to the prospect that community policing will deliver more good things to society's have-nots. Even if community policing were not more effective, if it redistributed services more equitably, one could argue that it had produced a net good for society. However, community policing calls for an alteration in the mechanisms of service delivery, shifting from one that relies on reacting to individual calls for service, to one that reacts to priorities established by organized elements of the community – neighborhood organizations, businesses, churches, victim groups, and the like. As previously noted, some research shows that when society's disadvantaged are well organized for collective action in these ways, greater benefits do come their way, but the problem remains: the disadvantaged are less likely to organize effectively for collective action (Skogan 1994: 179). The question then is whether community policing invests in society's have-nots a greater capacity to engage the police and lobby for the benefits they can bestow. If it does not, then by virtue of its distributional biases, giving more to those who can organize effectively, it may actually exacerbate service quantity and quality differentials between the haves and have-nots.

Skogan (2004; and Skogan *et al.* 2004: 26–37) provides the most focused research on this question, confirming that those most active in neighborhood beat meetings and district advisory committees in Chicago are indeed those who are better off, especially in Latino areas. In Chicago there is only a weak correspondence between what concerns the residential population of neighborhoods and those active in beat meetings, and activists tend to be more positive about the quality of police services (Skogan 2004: 65–67). However, there is some evidence that where neighborhood organizations work most energetically with the police, they will receive more service and that the city's response does tend to correspond to the priorities of both residents in general and especially activists. Yet this research does not provide a comparison of whether Chicago's reorganization of police service delivery to respond to neighborhood organization priorities works as well for the disadvantaged as it does for the advantaged, much less whether the disadvantaged are "gaining ground" compared to the more advantaged neighborhoods. Ultimately, we do not know whether Chicago's disadvantaged are better off under the community policing arrangements for mobilizing police responses than what preceded them.[4]

The research seems to tell us that where police-community partnerships flourish, there is a greater possibility of improving the quality of life, but that community policing's benefits will least likely be delivered to society's most afflicted. Researchers have not yet demonstrated that community policing helps them gain ground, but it does suggest that in a community policing environment, collective action is an important element for doing so. The challenge is in finding how to infuse the disadvantaged with the will and resources to organize effectively, and how to develop a community will to make the necessary investments to make that happen. If there is a magic wand to do this, community policing has not yet found how to activate its software.

The success story: nothing exceeds like success

When Americans want ever so badly to have a success, there are always many willing to seize upon an emblematic example, a "poster child" that inspires us to see what *can* be done, and from that infer that it *is* being done. Public officials, ever sensitive to the state of police legitimacy, surely welcome these success stories and understandably embrace them as good omens. Following in the wake of the crises of legitimacy that helped to ring down the curtain on the "professional" era of police reform, community policing success stories have proven to be a powerful force for sustaining the reform. They fuel the engines of "institutional isomorphism" in policing – as evidenced by the rapidity with which contemporary reforms are adopted. Obversely, skepticism is not all that palatable when people seek to nourish their hopes from such success stories. There are several such community policing success stories around the nation, and perhaps the most chronicled of these is Chicago's. I will focus on it, because it has the added advantage of being the object of over a decade's intense empirical evaluation.

The large body of studies published on Chicago's community policing effort comes from a consortium of researchers led by Wesley Skogan. As he has written the companion chapter to mine in this volume, I will not offer a detailed review of this careful, impressive body of work, but from it I will draw my own conclusions. Does community policing in Chicago work? Not like a Swiss clock, but it is a worthy effort that seems to have rendered many significant improvements over what preceded it (Skogan *et al.* 2004). That seems to me cause for encouragement, but my skeptic responsibilities lead me to take a second lesson from the Chicago story, which is that effective implementation of community policing is not a walk in the park; it is hard work that requires identifying and correcting mistakes and a sustained commitment at many levels inside and outside the organization (DuBois and Hartnett 2002; Skogan *et al.* 2004). Repeatedly, Chicago's evaluators note that there are many obstacles to full and effective implementation, they are not always overcome, and often the successes are mixed. Is this the model for the nation? I think not. Like running a sub-four-minute mile, we know it can be done, but we also know that few have the will and resources to do it. Early adopters may have that degree of commitment, but later adopters often rely upon the notoriety of the early adopters' success, and fail to attend to the challenges that must be overcome to secure that success in their case (Tolbert and Zucker 1983; Ritti and Mastrofski 2002). In fact, it seems likely that most police departments and their communities are unwilling or unable to make the sorts of commitments it takes to go beyond the fairly superficial transformations that come from adopting canned programs that are pale replicas of the "real deal." Even as early as 1993, only half of the top executive respondents to a national survey indicated that community policing would require major changes in policies, goals, mission statements, and training, and only 27 percent indicated that it would require extensive reorganization (Wycoff 1994). Thus, it seems unlikely that large numbers were committed to the kind of effort that Chicago's experience suggests is necessary to show substantial gains.

Enhanced police legitimacy

At first blush, the answer to the question, "Did community policing increase police legitimacy?" appears to be a no-brainer. Its rampant popularity among police agencies and elected officials, and the virtual absence of negative publicity point to a hearty, "Yes!" But if we apply the same standard of evidence to this issue as to others, the answer becomes less obvious.

We do not have anything resembling an experimental or quasi-experimental design by which we might judge the impact of the reform on legitimacy, so we need to rely on less rigorous methods. One approach is to measure legitimacy using public opinion surveys of the police. If community policing were enhancing police legitimacy, we should note that as its implementation increased in popularity over time, the public should render more positive views of the police, and we should expect to see a pronounced acceleration in positive evaluations in the years following 1994, when the availability of COPS funds added incentives for departments to implement or at least claim to implement community policing programs. National public opinion surveys offer no evidence of a nation-wide trend of this sort (Gallagher, Maguire, Mastrofski, and Reisig 2001). A variety of indicators (confidence, respect, satisfaction, fairness, honesty, brutality) suggest that during the era of community policing, the public's evaluations of police have remained stable, fluctuated considerably according to no distinct pattern, or have declined. Cross-sectional comparisons of public opinion about departments that vary in their degree of community policing implementation or symbolic commitment to community policing could provide another indicator. Unfortunately, no such study has been conducted. A 1998 national survey of citizens' satisfaction with the police serving their neighborhood compared twelve cities, finding that cities ranged from 78–97 percent reporting that they were satisfied. However, eight of the twelve varied little, only 84–89 percent.

Among those cities at the high and low levels of satisfaction there were no obvious patterns related to community policing.

An alternative view is that American police do not need to heighten the public's support beyond normal levels but are keen to ensure that it is sustained at an *acceptable* level, one that provides a stable environment in which organizations can operate without the need for radical change. In this regard, the above survey evidence suggests that community policing may have served admirably, because support for the police as an American institution has remained remarkably stable over the last two decades. This argument is subsumed under the claim that community policing is but the most recent manifestation of a long series of reforms designed to sustain the legitimacy of police (militarization, legalization, and professionalization), all circumlocutions that conceal or palliate the coercive nature of police work about which society is so ambivalent (Bittner 1970; Klockars 1988).

The two legs on which the legitimacy of community policing stands are responsiveness to the public and delivering results, and in both cases American society has not demanded rigorous scientific evidence to find value in this reform. While strong and consistent scientific evidence of its performance has not been available, the reform has prospered, at least if one judges by the eagerness with which communities around the nation have signed up for COPS grants (Maguire and Mastrofski 2000; Roth *et al.* 2000; Worrall and Zhao 2003), police leaders have employed its rhetoric and adopted its programs. Indeed, the very adoption of community policing programs seems to have provided a sufficiently strong signal to community leaders and the public at large that their police are doing the "right" thing (Committee to Review Research 2004: 308–12), and in this sense, community policing must be considered successful. This state of affairs is predicted by institutional organization theory (Scott 1992), and is likely to remain that way unless a different environment for legitimacy evolves, such as the "evidence-based" policing environment advocated by Sherman (1998).

The future of community policing: terrorist-oriented policing

Despite the contribution that community policing has made to the legitimacy of the American police, it is on hard times. The COPS Office, financial engine of the American reform movement, has had its budget slashed, and it is struggling to remain viable by demonstrating the utility of community policing to what one police chief recently called "terrorist-oriented policing" (Kerlikowske 2004). Meanwhile, the Department of Homeland Security is distributing billions of dollars to state and local police agencies to join the federal government in the war against terror. Here community policing demonstrates its worth to the extent that it encourages citizens to be forthcoming with information useful to counterterrorist measures. This conjures up the vision of an eager public of amateur informants, voluntarily feeding information to the police, who carefully sift through it to guide their efforts to undermine terrorist threats.

The skeptic understandably wonders how realistic this terrorist-oriented, community policing vision is. Neighborhood Watch and similar crime prevention efforts have failed to demonstrate substantial benefits in reducing "regular" crime, so these canned, off-the shelf approaches seem even less likely to be effective in developing reliable sources on terrorism in those neighborhoods where the most valuable information may reside – immigrant communities, and especially, Islamic-American communities (Lyons 2002). Here the challenges for eliciting voluntary terrorist-oriented information are great. To the extent that local police respond to the federal government's desire to be an intelligence conduit, how are local police to distinguish themselves from the federal enforcement practices that make immigrant and Islamic citizens and residents so fearful (dragnets, interrogations, secret trials and incarcerations, and deportation of undocumented aliens)? And how are local police to manage the tension between placating the fears of a public that supports profiling Islamic persons for terrorism, while demonstrating to those targeted groups an equitable sensitivity to the civil rights of all citizens (Davies 2002)?

Community policing advocates are rushing to assure Congress that community policing is essential to the success of this effort. Some have argued that this form of intelligence brokering has long been the hallmark of community policing (Ericson and Haggerty 1997), but the enlistment of community policing in the domestic war against terror marks a distinct change in the bases for justifying the reform. This transformation further subordinates the community to the police in this partnership, relegating police responsiveness and accountability to the public to the hinterlands of the police mission. The partnerships that matter most to police under terrorist-oriented policing are those that promote the more efficient exchange of information with federal law enforcement, intelligence, and various disaster response agencies at all levels of government (Committee to Review Research 2004: 209–214). And many are concerned that the terrorist-oriented mission and close association with military and intelligence agencies will accelerate the militarization and isolation of state and local police forces, rather than bringing them closer to the police-community partnerships that served as the source of legitimacy for community policing in the past. Can this be the end of community policing? To the extent that the war against terror shapes community policing, it will end it as we have known it.

Most troubling in the way that community policing is being bent to federal priorities in the war against terror is the limited role envisioned for the community – primarily one of serving the state as its eyes and ears. Virtually absent from the discussion is the great need for community-based self-help responses to disaster, especially when state responses fall short, as they most assuredly will (Clarke 2003). The current obsession with establishing government command and control overplays the state's capacity to do all that must be done, and it overlooks the potential of citizen grassroots organizations both to reduce vulnerability and to respond to crisis. I would prefer to see more emphasis on a form of community policing that sought a role for the government in strengthening the capacity of citizens to engage in collectively efficacious action in crisis conditions.

Conclusion

Community policing's advocates have promised a great deal, and they may have thereby contributed to a rising sense of entitlement to better service. But after a few decades of reform, those looking for evidence of a "quiet revolution," a "new blue line," or a "paradigm shift," should be disappointed by the state of affairs. The quantity and quality of the evidence is itself disappointing, but considering that which is available, the skeptic must conclude that the glass of community policing's benefits is closer to empty than full. Its implementation has not transformed the structure and operations of American policing so much as it has altered its rhetoric. While there may be a few community policing exemplars among the nation's police departments, there is little in the national policing landscape to assure us that structures and practices have been strikingly altered. The evidence of its effectiveness resides primarily in its capacity to make the public less fearful of crime, while doing little to reduce crime itself. While collective action promises to provide real benefits to the nation's neighborhoods and communities, community policing advocates are still struggling to find the elixir that will transform quiescent and alienated citizens into virtuous civic actors. While perhaps shifting the bases of police and government resource mobilization toward those who engage in collective action, community policing has not necessarily been effective in spreading these benefits to those who need them most, society's disadvantaged. Its capacity to serve effectively as a bulwark in the defense of the homeland against terrorism remains at present only wishful thinking.

To say that community policing's performance has been disappointing does not lead to the conclusion that it was the wrong path, but it is one that has for many meandered into a stagnant swamp of tepid programs and amorphous "philosophies," too often run by and for the police more than the community. Its greatest weakness, to adapt Gertrude Stein's famous line, is that there is often so very little there. Most police departments treat it as an add-on rather than something that requires a radical transformation of how the police and public organize to do policing. Such a transformation would require that the police first engage a community that can serve as an effective partner, and once that is accomplished, the police will inevitably require sharing far more power with the community than they have thus far been willing to do – the political equivalent of the loving, but oft-contentious partnerships portrayed in film by Spencer Tracy and Katherine Hepburn. This is risk-taking of a major sort, because our police have long struggled, often with good reason, to build effective buffers from community pressure (Reiss 1992), and it is not at all clear that enough citizens are willing to commit the necessary degree of effort, especially in the most afflicted areas. These partnerships, even those most earnestly pursued, have been constructed, often with the acquiescence of citizens, to prevent truly potent political organizing to evolve (Skogan 2004: 59). A cynic might even suggest that this is their intended purpose. Whether that is so, or not, they represent a bland version of the ideals of a democratically invigorated policing in America. Without a piquant dish of community policing, we lack a true test of its potential to flavor our communities with beneficial outcomes. American police and their communities would be better served spending less time celebrating community policing and more time figuring out how to do it in a meaningful way.

NOTES

The author thanks David Klinger, Edward Maguire, Roger Parks, and David Weisburd for their helpful suggestions in the preparation of this manuscript.
1. Respondents to a 1999 national survey of municipal police agencies of ten or more full-time officers showed that 29 percent provided their recruits with sixteen or more hours of training on community policing concepts and principles, while 54 percent provided that much training on traffic accident investigation, and 67 percent provided that much training in physical tactics and martial arts. Only 59 percent provided any training on organizing community groups, and the vast majority of these provided less than eight hours of such

training. These figures have not been published heretofore. They are taken from "Community Policing in America: National Survey of Police Executives and Agencies," which is described in Mastrofski, Parks, and Wilson (2003).

2. The Project on Policing Neighborhoods found that general patrol officers spent only about a quarter of their time in face-to-face public encounters and community policing specialists spent less than 20 percent (Parks, Mastrofski, DeJong, and Gray 1999: 499–500; see also Mastrofski, Parks, Reiss *et al.*, 1998). On average, patrol generalists spent less than a handful of minutes at community meetings, while specialists averaged only somewhat more (see also Frank, Brandl, and Watkins 1997: 721, 724). Despite the best management intentions to keep officers in their permanent beat assignments, officers seem to have difficulty remaining in their assigned beats for extended periods (Parks, Mastrofski, Reiss *et al.* 1998: 2–18). Finally, community policing specialists appear inclined to spend more of their time with citizens who are more respectable and less likely to present them with elevated emotions (Parks *et al.* 1999).

3. Officers' attitudes toward developing partnerships with the community had no significant bearing on the inclination to use verbal or physical force with suspects in the two departments studied. The effects of training and community policing specialist assignment did not show consistent effects in the two departments.

4. However, research on Indianapolis and St. Petersburg does suggest that police–citizen partnerships did have the desired effects on levels of perceived safety, regardless of the degree of structured disadvantage in the neighborhood, but modest differences did remain across socioeconomic categories at the individual level (Reisig and Parks 2004).

REFERENCES

Ajzen, I. (1987). Attitudes, traits, and actions: Dispositional prediction of behavior in personality and social psychology. *Advances in Experimental Social Psychology, 20*, 1–63.

Bittner, E. (1970). *The functions of police in modern society.* Washington, DC: National Institute of Mental Health.

Bratton, W. (1998). *Turnaround: How America's top cop reversed the crime epidemic.* New York: Random House.

Buerger, M. (1998). Police training as a pentecost: Using tools singularly ill-suited to the purpose of reform. *Police Quarterly, 1*, 27–63.

Chermak, S. and Weiss, A. (2002). *Identifying strategies to market police in the news.* Final report to the National Institute of Justice. Retrieved from: http://www.ncjrs.ors/pdffiles1/nij/grants/194130.pdf.

Clarke, L. (ed.). (2003). Terrorism and disaster: New threats, new ideas. *Research in Social Problems and Public Policy, 11.* Oxford: Elsevier.

Cochran, J. K. and Bromley, M. L. (2003). The myth(?) of the police subculture. *Policing: An International Journal of Police Strategies and Management, 26*, 88–117.

Committee to Review Research on Police Policy and Practices. (2004). *Fairness and effectiveness in policing: The evidence.* Washington, DC: National Academies Press.

Crank, J. P. (1994). Watchman and community: Myth and institutionalization in policing. *Law and Society Review, 28,* 325–351.

(2003). Institutional theory of police: A review of the state of the art. *Policing: An International Journal of Police Strategies and Management, 26,* 186–207.

Davies, S. L. (2002). Profiling terror. Paper delivered at the 16th International Conference of the International Society for the Reform of Criminal Law, Charleston, SC. Retrieved from: http://www.isrcl.org/Papers/Davies.pdf.

DiMaggio, P. J., and Powell, W. W. (1983). The iron cage revisited: Institutional isomorphism and collective rationality in organizational fields. *American Sociological Review, 48,* 147–160.

DuBois, J. and Hartnett, S. M. (2002). Making the community side of community policing work. In Dennis J. Stevens (ed.), *Policing and community partnerships* (pp. 1–16). New York: Prentice Hall.

Ericson, R. V. and Haggerty, K. D. (1997). *Policing the risk society.* Toronto, Canada: University of Toronto Press.

Fogelson, R. M. (1977). *Big city police.* Cambridge, MA: Harvard University Press.

Frank, J., Brandl, S. G., and Watkins, R. C. (1997). The content of community policing: A comparison of the daily activities of community and "beat" officers. *Policing: An International Journal of Police Strategy and Management, 20,* 716–728.

Gallagher, C., Maguire, E. R., Mastrofski, S. D., and Reisig, M. D. (2001). *The public image of the police.* Final report to the International Association of Chiefs of Police. Retrieved from: http://www.theiacp.org/profassist/ethics/public_image.htm.

Goldstein, H. (1990). *Problem-oriented policing.* New York: McGraw-Hill.

Gottfredson, D. C. (1997). School-based crime prevention. In L. W. Sherman, D. Gottfredson, D. MacKenzie, J. Eck, P. Reuter, and S. Bushway (eds.), *Preventing crime: What works, what doesn't, what's promising?* (pp. 5–74). Washington, DC: National Institute of Justice.

Gottfredson, D. C., Wilson, D. B., and Najaka, S. S. (2002). School-based crime prevention. In L. W. Sherman, D. P. Farrington., B. C. Welsh., and D. L. MacKenzie (eds.), *Evidence-based crime prevention.* London: Routledge.

Gould, J. B. and Mastrofski, S. D. (2004). Suspect searches: Assessing police behavior under the US Constitution. *Criminology and Public Policy, 3* (3), 315–362.

Greene, J. R. (2004). Community policing and organization change. In Wesley G. Skogan (ed.), *Community policing: Can it work?* (pp. 30–53). Belmont, CA: Wadsworth.

Greene, J. R., Bergman, W. T., and McLaughlin, E. J. (1994). Implementing community policing: Cultural and structural change in police organizations. In D. Rosenbaum (ed.), *The challenge of community policing: Testing the promises* (pp. 92–109). Thousand Oaks, CA: Sage Publications.

Haar, R. N. (2001). The making of a community policing officer: The impact of basic training and occupational socialization on police recruits. *Police Quarterly, 4,* 402–433.

Harris Poll. (1999). Study 828460. Retrieved from: ftp://ftp.irss.unc.edu//pub/
search_results/POLL..7Jun2004.09.38.53.txt

Kerik, B. B. (2001). *The lost son: A life in pursuit of justice.* New York: Regan Books.

Kerlikowske, R. G. (2004). The end of community policing: Remembering the
lessons learned. *FBI Bulletin,* April 6–10.

Klockars, C. B. (1988). The rhetoric of community policing. In J. R. Greene and
S. D. Mastrofski (eds.), *Community policing: Rhetoric or reality?* (pp. 239–258).
New York: Praeger.

LaFree, G. (1998). *Losing legitimacy: Street crime and the decline of institutions in
America.* Boulder, CO: Westview Press.

Lyons, W. (1999). *The politics of community policing: Rearranging the power to punish.*
Ann Arbor, MI: University of Michigan Press.

   (2002). Partnerships, information and public safety: Community policing in a
time of terror. *Policing: An International Journal of Police Strategies and Management, 25,* 530–542.

Maguire, E. R. (1997). Structural change in large municipal police organizations
during the community policing era. *Justice Quarterly, 14,* 547–576.

   (2002). Multiwave establishment surveys of police organizations. Special Issue,
Justice Research and Policy, 4, 39–60.

Maguire, E. R. and Katz, C. M. (2002). Community policing, loose coupling,
and sensemaking in American police agencies. *Justice Quarterly, 19,* 501–
534.

Maguire, E. R. and King, W. R. (2004). Trends in the policing industry. *The
Annals of the American Academy of Political and Social Science, 593,* 15–
41.

Maguire, E. R. and Mastrofski, S. D. (2000). Patterns of community policing in
the United States. *Police Quarterly, 3,* 4–45.

Maguire, E. R., Shin, Y., Zhao, J., and Hassell, K. D. (2003). Structural change
in large police agencies during the 1990s. *Policing: An International Journal
of Police Strategies and Management, 26,* 251–275.

Manning, P. K. (1984). Community policing. *American Journal of Police, 3,* 205–
227.

Mastrofski, S. D. (1998). Community policing and police organization structure.
In J. Brodeur (ed.), *Community policing and the evaluation of police service
delivery* (pp. 161–189). Thousand Oaks, CA: Sage Publications.

   (1999). *Policing for people. Ideas in American Policing Series.* Washington, DC:
Police Foundation.

   (2002). The romance of police leadership. In E. Waring, D. Weisburd, and
L. W. Sherman (eds.), *Theoretical advances in criminology: Crime and social
organization* (pp. 153–196). New Brunswick: Transaction Publishers.

   (2004). Controlling street-level police discretion. *The Annals of the American
Academy of Political and Social Sciences, 593,* 100–118.

Mastrofski, S. and Parks, R. (1990). Improving observational studies of police.
Criminology, 28, 475–496.

Mastrofski, S. D. and Ritti, R. R. (1999). *Patterns of community policing: A view
from newspapers in the United States.* COPS Working Paper #2. East Lansing,
Michigan State University.

   (2000). Making sense of community policing: A theoretical perspective. *Police
Practice and Research Journal, 1,* 183–210.

Mastrofski, S. D., Parks, R. B., and Wilson, D. B. (2003). *Influences on the adoption of community policing in the United States.* Report to the National Institute of Justice. Manassas, VA: George Mason University.

Mastrofski, S. D., Snipes, J. B., and Supina, A. (1996). Compliance on demand: The public's response to specific police requests. *Journal of Research in Crime and Delinquency, 33,* 269–305.

Mastrofski, S. D., Worden, R. E., and Snipes, J. B. (1995). Law enforcement in a time of community policing. *Criminology, 33,* 539–563.

Mastrofski, S. D., Snipes, J. B., Parks, R. B., and Maxwell, C. D. (2000). The helping hand of the law: Police control of citizens on request. *Criminology, 38,* 307–342.

Mastrofski, S. D., Parks, R. B., Reiss, A. J., Jr., Worden, R. E., DeJong, C., Snipes, J. B., and Terrill, W. (1998). *Systematic observation of public police: Applying field research methods to policy issues.* Washington, DC: National Institute of Justice.

McCluskey, J. D. (2003). *Police requests for compliance: Coercive and procedurally just tactics.* New York: LFB Scholarly Publishing, Inc.

McCluskey, J. D., Mastrofski, S. D., and Parks, R. B. (1999). To acquiesce or rebel: Predicting citizen compliance with police requests. *Police Quarterly, 2,* 389–416.

Meyer, J. W. and Rowan, B. (1977). Institutionalized organizations: Formal structure as myth and ceremony. *American Journal of Sociology, 83,* 340–363.

Moon, Y. (2004). Police organizations' response to institutionalized pressure for community policing. Ph.D. Dissertation. Bloomington, IN: Indiana University.

Moore, M. H. (1992). Problem-solving and community policing. In M. Tonry and N. Morris (eds.), *Modern policing* (pp. 99–158). Chicago: University of Chicago Press.

Moore, M. H. and Stephens, D. (1991). *Police organization and management: Towards a new managerial orthodoxy.* Washington, DC: Police Executive Research Forum.

Muir, W. K., Jr. (1977). *Police: Streetcorner politicians.* Chicago: University of Chicago Press.

Novak, K. J., Hartman, J. L., Holsinger, A. M., and Turner, M. G. (1999). The effects of aggressive policing of disorder on serious crime. *Policing: An International Journal of Police Strategies and Management, 22,* 171–190.

O'Shea, T. C. and Nicholls, K. (2003). *Crime analysis in America: Findings and recommendations.* Washington, DC: Office of Community Oriented Policing Services.

Parks, R. B., Mastrofski, S. D., DeJong, C., and Gray, M. K. (1999). How officers spend their time with the community. *Justice Quarterly, 16,* 483–518.

Parks, R. B., Mastrofski, S. D., Reiss, A. J., Jr., Worden, R. E., Terrill, W. C., DeJong, C., Stroshine, M., and Shepard, R. (1998). *St. Petersburg project on policing neighborhoods: A study of the police and the community.* Report to the National Institute of Justice. Bloomington, IN: Indiana University.

Reisig, M. D. and Chandek, M. S. (2001). The effects of expectancy disconfirmation on outcome satisfaction in police–citizen encounters. *Policing: An International Journal of Police Strategies and Management, 24,* 88–99.

Reisig, M. D. and Parks, R. B. (2004). Community policing and quality of life. In W. G. Skogan (ed.), *Community policing: Can it work?* (pp. 207–227). Belmont, CA: Wadsworth.

Reiss, A. J., Jr. (1971). *The police and the public.* New Haven: Yale University Press.

(1992). Police organization in the twentieth century. In M. Tonry and N. Morris (eds.), *Modern policing* (pp. 51–98). Chicago: University of Chicago Press.

Ritti, R. R. and Mastrofski, S. D. (2002). *The institutionalization of community policing: A study of the presentation of the concept in two law enforcement journals.* Final report to the National Institute of Justice. Manassas, VA: George Mason University.

Rosenbaum, D. P. (1988). Community crime prevention: A review and synthesis of the literature. *Justice Quarterly, 5,* 323–395.

Rosenbaum, D. P. and Hanson, G. S. (1998). Assessing the effects of school-based drug education: A six-year multi-level analysis of project D.A.R.E. *Journal of Research in Crime and Delinquency, 35* (4), 381–412.

Rosenbaum, D. P. and Wilkinson, D. L. (2004). Can police adapt? Tracking the effects of organizational reform over six years. In W. Skogan (ed.), *Community policing: Can it work?* (pp. 79–108). Belmont, CA: Wadsworth.

Roth, J. A., Roehl, J., and Johnson, C. C. (2004). Trends in community policing. In W. Skogan (ed.), *Community policing: Can it work?* (pp. 3–29). Belmont, CA: Wadsworth.

Roth, J. A., Ryan, J. F., Gaffigan, S. J., Koper, C. S., Moore, M. H., Roehl, J., Johnson, C. C., Moore, G. E., White, R. M., Buerger, M. E., Langston, E. A., and Thacher, D. (2000). *National evaluation of the COPS program – Title I of the 1994 Crime Act.* Washington, DC: National Institute of Justice.

Sadd, S. and Grinc, R. (1994). Innovative neighborhood oriented policing: An evaluation of community policing programs in eight cities. In D. P. Rosenbaum (ed.), *The challenge of community policing: Testing the promises* (pp. 27–52). Thousand Oaks, CA: Sage Publications.

Sampson, R. J. and Groves, W. B. (1989). Community structure and crime: Testing social-disorganization theory. *American Journal of Sociology, 94,* 774–802.

Sampson, R. J. and Raudenbush, S. W. (1999). Systematic social observation of public spaces: A new look at disorder in urban neighborhoods. *American Journal of Sociology, 105,* 603–651.

Sampson, R. J., Raudenbush, S. W., and Earls, F. (1997). Neighborhoods and violent crime: A multilevel study of collective efficacy. *Science, 277,* 918–924.

Sandburg, C. (1970). Washington monument by night. Stanza 4, *The complete poems of Carl Sandburg,* rev. and expanded ed. (p. 282). New York: Harcourt Press.

Schafer, J. A. (2001). *Community policing: The challenges of successful organizational change.* New York: LFB Scholarly Publishing LLC.

Scott, W. R. (1992). *Organizations: Rational, natural, and open systems* (3rd ed). Englewood Cliffs, NJ: Prentice Hall.

Sherman, L. W. (1997a). Communities and crime prevention. In L. W. Sherman, D. Gottfredson, D. MacKenzie, J. Eck, P. Reuter, and S. Bushway (eds.), *Preventing crime: What works, what doesn't, what's promising?* (pp. 3–1–3–49). Washington, DC: National Institute of Justice.

(1997b). Policing for crime prevention. In L. W. Sherman, D. Gottfredson, D. MacKenzie, J. Eck, P. Reuter, and S. Bushway (eds.), *Preventing crime: What works, what doesn't, what's promising* (pp. 8-1–8-58). Washington, DC: National Institute of Justice.

(1998). Evidence-based policing. *Ideas in American policing series.* Washington, DC: Police Foundation.

Skogan, W. G. (1994). The impact of community policing on neighborhood residents. In D. Rosenbaum (ed.), *The challenge of community policing: Testing the promises* (pp. 167–81). Thousand Oaks, CA: Sage Publications.

(2004). Representing the community in community policing. In W. G. Skogan (ed.), *Community policing: Can it work?* (pp. 57–75). Belmont, CA: Wadsworth.

Skogan, W. G. and Hartnett, S. M. (1997). *Community policing, Chicago style.* New York: Oxford University Press.

Skogan, W. G., Steiner, L., Benitez, C., Bennis, J., Borchers, S., DuBois, J., Gondocs, R., Hartnett, S., Kim, S. Y., and Rosenbaum, S. (2004). *Community policing in Chicago, year ten: An evaluation of Chicago's alternative policing strategy.* Springfield, IL: Illinois Criminal Justice Information Authority.

Snipes, J. B. (2002). Police response to citizen requests for assistance: An assessment of deservedness, workload, social status, and officer predisposition perspectives. Ph.D. Dissertation. University of Albany, State University of New York.

Snipes, J. B. and Mastrofski, S. D. (1990). An empirical test of Muir's typology of police officers. *American Journal of Criminal Justice, 14,* 268–296.

Sparrow, M. K., Moore, M. H., and Kennedy, D. M. (1990). *Beyond 911: A new era for policing.* New York: Basic Books.

Terrill, W. and Mastrofski, S. D. (2004). Working the street: Does community policing matter? In W. G. Skogan (ed.), *Community policing: Can it work?* (pp. 109–135). Belmont, CA: Wadsworth.

Terrill, W., Paoline, E. A., III, and Manning, P. K. (2003). Police culture and coercion. *Criminology, 41,* 1003–1034.

Tien, J. M. and Rich, T. F. (1994). The Hartford COMPASS Program: Experiences with a weed and seed-related program. In D. Rosenbaum (ed.), *The challenge of community policing: Testing the promises* (pp. 192–206). Thousand Oaks, CA: Sage Publications.

Tolbert, P. S. and Zucker, L. G. (1983). Institutional sources of change in the formal structure of organizations: The diffusion of civil service reform, 1880–1935. *Administrative Science Quarterly, 28,* 22–39.

Tyler, T. R. (2004). Enhancing police legitimacy. *Annals of the American Academy of Political and Social Science, 593,* 84–99.

Tyler, T. R. and Huo, Y. J. (2002). *Trust in the law: Encouraging public cooperation with the police and courts.* New York: Russell Sage Foundation.

Weisburd, D. and Eck, J. E. (2004). What can police do to reduce crime, disorder, and fear? *Annals of the American Academy of Political and Social Science, 593,* 42–65.

Weisburd, D., Greenspan, R., Hamilton, E. E., Bryant, K. A., and Williams, H. (2001). *The abuse of police authority: A national study of police officers' attitudes.* Washington, DC: Police Foundation.

Weisel, D. L. and Eck, J. E. (1994). Toward a practical approach to organizational change: Community policing initiatives in six cities. In D. P. Rosenbaum (ed.), *The challenge of community policing: Testing the promises* (pp. 53–72). Thousand Oaks, CA: Sage Publications.

Wilson, J. Q. (1968). *Varieties of police behavior*. Cambridge, MA: Harvard University Press.

Wood, R. L., Davis, M., and Rouse, A. (2004). Diving into quicksand: Program implementation and police subcultures. In W. G. Skogan (ed.), *Community policing: Can it work?* (pp. 136–161). Belmont, CA: Wadsworth.

Worden, R. E. (1989). Situational and attitudinal explanations of police behavior: A theoretical reappraisal and empirical assessment. *Law and Society Review*, 23, 667–711.

     (1995). Police officers' belief systems: A framework for analysis. *American Journal of Police*, 14, 49–81.

Worrall, J. L. and Zhao, J. (2003). The role of the COPS Office in community policing. *Policing: An International Journal of Police Strategies and Management*, 26, 64–87.

Wycoff, M. A. (1994). *Community policing strategies: Draft final report*. Washington, DC: Police Foundation.

Zhao, J., He, N., and Lovrich, N. P. (1999). Value change among police officers at a time of organizational reform: A follow-up study using Rokeach values. *Policing: An International Journal of Police Strategies and Management*, 22, 152–170.

Part II

Broken windows policing

4   *Advocate*
Of "broken windows," criminology, and criminal justice

William H. Sousa and George L. Kelling

Introduction: a few up-front discourses

Despite attacks from the criminological, legal, and academic left, "broken windows" theory is a robust policy option in criminal justice practice and crime prevention. It has not only fueled the community policing movement, it has also informed the evolution of community courts, community prosecution, and community probation and parole. The Midtown Community Court in Manhattan, to give just one example, emphasizes that broken windows is integral to its philosophy and practice. Moreover, the ideas embodied in broken windows have moved beyond criminal justice and criminology to areas like public health, education, parks, and business improvement districts (BIDs).

The original article (Wilson and Kelling 1982), published in the *Atlantic*, has had surprising "legs." Although exact figures are not available, circulation staff of the *Atlantic* have told both James Q. Wilson and Kelling (one of the authors of this paper), that "Broken Windows" has been reproduced more than any other article in *Atlantic*'s history. Moreover, familiarity with broken windows is widespread internationally: *Fixing Broken Windows*, published by Kelling and Catherine M. Coles in 1996, has been translated into Spanish, Polish, and Japanese. The vast publicity, of course, associated with both the restoration of order in New York's subways during the early 1990s and the crime reduction in the city itself in the mid-1990s contributed to the popularization of broken windows, especially since both then Mayor Rudolph Giuliani and Police Commissioner William Bratton repeatedly identified it as a key part of their policing strategy.

Of metaphors

As background, the term "broken windows" is a metaphor. Briefly, it argues that just as a broken window left untended is a sign that nobody

77

cares and invites more broken windows, so disorderly behavior left untended is a sign that nobody cares and leads to fear of crime, more serious crime and, ultimately, urban decay. ("Broken windows policing" refers to a police emphasis on disorderly behavior and minor offenses, often referred to as "quality of life" offenses like prostitution, public urination, and aggressive panhandling.)

Its expression as a metaphor partially explains the rapid spread of ideas embodied in broken windows. A metaphor, as defined in the *Oxford English Dictionary*, is "(T)he figure of speech in which a name or descriptive term is transferred to some object different from, but analogous to, that to which it is properly applicable" (1989: 676). Its origins are from the Greek, "to transfer," "to carry," or "to bear." Breaking it down, the broken windows metaphor transfers the "common wisdom" that a minor happening like a broken window can lead to increased damage if not taken care of, to the presumed consequences of uncivil and petty criminal behaviors: fear, serious crime, and urban decay.

The strength of a good metaphor is that it puts forward complex and nuanced ideas in simple and original ways that are easily communicated and readily recalled. When fresh and vivid, metaphors shock readers into attention. Criminal justice and criminology are riddled with metaphors – "white-collar" crime, criminal justice "system," "wars" against crime and drugs, "blind justice," and the "thin blue line" are just a few examples. Metaphors, however, cut both ways. As the poet Robert Frost has noted: "All metaphor breaks down somewhere. That is the beauty of it. It is touch and go with the metaphor, and until you have lived with it long enough you don't know where it is going. You don't know how much you can get out of it and when it will cease to yield. It is a very living thing."[1]

Using metaphors, as a consequence, is risky. Because they simplify, metaphors distort as well as reveal. They mask complexity; they call attention to some aspects of an issue and ignore others; they age; they "break down somewhere" as Frost puts it; and soon, "everybody knows what they mean," regardless of whether everybody does or does not. As a result, metaphors also easily lend themselves both to misstatement or misrepresentation, either out of ignorance or to serve some purpose.

Complicating this issue for a metaphor like broken windows, is that the ideas in broken windows have policy implications and have come to be *practiced*: that is, the broken windows metaphor is expressed not just in words, but in day-to-day action by agencies – most often by public police, but by other sectors as well. The extent to which these practices adhere to the spirit, philosophy, and intent of the original broken windows argument is, of course, open to debate. We have seen many applications of what is called a broken windows approach that we have found worrisome. We have also seen and participated in applications of broken windows of which we are proud: the New York City subway, to give just one example.

Of broken windows: what are the ideas of broken windows?

Although one can find many of the core ideas of broken windows in earlier works by James Q. Wilson and Kelling (Wilson 1968; Kelling, Pate, Ferrara *et al.* 1981) – as well as many other authors (see, for example, Jacobs 1961; Glazer 1979) – the most important presentation was the *Atlantic* article. What are these core ideas?

1. Disorder and fear of crime are strongly linked; (29–30)
2. Police (in the examples given, foot patrol officers) negotiate rules of the street. "Street people" are involved in the negotiation of those rules; (30)
3. Different neighborhoods have different rules; (30)
4. Untended disorder leads to breakdown of community controls; (31)
5. Areas where community controls break down are vulnerable to criminal invasion; (32)
6. "The essence of the police role in maintaining order is to reinforce the informal control mechanisms of the community itself." (34)
7. Problems arise not so much from individual disorderly persons as from the congregation of large numbers of disorderly persons; (35) and,
8. Different neighborhoods have different capacities to manage disorder. (36)

Additionally, the article raises some of the complexities associated with order maintenance. They include:

1. To what extent can order maintenance be shaped by the rules of neighborhoods rather than criminal law? (34)
2. How do we ensure equity in the enforcement of ordinances so "that police do not become the agents of neighborhood bigotry"? (35)
3. How is the balance maintained between individual rights and community interests? (36)
4. How do we ensure that community controls do not turn into neighborhood vigilantism? (36)

In 1996, these ideas and issues were again discussed in considerable detail in *Fixing Broken Windows* by Kelling and Catherine M. Coles (1996, with a Foreword by James Q. Wilson). *Fixing* not only restated these ideas, it discussed in detail many of the complexities and issues raised by the ideas of broken windows and their implementation in many communities. For example, Chapter 2, "The growth of disorder," is a detailed discussion of the historical and legal issues involved in defining disorder and balancing individual rights with community interests. We will not bother here to provide more details about *Fixing* except to make two points: first, *Fixing* explicitly located order maintenance within the context of community policing and the emerging community prosecution movement. (It will be remembered that community policing was in inchoate stages in 1981 when the original article was written.) Second, it heavily emphasized the differential strengths of neighborhoods – the important consequence of this was that order maintenance policies and activities were highly discretionary, from administrative policymaking to officers on the street.

An important question here is: do we (Wilson, Kelling, Coles, and, more recently, Sousa (see Kelling and Sousa 2001; Sousa 2003)) own these ideas? Obviously not, in two senses: first, many authors and programs emphasized police order maintenance long before the original article was written. Second, the ideas in broken windows are now "out there" and readers, academicians, and policymakers are free to make of them what they wish. Ideas have a life of their own and such is as it should be. The fact that some broken windows programs are a far cry from anything any of us ever had in mind is simply what happens in the policy arena. On the other hand, we do have a special claim when critics attack our written work – especially the original article and *Fixing*. Critics, at least academic critics, of broken windows are obligated to "second-order agreement": that is, the obligation to reproduce the ideas under question faithfully, if not enthusiastically. This is not only a matter of good scholarship, it is also a matter of professional ethics. Alas, this has not always happened.

Indeed, many of the academic and legal critiques have not only distorted broken windows, but they have done so with considerable zeal and passion. Among other charges, broken windows gives rise to "wars" on the poor, racism, and police brutality. For one author, Wilson and Kelling are "aversive racists" (Stewart 1998). Another argues that Wilson's and Kelling's main policy recommendation to police is that they should "kick ass" (Bowling 1999). To give just one other example, one of our Rutgers colleagues (not a criminal justice faculty member) while leading a campus demonstration held up *Fixing Broken Windows*, indicating that it was then Mayor Rudolph Giuliani's blueprint for policing New York City and, as such, responsible for police killings of citizens. The question is: Why such misrepresentation and passion?

Of the special ire of criminologists

To answer the question posed above some background is needed. The dominant criminological and criminal justice paradigm of the past half-century is that formulated by President Lyndon Johnson's Presidential Commission on Law Enforcement and the Administration of Justice. Its 1967 publication, *The Challenge of Crime in a Free Society*, endorsed the "system" model of criminal justice and gave rise to, and framed, criminal justice education to this day (President's Commission 1967).² The underlying assumption that shapes the entire report and its policy and educational consequences is that crime is caused by structural features of society: racism, poverty, and social injustice – the "root causes" of crime.

The assumed causal links among poverty, racism, and crime are woven throughout the President's Commission reports. Moreover, the report is laced with recommendations that deal with such broad societal problems: schools should be improved; youth should be prepared for employment; barriers to employment posed by discrimination should be eliminated; housing and recreational facilities should be improved; minimum family income should be provided – many, if not all, highly desirable social policies with which we have no quarrel.

The criminal justice "system" in this model is largely reactive. Police may patrol neighborhoods, but they do so in a largely non-intrusive fashion: in cars, remaining "in-service" – that is driving around in a random fashion – to ensure that they are available for calls. As the "front end" of the system, their primary responsibility is to respond to serious crime through enhanced communication systems. In this view, minor offenses are either formally decriminalized or virtually decriminalized as a matter of priorities and policies. Finally, the report is basically silent on the role of citizens and the community (except to support police), takes no notice of private security, and disregards the private sector. Crime control is achieved through broad social/political action to redress the structural inequities in society and by the activities of a public criminal justice system that processes offenders.

Crime *prevention* in this model is equated with grand ideas of social change: basic societal problems will have to be resolved. As the report indicates:

Warring on poverty, inadequate housing, and unemployment is warring against crime. A civil rights law is a law against crime. Money for schools is money against crime. Medical, psychiatric, and family-counseling services are services against crime. More broadly and most importantly every effort to improve life in the "inner city" is an effort against crime. A community's most enduring protection against crime is to right the wrongs and cure the illnesses that tempt men to harm their neighbors. (President's Commission 1967: 6)

In this view then, we are left with two policy options: change society and/or process cases. Liberals and conservatives (they have their own macro approach – restore the family and its values) alike largely accept this framework. Thus we get extensive debates about sentencing, capital punishment, the exclusionary rule, mandatory sentencing, "three strikes you're out," prison construction, and so forth, but virtually the entire debate is within the bounds of the paradigm first put forward by President Johnson's Crime Commission.

As such, the criminal justice system paradigm was integral to the 1960s Great Society.[3] Government *could* solve the problems of poverty, racism, and social injustice. The Great Society was not just a set of programs, linked as it was to civil rights, it was a moral cause to which social scientists were intensely committed and in which they were deeply involved. Crime prevention was to be a by-product of solving society's major problems. In the opinion of many championing this view, disloyalty to the root causes theory is evidence that one disregards the problems of poverty, racism, and social injustice. The liberal/left fear is that if disorder, fear, and crime are uncoupled from root causes, society's motivation to manage its ills will be reduced. Whether intended or not, crime prevention is held hostage to the pursuit of extremely broad social goals, some of which are only attainable over decades, at best.

So then to return to the question, what explains the special attention that broken windows has gotten from critics? First, broken windows defies root cause orthodoxy: that is, to prevent crime one must alleviate these social ills. It also questions corollary issues and policies: decriminalization, deinstitutionalization, "victimless" crime, and the views that only individuals and not neighborhoods can be victims and that individual rights almost always trump community interests. Second, broken windows and crime control success in New York City came out of the political right (e.g., James Q. Wilson and Mayor Rudolph Giuliani). This was a hard dose for liberal social scientists to swallow. Hence, the heated debates about why crime declined in New York City.[4] Finally, because of New York City, broken windows has become widely known, both in professional circles and in the popular media. It has become so well known that often when cited in the popular media it is neither attributed nor defined. Consequently, a press release or title that "refutes" broken windows, or implies something like it, is more likely to gather attention than it would otherwise. In other words, some authors are "piggybacking" on broken windows. We have no quarrel with this – we are in a marketplace of ideas; we would just caution such authors to represent broken windows and its implications accurately.

Of research into broken windows

Research on broken windows can be loosely divided into two categories. The first includes studies that examine the theoretical underpinnings of the hypothesis, such as the link between disorder and fear or the association between incivilities and serious crime. The second includes research that evaluates policies that are derived from or otherwise influenced by broken windows, such as quality-of-life programs or order maintenance enforcement practices. We briefly discuss these two categories.

Broken windows research: the disorder–fear and disorder–crime connections Broken windows argues that disorderly conditions and behaviors are linked both to citizen fear and to serious crime. Few criminologists have concern with this disorder-fear portion of the hypothesis, and a fair amount of empirical research – some of which goes as far back as research conducted by the President's Commission during the 1960s – demonstrates an association between incivilities and fear (see Skogan and Maxfield 1981 and Ross and Jang 2000 for two more recent examples). Some debate continues regarding measurement concerns, causal order, and individual versus ecological level influences on fear. LaGrange, Ferraro, and Supancic (1992), for instance, suggest that while incivility is related to fear, the effect is mediated through perceptions of risk. More recently, Taylor (2001) concludes that the incivility–fear connection is stronger at the individual level (one's perception of incivilities in the neighborhood has a greater impact than the actual amount of incivilities in the neighborhood) and that the connection is weak when examined longitudinally (incivilities influence later changes in fear, but not as strongly or consistently as other factors). Overall, however, most research to date agrees that disorder is, at least in some way, positively associated with fear.

Unlike the disorder–fear hypothesis, the disorder-serious crime connection is much more controversial – and far less studied. Skogan (1990) was the first to find support for the link empirically in *Disorder and Decline*. Using primarily survey data from forty neighborhoods in six cities (Chicago, Atlanta, San Francisco, Philadelphia, Houston, and Newark (NJ)), Skogan found a highly significant disorder–crime connection while taking into account other factors such as poverty, instability, and race. Harcourt (1998) has since challenged these findings, claiming among other concerns that Skogan's inclusion of several neighborhoods with particularly strong disorder–crime connections (from the city of Newark) manipulated the overall results. After reproducing the analyses and removing these neighborhoods from Skogan's dataset, Harcourt finds that the relationship between disorder and serious crime disappears.[5] Harcourt's results, however, have also been questioned (see Xu, Fiedler, and Flaming 2005). Harcourt removed several neighborhoods from the analysis to produce the no-association result, but the removal of several *different* neighborhoods from the dataset may have *strengthened* the disorder-crime connection found by Skogan (Eck and Maguire 2000; see also Katz, Webb, and Schaefer 2001). Harcourt's manipulation of the data, therefore, does less to disprove Skogan's results and more to point out a limitation to the original dataset: its sensitivity to outliers (Eck and Maguire 2000).

Often cited as the most convincing evidence against the disorder-crime association (and to the broken windows hypothesis overall) is Sampson and Raudenbush's (1999) assessment of the relationship between "collective efficacy,"[6] disorder, and serious crime. The authors use a variety of methods for their investigation, including systematic social observations designed to capture disorderly behaviors and conditions on the streets of Chicago. They challenge the connection between disorder and serious crime by suggesting that while disorder is moderately correlated with predatory crime, once antecedent neighborhood constructs (such as collective efficacy) are considered, the direct relationship between the two all but disappears. Sampson and Raudenbush conclude that the level of collective efficacy is a strong predictor of both disorder and predatory crime and that the relationship between incivilities and crime is spurious except for officially measured robbery. According to the authors, these results "contradict the strong version of the broken windows thesis" (1999: 637).[7]

We have several difficulties with the Sampson and Raudenbush study that involve the authors' methodological decisions (such as their failure to observe night-time activities) and their interpretation of the data (such as their casual dismissal of the robbery finding) (see Kelling 2001), but others have challenged their analyses as well (see Xu *et al.* 2005). Jang and Johnson (2001), for example, argue that Sampson and Raudenbush have not tested the broken windows theory at all because they misinterpreted the original thesis and therefore mis-specified their analyses. As Jang and Johnson point out, broken windows postulates that disorder *indirectly* leads to crime via weakened community and neighborhood controls (stated somewhat differently, Wilson and Kelling (1982) argue that disorder, *left unchecked by community and neighborhood controls*, will lead to more serious crime). Sampson and Raudenbush, however, assume the thesis proposes that disorder is *directly* associated with crime, and so test a model in which disorder mediates the effects of neighborhood characteristics (including collective efficacy) on crime rather than neighborhood characteristics mediating the effects of disorder (Jang and Johnson 2001). Taking into account this misinterpretation, Jang and Johnson estimate that Sampson and Raudenbush's assessment actually provides *positive* rather than negative support for broken windows.[8]

In any event, the debate over the link between disorder and crime remains contentious and research on the topic has produced mixed results. Interestingly enough, Taylor's (2001) examination of the incivility–crime connection seems to verify the inconsistency of previous research. His longitudinal assessment of Baltimore neighborhoods provides qualified support for the idea that "grime" leads to crime. He finds, however, that while disorder influences some later changes in criminal activity (as well as changes in neighborhood decline and fear), the results differ across indicators (types of disorder) and across outcomes (types of crime). Additionally, Taylor finds that other indicators, such as initial neighborhood status, are more consistent predictors of later crime.[9]

Broken windows research: policy evaluation A primary policy implication derived from the original *Atlantic* article is that if police and communities are able to manage minor disorders, the result can be a reduction in criminal activity. As such, activities that can be classified as broken windows policing,[10] which emphasize the assertive enforcement of minor offenses, continue to be implemented in communities across the country. Subsequent evaluations of broken windows policing activities and their impact on crime typically consider whether measures of minor offense enforcement are significantly related with measures of serious crime reduction.

The New York City Police Department provides perhaps the most obvious example of a macro policy of order maintenance, as it is well known that officers were asked to be more assertive in the management of minor offenses (i.e., typically those offenses that were virtually ignored in the past).[11] That an increase in minor offense enforcement accompanied a reduction in serious crime in New York helped to spark a continuing debate: did the strategy contribute to the reduction, or were other factors involved?

Numerous factors have been offered as potential causes for crime reduction in New York: changes in demographic and economic trends, shifts in drug use patterns, statistical regression to the mean, changes in the cultural values of at-risk populations, and many others.[12] Few studies, however, have examined the extent to which a general order maintenance strategy has contributed to the crime drop relative to other factors. Previously, we found that NYPD order maintenance activities in the 1990s (proxied by arrests for misdemeanor offenses) had a significant effect on violence reduction in New York net of economic, demographic, and drug-use variables (Kelling and Sousa 2001). Similarly, Corman and Mocan (2002), using the same proxy for broken windows policing, found that misdemeanor arrests had a significant impact on robbery and motor vehicle theft in New York during the 1990s after controlling for economic and other criminal justice factors (they do not find a significant impact on murder, assault, or burglary, however). Further support for a general strategy of order maintenance is also provided by Worrall (2002), though not using data from New York. Worrall's analysis of county-level data from California demonstrates that an increase in arrests for misdemeanors is associated with a reduction in felony property offenses independent of demographic, economic, and deterrence variables.

While these investigations of general broken windows strategies offer policy insight, the data available for such analyses are often less than ideal. The limitations of macro level data – often put forward by the authors themselves – therefore prohibit conclusive statements from these analyses alone. Several field evaluations, however, have examined the effectiveness of the strategy as implemented in focused, place-specific initiatives. Green (1996), for instance, examined Oakland's Specialized Multi-Agency Response Team (SMART) program – a problem-solving, place-oriented strategy that emphasized police coordination with city agencies to enforce drug nuisance abatement ordinances and other civil laws. Green's analysis demonstrates that these tactics helped to decrease disorder and drug problems without significant displacement. Braga, Weisburd, Waring *et al.* (1999), in another example, designed a field experiment in Jersey City, NJ, to assess the impact of problem-oriented policing strategies focused on social and physical disorders in violent places. They concluded that these strategies were associated with decreases in observed disorders, citizen calls for service, and criminal incidents.

Other field studies, though perhaps less detailed than those of Green (1996) and Braga *et al.* (1999), are less supportive of broken windows policies. Novak, Hartman, Holsinger, and Turner (1999) analyzed a police enforcement effort designed to reduce specific disorders – primarily alcohol and traffic-related offenses – in a community in a Midwestern city (although it was not designed to necessarily impact serious crime). The authors determined that the effort was not associated with a decrease in either robbery or burglary (the two serious crimes they analyzed) at the target site, although they acknowledge the result may be due to the duration (one month) and dosage level of the intervention. More recently, Katz, Webb, and Schaefer (2001) evaluated the impact of a police quality-of-life program in Chandler, AZ, designed to reduce social and physical disorders with the intent of decreasing serious crime. The authors found that, in general, the program had an impact on public morals disorders (such as prostitution and public drinking) and physical disorders in the target area. However, the impact on serious crime was minimal and changes in criminal activity varied by section of the target area.

Discussion

Whether regarding theory or policy, empirical research on broken windows has produced mixed results. Some academics, attorneys, and criminologists, however, have used the "mixed" results to mount offensives against the thesis. Their argument goes something like the following:

Studies are inconsistent when it comes to broken windows. Some find the necessary link between disorder and crime, some do not, and some find it only in certain places and/or for certain types of criminal activity. Because there are statistically better predictors of crime – such as neighborhood collective efficacy, neighborhood stability, etc. – policies should concentrate on improvements in those areas rather than on "fixing broken windows." Policies based on these better predictors can be more effective and are less morally objectionable than the management of minor offenses.

We argue three points in the remainder of this paper: (1) broken windows may have merit beyond the link between disorder and crime; (2) claims that broken windows is morally objectionable, to date, are based on little actual knowledge of order maintenance in practice; (3) despite criticisms, broken windows offers a viable policy option within communities.

Broken windows and strong causal reasoning The concepts of disorder and serious crime each capture extremely complex sets of activities – the fact that research is inconsistent concerning the link between the two is of little wonder. Indeed, it is difficult for us to argue that all instances of serious crime are the result of social and/or physical incivilities. Our guess is that as investigations continue into the relationship between disorder and crime, research will find stronger or weaker associations as both concepts are disaggregated into their numerous components. Current research foreshadows this conclusion. In several studies, for example, robbery has been linked to disorder where other serious crimes have not (Skogan 1990; Harcourt 1998; Sampson and Raudenbush 1999;

but see Taylor 2001). We also suspect that even different types of robbery are more or less associated with disorderly conditions and/or behaviors.[13]

In any event, debates will likely continue as to the strength of the causal connections between disorder and crime and the policy relevance behind these connections. But as Thacher (2004) indicates, both proponents and opponents of "broken windows" have become preoccupied with the search for strong causal relationships between disorder and criminal activity – a type of connection that is rarely (if ever) clearly understood in criminology despite the best efforts of objective social science. Thacher suggests that by basing the merits of order maintenance on the results of causal connection studies, criminology avoids a more important moral question: Is the management of minor offenses justified regardless of its indirect effects on crime? In other words, is the direct effect of order maintenance on public order a legitimate public policy goal?

In his analysis, Thacher argues that at least some types of order maintenance policing practices are important as ends unto themselves – regardless of their impact on serious crime – because "they address important instances of accumulative harms and offenses" (2004: 101). Indeed, some police order maintenance strategies are implemented with no original intent to reduce serious crime but instead with the goal of restoring public order. Restoration of order in the New York City subway provides an example. While evidence indicates that reductions in both disorder and serious crime (i.e., robberies) were linked to police order maintenance efforts (especially against fare-beating and aggressive begging), the policing effort was initially implemented as an attempt to bring control to an environment that had grown chaotic (Kelling and Coles 1996). Similarly, the disorder-reduction program described by Novak *et al.* (1999) did not have a substantial impact on serious crime, but it was only intended to reduce specific incivilities (primarily alcohol and traffic violations) in response to community complaints about these minor offenses (unfortunately, the authors were unable to assess the intervention's impact on these disorders). Even when an order maintenance intervention that is designed to reduce serious crime fails to do so, this does not necessarily mean the intervention is without merit. For instance, although Katz *et al.* (2001) concluded that a disorder reduction program did not have the intended impact on serious crime, they suggest that the intervention may still have been worthwhile because it had a significant effect on both social and physical disorders in the target area.

Broken windows and morally complex policing Of course, even if we build an argument that public order is a legitimate goal for public policy and that order maintenance policing can directly benefit public order, this still leaves the question of whether such a policing strategy is morally appropriate (Thacher 2004). It is true that broken windows is morally complex. In the original *Atlantic* article – as we outlined above – Wilson and Kelling were greatly concerned with the ambiguities, complexities, and controversies concerning order maintenance. Likewise Kelling and Coles discussed the legality and constitutionality of order maintenance throughout Chapter 2 – the longest chapter in *Fixing Broken Windows*. Some critics of broken windows, however, have literally ignored what was written in the original article and in *Fixing* and have instead argued that order maintenance is morally reprehensible. Among other concerns, they claim that order maintenance policies encourage heavy-handed, "zero-tolerance" police tactics, or that they criminalize relatively innocuous behaviors deemed acceptable in communities, or that they disproportionately affect citizens living in poor and minority neighborhoods.

The difficulty with critics' arguments, however, is that their assertions are based on little actual knowledge of order maintenance as implemented by police managers or as performed by line officers. Thacher (2004) makes this point strongly. Certainly many critics claim to "know" about broken windows policing, but their understanding of it appears to come from dramatized media accounts and either deliberate or careless distortions of the broken windows metaphor.[14] In fact, few have actually examined order maintenance in practice. Most criminologists/lawyers, for example, who have attacked the NYPD's practices, claimed that broken windows as practiced was morally reprehensible, and dismissed New York's crime reductions as due to structural variables, have spent little or no time "on the ground" either in neighborhoods or with police.

We recently analyzed broken windows policing in New York City (Kelling and Sousa 2001; Sousa 2003). One of us (Sousa) spent considerable time riding with NYPD and recording observations of officers as they performed various tasks including those that can be considered order maintenance. The observations suggest that order maintenance, at least as performed by NYPD, can best be described as officers *paying attention* to minor offenses that were essentially ignored in the past. Sometimes "paying attention" to minor offenses involved formal action – such as arrest or citation – but more often than not it involved no official action at all. While officers did not ignore disorderly behavior, they were much more likely to informally warn, educate, scold, or verbally reprimand citizens who violated minor offenses. Contrary to the claims of critics, we concluded that officers were mindful of the moral complexities behind their activities, considered the contexts and circumstances surrounding incivilities and minor offenses before taking action, and exercised careful discretion while performing order maintenance tasks.

All may not agree with our assessment of order maintenance in New York and all are free to disagree with our interpretations of the observations. The point, however, is that these observations were made with the intent to develop a more thorough understanding of broken windows in practice – at least in New York. We share with Thacher (2004) the view that the merits of broken windows should be evaluated less on causal connection studies (which are unlikely to produce definitively conclusive advice for policy) and more on detailed descriptions of order maintenance as it is practiced. Only the accumulation of more detailed investigations is likely to shed light on the ethical considerations of applied order maintenance and its impact on disorder in communities. Critics rightly point out that broken windows policies are morally complex, but until they begin to develop a more substantive understanding of that which they criticize, their claims that order maintenance policies are objectionable are nothing more than assertions based on questionable media accounts, dubious suspicions, and often politically driven speculations. In the end, research may find that order maintenance, as interpreted by some police departments or implemented by some police officers, is morally questionable, but for critics to condemn the practice without sufficient knowledge of it or on the basis of media representations is professionally irresponsible.

Broken windows and policy options   Finally in this section, we wish to briefly address two points made by some critics of broken windows. The first is that other policy options, such as problem-oriented policing, situational crime prevention, and community crime prevention, are available in lieu of broken windows policies. The second is that because there are better indicators of crime and crime reduction – for example, "collective efficacy," neighborhood stability, etc. – focus should be on policy improvements in those areas rather than on policies derived from broken windows.

Regarding the first point, we want to acknowledge that research continues to show that crime control efforts resulting from problem-solving, situational crime prevention, and community crime prevention demonstrate potential at reducing crime and restoring order in communities.[15] We do not, nor have we ever, suggested that order maintenance policing should be implemented instead of these efforts. Quite the contrary, we believe that order maintenance should represent a policy option in support of police and community efforts to be implemented as problem-analysis and problem-solving dictates. In fact, close examination reveals that this is the reality even in an organization that has a reputation as an "order maintenance" department: we found numerous examples of successful NYPD problem-solving efforts driven by the Compstat process – some of which had virtually no order maintenance quality to them at all (Kelling and Sousa 2001; Sousa 2003).

Regarding the second point, we wish to point out that many of the "better" statistical predictors of crime essentially offer little in the way of policy options. No one will argue, for example, against the desire to improve neighborhood "collective efficacy," but notions such as this are nebulous in both concept and practice. Easing unemployment, poverty, and racial tensions are highly desirable goals to be sure, but the methods by which these goals are to be attained are far from certain. Even if practitioners possessed the knowledge, skill, and resources to effect change in these areas, it is unclear whether, when, and to what extent these changes would later impact crime. The "better" statistical predictors of crime may be intellectually informative, but they represent vague concepts and/or unachievable goals to the practitioner who is tasked with implementing realistic crime control policies. Broken windows policies, in contrast, are *practical options*. They can be implemented as part of a larger problem-solving agenda, can be employed in a timely fashion, and can offer the potential for timely results.

Conclusion: of crime, criminology, and criminal justice

The contrast between the response to broken windows by policymakers and practitioners on the one hand, and a good portion of criminologists, on the other, is stark. In the world of policy and practice broken windows has become, for the most part, integral to the conventional wisdom of community justice – whether it be policing, prosecution, probation and parole, or community courts. The same largely holds true for the BID movement and the neighborhood community anticrime movement. Indeed many of our policymaking and practitioner colleagues find the responses of many criminologists to broken windows mystifying – for them a sign that criminologists are simply out of touch with the real world. They have a point. In fact, they have several points.

First, the root cause ideology has locked criminology and criminal justice into a practical dead end (it probably is a theoretical dead end as well, but that is another story). Until the past ten or fifteen years or so, criminology and criminal justice has had little to offer to crime prevention than political advocacy/action to achieve a liberal/left version of a "just society." If one thinks of the "big ideas" in criminal justice that have enriched the recent past, the story is telling. *Community policing* had its origins in the work of the American Bar Foundation, the early Police Foundation (1970–80), and policing itself. *Problem-solving*, too, had its origins in the work of the American Bar Foundation, but as refined and articulated by Herman Goldstein, a public administrator. *Situational crime prevention* was originated and largely formulated by a psychologist, Ronald Clarke. *Pulling levers* – the ideas that led to the dramatic drop in gang killings in Boston – was largely the product of line police in the Boston Police Department and shaped by public policy scholar, David Kennedy. *Compstat* – the administrative mechanism that addresses problems of information sharing and accountability in policing – was a product of the private sector and an entrepreneurial police chief, William Bratton and some of his closest colleagues in the NYPD (Simons 1995). *Broken windows* grew out of work by a political scientist, James Q. Wilson, and a social worker turned police researcher, Kelling. It can be argued that the notion of *hot spots*, rooted in the work of Glenn Pierce (see Pierce, Spaar, and Briggs 1984), was quickly enhanced and broadly promulgated through the work of contemporary criminologists (see Sherman 1989; Sherman, Gartin, and Buerger 1989; Weisburd, Maher, and Sherman 1993), but the initial work, both theoretical and practical, was developed outside of traditional criminological/criminal justice circles. With few exceptions, it is difficult to come up with recent criminal justice innovations that have their origins in criminology.

Second, and this is closely linked to the above, criminology, with its special interest in *why* people commit crimes, has co-opted schools of criminal justice. We have no quarrel with the academic study of why people commit crimes, it is a legitimate and important inquiry; however, we believe it should be properly lodged within sociology (within which criminology is a specialty). Why criminal justice has been co-opted by criminology is complex but includes the newness of criminal justice as a field, the status and tenure structures of universities, the ascendancy of "Great Society" theoreticians in crime control thinking, and the dominance of root causes ideology during the post-President's Commission era. Nonetheless, the idea that university units dedicated to crime control – after all, it was the crime problem that spurred their origin under the 1970s Law Enforcement Assistance Administration – should be dedicated to criminological pursuits, rather than crime control, was a turn of events that mired such units into relatively fruitless pursuits – at least from a public policy point of view.

Finally, criminology and criminal justice have confused scientific standards of evidence with the evidence that policymakers and practitioners require in the real world. To be sure, policymakers would love to live in a world where they were 95 per cent certain that implementing particular policies or practices would have the desired outcome. As a matter of fact, they do not and will not. Policymakers live in a world in which they have to make decisions – many of them, life and death – in which they are confronted with mixes of problems and programs that do not lend themselves to clean experiments, bad data, and often conflicting and/or uncertain research findings. In such a world, 70 or 80 percent certainty would be a happy thing. Broken windows looks pretty good in this world: if properly done, it will most probably be approved of by neighborhood residents, it will probably also reduce their fear of crime, and it looks like it will reduce some street crimes. Not a bad bet for policymakers and practitioners.

NOTES

We wish to thank Michael Wagers, Anthony Braga, and David Weisburd for their helpful comments on earlier drafts of this paper. Thanks also to Huan Gao of Rutgers University and Jodi Olson of UNLV for their assistance.

1. This quote is taken from Frost's "Education by poetry." It can be found on page 41 of *Selected Prose of Robert Frost*, ed. Hyde Cox and Edward Connery Lathem (Holt, Rinehart, and Winston; New York).

2. The idea of a criminal justice "system" was first promulgated by the American Bar Foundation during the 1950s. Many of the staff persons of the Bar Foundation, e.g., Lloyd Ohlin, Frank Remington, and Herman Goldstein, were important contributors to the President's Commission report.

3. Lloyd Ohlin, e.g., was not only the author (with Richard Cloward) of *Delinquency and Opportunity: A Theory of Delinquent Gangs* (1960), one of the key works giving rise to the War on Poverty and the Great Society, he was also a member of the President's Commission on Law Enforcement and the Administration of Justice.

4. It is interesting that neither the work of Ronald Clarke in *situational crime prevention* nor Marcus Felson in *routine activities* has engendered the hostility that broken windows has: both are as equally dismissive of root cause and motivational theories of crime control.

5. After reproducing Skogan's study, but before removing the Newark neighborhoods from the analysis, Harcourt acknowledges a statistically significant connection between disorder and robbery. When he eliminates the Newark neighborhoods, this disorder–robbery connection disappears.

6. Collective efficacy is defined as "the linkage of cohesion and mutual trust with shared expectations for intervening in support of neighborhood social control" (Sampson and Raudenbush 1999: 612–613). For purposes of their study, the collective efficacy measure was created by combining two measures from survey data: shared expectations for informal social control (represented by five survey items asking respondents to report the likelihood that their neighbors would take action given certain scenarios) and social cohesion/trust (represented by five survey questions asking residents to report on the trustworthiness, helpfulness, and collegiality of their neighbors).

7. What "the strong version of the broken windows thesis" is remains a mystery to us, but so be it.

8. Jang and Johnson (2001) themselves find support for broken windows, indicating in their analysis that neighborhood disorder is significantly related to illicit drug use among adolescents. However, individual "religiosity" (one's commitment to religion) and social networks weaken the effect of disorder on drug use.

9. Some research on the geographic distribution of crime also confirms the complex nature of the minor offense/serious offense relationship. Weisburd *et al.* (1993), for example, suggest that calls for service for minor offenses (public morals, drunks) correlate more strongly with certain serious offenses (i.e., robberies) than with others in crime "hot spots."

10. We use the terms "broken windows," "quality-of-life," and "order maintenance" interchangeably to describe a policing style that emphasizes the management of minor offenses. For reasons that are evident in this paper, we do not consider "zero tolerance" to be synonymous with these terms.

11. In some respects, the idea that "everyone knows" that NYPD is an "order maintenance" department is unfortunate. While it is true that the management of minor offenses is an important strategy in New York, the strategy is most prominent when used to support focused problem-solving activities that are often driven by the Compstat process (Kelling and Sousa 2001; Sousa 2003).

12. For a review of the potential causes of crime reduction in New York and elsewhere during the 1990s, see generally Karmen (1999) and Blumstein and Wallman (2000). See also Karmen (2000) and Kelling and Sousa (2001).

13. From our perspective, a finding that disorder is linked to robbery in these studies is both interesting and important for policy. Others, however, in their apparent zeal to disprove broken windows, gloss over the robbery finding. Because *only* robbery is related to disorder, so the argument goes, the thesis is inherently flawed (never mind that robbery is a "bellwether" crime and general gauge of violence in many communities). We believe that those who hold the disorder–crime connection up to such lofty standards suffer from a similar affliction as those who believe in what Hirschi and Selvin refer to as the first false criterion of causality: "Insofar as a relation between two variables is not perfect, the relation is not causal" (1966: 256). Among other reasons, Hirschi and Selvin argue that this criterion is false because perfect relations are virtually unknown in criminology. We agree, and thus those who will settle for little less than a perfect relationship between disorder and crime as "proof" of broken windows are not likely to find this proof in past, present, or future research.

14. An example of this comes from Greene (1999) who criticizes New York's order maintenance policing as brutal compared to other departments such as San Diego: "[the comparison] between New York City and San Diego offers compelling evidence that cooperative police-community problem solving can provide effective crime control through more efficient and humane methods" (1999: 185). Comparing New York to San Diego is troublesome at best, but even if such a comparison were possible, much of Greene's evidence for New York's less "humane" methods is based on little first-hand knowledge and comes instead from questionable and unreliable sources. For example, she cites politician Mark Green's opinions as authoritative on the subject of

New York's order maintenance policing, but fails to mention Green's transparent agenda as one of Giuliani's chief political rivals of the 1990s. Additionally, while she correctly points out that complaints against the police increased when order maintenance was introduced in New York (evidence that she claims supports the New York brutality position), Greene fails to place this point in its proper context. First, complaints against the police did increase from 1992 to 1995, but the number of officers also increased by nearly 10,000 during the same time period. Second, order maintenance policing necessarily requires more frequent contacts between officers and citizens – often in situations where the citizen is suspected of some sort of legal violation. Considering the number of officers added, combined with the increased frequency of contacts between police and citizens, one might be surprised if the number of complaints against police did not increase. Third, while the number of complaints against the police increased until 1995, the number *decreased* throughout the rest of the 1990s despite the fact that assertive enforcement of minor offenses continued. Greene's analysis exemplifies a general lack of knowledge of broken windows policing – particularly in New York – by those who claim a competency of it.
15. For a review of this research, see Eck and Maguire (2000) and Weisburd and Eck (2004).

REFERENCES

Blumstein, A. and Wallman, J. (eds.). (2000). *The crime drop in America*. Cambridge: Cambridge University Press.

Bowling, B. (1999). The rise and fall of New York murder: zero tolerance or crack's decline? *British Journal of Criminology, 39* (4), 531–554.

Braga, A. A., Weisburd, D. L., Waring, E. J., Mazerolle, L. G., Spelman, W., and Gajewski, F. (1999). Problem-oriented policing in violent crime places: a randomized controlled experiment. *Criminology, 37* (3), 541–580.

Cloward, R. A. and Ohlin, L. E. (1960). *Delinquency and opportunity: A theory of delinquent gangs*. New York: The Free Press.

Corman, H. and Mocan, N. (2002). *Carrots, sticks and broken windows*. NBER Working Paper 9061. Cambridge, MA: National Bureau of Economic Research.

Eck, J. E. and Maguire, E. R. (2000). Have changes in policing reduced violent crime? An assessment of the evidence. In A. Blumstein and J. Wallman (eds.), *The crime drop in America*. Cambridge: Cambridge University Press.

Glazer, N. (1979). On subway graffiti in New York. *The Public Interest, 54* (Winter), 3–11.

Green, L. (1996). *Policing places with drug problems*. Thousand Oaks, CA: Sage Publications.

Greene, J. A. (1999). Zero tolerance: a case study of police policies and practices in New York City. *Crime and Delinquency, 45* (2), 171–187.

Harcourt, B. E. (1998). Reflecting on the subject: a critique of the social influence conception of deterrence, the broken windows theory, and order-maintenance policing New York style. *Michigan Law Review, 97*, 291–389.

Hirschi, T. and Selvin, H. C. (1966). False criteria of causality in delinquency research. *Social Problems, 13,* 254–268.

Jacobs, J. (1961). *The death and life of great American cities.* New York: Vintage Books.

Jang, S. J. and Johnson, B. R. (2001). Neighborhood disorder, individual religiosity, and adolescent use of illicit drugs: a test of multilevel hypotheses. *Criminology, 39* (1), 109–144.

Karmen, A. (ed.). (1999). *Crime and justice in New York City.* New York: Primis Custom Publishing.

   (2000). *New York murder mystery: The true story behind the crime crash of the 1990s.* New York: New York University Press.

Katz, C. M., Webb, V. J., and Schaefer, D. R. (2001). An assessment of the impact of quality-of-life policing on crime and disorder. *Justice Quarterly, 18* (4), 825–876.

Kelling, G. L. (2001). Broken windows and the culture wars: a response to selected critiques. In R. Matthews and J. Pitts (eds.), *Crime, disorder, and community safety.* London: Routledge.

Kelling, G. L. and Coles, C. M. (1996). *Fixing broken windows: Restoring order and reducing crime in our communities.* New York: The Free Press.

Kelling, G. L. and Sousa, W. H. (2001). *Do police matter? An analysis of the impact of New York City's police reforms.* Civic Report No. 22. New York: Manhattan Institute.

Kelling, G. L., Pate, A., Ferrara, A., Utne, M., and Brown, C. E. (1981). *Newark foot patrol experiment.* Washington, DC: Police Foundation.

LaGrange, R. L., Ferraro, K. F., and Supancic, M. (1992). Perceived risk and fear of crime: role of social and physical incivilities. *Journal of Research in Crime and Delinquency, 29* (3), 311–334.

Novak, K. J., Hartman, J. L., Holsinger, A. M., and Turner, M. G. (1999). The effects of aggressive policing of disorder on serious crime. *Policing: An International Journal of Police Strategies and Management, 22* (2), 171–190.

Oxford English Dictionary (2nd ed.). (1989). Oxford: Clarendon Press.

Pierce, G. L., Spaar, S. A., and Briggs, L. R. (1984). *The character of police work: Implications for the delivery of services.* Boston: Center for Applied Social Research, Northeastern University.

President's Commission on Law Enforcement and the Administration of Justice (1967). *The challenge of crime in a free society.* Washington, DC: US Government Printing Office.

Ross, C. E. and Jang, S. J. (2000). Neighborhood disorder, fear, and mistrust: the buffering role of social ties with neighbors. *American Journal of Community Psychology, 28* (4), 401–420.

Sampson, R. J. and Raudenbush, S. W. (1999). Systematic social observation of public spaces: a new look at disorder in urban neighborhoods. *American Journal of Sociology, 105* (3), 603–651.

Sherman, L.W. (1989). Repeat calls for service: policing the "hot spots." In D. J. Kenney (ed.), *Police and policing: Contemporary issues.* New York: Praeger Publishers.

Sherman, L. W., Gartin, P. P., and Buerger, M. E. (1989). Hot spots of predatory crime: routine activities and the criminology of place. *Criminology*, *27*(1), 27–55.

Simons, R. (1995). Control in an age of empowerment. *Harvard Business Review* (March–April), 80–88.

Skogan, W. G. (1990). *Disorder and decline: Crime and the spiral of decay in American neighborhoods*. New York: The Free Press.

Skogan, W. G. and Maxfield, M. G. (1981). *Coping with crime: Individual and neighborhood reactions*. Beverly Hills, CA: Sage Publications.

Sousa, W. (2003). Crime reduction in New York City: The impact of the NYPD. Unpublished doctoral dissertation, Rutgers University, Newark, NJ.

Stewart, G. (1998). Black codes and broken windows: the legacy of racial hegemony in anti-gang civil injunctions. *Yale Law Journal*, *107* (7), 2249–2279.

Taylor, R. B. (2001). *Breaking away from broken windows*. Boulder, CO: Westview Press.

Thacher, D. (2004). Order maintenance reconsidered: moving beyond strong causal reasoning. *The Journal of Criminal Law and Criminology*, *94* (2), 101–133.

Weisburd, D. and Eck, J. E. (2004). What can police do to reduce crime, disorder, and fear? *The Annals*, *593*, 42–65.

Weisburd, D., Maher, L. and Sherman, L. (1993). Contrasting crime general and crime specific theory: the case of hot spots of crime. *Advances in Criminological Theory*, *4*, 45–70.

Wilson, J. Q. (1968). *Varieties of police behavior*. Cambridge, MA: Harvard University Press.

Wilson, J. Q. and Kelling, G. L. (1982). Broken windows: the police and neighborhood safety. *The Atlantic Monthly*, March, 29–38.

Worrall, J. L. (2002). *Does "broken windows" law enforcement reduce serious crime?* CICG Research Brief. Sacramento, CA: California Institute for County Government.

Xu, Y., Fiedler, M. L., and Flaming, K. H. (2005). Discovering the impact of community policing: the broken windows thesis, collective efficacy, and citizens' judgement. *Journal of Research in Crime and Delinquency*, *42* (2), 147–186.

5   *Critic*
Incivilities reduction policing, zero tolerance,
and the retreat from coproduction: weak
foundations and strong pressures

Ralph B. Taylor

A 2002 *New Yorker* cartoon depicts two grizzled prisoners whiling away
the day on their bunks. The one on the bottom bunk, presumably in reply
to a question from the inmate in the top bunk, explains, "There might
have been some carelessness on my part, but it was mostly just good police
work." The inmate on the top bunk seems startled by the admission.

The question to consider here is whether broken windows or incivility reduction policing is good police work. Broken windows policing is
conceptually grounded on the incivilities thesis. The incivilities thesis,
although it comes in several different guises, suggests that: physical deterioration and disorderly social conduct each contribute independently to
fear, neighborhood decline, and crime; by implication, incivility reducing
initiatives will contribute to neighborhood stability and safety, and lower
fear. To the extent that this logic model is inaccurate, inadequate, or
potentially misleading, incivilities reduction as a set of policing strategies
may fail to deliver. This chapter will summarize the conceptual limitations of that thesis, and the empirical limitations of the supporting work.
It will then broaden the discussion context in two ways: first, to provide
an alternate historical outline of where broken windows policing came
from and, second, to outline the elements of a police–citizen coproduced
process of public safety. Given that context, it sketches the specific challenges facing successful coproduction *over time* in an urban residential
context. Some current practices justified on the basis of the incivilities
thesis, such as zero tolerance policing, are probably exacerbating the very
problems earlier versions of these policing strategies sought to alleviate.

Incivilities thesis[1]

Evolution

As the data from the first National Crime Victimization Surveys appeared
in the early 1970s, researchers started realizing many more residents were

fearful than were victimized (Garofalo and Laub 1978). "Fear of crime" was more than "fear" of "crime." In addition to being worried about crime *per se*, people also were more frequently worried about untidy or disintegrating physical conditions they saw around them, as well as rowdy, decadent, or just misbehaving adults or teens (Wilson 1975). This version of the thesis is psychological and cross-sectional.

The best-known elaboration was contributed by Wilson and Kelling. They suggested, based in part on then-recent foot patrol evaluations in places like Newark, that unrepaired physical damage suggested an increasing and increasingly threatening level of "disorder" to local residents (Wilson and Kelling 1982). Over time, they proposed, residents and other street regulars who watched over the locale would retreat inside from their monitoring posts, leaving the street vulnerable to increasing domination by unruly teens and, later, invading serious offenders drawn in by decreasing guardianship. Wilson and Kelling made the thesis social psychological or group based, and suggested how consequences unfolded over time.

Skogan further ecologized the idea, suggesting that deteriorated physical conditions, and an unruly social climate, could contribute independently to community decline, in three different ways: crime rates should increase faster there, residents would outmigrate faster, leading to structural decline, and residents' fear or concern should go up faster (Skogan 1990).

Empirical evidence

This section briefly highlights what we know about the empirical support for the thesis (for more details, see Taylor 2001: 179–239).

The cross-sectional version of the incivilities thesis receives strong support at the individual level, especially if the incivilities indicators used are survey based. Those who see more problems in their locale are also more fearful, see local crime rates as higher, and are less sanguine about their neighborhood's future. These connections persist after controlling for demographics.

The cross-sectional version at the ecological level receives bivariate support. Incivilities connect with crime and with fear. Questions arise, however, when we attempt to partial out basic neighborhood social structure from incivilities *per se* because the two connect so strongly, especially if assessment-based indicators of incivilities are used (Taylor, Shumaker, and Gottfredson 1985; Taylor 1999). Some earlier cross-sectional, neighborhood-level analyses thought to support the connection

(Skogan 1990) have been extensively criticized for analytic mis-steps (Harcourt 2001: 76).

Two neighborhood-level studies examined the cross-sectional connections of incivilities and crime using data from the 1990s. In Chicago, results showed the effects of social disorders, captured through assessments, on robbery but not on homicide (Sampson and Raudenbush 1999). Re-analyses of data from five cities found connections between perceived social incivilities and robbery and assault rates, but the strength of the connection was much weakened after controlling for basic neighborhood structure – race, stability, and socioeconomic status (Taylor 1999). In addition, the strength of the connection varied by the crime in question and by city. Both these studies support the idea that incivilities and crime "share similar theoretical features and are consequently explained by the same constructs at the neighborhood level" (Sampson and Raudenbush 1999: 636). They label the antecedents "concentration of disadvantage and lowered collective efficacy" (*ibid.*: 636). Given the potential reciprocal relationship between incivilities and collective efficacy, it may be premature to conclude collective efficacy is an independent contributor to community crime rates. Nonetheless, the most important point is that "results such as these contradict the strong version of the broken windows thesis" (Sampson and Raudenbush 1999: 636).

The cross-sectional, ecological impacts of incivilities on responses to crime, such as fear, are still not fully understood, but collective efficacy does appear to be involved in these connections. Neighborhood-level analyses of several dozen Baltimore neighborhoods showed a bivalent impact of incivilities. Assessed incivilities directly elevated fear and behavioral restriction, while at the same time they depressed fear and restriction because they stimulated local involvement and attachment (Taylor 1996). At this juncture we cannot say with confidence that, at the ecological level, incivilities connect cross-sectionally with higher fear, as anticipated by the model; we do not yet have an analysis from one city, or from several cities, that looks at this connection while simultaneously considering not only structure, but also social networks, social climate, and collective efficacy.

When we turn to longitudinal work, we have only one neighborhood-level study with significant time elapsed between initial and follow-up measures (Taylor 2001). Work with several dozen neighborhoods in Baltimore showed that initial incivilities demonstrated some predicted lagged effects on crime, fear, and one pathway of neighborhood decline. Nonetheless, these impacts were not well patterned across multiple outcomes, depended on the type of incivility indicator used, and paled in comparison to the structural impacts of initial racial and status composition. Another longitudinal study at the streetblock level, using a shorter change time frame of one year, also finds weaker than expected lagged incivilities effects on responses to crime (Robinson, Lawton, Taylor, and Perkins 2003). In short, initial incivilities are not strongly and consistently determinative of later neighborhood crime or structure, or of later shifts in residents' responses to crime.

Such murky empirical outcomes naturally lead us back to questions about whether incivility reduction as a policing strategy will have a long-term payoff. It may be that "crime fighting" is far more important than "grime fighting" for improving future neighborhood quality (Taylor 2001: 372).

One final comment deserves mention before leaving questions of the causal impact of neighborhood incivilities. Some have recently suggested we should not worry whether order maintenance policing, based on the incivilities thesis, does or does not have the long-term causal impacts it is presumed to have (Thacher 2004). According to this view, the policing activities themselves are inherently worthwhile; they have "intrinsic merit" (412) as policy tools and deserve closer examination irrespective of potential impacts.

Such a proposal seems to ignore questions of policy selection. There are many different forms locale-based policing can take. Order maintenance policing is just one of those. It would seem more useful to find the police strategies that are the most effective for the long-term outcomes envisioned, and use those impact assessments to guide strategy selection, rather than to invest energy in describing strategies that may be less than optimal.

Empirical evidence speaks not only to questions of hypothesized impacts, but also to presumed measurement structures. If incivilities indeed reflect underlying conditions of disorder, different indicators, from different methods, should correlate strongly with one another. They don't always (Taylor 1999; Taylor 2001: 117–121), especially when we examine change rather than cross-sectional indicators. It is not unusual for neighborhoods changing in one direction on perceived incivilities to be changing in the opposite direction on assessed deterioration.

To expand on this last point, longitudinal versions of the incivilities thesis fail to describe the temporal sequence of described processes. How long does it take for increased social or physical incivilities to "inspire" additional serious crime? We currently have in place both the microecological principles (Taylor 1997), and the statistical procedures (Weisburd, Bushway, Lum, and Yang 2004) for understanding how different types of streetblocks change in different ways over time. We need a series of studies, with continuous longitudinal data available for independent, mediating, and outcome variables, to help us further specify the temporal component of the theory.

Evaluating police work

Considerable debate has ensued about the impacts of New York's broken windows policing implemented under Commissioner Bratton, and the extent to which it was responsible for dramatic crime reductions in the 1990s (Bratton 1998; Silverman 1999; Blumstein and Wallman 2000). Those arguments are too complex to summarize here. One piece of work cited in favor of the police strategies, however, uses New York City precinct and borough-level data to examine changes in crime over time, and links those changes to increased misdemeanor arrests by police (Kelling and Sousa 2001). Unfortunately, the statistical analysis in that work has numerous limitations.[2] Further, at that time in New York City the police were doing many things. In addition to broken windows policing they were implementing the Compstat process for organizational review and management of ongoing crime and reduction efforts. It is simply not possible to separate out the impacts of these different program components.

To resolve physical problems in a neighborhood related to housing or street conditions, police need to work alongside other agencies or key local actors like landlords or small business managers. Although often referred to as third-party policing rather than broken windows policing, the focus is often on physical or social incivilities, and lower crime and/or lower drug sales are an expected outcome. Several studies suggest these strategies work, although perhaps not as effectively as hoped (Green 1996; Mazerolle, Kadleck, and Roehl 1998). With such strategies, moreover, because they are usually multi-agency, working with housing inspectors and courts, it is often not clear what the contributions are of the police themselves.

Theoretical concerns

Space limitations preclude more than a brief summary of the major theoretical concerns raised by the incivilities thesis, and of the programs put into place based in part on its tenets (for more detail see Taylor 2001: 95–122; Harcourt 2001: 123–216). Some of the major points of this discussion are as follows.

What disorder where? As Wilson and Kelling (1982) originally anticipated, it is difficult to define one type of disorder deserving police attention in all locations. The focus of order maintenance policing efforts always will be context-sensitive. Presumably the focus that does emerge will be driven in large part by the officers' communications with citizen and business leaders in the community. Discretion always has been key to police conduct (Kelling 1999). To say police will focus on different non-crime problems in one location *vs.* another represents nothing new. It does, however, create challenges for police supervisors, and it does place a premium on police being closely enough connected with local citizen and business leaders so they have a sense of what is most disturbing to the community.

Collapse of the harm principle. Harcourt (2001) suggests that elevating minor misdemeanors to arrest-worthy behaviors, making the merely annoying dangerous because of its anticipated long-term harmful impacts on the community, results in a collapse of the harm principle. Stated differently, previously accepted orderings differentiating more *vs.* less serious criminal or deviant behavior get collapsed, creating confusion rather than changing normative views toward minor misdemeanors. A May 11, 2001 Associated Press story reported a fifth grader handcuffed and taken from Oldsmar Elementary School in Florida for drawing pictures of guns.

Increasing inequality. In addition, we know that those offenses where officers have the most discretion are often policed in a racially biased manner. Arrest patterns for minor misdemeanors are likely to introduce even greater levels of racial inequality into criminal justice processing (Tonry 1995). Increasing police activity around misdemeanors seems likely to increase overall racial inequality in this "front end" portion of criminal justice processing.

Subject creation. Focusing policing efforts on disorderly people widens the social gap between the haves and the have-nots, making the latter even less deserving, more criminal, and more dangerous than they are. It creates an "uncritical dichotomy between disorderly people and law abiders" (Harcourt 2001: 7). Such a binary schema is not only inaccurate, but also encourages further social divisiveness.

Where does broken windows policing come from?

George Kelling and others have placed the development of broken windows policing in a specific historical context (Kelling and Coles 1996; Kelling 1999). That perspective sees police in the 1970s and 1980s as hamstrung, unable to take care of the minor infractions they saw because of concerns about citizen complaints and lack of court follow-through. I propose here an alternate view, one that starts with the urban disorders of the 1960s, and the various types of policing innovations that followed

as a subsequent reform response. This amounts to further expanding
the above descriptive context by placing the theoretical evolution of the
broken windows thesis in a broader set of evolving police–citizen coproduction strategies. If my *mis en scene* is correct, then for broken windows
policing to work we must first attend to the essentials of the coproduction
process, and, second, understand the special longitudinal challenges to
that process posed by the urban residential fabric.

Although it is ancient history to anyone less than 50 in 2000, urban disorders rocked dozens of major US cities in the 1960s. Looting and citizen
riots in many cities, and police riots in some cities were later put under
the analytical microscope by high-profile commissions or sociologists
(Fogelson 1968). One of the most widely quoted reports from the time
by the Kerner Commission concluded that policing practices had contributed in part to some of the outbreaks (Kerner 1968).[3] The Commission also pinpointed increasing segregation and structural inequality as
facilitating factors as well, although these were perhaps less remediable.

Consequent concerns about police practices inspired not only federal
initiatives seeking to further professionalize the police; they also encouraged widespread thinking about ways in which police department structures and practices could reduce the distrust and antagonism between
police officers and citizens, especially citizens of lower-income urban
communities of color.

Structural changes emerging from such thinking included the rise of
police-organized community relations councils, often staffed by a community relations sergeant; additional police–citizen review commissions
with some oversight over some range of police matters; and, later, citizen
police academies. Whether these changes were just "window dressing" or
more substantive, and why the degree of citizen review or oversight varied
across locales are interesting questions, but not ones to be pursued given
the focus here.

More relevant to the focus are a host of strategies first appearing in
the very early 1970s. These can be grouped roughly into two classes –
those emphasizing citizens' and citizen groups' roles, and those emphasizing how patrolling police interact with citizens. Strategies emphasizing
citizens' roles included a broad range of community crime prevention
activities: Neighborhood Watch, Citizens on Patrol, Operation ID, security surveys, and Operation Whistlestop, to name a few (Rosenbaum
1988). Although the origins of some of these go back to Winchester,
England and the 1200s, the key feature as these emerged in the 1970s
was a neighborhood-based coordinating group working with a designated
police officer. The latter was often a crime prevention specialist or a
community relations officer. Much has been written about whether these

programs were successful or not, for what crimes, under what types of conditions (Rosenbaum 1986; 1987; 1988).

A second class of strategies also emerging in the early and mid-1970s addressed patrolling officers' relations with citizenry more generally. Many departments sought to develop more "stable" relationships between patrolling officers, local citizens, and local small business personnel. Patrolling officers were assigned to particular neighborhoods for an extended period of time with team policing and geographic- or neighborhood-based policing. The hope was that over time officers would develop an understanding of how local residents and business leaders viewed crime and related problems in those locations (Greene and Pelfrey 1997). To deepen this understanding, in the late 1970s researchers like Robert Trojanowicz suggested flattening the tires on the patrol cars, giving the police Nikes, and getting them out of their cars. Foot patrolling officers also were tasked to work cooperatively with local business and citizen leaders and identify the specific crimes, crime locations, and crime-related problems deserving attention. Police–citizen contact, coordination, and coproduction were seen as critical conditions for success (Greene and Taylor 1988). This model, in contrast to the typical community crime prevention model, links numerous police officers simultaneously with numerous local citizens and local business personnel without an intervening neighborhood organization.

Progressing into the 1980s and 1990s, these models morphed into related labels including third-party policing (Mazerolle, Kadleck, and Roehl 1997; Buerger and Mazerolle 1998), problem-oriented policing (Spelman and Eck 1987; Eck and Spelman 1989; Goldstein 1990; Mazerolle, Ready, Terrill, and Waring 2000), and, most difficult to define, community policing (Cordner 1997). Despite widespread disagreement about what constitutes community policing, and what its goals are (Greene and Mastrofski 1988), most would agree on the following underlying principles (Skogan and Hartnett 1997): "organizational decentralization" (6) permitting more autonomy to those officers most directly involved with the locals, and easier police–public communication; "a commitment to . . . problem-oriented policing" (7); "responsiveness to citizen input" (8); and building neighborhood capacity to prevent crime or solve crime-related problems, i.e., to help neighborhood groups become coproducers of safety (8).

Within this broader evolution, the development of both the practice and theory behind incivilities reduction policing proves intriguing as well. On the practice side, the initial policing focus was a variant of problem-oriented policing (Wilson and Kelling 1982). Following a problem-oriented SARA approach (Scanning, Analysis, Response and

Assessment) (Spelman and Eck 1987), police would identify trouble-some conditions in a locale, and work with citizenry and other agencies to resolve those. Oakland's "Beat Health" program was an excellent example of such an approach (Mazerolle, Kadleck, and Roehl 1998). In short, broken windows policing clearly started out as a coproduction model. Citizens were involved in problem identification, and other agencies were involved in problem resolution. It was not presumed the police would board up the abandoned houses themselves. To better understand this coproduction component, the following section outlines its essential elements.

Coproduction

Police rely on citizens and other agencies in numerous ways. Most simply, citizens must report incidents to the police if the police are not right there to see the crime taking place. So fundamentally, producing public safety is a coproduction process, wherein police and citizens, and other organizations working with the police all contribute to the outcome (Ostrom, Parks, Whitaker, and Percy 1979). Ostrom (1996: 1073) defines coproduction as: "the process through which inputs used to provide a good or service are contributed by individuals who are not 'in' the same organization." Further: "Coproduction implies that citizens can play an active role in producing public goods and services of consequence to them" (Ostrom 1996: 1073).

Various factors make coproduction more or less effective than a service provision model for achieving the intended outcome. Service recipients – in this case neighborhood residents, neighborhood leaders, and local business personnel – need to be active participants in the process (Ostrom 1996: 1079). In addition "both parties must be legally entitled to take decisions, giving them both some room for manoeuvre . . . [and] participants need to build credible commitments to one another (e.g., through contractual obligations, based on trust or by enhancing social capital)" (Jeffery and Vira 2001: 9).

Reputations, trust, and reciprocity play pivotal roles in increasing cooperation between members of the partnership (Ostrom 1998). A coproductive relationship between citizen leaders and police may create policing which is more responsive and more favorably viewed, and a citizenry more willing to report to the police (Ostrom and Whitaker 1973).

Clearly, significant structural impediments beyond the control of police departments limit the possibilities of effective police–citizen coproduction. Most importantly, police, in contrast to other public sector agencies, are charged with maintaining social control, and administering "law" (Black 1980). Reciprocity cannot emerge given such a condition, although mutual responsiveness can. In addition, the citizenry in locations where effective coproduction is most needed – low income, urban communities of color – are exactly the same places where distrust between the police and citizens is most profound (Weitzer 1999; Weitzer and Tuch 1999). The trust requisite for maximally effective coproduction will take much longer to grow in these locations.

The above limitations aside, in key ways police innovations emerging since the 1970s contained elements of a coproduction model. They attempted to increase citizen–police trust, to facilitate stable relationships between police and local leaders and citizens, and, by tuning police to local concerns, increase locality-based police responsiveness.

Zero tolerance policing, and back where we started

Unfortunately, some current police practices relying on the incivilities thesis as justification have moved completely away from a coproduction idea. The popular zero tolerance policing is a case in point. When police focus just on that subset of social incivilities – disorderly or drunk people, rowdy groups of teens, panhandlers or street vagrants – and seek to remove them from the street, either through aggressive policing, or fines, or even arrests, we have zero tolerance policing.

These behaviors are aggressively targeted by police in the belief that suppressing these street activities will reduce the occurrence in those places of more serious crimes. The primary focus is on social incivilities, with less attention given to physical conditions. For example, in his first year on the job Baltimore City Police Commissioner Kevin P. Clark increased misdemeanor citations about 500 percent (Davis 2004).

The movement toward zero tolerance strategies and away from coproduction has taken place gradually over the last twenty years (McArdle and Erzin 2001). This changing emphasis within the incivilities thesis may be driven in part by wider societal changes (Garland 2002; Ismaili 2003: 262). Putting the policing shifts in a broader context, we may be seeing a historic shift in American and Canadian policing back to the social control model of the late nineteenth century, and away from the crime control model which dominated in the second quarter of the twentieth century (Monkkonen 1981; Boritch and Hagan 1987).

Kelling (1999: 3) has recognized that incivilities models are used to support zero tolerance strategies, but he argues against such a connection: "it is an equation that I have never made."

Nevertheless, zero tolerance policing policies *are* widely accepted because they are legitimated, in the minds of many, by the incivilities thesis. Over time the police and the public expect these strategies to reduce serious crime rates. Police *themselves* believe this (see Kelling and Sousa 2001, ethnographic observation 2A).

There is some irony here. Post-urban disorder policing innovations spanning at least three decades have sought to defuse police–community antagonisms by moving closer to coproduction models. Scrutiny of police–community relations following the disorders of the 1960s led to a variety of coproduction models. With community crime prevention initiatives, police were to coordinate with citizenry through local citizen-led groups, and the members of those groups would serve as the "eyes and ears" of the police. In return, the police would keep those groups informed about local crime patterns. Geographic and team policing were department-based organizational strategies intended to increase trust of the police among local citizens, citizen leaders, and business personnel. In the mid-1980s departments sought closer connections with communities through community policing partnerships; they also sought to increase their effectiveness through third-party policing and problem-oriented policing initiatives. These latter innovations required police to coordinate much more closely than they had in the past with other local agencies. Such coordination was in recognition of the limits of police powers, coupled with the hope that solving problems related to crime could make residents feel better and might even reduce crime itself.

The perceived importance of problems related to crime such as social or physical incivilities, has increased steadily through the last two if not three decades, and this shift links to broader trends (Garland 2002). Although many of these incivilities require the police to coordinate with other agencies such as housing or licencing and inspections, there is a subset of social incivilities against which the police can act directly: people being disorderly.

Thus, this series of innovations has come full circle. Zero tolerance policies, ostensibly in the minds of some justified by the incivilities thesis, endorse and entrench the aggressive policing thought originally to contribute to civil disorders in the first place. Despite the ongoing debate about the sources – from the individual police department up to the changing social fabric – inspiring this evolution; despite scholars' refutation of the incivilities thesis/zero tolerance connection; and despite the empirical weaknesses and theoretical vagaries of the incivilities thesis, zero tolerance policing is currently popular and thought to be justified by that thesis.

Returning policing innovations to a coproduction model

What is needed at this juncture is to return policing innovations more generally to a coproduction model. What are the impediments to such a reintegration?

Major challenges to effective police–community coproduction *over time* emerge from the longitudinal texture of the urban residential fabric. These stumbling blocks, and the empirical evidence pointing them out, are described in more detail elsewhere (Taylor 2001: 303–357). In brief, the main points are these. Using qualitative interviews with over sixty Baltimore neighborhood leaders in the mid-1990s, and examining changes in official neighborhood boundaries sanctioned by the local planning department between 1979 and 1995, we gauged the types of changes in neighborhood names and boundaries taking place, and how those created challenges for coproduction. For a range of sociological reasons, neighborhood boundaries and names can change over time (Hunter 1971; 1974). We found that both type and extent of change were often linked to local racial differences, socioeconomic status, or political agendas from beyond the neighborhood itself (Logan and Molotch 1987). We suggested that those changes create substantial difficulties for police–citizen coproduction of public safety.

We saw that neighborhoods where stable police partnerships were most needed were those where significant changes were most likely to occur over a short time in both boundaries and representing organizations. In such locales police working with community leaders were in danger of collaborating with decreasingly representative community groups, or of being confused about the relevant spatial domain, or both.

Ideally, community–police partnerships should be organized at the neighborhood level. To do so would increase citizens' buy-in and stake in the outcome. Partnerships organized around police beats or districts (e.g., Skogan and Hartnett 1997) end up working with a cluster of local leaders in each beat, whose constituencies only partially overlap the police organizing unit. In these situations it is not surprising that local leaders' commitments often rapidly wane.

If police are to move to a neighborhood-based framework for organizing partnerships, some sort of stability of neighborhood would seem to be required. Ongoing neighborhood changes decrease police willingness to move to that organizing framework, and create difficulties in establishing working relationships between police and citizens. If police are to engage in problem reduction, and to be effective and respond in ways that best benefit the overall community, they need to understand a single spatial arena and the key players. It takes time working in one locale with one set of stakeholders to develop such understanding. Understanding, trust, and some element of reciprocity are key ingredients for effective coproduction (Ostrom 1998).

Given the volume and diversity of neighborhood boundary and name changes observed, and the understandable urban dynamics driving these changes (Hunter 1974), it appears that successful police-community coproducing relationships could be developed only in urban or suburban locations with strong overarching neighborhood governance structures. Many cities have such structures (Hallman 1984; Ferman 1996). To attempt to stabilize such partnerships *without* that broader, organizing and legitimizing political structure, effectively dooms these partnerships. It limits them to being no more than anemic relationships with no real commitment either from police or from citizen leaders. According to the coproduction model, it is extremely difficult if not impossible to coproduce community safety in such settings without that broader infrastructure.

Summary

The incivilities thesis and police work focusing on incivility reduction emerged from a preceding tradition of policing innovations, starting in the early 1970s, in response to urban riots of the 1960s. This emerging tradition sought to create successful police–community partnerships. The incivilities thesis has evolved, moving from initial psychological, cross-sectional formulations to ecological and longitudinal formulations. Empirical support documenting impacts of incivilities over time on crime, responses to crime, and neighborhood change, has been weaker and less consistent than hoped. Empirical investigations documenting salutary impacts of disorder reduction police work remain few and their rigor contested. Solid evidence of successful incivilities reduction nested within third-party policing has emerged, but the specific contribution of police work itself is not clear. A currently widely practiced version of disorder reduction policing is zero tolerance policing. It is thought by many to be justified by the incivilities thesis despite the latter's originator denying this connection, and despite the weak support for the thesis. Zero tolerance repudiates the police–community coproduction model on which the incivilities thesis, and earlier police–community innovations, were grounded. It is exacerbating the very problems these earlier policing innovations sought to reduce. To move back to a coproduction model of policing we will need to solve the problem of changing neighborhood identities, organizations, and boundaries.

NOTES

The author thanks the two editors and Ron Davis for helpful comments on earlier drafts of the chapter. Address correspondence to RBT, Department of Criminal Justice, Gladfelter Hall, Temple University, 1115 West Berks Street, Philadelphia, PA 19122 (tuclasses@rbtaylor.net).

1. More details on this material appear in Taylor (1999; 2001).
2. More specifically: the analysis confounds boroughs and precincts in one level of analysis rather than separating them out; there are no controls for spatial autocorrelation effects; and controls for basic ecological fabric appear to be underspecified, with no variables for racial composition or stability.
3. Of course, this is not the only decade of the twentieth century in which police activity has been linked to urban riots.

REFERENCES

Black, D. (1980). *The behavior of law*. New York: Academic Press.
Blumstein, A. and Wallman, J. (eds.). (2000). *The crime drop in America*. Cambridge: Cambridge University Press.
Boritch, H. and Hagan, J. (1987). Crime and the changing forms of class control: Policing public order in Toronto the Good, 1859–1955. *Social Forces, 66*, 307–335.
Bratton, W. (1998). *Turnaround*. New York: Random House.
Buerger, M. and Mazerolle, L. G. (1998). Third-party policing: A theoretical analysis of an emerging trend. *Justice Quarterly, 15*, 301–328.
Cordner, G. (1997). Community policing. In R. G. Dunham and G. P. Alpert (eds.), *Critical issues in policing: Contemporary readings*. Prospect Heights, IL: Waveland Press.
Davis, R. (2004). Quality of life crime splits police, prosecutors. *Baltimore Sun*, July 12, A1.
Eck, J. and Spelman, W. (1989). A problem-oriented approach to police service delivery. In D. J. Kenney (ed.), *Police and policing: Contemporary issues* (pp. 95–103). New York: Praeger.
Ferman, B. (1996). *Challenging the growth machine: Neighborhood politics in Chicago and Pittsburgh*. Lawrence: University of Kansas Press.
Fogelson, R. M. (1968). From resentment to confrontation: The police, the negroes, and the outbreak of the nineteen-sixties riots. *Political Science Quarterly, 83*, 217–247.
Garland, D. (2002). *The culture of control: Crime and social order in contemporary society*. Chicago: University of Chicago Press.
Garofalo, J. and Laub, J. (1978). The fear of crime: Broadening our perspective. *Victimology, 3*, 242–253.
Goldstein, H. (1990). *Problem-oriented policing*. Philadelphia: Temple University Press.
Green, L. (1996). *Policing places with drug problems*. Thousand Oaks, CA: Sage Publications.
Greene, J. R. and Mastrofski, S. D. (eds.). (1988). *Community policing: Rhetoric and reality*. New York: Praeger.

Greene, J. R. and Pelfrey, W. V. (1997). Shifting the balance of power between police and community. In R. G. Dunham and G. P. Alpert (eds.), *Critical issues in policing: contemporary readings*. Prospect Heights, IL: Waveland Press.

Greene, J. R. and Taylor, R. B. (1988). Community-based policing and foot patrol: Issues of theory and evaluation. In J. R. Greene and S. D. Mastrofski (eds.), *Community policing: Rhetoric or reality* (pp. 195–224). New York: Praeger.

Hallman, H. W. (1984). *Neighborhoods: Their place in urban life*. Beverly Hills, CA: Sage Publications.

Harcourt, B. E. (2001). *Illusion of order: The false promise of broken windows policing*. Cambridge, MA: Harvard University Press.

Hunter, A. (1971). The ecology of Chicago: Persistence and change, 1930–1960. *American Journal of Sociology*, *77*, 425–443.

    (1974). *Symbolic communities*. Chicago: University of Chicago Press.

Ismaili, K. (2003). Explaining the cultural and symbolic resonance of zero tolerance in contemporary criminal justice. *Contemporary Justice Review*, *6*, 255–264.

Jeffery, R. and Vira, B. (2001). Introduction. In R. Jeffery and B. Vira (eds.), *Conflict and cooperation in participatory natural resource management* (pp. 1–16). New York: Palgrave MacMillan.

Kelling, G. L. and Coles, C. M. (1996). *Fixing broken windows: Restoring order and reducing crime in our communities*. New York: Free Press.

Kelling, G. L. (1999). *Broken windows and police discretion*. Research Report NCJ17859. Washington, DC: National Institute of Justice.

Kelling, G. L. and Sousa, W. H., Jr. (2001). *Do police matter?: An analysis of the impact of New York City's police reforms*. Manhattan Institute Civic Report No. 22.

Kerner, O. (1968). *Report of the National Advisory Commission on Civil Disorders*. New York: Bantam.

Logan, J. R. and Molotch, H. (1987). *Urban fortunes*. Berkeley, CA: University of California Press.

Mazerolle, L. G., Kadleck, C., and Roehl, J. (1997). Controlling drug and disorder problems: The role of place managers. *Criminology*, *36*, 371–404.

Mazerolle, L. G., Ready, J., Terrill, W., and Waring, E. (2000). Problem oriented policing in public housing: The Jersey City evaluation. *Justice Quarterly*, *17*, 129–158.

Mazerolle, L. G., Kadleck, C., and Roehl, J. (1998). Controlling drug and disorder problems: The role of place managers. *Criminology*, *36*, 371–404.

McArdle, A. and Erzin, T. (2001). *Zero tolerance: Quality of life and the new police brutality in New York City*. New York: New York University Press.

Monkkonen, E. H. (1981). *Police in urban America, 1860–1920*. Cambridge: Cambridge University Press.

Ostrom, E. (1996). Crossing the great divide: Coproduction, synergy and development. *World Development*, *24*, 1073–1088.

(1998). A behavioral approach to the rational choice theory of collective action: Presidential address, American Political Science Association, 1997. *American Political Science Review, 92*, 1–22.

Ostrom, E. and Whitaker, G. (1973). Does local community control of police make a difference?: Some preliminary findings. *American Journal of Political Science, 17*, 48–76.

Ostrom, E., Parks, R. B., Whitaker, G. P., and Percy, S. L. (1979). The public service production process: A framework for analysing police services. In R. Baker and F. A. Meyer, Jr. (eds.), *Evaluating alternative law enforcement policies* (pp. 65–73). Lexington: DC Heath.

Robinson, J., Lawton, B., Taylor, R. B., and Perkins, D. D. (2003). Longitudinal impacts of incivilities: A multilevel analysis of reactions to crime and block satisfaction. *Journal of Quantitative Criminology, 19.*

Rosenbaum, D. P. (1986). *Community crime prevention: Does it work?, 22.* Beverly Hills: Sage Publications.

(1987). The theory and research behind neighborhood watch: Is it a sound fear and crime reduction strategy? *Crime and Delinquency, 33*, 103–134.

(1988). Community crime prevention: A review and synthesis of the literature. *Justice Quarterly, 5*, 323–395.

Sampson, R. J. and Raudenbush, S. W. (1999). Systematic social observation of public spaces: A new look at disorder in urban neighborhoods. *American Journal of Sociology, 105*, 603–651.

Silverman, E. (1999). *NYPD battles crime: Innovative strategies in policing.* Boston: Northeastern University Press.

Skogan, W. (1990). *Disorder and decline: Crime and the spiral of decay in American cities.* New York: Free Press.

Skogan, W. and Hartnett, S. (1997). *Community policing, Chicago style.* New York: Oxford University Press.

Spelman, W. and Eck, J. E. (1987). *Problem-oriented policing.* Washington, DC: National Institute of Justice.

Taylor, R. B. (1996). Neighborhood responses to disorder and local attachments: The systemic model of attachment, and neighborhood use value. *Sociological Forum, 11*, 41–74.

(1997). Social order and disorder of streetblocks and neighborhoods: Ecology, microecology and the systemic model of social disorganization. *Journal of Research in Crime and Delinquency, 33*, 113–155.

(1999). The incivilities thesis: Theory, measurement and policy. In R. L. Langworthy (ed.), *Measuring what matters* (pp. 65–88). Washington, DC: National Institute of Justice / Office of Community Oriented Policing Services.

(2001). *Breaking away from broken windows: Evidence from Baltimore neighborhoods and the nationwide fight against crime, grime, fear and decline.* New York: Westview Press.

Taylor, R. B., Shumaker, S. A., and Gottfredson, S. D. (1985). Neighborhood-level links between physical features and local sentiments: Deterioration, fear of crime, and confidence. *Journal of Architectural Planning and Research, 2*, 261–275.

Thacher, D. (2004). Order maintenance reconsidered: Moving beyond strong causal reasoning. *Journal of Criminal Law and Criminology*, *94*, 381–414.

Tonry, M. H. (1995). *Malign neglect: Race, crime and punishment in America*. New York: Oxford University Press.

Weisburd, D., Bushway, S., Lum, C., and Yang, S. M. (2004). Trajectories of crime at places: A longitudinal study of street segments in the city of Seattle. *Criminology*, *42*, 283–321.

Weitzer, R. (1999). Citizens' perceptions of police misconduct: Race and neighborhood context. *Justice Quarterly*, *16*, 819–846.

Weitzer, R. and Tuch, S. A. (1999). Race, class, and perceptions of discrimination by the police. *Crime and Delinquency*, *45*, 494–507.

Wilson, J. Q. (1975). *Thinking about crime*. New York: Basic.

Wilson, J. Q. and Kelling, G. L. (1982). Broken windows. *Atlantic Monthly*, *211*, 29–38.

Part III

Problem-oriented policing

6 *Advocate*
Science, values, and problem-oriented policing: why problem-oriented policing?

John E. Eck

Problem-oriented policing is so logical it is surprising it needs justification. Problem-oriented policing is based on the premises that (a) the public demands much of police; (b) the causes of these demands are often complex; (c) the police serve the public better when they make systematic inquiries into these complexities; (d) knowledge helps build new approaches to police services; and (e) learning from successful and unsuccessful innovations makes police more effective in handling the demands of the public. The validity of these premises can be seen if we pause to look at their opposites: (a) the public demands little of police; (b) the causes of these demands are simple; (c) systematic inquiry into the demands is of little use; (d) knowledge will not help build new approaches to police services; and (e) there is little to be learned from successes or failures, so examining them will not improve police effectiveness. None of these stand up to close scrutiny.

So why is problem-oriented policing often misinterpreted? One reason is that problem-oriented policing fundamentally redefines policing. It restates the police mission by creating a new unit of analysis for evaluating police actions: the "problem." It shifts policing to a scientific approach to preventing crime and away from the routine application of the law. And it replaces the notion of the police as gatekeepers to the criminal justice system with the idea that police are central to many networks that affect public well-being.

This chapter describes the evolution of problem-oriented policing. I begin at its origins and then describe its progress. Then I explain why it is difficult to evaluate. Finally, I describe why there is no viable alternative to problem-oriented policing.

What is problem-oriented policing?

Shot while playing basketball, a teenager lay bleeding to death just steps away from a hospital as emergency room workers refused to treat him, saying it was against policy to go outside. Hospital officials rescinded the policy later today. (Associated Press 1998)

Goldstein created problem-oriented policing to address police discretion. Police officers are given wide latitude to handle incidents. This gives them the ability to tailor decisions to the specific needs of situations, but it allows officers to take inappropriate actions. Unguided discretion is at the heart of most of the maladies facing policing – for example, over and improper use of force, ineffective crime reduction procedures, corruption, and discriminatory practices. Goldstein claimed that discretion could be guided if more were known about the types of problems police handle. Unfortunately, police administrators focus disproportionately on what the police do rather than on what the police are supposed to accomplish. This is the "means-over-ends syndrome" (Goldstein 1979). Goldstein suggested that if police focused more on what they were supposed to accomplish – addressing problems – officers could be provided with meaningful guidance in how to use their discretion, thus reducing the chances of inappropriate actions.

The means-over-ends syndrome can be seen best in police use of the law. Law enforcement is a tool, according to Goldstein (1979), not a goal. Police and citizens often confuse applying the law with reduction in trouble circumstances. This occurs when policymakers use the application of the law as the measure of success. In the mid-1990s I heard a new police chief speak to a group of citizens in my county. After his speech he took questions. One resident asked why police were arresting homeless men in the old downtown. The chief answered, "Were they drunk in public? If they were, they were violating the law and should be arrested." The chief did not try to show how these arrests addressed the legitimate concerns the public might have with homeless men – from unsightliness, to aggressive panhandling, to the health of the homeless men themselves. The chief implied that enforcing the law trumped the concerns of the public.

What are the ends that the police should attend to? The police role is to address the diverse array of troublesome circumstances brought to it by the public. Goldstein called these circumstances "problems." The criminal law is one of many tools the police could apply. How should police select the right tools for a particular problem? The answer is to examine the problem, learn why it continues, and select tools that fit the problem. Success should be measured by problem reduction – fewer, less serious, and less harmful problems.

Notice that problem-oriented policing contains three principles. The *empirical* principle states that the public demands that the police handle a diverse range of problems. The public is not wedded to a particular means to reduce problems, but it does demand that they be addressed. This is widely accepted and will not be examined further.

The *normative* principle claims that police are supposed to reduce problems rather than simply respond to incidents and apply the relevant criminal law. One can agree that the public demands a great deal of the police, but it does not follow automatically that the police should deliver all that is demanded of them. I will come back to this important point later.

The *scientific* principle asserts that police should take a scientific approach to problems. Police should apply analytical approaches and interventions based on sound theory and evidence, just as decisions of doctors are supposed to be based on medical science. This has implications for how one scientifically assesses problem-oriented policing. I will come back to this important point as well.

How has problem-oriented policing evolved?

These principles have remained constant, but problem-oriented policing has evolved in four ways: its position within police agencies; its theoretical underpinnings; its definition of "problem"; and in the amount of technical advice.

Location, scale, and quality

Problem-oriented policing was originally to be located in a headquarters unit. This unit would examine problems with the goal of providing advice as to what officers could do to improve their handling of these situations. A succession of pilot tests in Madison, Wisconsin (Goldstein and Susmilch 1982b), London (Hoare, Stewart, and Purcell 1984), Baltimore County, Maryland (Cordner 1986), and Newport News, Virginia (Eck and Spelman 1987) moved the location of analysis from headquarters to police officers assigned to operational units.

Decentralization of problem-solving had consequences. It increased the number of problems handled by increasing the officers who addressed them. This reduced the scale of problem analysis from problem classes to individual manifestations of problem classes – from how to handle street prostitution, for example, to how to handle street prostitution on a particular street corner. Decentralization and reduction in scale truncated inquiry into problems, from the extensive analysis originally envisioned, to limited probing by busy street cops. These changes reduced the quality of the average problem-solving effort.

Though the average quality declined, the range of quality probably widened. At the upper levels some important inquiries have been undertaken resulting in reductions of serious problems, for example, Boston's youth homicide reduction effort (Kennedy, Braga, and Piehl 1997; Braga,

Kennedy, Waring, and Piehl 2001), Liverpool's reduction of glass bottle injuries (Hester and Rice 2001), and the California Highway Patrol's project to reduce farm worker highway deaths (Helmick 2002). At the bottom level, what is called "problem solving" may simply be targeted enforcement or referrals to other agencies.

Recently, there has been renewed interest in centralized problem inquiries to improve quality. Advances in crime analysis have propelled these units to the center of problem-oriented policing, both as support for line officers engaged in problem solving, and as leaders of major inquiries (Boba 2003; Clarke and Eck 2003).

Theoretical underpinnings

Problem-oriented policing requires a theory of problems. By 1987, the link between problem solving and routine activity theory was apparent (Eck and Spelman 1987). By the early 1990s, routine activity theory became incorporated within problem-solving training through the "problem-analysis triangle." The triangle is now a standard part of problem analysis (Office of Community Oriented Policing Services 1998; Read and Tilley 2000; Braga 2002; Clarke and Eck 2003). Today, problem-oriented policing uses a variety of concepts, tools, and procedures from environmental criminology: repeat victim and place analysis, examining property ownership and street configurations, situational crime prevention and crime mapping, to name but a few (Braga 2002; Clarke and Eck 2003).

Problem definition

Problem-oriented policing is unique in creating an entirely new concept defining the goals of policing. Despite its centrality, "problem" was left undefined at first. Instead, Goldstein provided examples. The term was used as shorthand for the wide array of issues the public calls upon the police to handle.

A more precise definition was needed to operationalize problem-oriented policing. In 1998, the Office of Community Oriented Policing Services (COPS) of the US Justice Department defined a problem as "two or more incidents similar in one or more ways that is of concern to the police and a problem for the community" (Office of Community Oriented Policing Services 1998: 4). Recently, a problem has been defined as a reoccurring set of similar events, harmful to members of the community, that members of the public expect the local police to address. This definition is summarized by the acronym, CHEERS, for *C*ommunity,

*H*arm, *E*xpectations, *E*vents, *R*ecurring, and *S*imilarity (Clarke and Eck 2003).

There are many different types of problems. To describe how problems are related to each other, Ronald V. Clarke and I developed a classification system that identifies sixty-six forms of problems on the basis of the behaviors involved and the environments within which these behaviors take place (Eck and Clarke 2003).

Improvements in guidance

The transition of problem-oriented policing from theory to practice necessitated the development of technical advice. The SARA process (Scanning, Analysis, Response, Assessment), a first effort in this direction (Eck and Spelman 1987), has become almost synonymous with problem-oriented policing (Scott 2000). Later, Rana Sampson spearheaded the dissemination of a problem analysis framework known as the crime or problem triangle (Office of Community Oriented Policing Services 1998: 9). The triangle was expanded further to include people who can exercise control over situations (Eck 2003).

There has been a dramatic increase in the number of publications providing problem-solving guidance. These include general-purpose guides (Office of Community Oriented Policing Services 1998; Bynum 2001), as well as Anthony Braga's (2002) in-depth text on problem solving. There is now a small library of manuals on technical areas, such as surveys (Eck and LaVigne 1993; Weisel 1999), evaluations (Eck 2002a), and mapping (Harries 1999; Eck, Chainey, and Cameron 2005). Recently, the Jill Dando Institute for Crime Sciences published a guide to problem solving for British crime analysts (Clarke and Eck 2003).[1] And in 2004 the Center for Problem-Oriented Policing implemented a website with an on-line problem-solving simulation and a theory-based protocol (InPART) to facilitate individual and group problem solving (Center for Problem-Oriented Policing 2004). Much of this guidance is rooted in environmental criminology.

The COPS office has also funded a series of problem-specific guides. Each guide uses research and practices on a problem type (burglaries of single family homes (Weisel 2002), for example, or rave parties (Scott 2002)) to suggest methods for handling that type of problem.

A quarter of a century since it was first articulated important changes have taken place in the location of problem-oriented policing, the theory of problem-oriented policing, the concept of "problem," and in problem-solving guidance. Except for organizational location, these changes have been toward increasing specificity. This stands in stark contrast to other police reforms, such as community policing, broken windows theory, and Compstat, which have become less defined over time (Eck and Rosenbaum 1994; Harcourt 2001; Weisburd, Mastrofski, McNally, Greenspan *et al.* 2003).

Should police adopt a problem-oriented approach?

Any social innovation should be judged on the basis of its utility. Though there is substantial evidence for its effectiveness (Committee to Review Research 2004; Weisburd and Eck 2004), there is no simple test for the utility of problem-oriented policing. Unlike a program designed to address a narrow set of objectives (such as DARE or arrests in misdemeanor domestic violence calls), any particular evaluation can examine only a piece of a problem-oriented strategy. Developments in problem-oriented policing make the strategy a moving target. In addition to these standard limits on empirical evaluations there are limits particular to problem-oriented policing.

Problem-oriented policing as a values statement

Policing can be about many things. So the decision to assert that the police are about addressing problems is a choice among alternative values.

One could claim that the police should only provide emergency services. The prevention of crime, disorder, and other public concerns should be left to individuals, community groups, private markets, other professions, and other government entities. One could claim that this is today's standard form of policing and that this is how policing *should* be carried out.

Alternatively, one could claim that policing *should* be about fighting crime – both handling its aftermath and reducing future occurrences. Everything else is a sideshow created by historical accident, inept public administration, and other correctable factors. Police have shed many former police functions and so should shed remaining non-crime functions.

One could also assert that police should focus only on separating violators from non-violators and help to bring the violators before the courts. From this perspective, decreasing crime is not a police function at all, but the responsibility of others. If police actions prevent crime this is only an unintended side benefit.

These normative positions stand independent of the fact that they may be difficult to achieve. Empirical evidence only helps show what will need to change in order to achieve these goals.

Similarly, taking a problem-oriented approach is an assertion that the police *should* focus on diminishing the harm from the diverse array of issues brought to police attention. People demand a great deal of the police because other institutions fail. The police must be the agency that takes the lead in preventing future occurrences because they are the sole 24-hour general-purpose public trouble-shooting agency and have the greatest capacity to spearhead problem-solving-based prevention.

From a normative perspective problem-oriented policing is untestable. It is what the police should be doing because it is a natural outgrowth of the definition of policing. There will always be a need for an organization that deals with things that go wrong. Fixing these failures often raises the likelihood that force may be required. So a general-purpose agency with the ability to use the coercive powers of the state will always be required. This is policing (Bittner 1980). And if we desire policing to be effective and responsive to the public, then scientific examination of the problems is necessary.

Problem-oriented policing as science

Police have used science for decades, most obviously in forensics. That does not make policing a science, but makes science a tool of policing.

Problem-oriented policing goes further. A problem-oriented approach attempts to make policing an applied social science. On what grounds does this statement rest? There are two. First, Goldstein (1979) laid out four principles: (1) define problems with specificity; (2) study problems in depth; (3) conduct a broad search for solutions; and (4) focus on outcomes. These are basic empirical principles of any scientific inquiry.

That problem-oriented policing is an applied science can be seen when it is put into practice (beyond a cosmetic application). Problem-solving projects look like applied science. Good problem-solving efforts involve theory, systematic measurement, comparison, and analysis (Clarke and Eck 2003). Inquiries into problems were originally envisioned to be joint police–social scientists endeavors (Goldstein 1990). There are a number of well-documented case studies illustrating such collaborations (for example, Goldstein and Susmilch 1982a; Goldstein and Susmilch 1982c; Eck and Spelman 1987; Forrester, Chatterton, and Pease 1988; Kennedy et al. 2001; Clarke and Goldstein 2002; Clarke and Goldstein 2003). Much problem solving may be deficient, but so is much applied science.

This puts problem-oriented policing, as a whole, outside of the domain of scientific evaluations. Evaluations cannot determine if problem-oriented policing is effective because to attempt to scientifically evaluate problem-oriented policing as a single entity invokes Epimenides' paradox.[2] If problem-oriented policing is scientifically testable, one must be able to envision a test that could show that it fails to deliver what it claims. If such a test were conducted, and the core principles of problem-oriented policing were refuted, then the test also would refute the scientific procedures used to conduct the test. This calls into question the test's conclusions. So we have a circular argument.

Scientific tests can show that theories, methods, and interventions used within a problem-oriented approach do not deliver what they are supposed to deliver, and that other theories, methods, and interventions hold greater promise. Studies could show that a particular theory of problems is not as helpful as another theory (social disorganization theories, for example, are probably of limited utility, but environmental criminological theories show great promise). They could show that particular analytical techniques (e.g., mapping) produce more information about some problems than other problems. Experiments, for example, can demonstrate that crackdowns on drug hot spots have limited utility (Sherman and Rogan 1995a; Weisburd and Green 1995; Cohen, Gorr, and Singh 2003), and interventions with landlords at such places have greater effectiveness (Weisburd and Green 1995; Eck and Wartell 1998; Mazerolle, Roehl, and Kadleck 1998). Scientific studies could show that locating problem analysis in one part of the police organization is dysfunctional, while locating it in other parts of the organization is highly productive.

A problem-oriented approach as effective policing

Evidence can address important questions about problem-oriented policing. Two questions in particular are critical. How much analysis is needed for problem-oriented policing to be more effective than standard policing? And does expanding police actions beyond law enforcement improve its effectiveness? If limited analysis and diversity of actions improve police effectiveness, then incremental adoption of a problem-oriented approach is feasible. If analysis and diversity of action must increase dramatically to get a useful payoff, then implementing problem-oriented policing will be very difficult.

How much analysis is required? Findings from numerous studies show that even a little analysis makes detectable improvements in police effectiveness. Let's examine this question by looking at three unidimensional analyses of problems: repeat places, repeat offenders, and repeat victims (Eck 2001).

Detecting crime hot spots of is one of the most basic forms of analysis and evidence shows that acting on such limited analysis helps reduce crime – compared to acting without such analysis (Braga 2001; Sherman and Rogan 1995b; Sherman and Weisburd 1995). Is there additional utility for analysis *after* detecting hot spots? When hot spots are randomly assigned to problem-solving (treatment) and standard policing, the hot spots receiving the problem solving fared better on average than those receiving standard policing (Weisburd and Green 1995; Braga, Weisburd, Waring *et al.* 1999). Based on the published descriptions, the analysis undertaken in the treatment hot spots was relatively limited. So, even small amounts of analysis improve police effectiveness.

Deterrence works, if it can be applied to specific people. This is a basic lesson of one of the most ambitious case studies in problem-oriented policing, the Boston Ceasefire project (Braga *et al.* 2001; Kennedy *et al.* 1997). Similar results were found in the Indianapolis Gun Patrol Experiment (McGarrell, Chermak, Weiss, and Wilson 2001). Though the analysis applied is below the threshold for a problem-oriented approach, it shows that even a bit of analysis is better than none.

Focusing on repeat victims also reduces crime. Several quasi-experiments point to the effectiveness of focusing on people who have previous victimization experience (Farrell 1995). Repeat victimization programs typically use non-traditional interventions and often apply law enforcement as a last resort (Anderson, Chenery, and Pease 1995), so it is difficult to disentangle the effects of analysis from the effects of the use of alternatives to enforcement. Nevertheless, the conclusions from the repeat victimization experiences mirror those from repeat place and repeat offending – even a small amount of analysis is helpful.

How productive is diversifying responses? Repeat victimization programs show that the use of alternatives to enforcement improves effectiveness. There is evidence from other programs that diversifying police action beyond enforcement has payoffs. Crackdowns on drug hot spots produce small to modest crime or disorder reduction (Sherman and Rogan 1995a), but when coupled with landlord interventions, the impact is larger (Hope 1994; Green 1995; Eck and Wartell 1998; Mazerolle, Roehl, and Kadleck 1998). Matthews (1997) noticed a similar phenomenon with prostitution. Early enforcement resulted in short-term improvements but not sustained change. When enforcement was coupled with changes in street layout he noted longer-lasting and deeper impacts (Matthews 1993). Recently, Cohen and colleagues (2003) found that police crackdowns on illegal drug dealing at bars had noticeable but temporary effects. What would have occurred if the interventions had targeted the bar owners using a wider variety of interventions? There is a small but useful set of evaluations suggesting that the impact would have been greater (Homel, Hauritz, Wortley *et al.* 1997; Eck 2002b).

In conclusion, even rudimentary application of a problem-oriented approach produces meaningful positive results, relative to alternatives (Weisburd and Eck 2004). Though I have separated the effects of analysis from the application of alternative interventions, alternative interventions may not be much more effective than enforcement *unless* coupled with analysis. Without analysis it is difficult to determine which alternatives should be applied. So to be really effective both analysis *and* diversity of intervention need to be applied.

These conclusions are conservative. The payoff to careful analysis and diversifying responses may be greater. This is because policing is a human activity. In every human activity fine distinctions improve effectiveness because fine distinctions allow carefully tailored actions. And analysis allows the development of complex sets of actions. Some claim that the progression from simple to complex is a universal part of all life (Solè and Goodwin 2000). It would be odd if paying attention to detail and acting on knowledge did not improve police effectiveness when it improves all other endeavors.

Additionally, I have assumed that there is a stable body of knowledge. As noted earlier, the volume and specificity of problem analysis and intervention guidance has increased over the last decade. Problem analysis will become more penetrating as the knowledge grows and guidance becomes more specific.

Problem-oriented policing itself is a source of innovation. When police make systematic inquiries into a problem we learn things. Often what we learn are small details. On occasion we learn general principles. Two examples of problem-oriented policing creating new principles are examined in this volume: focused deterrence (Kennedy in this volume) and third-party policing (Mazerolle in this volume). Thus, the more problem-oriented the police become, the more they will learn about problems and appropriate responses. In short, the practice of problem-oriented policing produces a positive feedback that creates an increase in police effectiveness.

All of this suggests that problem-oriented policing can be implemented incrementally, in small steps.

Is there an alternative to problem-oriented policing?

Problem-oriented policing is not an historical necessity. There is no logical reason that others could not apply problem solving to prevent crime. High-school students have successfully undertaken problem-solving activities (Kenney and Watson 1996). Some have argued that the security industry is far better poised to analyze and address crime problems (Professional Security 2004). Policing could move away from a problem-oriented approach. But if it does, it will become increasingly marginalized (Eck 1993).

We have seen this occur with other emergency services. Fire and emergency medical services mitigate the harmful effects of incidents rather than prevent the incidents. Modern fire services focus on fire suppression with most prevention left to other private and public agencies. Emergency medical services respond to vehicle accidents, shooting injuries, and heart attacks, but do little to prevent these events. Policing could go this route as well.

But if policing is to have a prevention role, then there is no alternative to a problem-oriented approach. The standard model of policing currently applied has limited effect on preventing crime and disorder (Committee to Review Research 2004; Weisburd and Eck 2004). There is only limited evidence for the prevention effectiveness of community policing when a problem-oriented approach is not also used. Community policing's value may be in fostering better police–community relations, improving the legitimacy of police, and promoting democratic principles. It is a complementary innovation to a problem-oriented approach instead of a competitor to it. Other innovations, such as hotspots policing, third-party policing, focused deterrence, and Compstat highlight aspects of a problem-oriented approach. These are not alternatives, but elaborations on problem identification, interventions, and management systems that have been or could be adapted to a problem-oriented approach.

Broken windows theory also may be complementary to a problem-oriented approach (Kelling and Sousa 2001). If broken windows theory can incorporate analysis and innovation, then it too can be applied within a problem-oriented approach. This theory is only antithetical to a problem-oriented approach if it fosters a single response to all police problems. Because broken windows theory makes no suggestions regarding a variety of police problems such as civil disturbances and traffic accidents it is more limited than a problem-oriented approach. Another limitation is that broken windows theory is at best only weakly supported by evidence (Harcourt 2001; Committee to Review Research 2004).

In the end, there is only one criticism of problem-oriented policing: a problem-oriented approach is too difficult to implement. If this were valid then an alternative to a problem-oriented approach would be needed. Any alternative would have to be simpler than a problem-oriented approach. But then it will be too simple to be effective for the demands on policing. And that will bring us back to where we were when Goldstein proposed a problem-oriented approach.

Fortunately, this criticism is invalid. As we have seen, problem-solving "light" is better than no problem-solving at all. Progress in policing may be one baby step after another. Even if change is incremental and slow that does not make problem-oriented policing unrealistic. Enacting a problem-oriented approach just requires diligence, hard work, and a great deal of patience. But then, there is no real alternative.

NOTES

This paper is the result of twenty years of hanging out with some very smart people. Each deserves thanks. Unfortunately, space and memory limit those I can mention. So in alphabetical order, "thank you" to Anthony Braga, Ronald Clarke, Ron Glensor, Herman Goldstein, Johannes Knutsson, Gloria Laycock, Lorraine Mazerolle, Nancy McPherson, Andy Mills, Graeme Newman, Rana Sampson, Karin Schmerler, Michael Scott, Lawrence Sherman, William Spelman, Darrel Stephens, Nick Tilley, Julie Wartell, David Weisburd, and Deborah Weisel. Tamara Madensen deserves special credit for helping prepare the manuscript for publication. I alone am responsible for any errors, omissions, and illogical leaps.
1. The COPS office has funded a companion guide for US crime analysts.
2. Epimenides was a sixth-century BC scholar from Crete who said, "All Cretans are liars." This has been sharpened to the Liars paradox, "This statement is false" (Hofstadter 1979).

REFERENCES

Anderson, D., Chenery, S., and Pease, K. (1995). *Preventing repeat victimization: A report on progress in Huddersfield*. London: Home Office, Police Research Group.
Associated Press. (1998, May 19). As dying teen bleeds nearby, hospital staff stays inside – incident prompts change in policy. *Washington Post*, p. A9.
Bittner, E. (1980). *The functions of police in modern society*. Rockville, MD: National Institute of Mental Health.
Boba, R. (2003). *Problem analysis in policing*. Washington, DC: Police Foundation.
Braga, A. A. (2001). The effects of hot spots policing on crime. *Annals of the American Academy of Political and Social Science, 578*, 104–125.
     (2002). *Problem-oriented policing and crime prevention*. Monsey, NY: Criminal Justice Press.
Braga, A. A., Kennedy, D. M., Waring, E. J., and Piehl, A. M. (2001). Problem-oriented policing, deterrence, and youth violence: An evaluation of Boston's operation ceasefire. *Journal of Research in Crime and Delinquency, 38* (3), 195–225.
Braga, A. A., Weisburd, D. L., Waring, E. J. Mazerolle, L. G., Spelman, W., and Gajewski, F. (1999). Problem-oriented policing in violent crime places: A randomized controlled experiment. *Criminology, 37* (3), 541–580.
Bynum, T. (2001). *Using analysis for problem-solving: A guidebook for law enforcement*. Washington, DC: Office of Community Oriented Policing Services.

Center for Problem-Oriented Policing. (2004). *InPART: Interactive problem analysis and response tool.* Retrieved from www.popcenter.org.

Clarke, R. V. and Eck, J. E. (2003). *Become a problem-solving crime analyst: In 55 small steps.* London: Jill Dando Institute of Crime Science.

Clarke, R. V. and Goldstein, H. (2002). Reducing theft at construction sites: lessons from a problem-oriented project. In N. Tilley (ed.), *Analysis for crime prevention,* 13 (pp. 89–130). Monsey, NY: Criminal Justice Press.

(2003). Thefts from cars in center-city parking facilities: A case study in implementing problem-oriented policing. In J. Knutsson (ed.), *Problem-oriented policing: From innovation to mainstream,* 15 (pp. 257–298). Monsey, NY: Criminal Justice Press.

Cohen, J., Gorr, W., and Singh, P. (2003). Estimating intervention effects in varying risk settings: Do police raids reduce illegal drug dealing at nuisance bars? *Criminology, 41* (2), 257–292.

Committee to Review Research on Police Policy and Practices. (2004). *Fairness and effectiveness in policing: The evidence.* Washington, DC: National Academies Press.

Cordner, G. W. (1986). Fear of crime and the police: An evaluation of a fear-reduction strategy. *Journal of Police Science and Administration, 14* (2), 223–233.

Eck, J. E. (1993). Alternative futures for policing. In D. Weisburd and C. Uchida (eds.), *Police innovation and control of the police* (pp. 59–79). New York: Springer Verlag.

(2001). Policing and crime event concentration. In R. Meier, L. Kennedy, and V. Sacco (eds.), *The process and structure of crime: criminal events and crime analysis* (pp. 249–276). New Brunswick, NJ: Transactions.

(2002a). *Assessing responses to problems: An introductory guide for police problem-solvers.* Washington, DC: Office of Community Oriented Policing Services, US Department of Justice.

(2002b). Preventing crime at places. In L. W. Sherman, D. Farrington, B. Welsh, and D. L. MacKenzie (eds.), *Evidence-based crime prevention* (pp. 241–294). New York: Routledge.

(2003). Police problems: The complexity of problem theory, research and evaluation. In J. Knutsson (ed.), *Problem-oriented policing: From innovation to mainstream,* 15 (pp. 67–102). Monsey, NY: Criminal Justice Press.

Eck, J. E. and Clarke, R. V. (2003). Classifying common police problems: A routine activity approach. In M. J. Smith and D. B. Cornish (eds.), *Theory for practice in situational crime prevention,* 16 (pp. 7–40). Monsey, NY: Criminal Justice Press.

Eck, J. E. and LaVigne, N. (1993). *A police guide to surveying citizens and their environment.* Washington: DC: Bureau of Justice Assistance.

Eck, J. E. and Rosenbaum, D. (1994). The new police order: Effectiveness, equity and efficiency in community policing. In D. Rosenbaum (ed.), *The challenges of community policing: Testing the promises* (pp. 3–26). Thousand Oaks, CA: Sage Publications.

Eck, J. E. and Spelman, W. (1987). *Problem-solving: Problem-oriented policing in Newport News.* Washington, DC: Police Executive Research Forum.

Eck, J. E. and Wartell, J. (1998). Improving the management of rental properties with drug problems: A randomized experiment. In L. G. Mazerolle and J. Roehl (eds.), *Civil Remedies and Crime Prevention*, 9 (pp. 161–83). Monsey, NY: Criminal Justice Press.

Eck, J. E., Chainey, S., and Cameron, J. (2005). *Mapping crime: Understanding hot spots*. Washington, DC: US Department of Justice, National Institute of Justice.

Farrell, G. (1995). Preventing repeat victimization. In M. Tonry and D. P. Farrington (eds.), *Building a safer society: Strategic approaches to crime prevention*, 19 (pp. 469–534). Chicago, IL: University of Chicago Press.

Forrester, D., Chatterton, M., and Pease, K. (1988). *The Kirkhold burglary prevention project, Rochdale*. London: Home Office.

Goldstein, H. (1979). Improving policing: A problem-oriented approach. *Crime and Delinquency*, 25 (2), 236–258.

(1990). *Problem-oriented policing*. New York: McGraw-Hill.

Goldstein, H. and Susmilch, C. E. (1982a). The drinking-driver in Madison: A study of the problem and the community's response. Madison, WI: Law School, University of Wisconsin.

(1982b). Experimenting with the problem- oriented approach to improve police service: A report and some reflections on two case studies. Madison, WI: Law School, University of Wisconsin.

(1982c). The repeat sexual offender in Madison: A memorandum on the problem and the community's response. Madison, WI: Law School, University of Wisconsin.

Green, L. (1995). Policing places with drug problems: The multi-agency response team approach. In J. E. Eck and D. Weisburd (eds.), *Crime and place*, 4 (pp. 199–216). Monsey, NY: Criminal Justice Press.

Harcourt, B. E. (2001). *Illusion of order: The false promise of broken windows policing*. Cambridge, MA: Harvard University Press.

Harries, K. (1999). *Mapping crime: Principle and practice*. Washington, DC: National Institute of Justice, Crime Mapping Research Center.

Helmick, D. O. (2002). *Safety and farm labor vehicle education program*. Sacramento, CA: California Highway Patrol.

Hester, J. and Rice, K. (2001). Operation crystal clear: In an effort to reduce glass related street violence, the message remains 'crystal clear'. Liverpool, UK: Merseyside Police.

Hoare, M. A., Stewart, G., and Purcell, C. M. (1984). The problem oriented approach: Four pilot studies. London: Metropolitan Police, Management Services Department.

Hofstadter, D. R. (1979). *Gödel, Escher, Bach: An eternal golden braid*. New York: Vintage.

Homel, R., Hauritz, M., Wortley, R., McIlwain, G., and Carvolth, R. (1997). Preventing alcohol-related crime through community action: The surfers paradise safety action project. In R. Homel (ed.), *Policing for prevention: Reducing crime, public intoxication and injury*, 7 (pp. 35–90). Monsey, NY: Criminal Justice Press.

Hope, T. (1994). Problem-oriented policing and drug market locations: Three case studies. In R. V. Clarke (ed.), *Crime prevention studies*, 2 (pp. 5–31). Monsey, NY: Criminal Justice Press.

Kelling, G. L. and Sousa, W. H., Jr. (2001). Do police matter? An analysis of the impact of New York City's police reforms. *Civic Report*. New York: Manhattan Institute for Policy Research.

Kennedy, D. M., Braga, A. A., and Piehl, A. M. (1997). The (un)known universe: Mapping gangs and gang violence in Boston. In D. Weisburd and T. McEwen (eds.), *Crime mapping*, 8 (pp. 219–262). Monsey NY: Criminal Justice Press.

(2001). Developing and implementing operation ceasefire. In National Institute of Justice (ed.), *Reducing gun violence: The Boston gun project's operation ceasefire*. Washington, DC: National Institute of Justice.

Kenney, D. and Watson, T. S. (1996). Reducing fear in the schools: Managing conflict through student problem solving. *Education and Urban Society*, 28 (4), 436–455.

Matthews, R. (1993). *Kerb-crawling, prostitution and multi-agency policing*. London: Home Office.

(1997). Developing more effective strategies for curbing prostitution. In R. V. Clarke (ed.), *Situational crime prevention: Successful case studies*, 2nd ed. (pp. 74–82). Guilderland, NY: Harrow and Heston.

Mazerolle, L.G., Roehl, J., and Kadleck, C. (1998). Controlling social disorder using civil remedies: Results from a randomized field experiment in Oakland, California. In L. Mazerolle and J. Roehl (eds.), *Civil remedies and crime prevention*, 9 (pp. 141–160). Monsey, NY: Criminal Justice Press.

McGarrell, E. F., Chermak, S., Weiss, A., and Wilson, J. (2001). Reducing firearms violence through directed police patrol. *Criminology and Public Policy*, 1 (1), 119–148.

Office of Community Oriented Policing Services. (1998). *Problem-solving tips: A guide to reducing crime and disorder through problem-solving partnerships*. Washington, DC: US Department of Justice, Office of Community Oriented Policing Services.

Professional Security. (2004, January). Manual of crime science: New breed aims to outwit the criminals. *Professional Security*, 64.

Read, T. and Tilley, N. (2000). *Not rocket science? Problem-solving and crime reduction*. London: Home Office.

Scott, M. S. (2000). *Problem-oriented policing: Reflections on the first 20 years*. Washington, DC: US Department of Justice, Office of Community Oriented Policing Services.

(2002). *Rave parties*. Washington, DC: Office of Community Oriented Policing Services.

Sherman, L. W. and Rogan, D. P. (1995a). Deterrent effects of police raids on crack houses: A randomized, controlled, experiment. *Justice Quarterly*, 12 (4), 755–781.

(1995b). Effects of gun seizures on gun violence: 'Hot spots' patrol in Kansas City. *Justice Quarterly*, 12 (4), 673–693.

Sherman, L. W. and Weisburd, D. (1995). General deterrent effects of police patrol in crime "hot spots": A randomized, controlled trial. *Justice Quarterly*, *12* (4), 625–648.

Solè, R. and Goodwin, B. (2000). *Signs of life: How complexity pervades biology.* New York: Basic Books.

Weisburd, D. and Eck, J. E. (2004). What can police do to reduce crime, disorder and fear? *Annals of the American Academy of Political and Social Science, 593*, 42–65.

Weisburd, D. and Green, L. (1995). Policing drug hot spots: The Jersey City drug market analysis experiment. *Justice Quarterly, 12* (4), 711–735.

Weisburd, D., Mastrofski, S., McNally, A. M., Greenspan, R., and Willis, J. J. (2003). Reforming to preserve: Compstat and strategic problem solving in American policing. *Criminology and Public Policy, 2* (3), 421–456.

Weisel, D. (1999). *Conducting community surveys: A practical guide for law enforcement agencies.* Washington, DC: Bureau of Justice Statistics and Office of Community Oriented Policing.

(2002). *Burglary of single-family homes.* Washington, DC: Office of Community Oriented Policing Services.

7 *Critic*
Problem-oriented policing: the disconnect between principles and practice

Anthony A. Braga and David Weisburd

Problem-oriented policing works to identify *why* things are going wrong and to frame responses using a wide variety of innovative approaches (Goldstein 1979). Using a basic iterative approach of problem identification, analysis, response, assessment, and adjustment of the response, this adaptable and dynamic analytic approach provides an appropriate framework to uncover the complex mechanisms at play in crime problems and to develop tailor-made interventions to address the underlying conditions that cause crime problems (Eck and Spelman 1987; Goldstein 1990). Researchers have found problem-oriented policing to be effective in controlling a wide range of specific crime and disorder problems, such as convenience store robberies (Hunter and Jeffrey 1992), prostitution (Matthews 1990), and alcohol-related violence in pubs and clubs (Homel, Hauritz, Wortley *et al.* 1997). Indeed, there is very promising evidence of the effectiveness of the approach (Braga 2002; Committee to Review Research 2004; Weisburd and Eck 2004).

But is the "problem-oriented policing" that researchers have evaluated similar to the model of problem-oriented policing that its originators proposed? There is substantial evidence that, too often, the principles envisioned by Herman Goldstein are not being practiced in the field. Deficiencies in current problem-oriented policing practices exist in all phases of the process. A number of scholars have identified challenging issues in the substance and implementation of many problem-oriented policing projects, including: the tendency for officers to conduct only a superficial analysis of problems and then rush to implement a response, the tendency for officers to rely on traditional or faddish responses rather than conducting a wider search for creative responses, and the tendency to completely ignore the assessment of the effectiveness of implemented responses (Cordner 1998; but also see Clarke 1998; Read and Tilley; Scott and Clarke 2000). Indeed, the research literature is filled with a long history of cases where problem-oriented policing programs tend to lean toward traditional methods and where the problem-solving process is weak (Goldstein and Susmilch 1982; Eck and Spelman 1987;

Buerger 1994; Capowich, Roehl, and Andrews 1995; Read and Tilley 2000). In his recent review of several hundred submissions for the Police Executive Research Forum's Herman Goldstein Award for Excellence in Problem-Oriented Policing, Clarke (1998) laments that many recent examples of problem-oriented policing projects bear little resemblance to Goldstein's original definition. Eck (2000) comments that the problem-oriented policing that is practiced today is but a shadow of the original concept.

In this chapter we examine the nature of problem solving and problem-oriented policing as it is practiced in the field. Our main conclusion is that there is a disconnect between the rhetoric and reality of problem-oriented policing, and that this is not likely to change irrespective of the efforts of scholars and policymakers. Indeed, we take a very different approach to this problem than others who have examined the deficiencies of problem-oriented approaches. We argue that there is much evidence that what might be called "shallow" problem-solving responses can be effective in combating crime problems. This being the case, we question whether the pursuit of problem-oriented policing, as it has been modeled by Goldstein and others, should be abandoned in favor of the achievement of a more realistic type of problem solving. While less satisfying for scholars, it is what the police have tended to do, and it has been found to lead to real crime prevention benefits.

Defining the problem

To understand our argument it is useful to review the problems that police encounter at each stage of the well-known SARA model (Scanning, Analysis, Response, Assessment) that was developed in Newport News, Virginia, to crystallize the problem-oriented process (Eck and Spelman 1987). In practice, many problem-oriented policing projects do not follow the linear and separate steps of the SARA model. The steps tend to occur simultaneously or in a fashion in which officers move back and forth between scanning, analysis, and responses (Capowich and Roehl 1994; Braga 1997). Nevertheless, the model provides a useful way to structure our discussion of the disconnect between principles and practice in the problem-oriented policing process.

Scanning

Scanning involves the identification of problems that are worth looking at because they are important and amenable to solution. Herman Goldstein (1990) suggests that the definition of problems be at the street level of analysis and not be restricted by preconceived typologies. Goldstein further clarifies what is meant by a problem by specifying the term as: "a cluster of similar, related, or recurring incidents rather than a single incident; a substantive community concern; or a unit of police business" (1990: 66). To ensure that problems are specified correctly, it is important to break down larger categories of crime into more specific kinds of offenses (Clarke 1997). For example, auto theft should be further specified into particular types of auto theft such as "joy riding" or "stripping for auto parts." Close analysis of these specific problems may lead to very different types of intervention that might be more appropriate for each component of an auto theft problem when compared to a more general approach.

There are many ways a problem might be nominated for police attention. A police officer may rely upon his or her informal knowledge of a community to identify a problem that he or she thinks is important to the well-being of the community. Another approach to identifying problems is through consultation with community groups of different kinds, including other government agencies. Another possibility is to identify problems from the examination of citizen calls for service coming into a police department. This approach is implicitly recommended by those who advocate "repeat call analysis" or the identification of "hot spots" (Sherman, Gartin, and Buerger 1989; Weisburd and Mazerolle 2000). The notion is that citizens will let the police know what problems concern them by making calls as individuals. Crime mapping has become a very popular way for police departments to identify existing crime problems (Weisburd and McEwen 1997). A recent Police Foundation report found that seven in ten departments with more than 100 sworn officers reported using crime mapping to identify crime hot spots (Weisburd, Mastrofski, and Greenspan 2001).

Relative to their performance in other phases of the process, police officers are generally good at identifying problems (Bynum 2001). However, Clarke (1998) suggests that problem-oriented police officers often fail to make appropriate specifications of the problems they are addressing in one of two ways: they undertake a project that is either too small or too big. Small, beat level projects, such as dealing with a confused lonely old man who is seeking some daily companionship by repeatedly calling the police for a variety of concerns, may be better handled as a citywide project addressing older citizens who live alone and who generate a large number of calls for trivial matters (Clarke 1998). Some overly ambitious initiatives, such as dealing with "gang delinquency" or focusing on a "problem neighborhood," do not represent a single problem, but a collection of problems. For example, in the "problem neighborhood," there could be a diverse set of problems such as drug markets, auto theft, and domestic violence. These are separate problems that require individual attention. Problems in problem-oriented policing programs are sometimes broadly identified; this destroys the discrete problem focus of the project and leads to a lack of direction at the beginning of analysis (Clarke 1998).

Analysis

The analysis phase challenges police officers to analyze the causes of problems behind a string of crime incidents or substantive community concern. Once the underlying conditions that give rise to crime problems are known, police officers develop and implement appropriate responses. The challenge to police officers is to go beyond the analysis that naturally occurs to them; namely, to find the places and times where particular offenses are likely to occur, and to identify the offenders who are likely to be responsible for the crimes. Although these approaches have had some operational success, this type of analysis usually produces directed patrol operations or a focus on repeat offenders. The idea of analysis was intended to go beyond this. Unfortunately, as Boba (2003) observes, while problem-oriented policing has blossomed in both concept and practice, problem analysis has been the slowest part of the process to develop. In his twenty-year review of problem-oriented policing, Michael Scott (2000) concludes that problem analysis remains the aspect of problem-oriented policing that is most in need of improvement. The Police Executive Research Forum's national assessment of the US Community Oriented Policing Services (COPS)-sponsored Problem Solving Partnerships program also found that problem analysis was the weakest phase of the problem-oriented policing process (Police Executive Research Forum 2000).

Bynum (2001) suggests that police have difficulty clearly defining problems, properly using data sources, conducting comprehensive analyses, and implementing analysis-driven responses. Some officers skip the analysis phase or conduct an overly simple analysis that does not adequately dissect the problem or does not use relevant information from other agencies (such as hospitals, schools, and private businesses) (Clarke 1998). Based on his extensive experience with police departments implementing problem-oriented policing, Eck (2000) suggests that much problem analysis consists of a simple examination of police data coupled with the officer's working experience with the problem. In their analysis of problem-oriented initiatives in forty-three police departments in England and Wales, Read, and Tilley (2000) found that problem analysis was generally weak with many initiatives accepting the definition of a problem at face value, using only short-term data to unravel the nature of the problem, and failing to adequately examine the genesis of the crime problems.

Analyzing problems at crime hot spots may present a particularly vexing challenge to problem-oriented police officers. Given the contemporary popularity of crime mapping in the identification of problems worthy of police attention, we feel that it is important to highlight the difficulties in analyzing problems at hot spots. High-activity crime places tend to have multiple problems and the problems at crime places can be quite complex and involved. In their close analysis of hot spots in Minneapolis, Weisburd and his colleagues (1992) suggest that a heterogeneous mix of crime types occur at high-activity crime places rather than a concentration of one type of crime occurring at a place. In their examination of problem-oriented policing in San Diego, Capowich and Roehl (1994) observed that multiple problems tend to coincide at places and report, "at the beat level, there are no pure cases in which the problem can be captured under a single classification. The range of problems is wide, with each presenting unique circumstances" (144). In Oakland's Beat Health program to deal with drug nuisance locations, officers encountered difficulties unraveling what was happening at a place and deciding how it should be addressed (Green 1996).

In the Jersey City (NJ) problem-oriented policing in violent crime hot spots experiment, the number of identified problems per place ranged from three to seven, with a mean of 4.7 problems per place (Braga 1997; Braga, Weisburd, Waring et al. 1999). Table 7.1 presents the problems identified by officers for further analysis and the key characteristics of violent crime hot spots in the Jersey City problem-oriented policing experiment. From their training and the reading materials made available to them, the problem-oriented officers expected that they would be preventing violence at each place by focusing on very specific underlying characteristics or situational factors. After examining places closely, the officers observed that they would be controlling a multitude of crime problems. All twelve places were perceived to suffer from social disorder problems such as loitering, public drinking, and panhandling; eleven places suffered from physical disorder such as trash-filled streets, vacant lots, and abandoned buildings. Seven places had problems with illicit drug selling and three places had problems with property crimes.

Across and within places in the Jersey City problem-oriented policing experiment, few problems were analyzed thoroughly (Braga 1997). Eck and Spelman (1987) suggest two classifications for the depth of problem analysis: limited analysis and extended analysis. Eck and Spelman (1987) grouped problem-solving efforts by the Newport News (VA) Police

Table 7.1 *Problems and characteristics of 12 violent crime places*

Place	Problems	Relevant Characteristics
1	Assault and robbery of commuters Shoplifting Pick-pocketing Drug selling Homeless loitering and panhandling Disorderly groups of youths Physical disorder	Train and bus terminal Restaurants and retail stores Abandoned buildings Abandoned automobiles Holes in fences around terminal Poor lighting Piles of lumber used by loiterers Piles of trash deposited by dumpers
2	Street fights Drug market Public drinking and drug use Disorderly groups of youths Physical disorder	Major thoroughfare Bodega Tavern Abandoned buildings Vacant lot
3	Assault and robbery of college students Burglary and larceny on campus Loitering Minor drug selling Physical disorder	College campus Multiple bus stops Trash-strewn vacant lot w/tall weeds Low-income apartment building Trash-strewn alley Poor lighting
4	Assault and robbery of students Car-jacking Homeless loiterers Disorderly groups of youths	Grammar/middle school Community college Retail stores Major intersection
5	Robbery of retail stores Street fights Disorderly groups of youths Public drinking Physical disorder	Retail stores Restaurants Major thoroughfare Trash-strewn streets
6	Drug market Loitering Public drinking Physical disorder	Liquor store Major thoroughfare Poor lighting
7	Robbery of elderly Disorderly groups of youths Physical disorder	Senior citizen housing complex Low-income housing project Interstitial area between middle-class and lower-class neighborhoods Poor lighting Bus stop
8	Drug market Street fights Bar fights Disorderly groups loitering Public drinking Physical disorder	Large low-income apartment building Tavern Retail stores

Table 7.1 (*cont.*)

Place	Problems	Relevant Characteristics
9	Active indoor and outdoor drug market Street fights Loitering Public drinking Physical disorder	Abandoned buildings Low-income apartment building Major thoroughfare Vacant lots
10	Robbery of convenience stores Disorderly groups of youths Loitering Burglaries Physical disorder	Retail stores Major thoroughfare Trash-strewn streets
11	Street fights Drug market Public drinking Loitering Physical disorder	Abandoned buildings Residential neighborhood Poor lighting Vacant lots Graffiti Trash-strewn street
12	Drug market Bar fights Street fights Public drinking Loitering Disorderly groups of youths Physical disorder	Park Taverns Poor lighting Retail stores and restaurants Trash-strewn streets

Department by determining whether there were obvious information sources that were not used, given the nature of the problem; if there were not any obvious unused sources, the effort was classified as extended. Using these definitions, slightly less than one third (31.1 percent; 19 of 61) of the identified problems in the Jersey City study received what could be described as an extended analysis. It must be noted that, for certain problems, a superficial analysis was all that was necessary (e.g., alleviating a trash problem by recognizing that there were no trash receptacles at the place). Weak problem analyses occurred for two reasons. First, at ten of the twelve places, the officers believed that they "knew what was going on" based on their working knowledge and "on the spot" appraisals of problems. Second, the officers believed that most of the street crime at the place could be linked directly or indirectly to the physical and social disorder of a place. From their problem-oriented policing training, the officers were familiar with the broken windows thesis and much preferred the simplicity of a general plan to restore order and reduce crime at places over the specifics of the SARA model to control the multiple and interrelated problems of a place. Rather than conducting rigorous analysis of crime problems and developing tailor-made solutions, the officers generally attempted to control their places via aggressive order maintenance and making physical improvements such as securing vacant lots or removing trash from the street.

Responses

After a problem has been clearly defined and analyzed, police officers confront the challenge of developing a plausibly effective response. The development of appropriate responses is closely linked with the analysis that is performed. The analysis reveals the potential targets for an intervention, and it is at least partly the idea about what form the intervention might take that suggests important lines of analysis. As such, the reason police often look at places and times where crimes are committed is that they are already imagining that an effective way to prevent the crimes would be to get officers on the scene through directed patrols. The reason they often look for the likely offender is that they think that the most effective and just response to a crime problem would be to arrest and incapacitate the offender. However, the concept of "problem-oriented policing" as envisioned by Herman Goldstein (1990), calls on the police to make a much more "uninhibited" search for possible responses and not to limit themselves to getting officers in the right places at the right times, or identifying and arresting the offender (although both may be valuable responses). Effective responses often depend on getting other people to take actions that reduce the opportunities for criminal offending, or to mobilize informal social control to drive offenders away from certain locations.

The available research evidence suggests that the responses of many problem-oriented policing projects rely heavily upon traditional police tactics (such as arrests, surveillance, and crackdowns) and neglect the wider range of available alternative responses (Clarke 1998). Many evaluations of problem-oriented policing efforts have documented a preponderance of traditional policing tactics (see e.g., Capowich and Roehl 1994; Cordner 1994). Read and Tilley (2000) found that officers selected certain responses prior to, or in spite of, analysis; failed to think through the need for sustained crime reduction; failed to think through the mechanisms by which the response could have a measurable impact; failed to fully involve partners; narrowly focused responses, usually on offenders; as well as a number of other weaknesses in the response development process. Cordner (1998) observed that some problem-oriented policing projects gravitate toward faddish responses rather than implementing a response that truly fits the nature of the problem.

As suggested above, the complexity of problems at crime hot spots may discourage police officers from developing innovative responses. For example, frustrated narcotics officers may choose to chase drug dealers at a place rather than implementing a plan to change the multiple underlying characteristics of a place that make it an attractive spot for illicit drug sales (Green 1996; Eck and Wartell 1998; Taylor 1998). In the Jersey City problem-oriented policing experiment, the numerous responses implemented at the violent crime hot spots mirrored the complexity of the problems they were intended to control (Braga 1997). Twenty-eight types of responses were implemented across the places (Table 7.2). The number of responses per place ranged from one to twelve, with a mean of 6.7 responses per place. Traditional policing tactics were used at all places and comprised between 14 percent (Place 7) and 100 percent (Place 4 and Place 10) of the responses per place. On average, almost a third (31.1 percent) of the responses implemented per place involved traditional enforcement. Situational interventions intended to modify the characteristics of a place were implemented at ten of twelve treatment places. The situational strategies varied according to the nuances of the problems at places (e.g., razing an abandoned building or the code inspection of a tavern). However, at all locations, a package of aggressive order maintenance interventions was used to control the social disorder of the places. These tactics included repeat foot and radio car patrols, dispersing groups of loiterers, issuing summons for public drinking, "stop and frisks" of suspicious persons, and so on. At nine places, drug enforcement was used to disrupt drug sales at the place. The officers believed that an increased presence and the harassment of illicit users of the place would quell egregious social disorder, at least temporarily, until a better plan could be developed and implemented. According to the officers, aggressive order maintenance was a treatment that could affect all illicit activity no matter what the variation: drug selling, loitering by disorderly youth, homeless panhandlers, predatory robbers – all could be affected by an increased presence in a bounded geographical area. The Jersey City officers much preferred this strategy to the additional work necessary to implement alternative situational responses (Braga 1997).

Assessment

The crucial last step in the practice of problem-oriented policing is to assess the impact the intervention has had on the problem it was

Table 7.2 *Responses to problems at violent crime places*

Place	Responses
1	Aggressive order maintenance to disperse loitering homeless and disorderly youths
	Drug enforcement to disrupt street-level drug sales around train and bus terminals
	Robbery investigation to apprehend robbery crew
	Public works removed trash at place to discourage illegal dumping
	Hung "No dumping – Police take notice" sign to discourage illegal dumping
	Fixed holes in fence to secure access to the bus and train terminal
	Boarded and fenced abandoned buildings to prevent drug activity and squatting
	Helped homeless find shelter and substance abuse treatment
	Dispensed crime prevention literature to commuters
	Removed piles of lumber to discourage loitering
2	Aggressive order maintenance to disperse groups of disorderly youths
	Drug enforcement to disrupt street-level drug sales on street corner and from bodega
	Required store owners to clean trash from store fronts
	Erected fences to secure vacant lot from illicit drug activity
	Cleaned vacant lot
	Boarded and fenced abandoned buildings to prevent drug activity
	Removed drug selling crew's stashed guns
	Housing code enforcement to repair dilapidated building
	Eviction of drug seller from low-income apartment at place
	Surveillance of drug offenders using videotapes
3	Aggressive order maintenance to disperse loiterers from vacant lot and apartment building area
	Drug enforcement to disrupt street-level drug sales from vacant lot, alley, and apartment building
	Robbery investigation to apprehend robbery crew
	Cut weeds and removed trash from vacant lot
	Erected fence around vacant lot to prevent drug sales and robberies
	Public works removed trash and drug paraphernalia from alley
	Public works trimmed trees to increase lighting around vacant lot, alley, and apartment building
	Dispensed crime prevention literature to students and campus security
	Improved apartment building security by adding new door locks; prevented access to drug dealers
4	Aggressive order maintenance to disperse vagrants and groups of disorderly youths
	Directed patrol before and after school hours
	Robbery investigation to apprehend robbery crew
5	Aggressive order maintenance to disperse groups of disorderly youths
	Required store owners to clean store fronts
	Changed style of trash cans to prevent loitering
6	Aggressive order maintenance to disperse loiterers
	Drug enforcement to disrupt street-level drug sales in front of liquor store
	Required store owners to clean store fronts
	Opened and cleaned vacant lot to allow neighborhood kids to play basketball
	Repaired street lights to increase lighting in area
	Housing code enforcement to clean apartment building used as stash house

Table 7.2 (*cont.*)

Place	Responses
7	Aggressive order maintenance to disperse loitering groups of disorderly youths
	Housing code enforcement to remove trash from within housing project
	Evicted squatters and drug sellers from unoccupied apartments in low-income housing project
	Public works removed trash from around low-income housing project
	Improved housing project security by adding new locks to doors; prevented access to drug dealers
	Improved lighting around housing project by installing floodlights and replacing streetlights
	Enforced parking ordinances around housing project to impound cars of drug sellers and buyers
8	Aggressive order maintenance to disperse loiterers
	Intensive drug enforcement to disrupt street-level sales and dismantle major drug organization
	Required store owners to clean store fronts
	Code investigation of taverns
9	Aggressive order maintenance to disperse loiterers
	Drug enforcement to disrupt street-level drug sales
	Housing code enforcement to clean up low-income property
	Evicted drug sellers from low-income apartment building
	Boarded and fenced abandoned buildings to prevent drug activity
	Razed abandoned buildings
	Cleaned vacant lots
	Public works removed trash from street
	Erected fences around vacant lots to secure from drug activity
	Surveillance of offenders at place using video tapes
	Hung sign "No drug selling – Area under video surveillance by police"
10	Aggressive order maintenance to disperse groups of disorderly youths
11	Aggressive order maintenance to disperse loiterers
	Drug enforcement to disrupt street-level drug sales
	Surveillance of offenders at place using video tapes
	Hung sign "No public drinking – Area under video surveillance by police"
	Public works trimmed trees to increase lighting in area
	Boarded and fenced abandoned buildings to prevent drug activity
	Cleaned vacant lot
	Erected fence around vacant lot to secure from drug activity
	Removed graffiti from building
	Mobilized residents to keep streets clean in front of their homes
	Public works removed trash from street
	Added trash receptacles to prevent litter
12	Aggressive order maintenance to disperse loiterers and groups of disorderly youth
	Drug enforcement to disrupt drug sales at park and in and around bars
	Code investigation of taverns; one bar shut down and other bar owners discontinue sales of "take-out" alcohol
	Required storeowners to clean storefronts

supposed to solve. Assessment is important for at least two different reasons. The first is to ensure that police remain *accountable* for their performance and for their use of resources. Citizens and their representatives want to know how the money and freedom they surrendered to the police are being used, and whether important results in the form of less crime, enhanced security, or increased citizen satisfaction with the police have been achieved. A second reason assessment is important is to allow the police to *learn* about what methods are effective in dealing with particular problems. Unless the police check to see whether their efforts produced a result, it will be hard for them to improve their practices. The degree of rigor applied to the assessment of problem-oriented initiatives will necessarily vary across the size and overall importance of the problems addressed (Clarke 1998). Serious, large and recurrent problems such as controlling gang violence or handling domestic disputes deserve highly rigorous examinations. Other problems that are less serious, or common, such as a lonely elderly person making repeat calls to the police for companionship, are obviously not worth such close examinations. Unfortunately, Scott and Clarke (2000) observe that assessment of responses is rare and, when undertaken, it is usually cursory and limited to anecdotal or impressionistic data.

Clarke's (1998) review of submissions for the Herman Goldstein award provides a good summary of the common limitations of assessments performed by police departments engaged in problem-oriented policing projects (319–320):

- Police report reductions in calls for service or arrests without relating the results to specific actions taken. In other words, the police frequently fail to examine whether variations in "dosage levels" of the response correlate with variations in relevant crime statistics.
- Police consider assessment only as an afterthought, rather than building it into the original outline of the project.
- Police fail to present any control data. For example, if some action has been taken in one location that appears to have produced a decrease in the number of calls for service, the police do not generally document what, if anything, happened in a similar nearby location where no action was taken.
- On the rare occasion when control data are presented, police fail to ensure that the control is adequate. For example, the control location may be so different from the original site that it is impossible to conclude anything from the comparison.
- Police fail to study displacement. Many agencies do not realize that their response may simply have pushed the problem elsewhere.

Is "shallow" problem solving enough?

Despite the gap between the desired application of the approach and its actual implementation, there is considerable evidence that problem-oriented policing is effective in preventing crime (see e.g., Braga 2002; Committee to Review Research 2004; Weisburd and Eck 2004). This suggests that problem-oriented policing interventions may not need to be implemented in the ways envisioned by Herman Goldstein in order to produce a crime prevention effect. Perhaps, simply focusing police resources on identifiable risks that come to the attention of problem-oriented policing projects, such as high-activity offenders, repeat victims, and crime hot spots, may be enough to produce crime control gains. This is a striking result considering the large body of research that shows the ineffectiveness of many police crime prevention efforts (see Visher and Weisburd 1998 for a review). Therefore, we think that it is critically important to refine and extend current definitions of police crime prevention efforts.

Given the long police tradition of responding to high-crime locations and the current popularity of hot spots policing, our concluding discussion focuses on police crime efforts at high-crime places. These concepts could also be applied to offender- and victim-focused responses. Figure 7.1 presents a continuum of strategies, ranging from traditional to innovative, that police can use to control crime at high-crime places. At one extreme, police departments use traditional, incident-driven strategies to control crime in the community. Although these activities coincidentally cluster in space and time, these *ad hoc* enforcement strategies are not specifically targeted at problem places and the limitations of this approach are, by now, well known. Based on Eck's (1993) examination of alternative futures for problem-oriented policing, problem-solving efforts can be divided into "enforcement" and "situational" problem-oriented policing programs. "Enforcement" problem-oriented policing interventions have moved the police response forward by focusing mostly traditional tactics at high-risk times and locations. Although these programs are "problem oriented" in a global way, their tactics do not employ the individualized treatments of crime problems advocated by Herman Goldstein (1990). These interventions have included optimizing patrol time in hot spots (Koper 1995; Sherman and Weisburd 1995), conducting aggressive *Terry* [1] searches for guns in areas that are known for high levels of firearms violence (Sherman, Shaw, and Rogan 1995), and implementing systematic crackdowns in street-level drug markets (Weisburd and Green 1995).

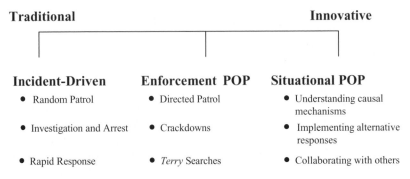

Figure 7.1 Continuum of police strategies to control high-crime places

These enforcement problem-oriented policing interventions focus mainly on the time and location of crime events, rather than focusing on the characteristics and dynamics of a place that make it a hot spot for criminal activity. Although these interventions have produced crime control gains and have added to law enforcement's array of crime prevention tools, it is commonly assumed that police could be more effective if they focused their efforts on the criminogenic attributes that cause a place to be "hot." In other words, adding an increased level of guardianship at a place by optimizing patrols is a step in controlling crime, but reducing criminal opportunities by changing site features, facilities, and the management at a place (e.g., adding streetlights, razing abandoned buildings, and mobilizing residents) may have a more profound effect on crime. At the innovative end of the continuum is Goldstein's (1990) vision of "situational" problem-oriented policing: members of police agencies undertake a thorough analysis of crime problems at places, collaborate with community members and other city agencies, and conduct a broad search for situational responses to problems.

Similar to other studies, translating problem-oriented policing theory into practice was difficult for Jersey City problem-oriented police officers. On the continuum of police strategies to control high-activity crime places, the program as implemented would fit between enforcement and situational problem-oriented interventions (see Figure 7.1). Despite falling short of Goldstein's vision, the Jersey City problem-oriented policing program was still found to be effective in preventing crime (Braga *et al.* 1999). Some scholars would describe the efforts of the Jersey City police officers as "problem solving" rather than problem-oriented policing (Cordner 1998). Problem solving is a "shallow" version of problem-oriented policing, as these efforts are smaller in scope, involve rudimentary analysis, and lack formal assessments. According to Cordner (1998),

problem solving better describes what an officer does to handle a particular dispute or drug house rather than initiatives to deal with problems of substantial magnitude like prostitution in a downtown area and
thefts from autos in parking lots. Enforcement problem-oriented initiatives would also fit what we would consider shallow problem solving.
When the complexities of crime problems at places and the difficulties
police officers experience in unraveling these problems and implementing
individualized responses are considered, shallow problem solving can be
a very practical way for police departments to prevent crimes at certain
places.

Should we expect police agencies to develop more in-depth problem solving?

Problem-oriented policing advocates lament the current state of the art
in problem solving and offer a laundry list of suggestions to improve the
capacity of police agencies to engage in strategic problem solving (see
e.g., Scott 2000; Braga 2002; Boba 2003). Is it realistic to expect police
agencies to develop their capacity to conduct more in-depth problem-
oriented policing so their officers can go beyond the shallow problem
solving that is currently practiced in the field? We believe that it is unlikely
that police agencies will enhance their problem-solving efforts in the
foreseeable future. There seem to be, at least, two obstacles. First, the
hierarchical organizational structure of policing in itself tends to inhibit
innovation and creativity. In their close examination of Compstat, Willis,
Mastrofski, and Weisburd (2004) found that, while the program holds out
the promise of allowing police agencies to adopt innovative technologies
and problem-solving techniques, it actually hindered innovative problem
solving while strengthening the existing hierarchy through the added pressure of increased internal accountability. Officers were reluctant to brainstorm problem-solving approaches during Compstat meetings for fear of
undermining authority or the credibility of their colleagues. Moreover,
the danger of "looking bad" in front of superior officers discouraged middle managers from pursuing more creative crime strategies with a higher
risk of failure.

Second, the organizational culture of policing is resistant to this in-
depth approach to problem solving. The community policing movement that emerged in the 1980s stressed greater police recognition
of the role of the community and emphasized "decentralization" and
"debureaucratization" to empower rank-and-file officers to make decisions about how better to serve the neighborhoods to which they were
assigned (Skolnick and Bayley 1986; Mastrofski 1998). Weisburd and

his colleagues (2003) suggest that the popularity and rapid diffusion of Compstat programs across larger police departments in the United States during the 1990s could be interpreted as an effort to maintain and reinforce traditional police structures rather than an attempt to truly reform American policing. The rapid rise of Compstat within police agencies did not enhance their strategic problem-solving capacity at the beat level as Compstat departments were found to be reluctant to relinquish power that would decentralize some key elements of decisionmaking such as allowing middle managers to determine beat boundaries and staffing levels, enhancing operational flexibility, and risking going beyond the standard tool kit of police tactics and strategies (Weisburd *et al.* 2003). The overall effect of the spread of Compstat, whether intended or not, was to reinforce the traditional bureaucratic model of command and control.

More generally, the type of in-depth problem solving that Goldstein and other problem-oriented policing advocates have proposed seems unrealistic in the real world of policing, especially at the street level where it is often envisioned. In the real world of police organizations, community and problem-oriented police officers rarely have the latitude necessary to assess and respond to problems creatively. As William Bratton (1998: 199) observed in his assessment of community policing in New York City at the beginning of his tenure, "street-level police officers were never going to be empowered to follow through." Compstat was offered as a solution to this problem, but the ability of the rank-and-file officer to make decisions changed little as middle managers were held accountable for achieving organizational goals of successful crime control (Willis *et al.* 2004). Of course, decentralizing decisionmaking power to line-level officers does not guarantee effective problem solving. In their assessment of problem solving in Chicago, a police department well known for its efforts to decentralize its organization to facilitate community policing, Skogan and his colleagues (1999: 231) gave a failing grade ranging from "struggling" to "woeful" for problem-solving efforts in 40 percent of the beats they studied. Inadequate management, poor leadership and vision, lack of training, and weak performance measures were among the operational problems identified as affecting problem solving in the poorly performing beats (Skogan *et al.* 1999).

Conclusion

Problem-oriented policing represents an important innovation in American policing. Unfortunately, the practice of problem-oriented policing too often falls short of the principles suggested by Herman Goldstein (1990). Given the extensive literature on the gap between principles and practice, it seems unrealistic to expect line-level officers to conduct in-depth problem-oriented policing as their routine way of dealing with crime problems. Successful applications of problem-oriented policing usually involve larger-scale problems, the involvement of academic researchers and crime analysis units, and the solid support of the police command staff to implement alternative responses. The Boston Police Department's Operation Ceasefire intervention to prevent gang violence (Braga *et al.* 2001), the Newport News Police Department's efforts to reduce thefts from cars parked in shipyard parking lots (Eck and Spelman 1987), and the Charlotte Mecklenburg Police Department's program to reduce theft from construction sites (Clarke and Goldstein 2002) involved resources that were far beyond the reach of the rank-and-file police officer.

Research evidence suggests that shallow problem-solving efforts, ranging from focused enforcement efforts in high-risk places and at high-risk times to problem solving with weak analyses, mostly traditional responses, and limited assessments, are enough to prevent crime. Perhaps it is time to stop trying to achieve the ideal of strategic problem-oriented policing at the street level and embrace the reality of what has been shown to lead to real crime prevention value – *ad hoc* shallow problem-solving efforts that focus police on high-risk places, situations, and individuals. We suggest that line-level officers should be encouraged to problem solve at the beat level and more sophisticated problem-oriented policing projects should be engaged higher up in the organization with the support of a crime analysis unit and in collaboration with other criminal justice agencies, academic researchers, and community-based groups. However, it is time for police practitioners and policymakers to set aside the fantasy of street-level problem-oriented policing and embrace the reality of what they can expect from the beat officer in the development of crime prevention plans at the street level.

NOTE

In Terry *v.* Ohio (1968), the Supreme Court upheld police officers' right to conduct brief threshold inquiries of suspicious persons when they have reason to believe that such persons may be armed and dangerous to the police and others. In practice, this threshold inquiry typically involves a safety frisk of the suspicious person.

REFERENCES

Boba, R. (2003). *Problem analysis in policing*. Washington, DC: Police Foundation.
Braga, A. A. (1997). Solving violent crime problems: An evaluation of the Jersey City Police Department's pilot program to control violent places. Doctoral

Dissertation, Rutgers University. Ann Arbor, MI: University Microfilm International.

(2002). *Problem-oriented policing and crime prevention.* Monsey, NY: Criminal Justice Press.

Braga, A. A., Kennedy, D., Waring, E., and Piehl, A. (2001). Problem-oriented policing, deterrence, and youth violence: An evaluation of Boston's Operation Ceasefire. *Journal of Research in Crime and Delinquency, 38,* 195–225.

Braga, A. A., Weisburd, D., Waring, E., Mazerolle, L. G., Spelman, W., and Gajewski, F. (1999). Problem-oriented policing in violent crime places: A randomized controlled experiment. *Criminology, 37,* 541–580.

Bratton, W. (1998). *Turnaround: How America's top cop reversed the crime epidemic.* New York: Random House.

Buerger, M. (1994). The problems of problem-solving: Resistance, interdependencies, and conflicting interests. *American Journal of Police, 13,* 1–36.

Bynum, T. (2001). *Using analysis for problem-solving: A guidebook for law enforcement.* Washington, DC: Office of Community Oriented Policing Services, US Department of Justice.

Capowich, G. and Roehl, J. (1994). Problem-oriented policing: Actions and effectiveness in San Diego. In D. Rosenbaum (ed.), *The challenge of community policing: Testing the promises.* Thousand Oaks, CA: Sage Publications.

Capowich, G., Roehl, J., and Andrews, C. (1995). *Evaluating problem-oriented policing outcomes in Tulsa and San Diego.* Final Report to the National Institute of Justice. Alexandria, VA: Institute for Social Analysis.

Clarke, R. (ed.) (1997). *Situational crime prevention: Successful case studies.* 2nd ed. Albany, NY: Harrow and Heston.

(1998). Defining police strategies: Problem solving, problem-oriented policing and community-oriented policing. In T. O'Connor Shelley and A. C. Grant (eds.), *Problem-oriented policing: Crime-specific problems, critical issues, and making POP work.* Washington, DC: Police Executive Research Forum.

Clarke, R. and Goldstein, H. (2002). Reducing theft at construction sites: Lessons from a problem-oriented project. In N. Tilley (ed.), *Analysis for crime prevention.* New York: Criminal Justice Press.

Committee to Review Research on Police Policy and Practices. (2004). *Fairness and effectiveness in policing: The evidence.* Washington, DC: National Academies Press.

Cordner, G. (1994). Foot patrol without community policing: Law and order in public housing. In D. Rosenbaum (ed.), *The challenge of community policing: Testing the promises.* Thousand Oaks, CA: Sage Publications.

(1998). Problem-oriented policing vs. zero tolerance. In T. O'Connor Shelley and A. C. Grant (eds.), *Problem-oriented policing: Crime-specific problems, critical issues, and making POP work.* Washington, DC: Police Executive Research Forum.

Eck, J. E. (1993). Alternative futures for policing. In D. Weisburd and C. Uchida (eds.), *Police innovation and control of the police: Problems of law, order, and community.* New York: Springer-Verlag.

(2000). Problem-oriented policing and its problems: The means over ends syndrome strikes back and the return of the problem-solver. Unpublished manuscript. Cincinnati, OH: University of Cincinnati.

Eck, J. E. and Spelman, W. (1987). *Problem-solving: Problem-oriented policing in Newport News.* Washington, DC: Police Executive Research Forum.

Eck, J. E. and Wartell, J. (1998). Improving the management of rental properties with drug problems: A randomized experiment. In L. G. Mazerolle and J. Roehl (eds.), *Civil Remedies and Crime Prevention,* 9 (pp. 161–183). Monsey, NY: Criminal Justice Press.

Goldstein, H. (1979). Improving policing: A problem-oriented approach. *Crime and Delinquency, 25,* 236–258.

(1990). *Problem-oriented policing.* Philadelphia, PA: Temple University Press.

Goldstein, H. and Susmilch, C. (1982). The drinking-driver in Madison: A study of the problem and the community's response. Madison, WI: University of Wisconsin Law School.

Green, L. (1996). *Policing places with drug problems.* Thousand Oaks, CA: Sage Publications.

Homel, R., Hauritz, M., Wortley, R., McIlwain, G., and Carvolth, R. (1997). Preventing alcohol-related crime through community action: The surfers paradise safety action project. In R. Homel (ed.), *Policing for prevention: Reducing crime, public intoxication, and injury.* New York: Criminal Justice Press.

Hunter, R. and Jeffrey, C. R. (1992). Preventing convenience store robbery through environmental design. In R. Clarke (ed.), *Situational crime prevention: Successful case studies.* Albany, NY: Harrow and Heston.

Koper, C. (1995). Just enough police presence: Reducing crime and disorderly behavior by optimizing patrol time in crime hot spots. *Justice Quarterly, 12,* 649–672.

Mastrofski, S. (1998). Community policing and police organization structure. In J. Brodeur (ed.), *How to recognize good policing: Problems and issues.* Thousand Oaks, CA: Sage Publications.

Matthews, R. (1990). Developing more effective strategies for curbing prostitution. *Security Journal, 1,* 182–187.

Police Executive Research Forum. (2000). *PSP National Evaluation Final Report.* Washington, DC: Police Executive Research Forum.

Read, T. and Tilley, N. (2000). *Not rocket science? Problem-solving and crime reduction.* Crime Reduction Series Paper 6. London: Policing and Crime Reduction Unit, Home Office.

Scott, M. (2000). *Problem-oriented policing: Reflections on the first 20 years.* Washington, DC: US Department of Justice, Office of Community Oriented Policing Services.

Scott, M. and Clarke, R.V. (2000). A review of submission for the Herman Goldstein Excellence in Problem-Oriented Policing. In C. Sole Brito and E. Gratto (eds.), *Problem-oriented policing: Crime-specific problems, critical issues, and making POP work,* 3. Washington, DC: Police Executive Research Forum.

Sherman, L. W., Gartin, P., and Buerger, M. (1989). Hot spots of predatory crime: Routine activities and the criminology of place. *Criminology, 27,* 27–56.

Sherman, L. W. and Weisburd, D. (1995). General deterrent effects of police patrol in crime hot spots: A randomized controlled trial. *Justice Quarterly, 12,* 625–648.

Sherman, L. W., Shaw, J., and Rogan, D. (1995). *The Kansas City gun experiment.* Washington, DC: National Institute of Justice, US Department of Justice.

Skogan, W., Hartnett, S., DuBois, J., Comey, J., Kaiser, M., and Lovig, J. (1999). *On the beat: Police and community problem solving.* Boulder, CO: Westview Press.

Skolnick, J. and Bayley, D. (1986). *The new blue line: Police innovations in six American cities.* New York: Free Press.

Taylor, R. (1998). *Crime and small-scale places: What we know, what we can prevent, and what else we need to know.* In Crime and Place: Plenary Papers of the 1997 Conference on Criminal Justice Research and Evaluation. Washington, DC: National Institute of Justice, US Department of Justice.

Visher, C. and Weisburd, D. (1998). Identifying what works: Recent trends in crime prevention strategies. *Crime, Law and Social Change, 28*, 223–242.

Weisburd, D. and Eck, J. E. (2004). What can police do to reduce crime, disorder, and fear? *Annals of the American Academy of Political and Social Science, 593*, 42–65.

Weisburd, D. and Green, L. (1995). Policing drug hot spots: The Jersey City DMA Experiment. *Justice Quarterly, 12*, 711–736.

Weisburd, D. and Mazerolle, L. (2000). Crime and disorder in drug hot spots: Implications for Theory and Practice in Policing. *Police Quarterly, 3* (3), 331–349.

Weisburd, D. and McEwen, J. T. (eds.). (1997). *Crime mapping and crime prevention.* Monsey, NY: Criminal Justice Press.

Weisburd, D., Maher, L., and Sherman, L. W. (1992). Contrasting crime general and crime specific theory: The case of hot spots of crime. *Advances in Criminological Theory, 4*, 45–69.

Weisburd, D., Mastrofski, S. D., and Greenspan, R. (2001). *Compstat and Organizational Change.* Washington, DC: Police Foundation.

Weisburd, D., Mastrofski, S. D., McNally, A. M., Greenspan, R., and Willis, J. (2003). Reforming to preserve: Compstat and strategic problem solving in American policing. *Criminology and Public Policy, 2* (3), 421–456.

Willis, J., Mastrofski, S. D., and Weisburd, D. (2004). Compstat and bureaucracy: A case study of challenges and opportunities for change. *Justice Quarterly, 21* (3), 463–496.

Part IV

Pulling levers policing

8   *Advocate*
    Old wine in new bottles: policing and the
    lessons of pulling levers

David M. Kennedy

Introduction

Pity the poor soul who, ten years ago, would have predicted that hard-core street cops would be making a practice of sitting down with serious violent offenders and telling them politely to cease and desist. Yet, increasingly, that is what cops are doing: and, more to the point, doing successfully. The "pulling levers" strategies piloted in Boston in the mid-1990s and implemented since then in a range of other jurisdictions are racking up impressive results in preventing violent crimes. From one vantage, these strategies are innovative, sometimes bordering on the bizarre, as in the face-to-face meetings between authorities and offenders that many rely upon. From another, they are really very traditional, relying on old and simple ideas about offenders and their motivations, and about authorities and their powers, and how the latter can influence the former. Old and new meet in the design of the strategies, where ivory-tower research methods rely on the street savvy of front-line cops; in images of offenders, where very traditional and concrete ideas about serious crime meet new and abstract notions; in the partnerships that carry out the work, where traditional actors do some very traditional things in significantly new ways; and in the underlying logic of the strategies, which seeks to do something entirely old-fashioned – deter crime – in a strikingly original way.

Pulling levers strategies are one fruit of the problem-oriented policing movement. The approach first emerged as part of the Boston Gun Project, a problem-oriented policing project aimed at "gang" violence in Boston, and has since spread to other jurisdictions and settings (Kennedy 1997; 1998; Kennedy and Braga 1998; Braga, Kennedy, Waring, and Piehl 2001; Braga, Kennedy, and Tita 2002; Kennedy 2002a; Dalton 2003; McGarrell and Chermak 2003; Tita, Riley, Ridgeway *et al.* 2003; Wakeling 2003). It was, in that sense, straight from the problem-oriented copybook: it focused on a relatively narrow problem, utilized a wide variety of information sources and analytic techniques, relied heavily on the experience and insight of front-line law enforcement and community actors, and sought a strategic intervention that would have a substantial impact. It is also one of a growing number of policing interventions that combines a set of relatively traditional tactics with a new strategic focus, and adds to that mix new operational tools, resulting in a strategy that looks both very traditional and quite new and different (Weisburd and Eck 2004).

The best news about these strategies is that they seem to have worked in a number of jurisdictions against serious crime problems that have traditionally been regarded as intractable, and even in principle impossible for criminal justice actors to address. But beyond that, they suggest a bridge between traditional and powerful – but often, in practice, unhappily limited – ideas and actions, and variations on those ideas and actions that can lead to potent, practical applications. This chapter looks at the experience to date with pulling levers strategies. It is not a review of the operational idea, its intellectual roots, particular interventions, or the formal evaluation of impacts; those things have been done elsewhere. Rather, it treats another set of concerns: what these strategies seem to have meant to police departments and other criminal justice agencies, and why, and what that experience suggests about next steps.

What it is

Pulling levers or focused deterrence strategies deploy enforcement, services, the moral voice of communities, and deliberate communication in order to create a powerful deterrent to particular behavior by particular offenders. First deployed in Boston in the mid-1990s to prevent youth violence, pulling levers operations have tended to follow a basic framework that includes:

- Selection of a particular crime problem, such as youth homicide or street drug dealing.
- Pulling together an interagency enforcement group, typically including police, probation, parole, state and federal prosecutors, and sometimes federal enforcement agencies.
- Conducting research, usually relying heavily on the field experience of front-line police officers, to identify key offenders – and frequently *groups* of offenders, such as street gangs, drug crews, and the like – and the context of their behavior.
- Framing a special enforcement operation directed at those offenders and groups of offenders, and designed to substantially influence that context, for example by using any and all legal tools (or levers) to

sanction groups such as crack crews whose members commit serious violence.

- Matching those enforcement operations with parallel efforts to direct services and the moral voices of affected communities to those same offenders and groups.
- Communicating directly and repeatedly with offenders and groups to let them know that they are under particular scrutiny, what acts (such as shootings) will get special attention, when that has in fact happened to particular offenders and groups, and what they can do to avoid enforcement action. One form of this communication is the "forum," "notification," or "call-in," in which offenders are invited or directed (usually because they are on probation or parole) to attend face-to-face meetings with law enforcement officials, service providers, and community figures.

In Boston, for example, probation officers pulled members of street drug groups into meetings with authorities, service providers, and community figures where they were told that violence had led to comprehensive enforcement actions – such as federal drug investigations – against several violent groups, that violence by their groups would provoke the same enforcement actions, that services were available to those who wished them, that the affected communities desperately wanted the violence to stop, and that groups that did not act violently would not get such unusual, high-level enforcement attention. Similar efforts in other jurisdictions followed. Pulling levers has been a central theme in the Justice Department's Strategic Approaches to Community Safety Initiative and Project Safe Neighborhoods initiative, and the basic ideas are increasingly showing up in local operations (Dalton 2003). In general, "pulling levers" operations seem to be well received by the affected communities, apparently due at least in part to the usually wide array of community actors involved and to the clear notice and options provided to offenders (Winship and Berrien 1999).

Evidence of impact

There is good reason to believe that such efforts can work. These interventions do not lend themselves to the kind of high-level random assignment experimental designs that would give the strongest evaluations of their impact. Short of that, the available evaluations and a growing body of site experience suggest strong effects. The best statistical evaluations come from Boston and Indianapolis and show strikingly parallel results: citywide reductions in homicide of around 50 percent, with larger effects on gun homicides of younger minority males at which both interventions were primarily directed (Braga *et al.* 2001; McGarrell and Chermak 2003). In each case, the reductions were very sudden and sharp: what Professor Edmund McGarrell, now of Michigan State University, who helped organize the Indianapolis project, calls the "light switch" effect. The same pattern has been seen in Minneapolis (Kennedy and Braga 1998); Stockton, California (Wakeling 2003); High Point and Winston-Salem, North Carolina (Dalton 2003); Portland, Oregon (Dalton 2003); and Rochester, New York.[1] A weak, because only partially implemented, version even appears to have been somewhat effective in East Los Angeles (Tita *et al.* 2003). The range of cities now suggests that the basic model is effective against violence by more informal, neighborhood-based drug groups, as in Boston; by more structured, Chicago-style "gangs," as in Minneapolis and Indianapolis; and by West coast gangs, as in Stockton and Los Angeles. It has been effective in jurisdictions in which violence was more or less stable, as in Boston, and in which it was escalating, as in Minneapolis and Indianapolis. Not all of the news is good. Several jurisdictions have failed to sustain what were apparently successful interventions. Serious efforts in Baltimore and San Francisco did not reach the point of full implementation (about which more later). There does seem good reason to believe, however, that these strategies hold promise of real effectiveness. Taken separately, as is often – perhaps always – the case, there are plausible doubts about what might have happened in each site. Taken together, the experience to date suggests the strategy has both power and legs.

There is less experience with pulling levers interventions aimed at other crime problems. The author is involved in pulling levers drug market interventions in High Point and in Rochester, New York, both aimed at eliminating particularly troublesome public forms of drug dealing such as street markets and crack houses by warning dealers, buyers, and their families that focused enforcement is imminent (Kennedy 1998). There is as yet no experience with such interventions, but it is possible to revisit provocative and successful earlier drug market operations and view them in that light. The Houston Police Department's Link Valley operation, for example, used the deliberate announcement of a massive interagency sweep to dry up a large open-air powder cocaine market without making a single arrest (Kennedy 1990). The San Diego Police Department eliminated a substantial crack market by reaching out to both dealers and buyers and informing them of forthcoming special enforcement efforts (San Diego Police Department 1998). The author has framed pulling levers approaches to domestic violence (Kennedy 2002b). While there is no evidence that these strategies would be successful on a large scale, they do pass the law enforcement "laugh test": police, prosecutors, and other enforcement personnel tend to think that they're worth exploring. Pulling levers operations, then, are slowly being accepted in enforcement circles as useful additions both to the traditional operational repertoire and to newer frameworks such as "broken windows" policing.

What cops know

As innovative, odd, and apparently self-defeating as these strategies may be – just try telling a grizzled street cop that the way to stop violent crime is to tell hard-core offenders exactly what your enforcement plans are – their conditional appeal to practitioners makes a certain amount of sense. These are interventions that are based on what cops (and many others in law enforcement) know to be true. The whole of the strategy is certainly not familiar, and frequently meets with deep skepticism: the idea that offenders will pay any attention to a "stop it" message, for example – no matter how direct, credible, and backed up by action – often provokes stark disbelief. At the same time, though, much of what goes into these operations, and what sets them apart from other operations, is knowledge and outlook deeply ingrained in enforcement circles. Those sensibilities both shape the strategies and shape the law enforcement response to adopting them.

Police officers (and prosecutors, probation officers, and the like) know, for example, that for many crime problems, repeat offenders and repeat victims are at the center of the action. They know that much of that action is in particular neighborhoods, and particular places within those neighborhoods. They know that different kinds of groups, and various kinds of problems within and between those groups, drive a lot of what happens. They know that these groups and their members commit vast numbers of crimes, probation and parole violations, and other offenses, from failing to show up in court to not paying fines and child support to drinking and drugging to driving illegally. They know this not from reading criminology and social science – though all these threads are to be found there (Kennedy 2003) – but from their own experience. They know that if those groups and individual offenders were controlled, it would make a big difference. Experienced practitioners know that our usual attempts to shape offenders' behavior, whether through traditional enforcement or through services, counseling, social work, or such means, are hugely ineffective: most experienced law enforcement personnel hold out little or no hope that serious offenders will be influenced by anything short of a cop standing at arm's length. That frequently, perhaps usually, makes them despair of doing *anything* effective. But they want to, and their inclination is to do so through enforcement: police officers and their kin in other agencies believe in good guys and bad guys, and they believe in the exercise of authority, and they want to draw lines in the sand and enforce them. "Pulling levers" interventions speak to this orientation. It suits cops to say, Stop it! They need to be persuaded that it can work, but this mindset at least opens the door. It sets these interventions, and other largely authority-based interventions such as broken windows strategies, apart from other innovative problem-solving frameworks such as, for example, crime prevention through environmental design.

Operationally, the wealth of very particular street knowledge at the front lines of these agencies is an invaluable resource. Police officers, in particular – but also frequently probation and parole officers, line prosecutors, the sheriff's officers who manage jail populations, and others – frequently have extraordinary insight into who is doing what, and why, and very often what will happen next. What from even a small distance looks chaotic, senseless, and unpredictable is often known to these practitioners as comprehensible and in its own way coherent. They know who is in what street groups, and who is fighting with whom; what last year's antecedent to yesterday's shooting was; who is committing the drug robberies that are not even being reported to the police; who is selling drugs on the corners; what mid-level dealer is running the crack houses operated only by juveniles; what turf is claimed by which groups, and who is allowed there and who is not; which domestic violence offenders are currently most dangerous to what women. Police departments and other enforcement agencies generally make little or no use of this front-line knowledge, partly because it is often of no use in making cases – an unreported drug robbery, to take a particularly clear example, cannot be prosecuted – and partly because of the top-down management typical of police agencies. As a result, what is common knowledge at the street level can be utterly obscure just a few steps away. In Washington, DC, for example, even some career homicide prosecutors argued vehemently that that city's extraordinary homicide rate was the product of solo gunslingers bumping into each other on the streets; there was, they believed, no more sense to it than that, and no logic or context beyond chaotic social breakdown. That was what they saw in the formal fact patterns they reviewed and presented in prosecutions. Police officers were incredulous, and for good reason; a review of homicide incidents based on front-line knowledge showed clearly that homicide was rooted in very patterned behavior by a fairly small number of very active and well-known, mostly neighborhood-based drug crews (Travis, Kennedy, Roman *et al.* 2003). But until what they knew was deliberately gathered and recorded, it had no formal existence and could not shape policy or operations.

Qualitative research can draw this information out. These methods – incident reviews, gang and group mapping exercises, systems to gather front-line knowledge about "hidden" crimes like drug robberies and domestic violence – have become central both to unpacking particular crime problems and to implementing pulling levers interventions (Kennedy, Braga, and Piehl 1997; Kennedy and Braga 1998; Dalton 2003; McGarrell and Chermak 2003; Wakeling 2003). The information they produce is vital, and frequently astonishes both agency executives and outsiders. In San Francisco, for example, a surge in homicide that shocked the city and led to, among other things, a high-profile public forum by the mayor, was the product, by front-line consensus, of perhaps a hundred or fewer particularly dangerous, influential – and quite well-known – offenders. The process of gathering and utilizing such knowledge honors the front lines and greatly enhances the salience of subsequent operations.

Reclaiming deterrence: futility and displacement

Pulling levers strategies are deterrence strategies. Most criminal justice practitioners, most of the time, do not believe in deterrence. That the strategies work, and beyond that work with offenders and crime problems that have demonstrably been particularly resistant to ordinary enforcement, is helping reclaim the idea and the practice of deterrence.

The failure of deterrence is everywhere in law enforcement. Practitioners certainly believe that it is operating at some level – if police shut down operations, crime would certainly go up – but they do not much believe that it is operating at the margin. They do not believe that offenders, particularly serious offenders, much care about official consequences for their crimes or that those consequences can be increased such that offenders will care. The evidence for this is manifest. Many offenders are arrested and sanctioned repeatedly, and continue to offend. Many commit crimes such as drug dealing in full public view. Many routinely violate the terms and conditions of probation and parole. And many, by their actions and words, show their apparent disregard for extreme and predictable consequences of their behavior, such as being hurt or killed on the street. When offenders don't mind dying, authorities frequently say, what can we possibly do that they will care about?

This does not undercut the faith police and other authorities have in *enforcement*. But it severely limits the ways in which they think enforcement can be effective. It may work to swamp an area with officers; as long as that persists, offenders will keep their heads down. It will certainly work to take an offender off the streets; while he's inside, he won't commit any crimes outside. But authorities tend to have little or no faith in their ability to persuade offenders to change their behavior, or in fact to do anything at all; one of the predictable hurdles in implementing "pulling levers" operations is police officers' conviction that probationers will not even bother to show up when directed to appear at call-ins. They violate their probation all the time, and nothing ever happens, officers say; why should this be any different? (In fact, compliance at call-ins is routinely very high, and in practice seeing probationers appear often opens the first chink in line officers' skepticism about the larger strategy.)

Closely linked is an absolute, nearly theological belief in displacement – that anything short of incarceration will simply move offenders around. The research on this point is by now pretty persuasive; displacement is far less universal than has long been thought, is virtually never complete, and in fact enforcement efforts frequently produce a "diffusion of benefits," the opposite of displacement (Clarke and Weisburd 1994; Braga 2002). Police and other enforcement practitioners remain unmoved. This is not what they see, and they do not believe it. One of the most important results of the manifest impact of pulling levers strategies, then, is that the basic idea of deterrence – a big and important idea – is to some extent being rehabilitated. The facts are quite clear, in jurisdiction after jurisdiction, the worst of offenders – gang members, violent offenders, shooters – are substantially changing their behavior without being taken off the street. It is but a short step to the provocative thought that it is not that offenders cannot be deterred, but that what we normally do is simply not deterring them, and that quite possibly we can do better.

The salience of groups and networks

Most pulling levers interventions have focused on various kinds of groups and networks: gangs, drug crews, and the like. This is not necessarily an essential part of the framework. Individual domestic violence offenders, for example, could be identified as being particularly dangerous; sanctioned using any available legal means (domestic violence charges, charges on other sorts of legal exposure, special probation and parole regimes); and that special focus marketed to other domestic violence offenders in order to shape their behavior (Kennedy 2002b). But in practice, pulling levers strategies have so far focused primarily on homicide and serious violence in urban settings, and in practice those problems are overwhelmingly concentrated in groups and networks of chronic offenders (Kennedy 1997; 1998; Kennedy and Braga 1998; Braga *et al.* 2001; Braga *et al.* 2002; Kennedy 2002a; Dalton 2003; McGarrell and Chermak 2003; Tita *et al.* 2003; Wakeling 2003). Various sorts of groups of offenders representing a tiny fraction of the population have repeatedly been shown to be responsible for most homicides and large shares of other violent crime (Kennedy 2003). The operational strategies have simply followed that presentation of the problem. Once again, the salience of groups and networks is a commonplace in the literature, and also a commonplace on the front lines. It has not, however, been a commonplace in official accounts of these problems or, frequently, in operational responses to them. Elevating their recognition and the attention paid to them is an important development.

There are a number of reasons groups and networks have gotten far less attention than they should have in law enforcement practice. Police and other authorities recognize the existence of gangs, but outside of a few jurisdictions most of these groups and networks are not what are generally thought of as gangs (Kennedy 2002a). Legal avenues rarely allow a group or network to be held legally responsible for a criminal act; a loose-knit drug group cannot in practice be charged collectively for the shooting committed by one of its members. Homicide investigators and prosecutors responsible for uncovering and presenting the fact pattern will themselves frequently not know about the rest of the group or the larger context of the shooting. Those who know the most about the group and its behavior, such as conflicts with other groups, will frequently be narcotics and precinct officers and have no role in the investigation, or in the gathering and interpreting of departmental intelligence. What results is a kind of open secret in which the existence of offender groups and networks, and the significance of their behavior, is both very well known to some practitioners and neither recognized nor acted upon elsewhere. In New Haven, for example, authorities concerned about gun crime insisted that gangs were not an issue; the Latin Kings, who had previously been a presence, had been eliminated through federal prosecutions. Work with front-line police officers, however, brought to the surface what they already knew – that loose neighborhood-based groups of chronic offenders were responsible for most of the violence (Dalton 2003). Similar findings are invariable in other jurisdictions.

Some of the implications are immediate and practical. These groups can in fact be attended to as groups, even when something like a conspiracy case or a RICO prosecution cannot be brought; a hand-to-hand drug buy from each member can put the whole group out of action. The prospect of using the many such legal avenues is in fact the origin of the pulling levers label. Once recognized, these groups can also be communicated with: they can be told, for example, that a shooting by one of their number will result in action against all. Their relations with other groups can be identified and monitored, so that allies and enemies in a simmering group-on-group vendetta get special attention.

A particularly interesting possibility – less immediate, but perhaps no less practical – is recognizing that such groups and networks of groups produce and enforce their own codes, rules, and expectations. This, again, is classic sociology, criminology, and psychology, which have always placed great emphasis on norms (Kennedy 2003). Police and other authorities have rarely matched this recognition. A drive-by shooting will typically be viewed as an expression of the shooter's character and choice, or, more remotely, as the product of more global forces such as neighborhood, class, or racial and ethnic factors. Authorities rarely consider that something intermediate might be operating, such as the imposition by the shooter's crew of norms that demand violence in certain circumstances, and the real benefits and risks that go along with complying or failing to comply. Nor do they consider the possibility of deliberately countering or even changing those norms, such as by letting all group members know that violence by one will impose costs on all, or by mobilizing respected community voices to challenge them. In Lowell, Massachusetts, for example, police responded to shootings by young Asian gang members, against whom they had very little legal leverage, by cracking down on the gambling parlors operated by older gang members and telling them explicitly that the shooting had triggered the crackdowns. The police could not control the shooters, but the older members could and did (Braga, McDevitt, and Pierce 2005). Recognizing groups and group processes opens up an enormous range of analysis and action that operates in between, and may be more productive than, the usual very particular attention to individuals and very broad attention to social factors.

The strategic use of traditional enforcement

Law enforcement likes enforcing the law. For better or for worse, the appeal of the traditional operational toolkit – patrol, rapid response, investigation, arrest, prosecution, jail, prison, and the like – remains strong. A large body of academic and, beyond that, practical experience suggesting that these tools are often very weak indeed has done little to change their primacy (Braga 2002; Weisburd and Eck 2004). Their failure in practice is much more likely to be ascribed to system or social failure – we're making the arrests, the prosecutors are letting us down; what can we do when nobody in the neighborhood is finishing school or working? – than it is to lead to fundamental reconsideration of how business is or ought to be done. Police, prosecutors, and others believe, even in the midst of great frustration, in what they do.

Pulling levers strategies appeal to practitioners partly because they make a virtue of those beliefs and of existing agency capacities. These tools, *as deployed*, are usually unsatisfactory. Deploying them in new ways may be very different. Law enforcement personnel, and many others, think that the logic and the actions of enforcement should matter. People should seek to avoid being arrested, should avoid going to prison, should not want probation officers in their bedrooms. The manifest failure of existing tools to win compliance from offenders fuels the common conclusion that they are, on that evidence, irrational. But what if here, too, there is a middle ground? It is true that chronic offenders are frequently arrested and sanctioned. But it is also true – and, again, well understood both from research and from practical experience – that most crimes are not reported, most that are reported are not cleared, most that are cleared are not met with stiff sanctions, sanctions such as probation are generally not rigorously enforced, and so on (Kennedy 2003). It is thus possible for there to be a great deal of enforcement without that enforcement being consistent, predictable, or very meaningful to offenders. A street drug dealer may have been arrested a number of times. But each day, when he considers whether to go work his corner, the chance that he will be arrested *today* will be both small and essentially random. This can be true even for very serious crimes. In one of the most violent areas of Washington, DC, nearly three-quarters of homicides go unsolved.[2] Police and others very often know what happened, but they cannot put cases together, and so there are no official consequences (Braga, Piehl, and Kennedy 1999).

Law enforcement personnel understand very well – better than most others, short of offenders – that this is in fact true. Their usual responses, which have to do with resources, dramatically altering the behavior of various criminal justice agencies and judges, enhancing the willingness of the public to come forward, and the like, are hopeless, and they know that as well. Pulling levers strategies offer a way out. It is in fact possible to warn each of sixty street gangs in a jurisdiction that the first to commit a homicide will get overwhelming attention, and to back that promise up. Experience shows that when offenders believe that promise, their behavior changes. It may be possible to make sure that the worst 100 domestic abusers in a jurisdiction get very special attention, and then let the next 1000 know that behavior on their part will win them a place in the top group. It may be possible to warn a dozen street drug markets that there will be a crackdown in a week, and that they can protect themselves by shutting down before it comes.

This is very much old wine in new bottles, traditional building blocks assembled in commonsense but original ways. It bows in both directions:

to the conviction on the part of police and other authorities that enforcement is (or should be) powerful, justified, and important, and to the painfully clear fact that enforcement as usual too often simply does not work. Many in criminal justice have long been aware of the latter without being willing or able to give up the former. These strategies, at least to some extent, offer a way forward.

Communication, relationship, and common ground

Communication with offenders is a central element in pulling levers strategies. Communication and persuasion have long been recognized as essential elements in the deterrence process; sanctions offenders do not know about cannot deter them, and sanctions offenders do not believe in will not deter them (Zimring and Hawkins 1973; Kennedy 2003). Communication has in practice gotten very little attention, however, either theoretically or practically. We tend to assume what we know in fact to be false: that offenders understand the complicated and often rapidly shifting enforcement environment they face. One central lesson of pulling levers operations is the clear power of direct communication with offenders. A city's-worth of drug crews may utterly ignore the fact – may not collectively even be aware of the fact – that one crew has just been taken off the street. But tell them all that this has happened, and beyond that, that attention to groups is now standard operating procedure, and beyond that, that the next group that commits violence will be treated likewise, and beyond that, that enforcement attention will be heightened if groups are active in street drug sales – and matters may change. The evidence is that matters do change.

As experience with these strategies has accumulated, two related themes have emerged. One is that *relationships* between authorities and offenders matter a great deal. There is no acceptable place for this notion in traditional enforcement thinking. The operational and legal conventions of traditional law enforcement and case processing – call by call, incident by incident, case by case – run counter. The atmosphere and resonances of policing and much of the rest of law enforcement, with its division of the world into white hats and black hats, also very much run counter. Where the idea of relationship does have a place, as is sometimes true in probation and parole, there is a tendency to partition out the exercise of authority – leading, for example, to the framing of supervisees as "clients," which leads to much eye-rolling by the more enforcement minded.

Pulling levers strategies structure a very different kind of relationship. Authorities meet with offenders, as in call-ins, in a setting that is respectful, civil, but also unabashedly about authority and consequences. Such contacts are often repeated. They are often supplemented as needed in other settings, such as pointed warnings on the street when front-line intelligence suggests that trouble is brewing between particular groups. They frequently include other elements, such as the offering of services and impassioned statements by community figures. One of the most striking features of call-ins for police officers and other enforcement figures is that offenders tend to be well behaved, attentive, and often visibly moved by what ministers, mothers who have lost their children to the street, and neighborhood elders have to say to them. It is not uncommon for offenders to applaud authorities who speak to them uncompromisingly but also respectfully. Once the call-in process becomes known on the streets, offenders sometimes show up uninvited and ask to be allowed to sit in. The contrast with the conventional wisdom – that offenders are wild, self-destructive, unreachable, and the like – is graphic.

It is but a short step to the idea that there is in fact *common ground* between authorities and offenders. There is also no place for this in traditional enforcement thinking, which assumes a constant, zero-sum struggle between the forces of good and bad. In fact, there is a great deal of common ground. Offenders do not wish to die; for the most part they do not wish to be arrested and go to prison; they do not want their mothers to grieve; they do not want their younger siblings following in their footsteps or walking deadly streets; they would, all else being equal, prefer to do their business quietly and safely. These are, at least sometimes, goals authorities and offenders can seek together. Each gang may put down its guns if it understands that all are putting them down. Drug dealers may shift the ways in which they do business if they understand that police will be paying particular attention to the street markets and crack houses that most damage and endanger communities. Such common ground is certainly not absolute, or always to be found, but it is also not unknown. The clear fact that offenders respond to, and sometimes quite evidently welcome, the new rules established in pulling levers strategies is beginning to suggest to authorities that offenders might *want* things to be different, or at least that they may be far less resistant than is invariably assumed. It is, like the rest of the pulling levers framework, a notion that is both commonsensical and radical.

The rest of the story

All this is promising and provocative. Not all the news, of course, is good. These strategies are demonstrably potent in addressing serious violence. Whether they can be extended to other substantive problems remains to be seen. Where they have been effective, they have had a large impact on very particular problems; they have not had broad effects on a whole range of crime issues, as has happened, for example, in New York City. While some police departments and other criminal justice agencies are intrigued by these ideas, resistance and skepticism remain deep. Their staying power within implementing agencies remains very much in question. Boston, where the strategy originated, let Operation Ceasefire wither, as did – after an even more striking apparent initial success – Minneapolis (Kennedy and Braga 1998). Others have done better; the initiative in Indianapolis, for example, remains healthy and continues to evolve. But the same elements that make these operations promising – the innovative thinking, the focused operations, the interagency partnerships, the structuring of new relationships with offenders – also present challenges to getting them off the ground and keeping them in place. Local political strife, for example, scuttled the enterprise in Baltimore just at the point that it was demonstrating initial success in the field (Braga, Kennedy, and Tita 2002). In particular, the lion's share of the work inevitably falls on police departments, who have most of the necessary street knowledge and enforcement capacity. Trying to mobilize and sustain police action frequently shows, in the rudest imaginable ways, the shockingly poor management and accountability mechanisms within police departments, and departments' consequent abilities simply to refuse – obviously and successfully – what their executive levels demand of them.

At this point, it seems fair to say that the "pulling levers" framework is a bright spot in the larger community and problem-solving policing agenda. That agenda is not being realized as one might wish: nearly all police agencies still do nearly all their work the same way they did twenty years ago at the beginning of the "new policing" movement (Goldstein 2002). Occasional standout initiatives do not change that clear truth. The spread of pulling levers strategies stands in some small way in opposition to that stasis. Like the other main exception, the spread of broken windows policing, the strategies have what appeal they have to law enforcement practitioners primarily because they allow mostly traditional tactics to be deployed in new ways with the promise of considerably greater results. We shall see whether even that movement is sustained, and beyond that whether the possibly quite considerable potential for even more innovative thought and action can be realized.

NOTES

1. These data are available upon request from author.
2. Matt Miranda, Office of the United States Attorney, personal communication.

REFERENCES

Braga, A. (2002). *Problem-oriented policing and crime prevention*. Monsey, New York: Criminal Justice Press.

Braga, A., Kennedy, D., and Tita, G. (2002). New approaches to the strategic prevention of gang and group-involved violence. In C. R. Huff (ed.), *Gangs in America*, 3rd ed. Thousand Oaks, CA: Sage Publications.

Braga, A., McDevitt, J., and Pierce, G. (2005). Understanding and preventing gang violence: Problem analysis and response development in Lowell, Massachusetts. *Police Quarterly, 8*.

Braga, A., Piehl, A., and Kennedy, D. (1999). Youth homicide in Boston: An assessment of supplementary homicide report data. *Homicide Studies, 3*, 277–299.

Braga, A., Kennedy, D., Waring, E., and Piehl, A. (2001). Problem-oriented policing, deterrence, and youth violence: An evaluation of Boston's operation ceasefire. *Journal of Research in Crime and Delinquency, 38*, 195–225.

Clarke, R. and Weisburd, D. (1994). Diffusion of crime control benefits: Observations on the reverse of displacement. *Crime prevention studies, 2*, 165–184.

Dalton, E. (2003). *Lessons in preventing homicide*. Project Safe Neighborhoods Report. Lansing, MI: School of Criminal Justice, Michigan State University.

Goldstein, H. (2002). On further developing problem-oriented policing: The most critical need, the major impediments, and a proposal. In J. Knutsson (ed.), *Mainstreaming problem-oriented policing*. Monsey, NY: Criminal Justice Press.

Kennedy, D. (1990). Fighting the drug trade in Link Valley. Case C16-90-935.0. Cambridge, MA: John F. Kennedy School of Government, Harvard University.

(1997). Pulling levers: Chronic offenders, high-crime settings, and a theory of prevention. *Valparaiso University Law Review, 31*, 449–484.

(1998). Pulling levers: Getting deterrence right. *National Institute of Justice Journal*, July 2–8.

(2002a). A tale of one city: Reflections on the Boston Gun Project. In G. Katzmann (ed.), *Securing our children's future: New approaches to juvenile justice and youth violence*. Washington, DC: Brookings Institution Press.

(2002b). *Controlling domestic violence offenders*. Report submitted to the Hewlett-Family Violence Prevention Fund. Cambridge, MA: John F. Kennedy School of Government, Harvard University.

(2003). *Reconsidering deterrence*. Final report submitted to the US National Institute of Justice. Cambridge, MA: John F. Kennedy School of Government, Harvard University.

Kennedy, D. and Braga, A. (1998). Homicide in Minneapolis: Research for problem solving. *Homicide Studies, 2*, 263–290.

Kennedy, D., Braga, A., and Piehl, A. (1997). The (un)known universe: Mapping gangs and gang violence in Boston. In D. Weisburd and J. T. McEwen (eds.), *Crime Mapping and Crime Prevention*. Monsey, NY: Criminal Justice Press.

McGarrell, E. and Chermak, S. (2003). *Strategic approaches to reducing firearms violence: Final report on the Indianapolis violence reduction partnership*. Final report submitted to the US National Institute of Justice. East Lansing, MI: School of Criminal Justice, Michigan State University.

San Diego Police Department. 1998. Operation "hot pipe/smoky haze/rehab." Paper published in the proceedings of the 9th Annual International Problem-Oriented Policing Conference. Washington, DC: Police Executive Research Forum.

Tita, G., Riley, K. J., Ridgeway, G., Grammich, C., Abrahamse, A., and Greenwood, P. (2003). *Reducing gun violence: Results from an intervention in East Los Angeles.* Santa Monica, CA: Rand Corporation.

Travis, J., Kennedy, D., Roman, C., Beckman, K., Solomon, A., and Turner, E. (2003). An analysis of homicide incident reviews in the District of Columbia. Unpublished report. Washington, DC: Justice Policy Center, The Urban Institute.

Wakeling, S. (2003). Ending gang homicide: Deterrence can work. *Perspectives on violence prevention, 1.* Sacramento, CA: California Attorney General's Office and the California Health and Human Services Agency.

Weisburd, D. and Eck, J. E. (2004). What can police do to reduce crime, disorder, and fear? *Annals of the American Academy of Political and Social Science, 593,* 42–65.

Winship, C. and Berrien, J. (1999). Boston cops and black churches. *The Public Interest, 136,* 52–68.

Zimring, F. and Hawkins, G. (1973). *Deterrence: The legal threat in crime control.* Chicago: University of Chicago Press.

9   *Critic*
     Partnership, accountability, and innovation:
     clarifying Boston's experience with pulling
     levers

Anthony A. Braga and Christopher Winship

The pulling levers focused deterrence strategy has been embraced by the US Department of Justice as an effective approach to crime prevention. In his address to the American Society of Criminology, former National Institute of Justice Director Jeremy Travis (1998) announced "[the] pulling levers hypothesis has made enormous theoretical and practical contributions to our thinking about deterrence and the role of the criminal justice system in producing safety." Pioneered in Boston to halt youth violence, the pulling levers framework has been applied in many American cities through federally sponsored violence prevention programs such as the Strategic Alternatives to Community Safety Initiative and Project Safe Neighborhoods (Dalton 2002). In its simplest form, the approach consists of selecting a particular crime problem, such as youth homicide; convening an interagency working group of law enforcement practitioners; conducting research to identify key offenders, groups, and behavior patterns; framing a response to offenders and groups of offenders that uses a varied menu of sanctions ("pulling levers") to stop them from continuing their violent behavior; focusing social services and community resources on targeted offenders and groups to match law enforcement prevention efforts; and directly and repeatedly communicating with offenders to make them understand why they are receiving this special attention (Kennedy 1997; Kennedy in this volume).

Despite the enthusiasm for the approach, there is relatively little rigorous scientific evidence that pulling levers deterrence strategies have been useful in preventing violence beyond the Boston experience (Wellford, Pepper, and Petrie 2005). Even in Boston, the exact contribution of pulling levers to the reduction of youth violence remains unclear (Wellford *et al.* 2005). Moreover, high-profile replications of the Boston approach have been difficult to implement and sustain. In Baltimore, local political problems undermined the implementation process (Braga, Kennedy, and Tita 2002). In Minneapolis, the strategy was abandoned as the participating agencies returned to their traditional methods of dealing with violence (Kennedy and Braga 1998).

We believe that the difficulties experienced by other jurisdictions stem from a limited understanding of the larger Boston story. Boston's success in reducing youth violence has been attributed to a wide variety of programs and strategies: public health interventions, police–probation partnerships, enhanced federal prosecutions, police–black minister partnerships, and the pulling levers focused deterrence strategy known as Operation Ceasefire. Many observers have suggested that these are isolated and competing explanations. For example, in his discussion of Operation Ceasefire and the Boston Police Department's collaboration with activist black ministers, Fagan (2002) describes these as "two distinct and contrasting narratives [that] comprise the Boston story" (136).

In reality, the Boston story consists of multiple interconnected layers. As we discuss below, the implementation of Ceasefire was possible because of newly formed relationships among the police and other law enforcement and social service agencies and between the police and the community, with the latter creating important mechanisms for police accountability. Thus, although available quantitative evidence suggests that Operation Ceasefire was the key initiative associated with a significant reduction in youth violence, a fuller and more nuanced description of the Boston experience is needed. A narrow and inappropriate interpretation of Boston's success as simply being due to Operation Ceasefire creates the danger of unrealistic expectations of success, serious implementation problems in replicating the Ceasefire program, and an inability to sustain implemented violence prevention programs.

In order to understand the innovations that took place in Boston's policing strategies during the 1990s it is necessary to examine the importance of two key elements that created the foundation that made change possible. First, in order for the Boston Police to develop an innovative program involving a variety of partners, it was essential to have established a "network of capacity" consisting of dense and productive relationships from which partners could be drawn. Second, because of the long history of perceived racism by the Boston Police, a new mechanism of police accountability was necessary in order to create trust that new programs would be beneficial to the community. This trust was essential for establishing needed community and political support for innovative efforts by the Boston Police. Operation Ceasefire simply could not have been launched without either a network of partners who were a central component of its design or the trust that derived from accountability.

This chapter begins by briefly describing the key elements of Ceasefire. It then examines the available evidence on Ceasefire's effect on serious violence in Boston and elsewhere. It subsequently discusses the implementation of Ceasefire within the changing political context of police–community relationships and evolving police partnerships with other agencies. Finally, it analyses the implications of the fuller Boston story for replicating and sustaining the Boston approach in other jurisdictions.

The Boston Gun Project and Operation Ceasefire

Like many American cities during the late 1980s and early 1990s, Boston suffered an epidemic of youth violence that had its roots in the rapid spread of street-level crack-cocaine markets (Kennedy, Piehl, and Braga 1996). The Boston Gun Project was a problem-oriented policing project aimed at preventing and controlling serious youth violence. The problem analysis phase of the Project began in early 1995 and the Operation Ceasefire strategy was implemented in mid 1996. The trajectory of the Project and of Ceasefire has been extensively documented (see e.g., Kennedy et al. 1996; Kennedy, Braga, and Piehl 2001; Kennedy in this volume). Briefly, a problem-solving working group of law enforcement personnel, youth workers, and researchers diagnosed the youth violence problem in Boston as one of patterned, largely vendetta-like hostility amongst a small population of highly active criminal offenders, and particularly amongst those involved in some sixty loose, informal, mostly neighborhood-based gangs. Based on the problem-analysis findings, the Boston Gun Project working group crafted the Operation Ceasefire initiative that was tightly focused on disrupting ongoing conflicts among youth gangs.

The Boston Police Departments's Youth Violence Strike Force (YVSF), an elite unit of some forty officers and detectives, coordinated the actions of Operation Ceasefire. An interagency working group, composed of law enforcement personnel, youth workers, and members of Boston's Ten Point Coalition of activist black clergy, was convened on a biweekly basis to address outbreaks of serious gang violence. Operation Ceasefire's pulling levers strategy was designed to deter gang violence by reaching out directly to gangs, saying explicitly that violence would no longer be tolerated, and backing up that message by "pulling every lever" legally available when violence occurred (Kennedy 1997). These law enforcement levers included disrupting street-level drug markets, serving warrants, mounting federal prosecutions, and changing the conditions of community supervision for probationers and parolees in the targeted group. Simultaneously, youth workers, probation and parole officers, and clergy offered gang members services and other kinds of help. If gang members wanted to step away from a violent lifestyle, the

Ceasefire working group focused on providing them with the services and opportunities necessary to make the transition.

The Ceasefire Working Group delivered their anti-violence message in formal meetings with gang members; through individual police and probation contacts with gang members; through meetings with inmates of secure juvenile facilities in the city; and through gang outreach workers (Kennedy *et al.* 2001). The deterrence message was not a deal with gang members to stop violence. Rather, it was a promise to gang members that violent behavior would evoke an immediate and intense response. If gangs committed other crimes but refrained from violence, the normal workings of police, prosecutors, and the rest of the criminal justice system dealt with these matters. But if gang members hurt people, the Working Group focused its enforcement actions on them.

A large reduction in the yearly number of Boston youth homicides followed immediately after Operation Ceasefire was implemented in mid-1996. This reduction was sustained for the next five years (see Figure 9.1). The Ceasefire program, as designed, was in place until 2000. During the early years of the new millennium, the Boston Police experimented with a broader approach to violence prevention by expanding certain Ceasefire tactics to a broader range of problems such as serious repeat violent gun offenders, the re-entry of incarcerated violent offenders back into high-risk Boston neighborhoods, and criminogenic families in hot spot areas. These new approaches, known broadly as Boston Strategy II, seemed to diffuse the ability of Boston to respond to ongoing conflicts among gangs. Homicide, most of which is gang related, has returned as a serious problem for the City of Boston. Homicide has been rising since 2001 with the sharpest increase among victims aged 25 and older (Figure 9.1). In Fall 2004, the Boston Police implemented a new violence prevention campaign, which borrows heavily from Ceasefire's tight focus on disrupting cycles of violent gang retribution (Winship forthcoming).

Evidence on the impact of Ceasefire on serious violence

A US Department of Justice (DOJ)-sponsored evaluation of Operation Ceasefire used a non-randomized control group design to analyze trends in serious violence between 1991 and 1998. The evaluation reported that the intervention was associated with a 63 percent decrease in the monthly number of Boston youth homicides, a 32 percent decrease in the monthly number of shots-fired calls, a 25 percent decrease in the monthly number of gun assaults, and, in one high-risk police district given special attention in the evaluation, a 44 percent decrease in the monthly number of youth gun assault incidents (Braga, Kennedy, Waring, and Piehl 2001). The

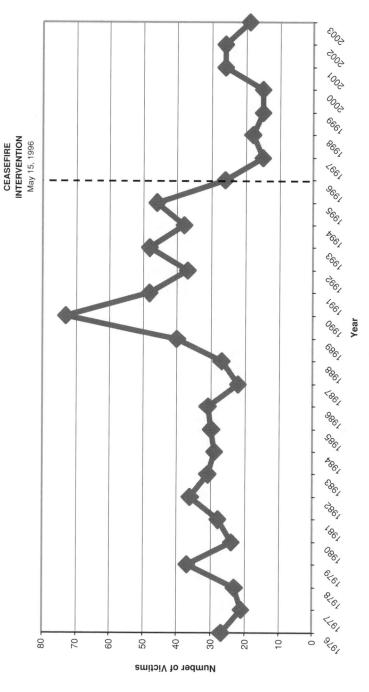

Figure 9.1 Youth homicide in Boston, 1976–2003, victims ages 24 and under

evaluation also suggested that Boston's significant youth homicide reduction associated with Operation Ceasefire was distinct when compared to youth homicide trends in most major US and New England cities.

Other researchers, however, have observed that some of the decrease in homicide may have occurred without the Ceasefire intervention in place as violence was decreasing in most major US cities. Fagan's (2002) cursory review of gun homicide in Boston and in other Massachusetts cities suggests a general downward trend in gun violence that existed before Operation Ceasefire was implemented. Levitt (2004) analyzed homicide trends over the course of the 1990s and concluded that the impact of innovative policing strategies, such as Operation Ceasefire in Boston and broken windows policing and Compstat in New York, on homicide was limited. Other factors, such as increases in the number of police, the rising prison population, the waning crack-cocaine epidemic, and the legalization of abortion, can account for nearly all of the national decline in homicide, violent crime, and property crime in the 1990s.

The National Academies' Panel on Improving Information and Data on Firearms (Wellford *et al.* 2005) concluded that the Ceasefire evaluation was compelling in associating the intervention with the subsequent decline in youth homicide. However, the Panel also suggested that many complex factors affect youth homicide trends and it was difficult to specify the exact relationship between the Ceasefire intervention and subsequent changes in youth offending behaviors. While the DOJ-sponsored evaluation controlled for existing violence trends and certain rival causal factors such as changes in the youth population, drug markets, and employment in Boston, there could be complex interaction effects among these factors not measured by the evaluation that could account for some meaningful portion of the decrease. The evaluation was not a randomized, controlled experiment. Therefore, the non-randomized control group research design cannot rule out these internal threats to the conclusion that Ceasefire was the key factor in the youth homicide decline.

Like the Panel, we believe that Ceasefire was responsible for a meaningful proportion of the youth homicide decline. However, it is difficult to determine the exact contribution of Ceasefire to the decline. Clearly, other factors were responsible for some of the decline. As Figure 9.2 reveals, there was a parallel decrease of approximately equal magnitude in adult homicide that can only be partly explained by Ceasefire's potential effect on the behavior of adults participating in violent gang dynamics. Figure 9.1 also presents a long-term picture of youth homicide that suggests some of the decline may result from a "regression to the mean" phenomenon. Youth homicides dramatically increase in 1989 and remain historically high through 1995. While post-Ceasefire youth homicide

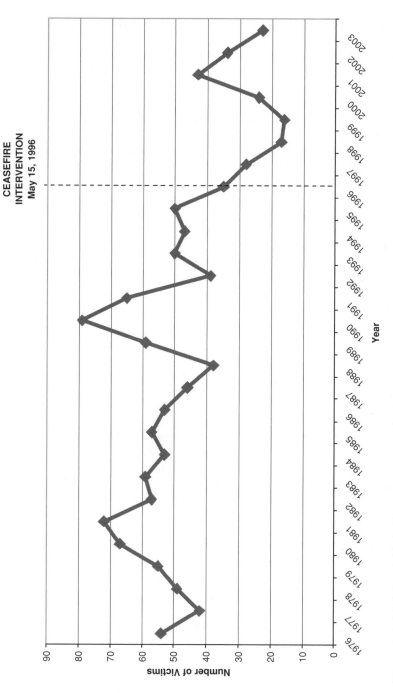

Figure 9.2 Adult homicide in Boston, 1976–2003, victims ages 25 and older

counts are lower than counts during the 1976–88 period, it seems plausible that some portion of the decline was part of a natural return to an average count of youth homicide. This certainly raises questions about the effectiveness of Ceasefire. Experimental research is necessary to uncover the true crime prevention benefits of engaging a pulling levers strategy.

The National Academies' Panel also found that the evidence on the effectiveness of the pulling levers focused deterrence strategy is quite limited (Wellford *et al.* 2005). The available evidence on the effects of pulling levers programs in other jurisdictions is scientifically weak. Assessments of these programs in other jurisdictions did not use control groups and usually consisted of simple pre-post measurements of trends in violence (see, e.g., Braga *et al.* 2002; McGarrell and Chermak 2003). In Baltimore and Minneapolis, two well-known replications of the Boston experience, violence prevention initiatives rapidly unraveled and were abandoned (Kennedy and Braga 1998; Kennedy in this volume). As discussed further below, we believe that the difficulty other jurisdictions have had in replicating and sustaining a pulling levers focused deterrence strategy may, in part, stem from a weak understanding of the context in which the Boston intervention was implemented.

The larger Boston story I: The development of a "network of capacity"

Missing from the account of Operation Ceasefire reported in most law enforcement circles is the larger story of an evolving collaboration that spanned the boundaries that divide criminal justice agencies from one another, criminal justice agencies from human service agencies, and criminal justice agencies from the community. Such collaborations are necessary to legitimize, fund, equip, and operate complex strategies that are most likely to succeed in both controlling and preventing youth violence (Moore 2002). The solid working relationships that were at the heart of the interagency working group process were developed long before the Boston Gun Project commenced in 1995. In essence, Boston created a very powerful "network of capacity" to prevent youth violence (Moore 2002). This network was well positioned to launch an effective response to youth violence because criminal justice agencies, community groups, and social service agencies coordinated and combined their efforts in ways that could magnify their separate effects. Ceasefire capitalized on these existing relationships by focusing the network on the problem of serious gang violence.

Criminal justice agencies work largely independent of each other, often at cross-purposes, often without coordination, and often in an atmosphere of distrust and dislike (Kennedy 2002). Until the height of the youth violence epidemic, this observation was certainly true in Boston. It was painfully apparent that no one agency could mount a meaningful response to the gang violence that was spiraling out of control in the city. The crisis forced Boston criminal justice agencies to work together and develop new approaches to deal with the violence problem. YVSF officers and detectives and line-level workers from other criminal justice agencies collaborated on a variety of innovative programs, including: Operation Night Flight – a police–probation partnership to ensure at-risk youth were abiding by the conditions of their release into the community (Corbett, Fitzgerald, and Jordan 1998); Safe Neighborhoods Initiatives – a community prosecution program that was rooted in a partnership between the Suffolk County District Attorney's Office, the Boston Police, and community members in hot spot neighborhoods (Coles and Kelling 1999); and a partnership between the Boston Police, the Bureau of Alcohol, Tobacco, and Firearms (ATF), and the US Attorney's Office to identify and apprehend illegal gun traffickers who were providing guns to violent gangs (Kennedy et al. 1996).

The YVSF also formed working relationships with social service and opportunity provision agencies. For certain prevention initiatives, the YVSF was the lead agency involved in the program such as the Summer of Opportunity program that provides at-risk youth with job training and leadership skills that could be transferred to workplace, school, or home settings. More often, however, the police supported the activities of youth social service providers from community-based organizations such as the Boston Community Centers' streetworker program and the Dorchester Youth Collaborative. YVSF officers and detectives would encourage at-risk youth to take advantage of these resources and also consider the input of youth workers in determining whether certain gang-involved youth would be better served by prevention and intervention actions rather than enforcement actions.

When the Boston Gun Project was initiated, the YVSF had already developed a network of working relationships that could be powerfully channeled by a more focused initiative like Operation Ceasefire. Criminal justice agency partnerships provided a varied menu of enforcement options that could be tailored to particular gangs. Without these partnerships, the available "levers" that could be pulled by the working group would have been limited. Social service and opportunity provision agencies were also integrated into Ceasefire interventions to provide a much-needed "carrot" to balance the law enforcement "stick." The inclusion of prevention and intervention programs in the Ceasefire intervention was vitally important in securing community support and involvement in the program. We believe that the legitimacy conferred upon the Ceasefire initiative by key community members was an equally important condition that facilitated the successful implementation of this innovative program.

The larger Boston story II: Accountability and police–community relations

There was a radical change in the relationship between the Boston Police and Boston's minority communities that pre-dated Ceasefire and had a profound influence on the trajectory of the Ceasefire intervention. This collaborative relationship, led by Ten Point Coalition activist black ministers, developed in the context of a high level of community dissatisfaction with policing strategies and tactics engaged by the Boston Police (Winship and Berrien 1999). When the violence epidemic started in the late 1980s, the Boston Police were ill equipped to deal with the sudden increase in serious youth violence. The Boston Police relied upon highly aggressive and reportedly indiscriminate policing tactics to deal with street gang violence (Winship and Berrien 1999; Berrien and Winship 2002; 2003). A series of well-publicized scandals emanating from an indiscriminate policy of stopping and frisking all black males in high-crime areas outraged Boston's black community. Perhaps the most important was the 1989 murder of Carol Stuart, a pregnant white woman on her way home from Boston City Hospital. Initially, Charles Stuart, the victim's husband who was the actual murderer, led Boston Police investigators to believe that the murderer was a black male. The police responded by blanketing the Mission Hill housing projects for a suspect. Abusive police conduct was reported to be widespread as coerced statements led to the wrongful arrest of a black male. The black community and the local media were outraged and condemned the discriminatory actions of the investigating officers. The Carol Stuart case and other scandals led to the establishment of the St. Clair Commission, an independent committee appointed to investigate the policies and practices of the Boston Police. In 1992 it released its report, which cited extensive corruption and incompetent management, and called for extensive reform including the replacement of top personnel.

In response, the Boston Police overhauled its organization, mission, and tactics during the early 1990s. The existing command staff, including the commissioner, were replaced with new officers who were known to be innovative and hardworking; investments were made to improve the department's technology to understand crime problems; a neighborhood policing plan was implemented; and beat-level officers were trained in the methods of community and problem-oriented policing. In 1991, the Anti-Gang Violence Unit (AGVU) was created and charged with disrupting ongoing gang conflicts rather than mounting an aggressive campaign to arrest as many offenders as possible. By 1994, the AGVU evolved into the YVSF and its mandate was broadened beyond controlling outbreaks of gang violence to more general youth violence prevention. While these changes were important in creating an environment where the police could collaborate with the community, residents of Boston's poor minority neighborhoods remained wary of and dissatisfied with a police department that had a long history of abusive and unfair treatment.

In 1992, a loosely allied group of activist black clergy formed the Ten Point Coalition after a gang invasion of the Morningstar Baptist Church. During a memorial for a slain rival gang member, mourners were attacked with knives and guns (Winship and Berrien 1999; Kennedy et al. 2001; Berrien and Winship 2002; 2003). In the wake of that outrage, the Ten Point Coalition ministers decided they should attempt to prevent the youth in their community from joining gangs, and also that they needed to send an anti-violence message to all youth, whether gang-involved or not.

Initially, the ministers assumed an adversarial role to the Boston Police and were highly critical in the public media of police efforts to prevent youth violence. However, as the ministers worked the streets, they started to form effective relationships with particular YVSF officers and developed a shared understanding of the nature of youth violence in Boston: only a small number of youths in the neighborhoods were involved in violence, many of these gang-involved youth were better served by intervention and prevention strategies, and only a small number of these gang-involved youths needed to be removed from the streets through arrest and prosecution strategies.

The Ten Point ministers also sheltered the police from broad public criticism while the police were engaged in activities the ministers deemed to be of interest to the community and its youth. In 1995, Paul McLaughlin, a local gang prosecutor who was white, was murdered on his way home from work. The initial description of the assailant ("young black male wearing a hooded sweatshirt and baggy pants") was vague enough to cause concern to many in the black community that an "open season on young black males" similar to that during the Carol Stuart investigation would occur (Grunwald and Anand 1995). Fortunately, these initial fears were unfounded as the black ministers and the Boston Police supported each other in the handling of the media and the ensuing investigation. The black ministers publicly praised the police for showing restraint in their conduct and the police praised the ministers for their willingness to provide help and keep the community calm (Berrien and Winship 2002; 2003).

Prior to Ceasefire, the Ten Point ministers also helped the Boston Police manage negative publicity by the local media after several potentially explosive events ranging from the beating of a black undercover officer by uniformed police officers (Chacon 1995) to the accidental death of 75-year-old retired minister who suffered a fatal heart attack after a botched drug raid (Mallia and Mulvihill 1994). In these cases, the ministers took two positions. First, they demanded that the police department take responsibility for its actions – investigate incidents thoroughly and hold those involved accountable. Second, after it was clear that the Boston Police was accepting responsibility, the ministers communicated to the community that the police were in fact reacting appropriately. This, in turn, prevented these situations from becoming racially explosive and provided the police with the continued political support they needed in order to undertake policy innovations, such as Ceasefire. In more recent years, the ministers have continued to play this dual role with regards to fatal police shootings, eight of which occurred over a 22-month period between 2000 and 2002 (Tench 2002; Winship forthcoming).

While the Ten Point ministers were not involved in the design of the Ceasefire intervention, they were influential as an informal "litmus test" of the types of enforcement actions that would and would not be tolerated by the community. The youth workers participating in the design of Ceasefire would voice their concerns about community reaction to any proposed enforcement tactics that could be viewed as overly aggressive. However, what usually ended discussions was the recognition of the political vulnerability of the Boston Police to the consequences of the Ten Point ministers potentially reporting any questionable practices to local media and, more importantly, exerting pressure on the Mayor's Office to deal with perceived inappropriate actions by the Department. For example, while discussing plausible interventions, the working group considered the notable gun violence reduction results of the Kansas City Gun Experiment, which involved intensive enforcement of laws against illegally carrying concealed firearms via safety frisks during traffic stops, plain view, and searches incident to arrest in gun violence hot spot areas (Sherman and Rogan 1995). After some discussion, the working group rejected the idea of engaging a hot spots policing strategy as the Boston Police did not want to adopt an enforcement program that could be viewed by the Ten Point ministers as a return to the indiscriminate "stop and frisk" policies of the past.

When Ceasefire was ready to be implemented, the commander of the YVSF presented the program to key black ministers to obtain their approval of and involvement in the initiative. The Boston Police knew that they would need the political support of the Ten Point Coalition to pursue aggressive enforcement actions against hardcore gang members who were central to violent conflicts. While the Ceasefire initiative was a violence prevention campaign, given the Carol Stuart case and other incidents, the community and local media could have easily misunderstood the enforcement tactics as simply another law enforcement initiative designed to arrest large numbers of young black men. The ministers recognized the value of the Ceasefire approach to violence prevention as it was carefully focused only on violent gang-involved youth and provided social services and opportunities to gang youth who desired them. After Ceasefire was implemented, Ten Point Coalition ministers became regular members of the working group. Ministers played key roles in working with the police to identify dangerous gang-involved youth, communicating the anti-violence deterrence message to all youth and, with the help of social service providers, offering assistance to gang youth who wanted to step away from their violent lifestyles.

By including the ministers in the Ceasefire working group, the Boston Police developed a mechanism for transparency and accountability that was very desirable to Boston's minority community. Through their involvement in Ceasefire, the ministers became part of the process of determining which gang interventions would be done and when. In addition, they, along with others, gave gang members the message that they had a choice: stop the violence and they would be helped – with school, a job, family; continue and the full weight of the law (and the community) would come down on them, with every possible lever being used to see that they were incarcerated. At a more general level, a shared understanding of the reality of youth violence and the actions that were necessary to prevent and control that violence emerged (Berrien and Winship 2002; 2003). The transparency and involvement in the enforcement process built trust and further solidified a functional working relationship between the community and the Boston Police. In turn, by engaging in a process through which they were meaningfully and appropriately accountable to the community, the Boston Police created the political support, or "umbrella of legitimacy," that they needed to pursue more focused and perhaps more aggressive intervention than would have been possible otherwise (Berrien and Winship 2002).

Implications of the larger story for other jurisdictions

Operation Ceasefire became a nationally recognized model for youth violence reduction programs and many jurisdictions quickly started to experiment with the approach (Kennedy in this volume). Unfortunately, despite some initially promising results, many of these replications were never fully implemented or were eventually abandoned. Braga has been involved in replication efforts in a number of cities, including Baltimore, Minneapolis, and San Francisco, and these jurisdictions simply did not have an adequate network of capacity in place before adopting a Ceasefire-like approach to youth violence. Operation Ceasefire was a "relationship intensive" intervention based on trust and the ability of a diverse set of individuals to work together toward a common goal. The narrow description of Ceasefire that currently circulates in criminal justice circles is, in many ways, a recipe for frustration and eventual failure as it simplifies the trajectory of the Boston experience.

Effective collaborations and the trust and accountability that they entail are essential in launching a meaningful response to complex youth violence problems. However, the fact that such collaborations are needed does not guarantee that they inevitably a rise or, once developed, that they are sustained. There are many significant obstacles to their development and maintenance such as giving up control over scarce resources that could compromise agencies' traditional missions, aligning agencies' individual work efforts into a functional enterprise, and developing a collective leadership among a group of individuals aligned with the needs of their individual organizations (Bardach 1998).

A central problem in creating and managing effective capacity-building collaborations is overcoming the problem of distrust (Bardach 1998). Distrust corrodes the creative process that criminal justice agencies and community-based organizations are necessarily engaged in. Like most cities, distrust characterized the relationship among criminal justice agencies and between criminal justice agencies and the inner city community in Boston. Practitioners and community members in Boston were able to overcome their historical distrust and form productive working relationships. These relationships existed before Ceasefire and were the foundation upon which it was built. Of course, working groups can be forced together and, sometimes, can implement short-term programs that have promising initial results. However, if the initiative is not based on a shared understanding of the problem and cemented through functional partnerships, the initiative will fall apart. These are key issues for other jurisdictions to consider in replicating Operation Ceasefire and in sustaining the collaborative effort once it has been launched.

In many community and problem-oriented policing projects, community members serve as informants who report to the police on unacceptable community conditions and the particulars of crime problems (Skogan and Hartnett 1997; Braga 2002). They are rarely engaged as "partners" or "co-producers" of public safety. Police officers remain the "experts" on crime who are primarily responsible for developing and managing interventions to address crime problems. Through their collaboration with Ten Point ministers, the Boston Police discovered a system whereby they were accountable to the community. This accountability to the community became a great asset to the police. By engaging the ministers in their violence prevention efforts and creating a sense of joint ownership of the youth violence problem, the Boston Police created the political support necessary for both innovation and more focused and aggressive intervention. With the Ten Point's approval of and involvement in Operation Ceasefire, the community supported the approach as a legitimate violence prevention campaign. Police strategies can acquire true legitimacy within the inner city only if the community partner supports police tactics when they are appropriate as well as publicly criticizes activities that are not (Berrien and Winship 2002; 2003; Winship forthcoming). Given the potentially harsh law enforcement levers that can be pulled as part of a Ceasefire-like program, we feel that community involvement is critical in replicating and sustaining such intensive violence prevention initiatives. Without the political support of the community, the police cannot pursue an innovative enforcement strategy that targets truly dangerous youth at the heart of urban youth violence problems.

REFERENCES

Bardach, E. (1998). *Getting agencies to work together*. Washington, DC: Brookings Institution Press.
Berrien, J. and Winship, C. (2002). An umbrella of legitimacy: Boston's Police Department – ten point coalition collaboration. In G. Katzmann (ed.), *Securing our children's future: New approaches to juvenile justice and youth violence*. Washington, DC: Brookings Institution Press.
(2003). Should we have faith in the churches? The ten-point coalition's effect on Boston's youth violence. In B. Harcourt (ed.), *Guns, crime, and punishment in America*. New York: New York University Press.
Braga, A. (2002). *Problem-oriented policing and crime prevention*. Monsey, NY: Criminal Justice Press.
Braga, A., Kennedy, D., and Tita, G. (2002). New approaches to the strategic prevention of gang and group-involved violence. In C. R. Huff (ed.), *Gangs in America* (3rd ed.). Thousand Oaks, CA: Sage Publications.
Braga, A., Kennedy, D., Waring, E., and Piehl, A. (2001). Problem-oriented policing, deterrence, and youth violence: An evaluation of Boston's operation ceasefire. *Journal of Research in Crime and Delinquency*, 38, 195–225.
Chacon, R. (1995). Boston police investigators seek cause of undercover officer's injuries. *The Boston Globe*, February 4, 22.

Coles, C. and Kelling, G. (1999). Prevention through community prosecution. *The Public Interest, 136,* 69–84.

Corbett, R., Fitzgerald, B., and Jordan, J. (1998). Boston's operation night light: An emerging model for police-probation partnerships. In J. Petersilia (ed.), *Community corrections: Probation, parole, and intermediate sanctions.* New York: Oxford University Press.

Dalton, E. (2002). Targeted crime reduction efforts in ten communities: Lessons for the Project Safe Neighborhoods initiative. *US Attorney's Bulletin, 50,* 16–25.

Fagan, J. (2002). Policing guns and youth violence. *The Future of Children, 12,* 133–151.

Grunwald, M. and Anand, G. (1995). Authorities praised; Some blacks wary. *The Boston Globe,* September 30, 80.

Kennedy, D. (1997). Pulling levers: Chronic offenders, high-crime settings, and a theory of prevention. *Valparaiso University Law Review, 31,* 449–484.

    (2002). A tale of one city: Reflections on the Boston gun project. In G. Katzmann (ed.), *Securing our children's future: New approaches to juvenile justice and youth violence.* Washington, DC: Brookings Institution Press.

Kennedy, D. and Braga, A. (1998). Homicide in Minneapolis: Research for problem solving. *Homicide Studies, 2,* 263–290.

Kennedy, D., Braga, A., and Piehl, A. (2001). Developing and implementing operation ceasefire. In *Reducing gun violence: The Boston gun project's operation ceasefire.* Washington, DC: National Institute of Justice, US Department of Justice.

Kennedy, D., Piehl, A., and Braga, A. (1996). Youth violence in Boston: Gun markets, serious offenders, and a use-reduction strategy. *Law and Contemporary Problems, 59,* 147–196.

Levitt, S. (2004). Understanding why crime fell in the 1990s: Four factors that explain the decline and six that do not. *Journal of Economic Perspectives, 18,* 163–190.

Mallia, J. and Mulvihill, M. (1994). Minister dies as cops raid wrong apartment. *The Boston Herald,* March 26, 1.

McGarrell, E. and Chermak, S. (2003). *Strategic approaches to reducing firearms violence: Final report on the Indianapolis violence reduction partnership.* Final report submitted to the US National Institute of Justice. East Lansing, MI: School of Criminal Justice, Michigan State University.

Moore, M. (2002). Creating networks of capacity: The challenge of managing society's response to youth violence. In G. Katzmann (ed.), *Securing our children's future: New approaches to juvenile justice and youth violence.* Washington, DC: Brookings Institution Press.

Sherman, L. and Rogan, D. (1995). Effects of gun seizures on gun violence: "Hot spots" patrol in Kansas City. *Justice Quarterly, 12,* 673–694.

Skogan, W. and Hartnett, S. (1997). *Community policing, Chicago style.* New York: Oxford University Press.

Tench, M. (2002). Group offers support for Evans, points to progress in curbing violence. *The Boston Globe,* September 21, 34.

Travis, J. (1998). *Crime, justice, and public policy*. Plenary presentation to the American Society of Criminology. Washington, DC: November 12. (http://www.ojp.usdoj.gov/nij/speeches/asc.htm).

Wellford, C., Pepper, J., and Petrie, C. (eds.). (2005). *Firearms and violence: A critical review*. Committee to Improve Research Information and Data on Firearms. Committee on Law and Justice, Division of Behavioral and Social Sciences and Education. Washington, DC: The National Academies Press.

Winship, C. (Forthcoming). The end of a miracle? Crime, faith, and partnership in Boston in the 1990s. In R. Drew Smith (ed.), *The public influence of black churches*, II. Durham, NC: Duke University Press.

Winship, C. and Berrien, J. (1999). Boston cops and black churches. *The Public Interest, 136*, 52–68.

Part V

Third-party policing

10 *Advocate*
The case for third-party policing

Lorraine Mazerolle and Janet Ransley

Third-party policing is defined as police efforts to persuade or coerce organizations or non-offending persons, such as public housing agencies, property owners, parents, health and building inspectors, and business owners to take some responsibility for preventing crime or reducing crime problems (Buerger and Mazerolle 1998: 301). In third-party policing, the police create or enhance crime control nodes in locations or situations where crime control guardianship was previously absent or non-effective. Sometimes the police use cooperative consultation with community members, parents, inspectors, and regulators to encourage and convince third parties to take on more crime control or prevention responsibility. Central, however, to third-party policing is the police use of a range of civil, criminal, and regulatory rules and laws, to engage, coerce (or force) third parties into taking some crime control responsibility. It is the regulatory and legal provisions that dictate the process for third-party intervention.

In third-party policing, laws and legal mechanisms are directed at willing or unwilling non-offending third parties, with the object of facilitating or coercing them into helping to control the behavior of offending ultimate targets. This type of policing, however, is not new. Some might argue that this is just good, proactive policing. Indeed, for many years the police have sought alternative solutions to regulate activities and solve crime problems (Eck and Spelman 1987; Goldstein 1990; Goldstein 2003). The police often create "place managers" to guard and protect problem places (Eck 1994; Felson 1994) and they have used situational responses for many years to deal with on-going crime problems (Clarke 1992). The police have been carrying out this mode of policing for years, whether as part of their routine patrol activities, their problem-oriented policing program, or as a crime prevention initiative.

A systematic review of third-party policing evaluations reveals that about less than a third of third-party policing initiatives occur within the context of problem-oriented policing (Mazerolle and Ransley 2005). We suggest, therefore, that third-party policing (e.g., legal levers, civil remedies, coercion of third parties) is more than a subset of problem-solving responses (see Goldstein 1990; Scott 2000; Goldstein 2003). We argue that third-party policing is distinguished from other models of policing through its intrinsic links with societal trends in regulation more generally and the legal/regulatory provisions that dictate the intervention processes. Indeed, we argue that the proliferation of third-party policing has not occurred in a vacuum as an idea born at the grassroots of policing or because the police have just gotten better at good, proactive policing. Rather, we argue that the pace, context, and prominence of third-party policing initiatives has escalated in recent years as one of many consequences in the move from centralized state control to a system of decentralized networks of governance and crime control agents. The proliferation and development of third-party policing is, we suggest, reflective of external pressure and the general transformation of government and governance taking place in contemporary society.

In this chapter we provide an analysis of third-party policing in a societal context. We begin with an overview of the trends in regulation more generally that have set the stage for third-party policing to emerge as a popular crime control tactic. We then describe the key dimensions of third-party policing and summarize the evaluation evidence. We conclude our chapter with a short examination of the side-effects, fairness, and equity concerns that are raised through third-party policing and propose ways in which third-party policing could be appropriately implemented into mainstream policing activities.

Governance, regulation, and third-party policing

The proliferation of third-party policing is part of a pattern of major change, indeed a transformation, of government and governance taking place in contemporary society. This political, legal, economic, and social transformation has affected the institutions of government and civil society and is also altering how we think about crime, its prevention, and its control (Braithwaite 2000). Big, organizing themes like governance, risk, and plurality are now intrinsically affecting crime control and policing and the rise of third-party policing has emerged in the context of these broader trends in governance and crime control.

Recent transformations of governance in Western democracies have involved a movement away from state sovereignty and control to networks of power (see Braithwaite 2000). These changes have influenced contemporary police practice and driven the societal push to third-party policing. In this contemporary model of governance the state provides only one of many nodes in a network of regulation.

The main mechanism for this transformation has been the development of the notion of risk – economic, social, and political activities are less subject to central control, and more likely to be monitored for risks that need to be managed (Ericson and Haggerty 1997; O'Malley 2000). Garland (1996; 1997) argues that risk and insurance promote a form of "responsibilized" autonomy (Garland 1996: 452–455). That is, the burden of managing risk has been shifted from governments to individuals, who must become responsible for the outcomes of their own decisions on risk. Prudent individuals will obtain insurance, identify and minimize risk, and manage their own security.

Feeley and Simon (1994) apply the concepts of risk to criminal justice, to develop the notion of actuarial justice. They describe an old and a new penology – the old marked by "concern for individuals, and preoccupied with such concepts as guilt, responsibility and obligation, as well as diagnosis, intervention and treatment of an individual offender" (Feeley and Simon 1994: 173). The new penology, however, is "concerned with techniques for identifying, classifying and managing groups assorted by levels of dangerousness. It takes crime for granted. It accepts deviance as normal" (Feeley and Simon 1994: 173). Interventions are less directed at determining responsibility or ensuring accountability, and more at managing and regulating risky groups of people or places.

The impact of these trends on crime control and policing has been to change the focus from state responsibility for preventing and correcting criminal behavior to a system where crime control and prevention networks are responsible for identifying and managing risks. Public police form one node of these networks, with private police, insurance companies, regulatory agencies, communities, schools, and parents as other nodes. These networks may exist within legislated frameworks, but are often episodic and *ad hoc*. The prime concern of police and the criminal justice system is less with the detection and rehabilitation of individual offenders, and more with identifying and corralling risky groups – repeat offenders, sex offenders, drug users, homeless or mentally ill people. The new technologies involve systematic identification of target groups or places (Eck and Weisburd 1995), and then new forms of surveillance, preventive detention, and incapacitation via longer or mandatory sentences.

It is now well documented that the rhetoric of market solutions and privatization espoused by Thatcherist and Reaganist proponents of the 1980s–90s was not deregulation, but rather a new form of regulation (Braithwaite 1999; 2000). For every privatized industry there was created a new regulatory agency to supervise, monitor, and investigate the new private players. But the new regulators differ from the old, state-centered models. They rely on regulatory techniques ranging from voluntary and enforced self-regulation through to selective use of the old command-and-control techniques and sanctions. They work with industry bodies, and increasingly as part of globalized regulatory networks (Braithwaite and Drahos 2000). The practical effect has been a shift in regulatory model, from state control to market models, from hierarchical systems of command and control to responsive regulation. The new forms of governance actually require state control of the direction of regulation and risk management, with many of the operational regulatory and compliance functions then shifted out to the market, community, and other social institutions.

The scope of regulation has been expanding significantly since the 1960s. In recent years traditional areas of regulation (such as health, education, and taxation) have been joined by new forms of social regulation (such as occupational health and safety, building codes, consumer protection, and environmental regulation). In many of these areas, formal regulation, or law, has been only one form of social control, with self, peer, and professional regulation also being significant. Recognition of this plurality of regulatory methods, coupled with ideologically inspired shrinkage of state activities, has led to a departure from reliance on command and control as the only way of securing compliance with regulation. Nowadays, the regulatory pyramid (Ayres and Braithwaite 1992) sets out a tiered ranking of techniques, beginning with persuasion and self-regulation, progressing through professional discipline, adverse publicity and fines, through to prosecution and the withdrawal of occupational licenses. Responsive regulation requires a logical working through of these techniques, resulting in the use of the most coercive only in a small number of cases of intransigence. Hence, regulation becomes a layered web, with strands contributed by public regulatory agencies, professional and community organizations and individuals, and international organizations.

The impact of these methods on regulatory agencies is to transform them from reactive, hierarchical command structures to problem-oriented, team-based units focused on risk management (Sparrow 1994; 2000). The emphasis moves from after the event use of formal legal sanctions, to cooperation, persuasion, and the creation of incentives for compliance. The attraction for the regulated is the comfort that the "big stick" of coercive sanctions will only be used as a last resort, and also that those who are regulated will have some input into the rule-making and compliance processes. The attraction for governments is also twofold – first, persuasion and the other techniques are cheaper and give quicker results than formal legal process (see Cheh 1998), but more importantly, they help build an image of government as supportive of business, rather than focused on bureaucracy and red tape.

These changes in societal context have far-reaching implications for police and the organization of police work. One oft-cited effect of the shift in regulation has been the movement away from state dominated policing to the situation where most developed economies have more private than state police (Shearing and Stenning 1987). As private security guards replace police in public and private buildings, community centers, even public spaces, and as private prison administration proliferates, the role of the state increasingly becomes one of regulating standards rather than actually controlling policing and criminal justice functions. The end result is a "reconstitution of policing as a mechanism of governance oriented to the *management* of conduct across civil society, and the advent of a loosely coupled network of policing agencies" (Loader 2000: 333–334, emphasis added) and a partial shift in the control of policing away from the state towards political subcenters (Shearing 1996).

Perhaps the most pervasive impact of the shift in governance is the assumption now that the public police no longer (if they ever did) have a monopoly over responding to and preventing crime, but are expected to work in partnership with a range of other institutions, agencies, and individuals. There is no clear framework for these types of partnerships, but rather a set of expectations that police will work cooperatively with their partners (what we define as "third parties") in identifying and responding to crime, in ways that are likely to vary from community to community and problem to problem. We note that the notion of police partnerships is now entrenched in legislation in the United Kingdom with the requirement for police and local authorities to cooperatively develop crime reduction policies.

Police have become, as Ericson and Heggarty (1997) describe, the brokers for these partnerships – coordinating, providing information and resources, and responding to the risks. Risks are identified through the analysis of statistical data and technologies such as computerized crime mapping systems and utilized systematically by the police through management systems like Compstat (see Weisburd, Mastrofski, McNally *et al.* 2003). Interagency task forces and intervention teams with multiagency membership all utilize these technologies for crime control purposes.

We argue that the proliferation of third-party policing is an intrinsic outcome of these transformations in governance and the rise of the new regulatory state. Third-party policing is the result of global, regulatory processes and the accompanying pressures on the police to conform to contemporary regulatory practice. It is no coincidence that cooperation, risk management, problem identification and solving, and partnerships are the new primary foci for regulatory practice, as well as policing.

Dimensions of third-party policing

Third-party policing is defined and distinguished from other models of policing through the intrinsic links it has with transformations in governance more generally and in regulatory trends more particularly. The general form of third-party policing includes the police forming willing (or unwilling) partnerships and using legal levers to control and prevent crime. We describe the key dimensions of third-party policing below.

Purpose of action

We identify two primary purposes of third-party policing activities: crime prevention or crime control. In crime prevention, the police seek to anticipate crime problems and reduce the probability of an escalation of the underlying conditions that may cause crime problems to develop. Third-party policing that has crime prevention as its purpose of action operates to control those underlying criminogenic influences that may (or may not) lead to future crime problems. By contrast, third-party policing that seeks to control existing crime problems explicitly aims to alter the routine behaviors of those parties that the police believe might have some influence over the crime problem.

Initiators of third-party policing

In our analysis of third-party policing we focus on the public police as the initiators of third-party policing. There are, however, a variety of collectivities and individuals that have (or could) initiate similar activities. We define these activities, however, as third-party crime control in order to distinguish the activities of the public police as initiators from other potential initiators such as prosecutors, individual citizens, private security, community groups, and law enforcement agents in regulatory agencies. Whilst we focus exclusively in this chapter on the public police as the initiators of third-party policing, we recognize the plurality of potential initiators of similar activities and that different communities, states, and countries will most likely emphasize different types of third-party initiators.

Focal point

The focal point of third-party policing can be people, places, or situations (see Mazerolle and Roehl 1998; Smith 1998). Sometimes third-party policing efforts are directed specifically at categories of people such as young people, gang members or drug dealers. To address some types of crime problems, the focal point of third-party policing efforts might be directed against specific places, more often than not places that have been defined by the police as hot spots of crime. Drug dealing corners, parks where young people hang out, and public malls are typically the focal point of third-party policing activities that address specific places as opposed to certain categories of people.

The third focal point of third-party policing activities includes situations that give rise to criminogenic activity. An example of a criminogenic situation that gives rise to third-party policing responses include fights occurring in entertainment precincts. In third-party policing licensees are encouraged (or coerced) into partnerships that induce them to control the supply of alcohol and the off-site conduct of patron behavior (see the Valley Alcohol Management Partnership, an interdepartmental initiative in Brisbane, Queensland). In this third-party policing example, the police draw on legal provisions to *coerce* third-party partners such as government agencies (e.g., Department of Communities, Brisbane City Council), statutory authorities (Liquor Licensing Authority), and businesses (local pubs, bars, and nightclubs) into signing onto an Alcohol Management Accord. The accord governs the training of bartenders, the ratio of trained versus untrained personnel working at any time, the supply of alcohol to patrons, and the assistance provided by the local businesses to better disperse patrons throughout the night.

Types of problems

Third-party policing can be directed against a broad range of crime and quality of life problems (see Finn and Hylton 1994; National Crime Prevention Council 1996). However, most examples and evaluations of third-party policing comprise police efforts to control drug problems (see Green 1996; Eck and Wartell 1998; Mazerolle, Kadleck, and Roehl 1998) and disorderly behavior.

There is one main reason why third-party policing tends to proliferate in efforts to control low-level, street types of crime activity. In the new regulatory state, nodes for crime control are created not in a vacuum but as the result of centralized state policymaking. A higher-order, complex crime problem such as child sexual assault is the type of crime that grabs newspaper headlines and challenges the state to create wide-ranging policies to guide intervention. The crime control partners (doctors, police, educators, child safety officers) and legal levers (e.g., mandatory notification) for these types of problems are usually initiated at a state level and generally not by the police. As such, the police are just one partner (albeit important) in the process, but not the initiator of the third-party intervention.

Ultimate targets

The ultimate targets of third-party policing efforts are people involved in deviant behavior. In theory, the ultimate targets of third-party policing could include those persons engaged in any type of criminal behavior including domestic violence, white-collar offending, street crime, and drug dealing. In practice, however, the ultimate targets of third-party policing are typically street level offenders. Young people (see White 1998), gang members, drug dealers (Green 1996), vandals, and petty criminals typically feature as the ultimate targets of third-party policing.

Proximate targets, burden bearers and third parties

A key, defining feature of third-party policing is the presence of some type of third person (or third collectivity or regulatory node) that is utilized by the police in an effort to prevent or control crime. The list of potential third parties is extensive and can include property owners, parents, bar owners, shop owners, local and state governments, insurance companies, business owners, inspectors, and private security guards. Indeed, any person or entity that is engaged by the police to take on some type of role in controlling or preventing crime could potentially be identified as a third-party or what Buerger and Mazerolle (1998) refer to as "proximate targets" and what Mazerolle and Roehl (1998) have referred to as "burden-bearers." These are the people or entities that are coerced by the police and who carry the burden for initiating some type of action that is expected to alter the conditions that allow crime activity to grow or exist.

Proximate targets of third-party policing are often stakeholders or regulators that are identified by the police as being useful levers in controlling a crime problem. Indeed, the roles in third-party policing can change rapidly, they vary depending on the situation, sometimes reciprocal in nature and idiosyncratic to the problem at hand. Indeed, the proximate targets of a third-party policing activity in one context may become the ultimate targets of third-party policing in another context. Moreover, cooperative police partners in one context might become hostile "partners" in another context. We suggest that the dynamic nature of third-party policing reflects the fluidity and chaotic nature of crime prevention and crime control more generally.

There are many potential partners in third-party policing including education authorities who prosecute the parents of truants, bar owners who work with police to reduce street drunkenness, and property owners who screen potential tenants and maintain the physical conditions of their properties. However, a predominant group involved with police in third-party policing networks comprises the regulatory authorities. These are government agencies or officials with a function of regulating and maintaining standards in some legal activity, such as housing, building, business, or industry. Typical regulatory officials who might become involved in third-party policing include building, health and safety inspectors, and environmental protection officers. These officials are attractive to police because their functions are often accompanied by coercive powers to enter properties, inspect and search, issue closure orders, or take other retaliatory action against people in breach of the regulatory scheme. For police, partnering with such officials can act as a *de facto* extension of their own powers, as well as increasing their potential weapons and sanctions against people they suspect of involvement in criminal activity. But it is important to remember that crime control and prevention are not the primary aims of regulators, who instead have specific statutory functions to fulfil.

Legal basis

In third-party policing, compliance is obtained through the threat, or actual use of, some type of legal provision. As such, a key defining feature of third-party policing is that there must be some sort of legal basis (statutes, delegated or subordinate legislation or regulations, contractual relationships, torts laws) that shapes police coercive efforts to engage a third-party to take on a crime prevention or crime control role. The most common legal basis of third-party policing includes local, state, and federal statutes (including municipal ordinances and town by-laws), health and safety codes, uniform building standards, and drug nuisance abatement laws, and liquor licensing. We point out that the legal basis does not necessarily need to be directly related to crime prevention or crime control. Indeed, most third-party policing practices utilize laws and regulations that were not designed with crime control or crime prevention in mind (e.g., Health and Safety codes, Uniform Building Standards). For the vast majority of third-party policing activities, the legal basis that provides the coercive power for police to gain the "cooperation" of third parties derives from delegated legislation and obscure, non-criminal sources.

The partnerships between police and third parties occur within a legal framework that authorizes the conduct of the third-party – the building inspector, local authority, licensing agency, or parent. This legal framework establishes the source of authority of the third-party, the extent to which they can partner with police, the contexts in which they can do that, the types of action they can take against targets (criminogenic places and individuals), and the limits of their legal ability to cooperate with, or be coerced by, police.

In third-party policing, laws and legal mechanisms are directed at willing or unwilling non-offending third parties, with the object of facilitating or coercing them into helping to control the behavior of offending ultimate targets. The types of law used can be criminal or civil, and the distinction between these two categories is becoming increasingly blurred (see also Cheh 1991). The laws or legal devices used may be established specifically for the relevant crime control purpose, or may be directed at some other issue but coopted, by police, community groups, victims, or regulators, to achieve crime control or prevention goals.

Much of what we describe as third-party policing has arisen as an unintended consequence of law, rather than as its specific object (notable exceptions include Britain's Crime and Disorder Act 1998, which specifically mandates police networks). Third-party policing has arisen largely in the space known as "the shadow of the law" – that is, it is influenced by the law, uses the law where necessary, is limited in scope by the law, but often occurs in practice as an extralegal activity.

Types of sanctions and penalties

Civil sanctions and remedies vary greatly including court-ordered repairs of properties, fines, forfeiture of property or forced sales to meet fines and penalties, eviction, padlocking or temporary closure (typically up to a year) of a rented residential or commercial property, license restrictions and/or suspensions, movement restrictions, lost income from restricted hours and ultimately arrest and incarceration (see Mazerolle and Roehl 1998). Oftentimes, several civil remedies and sanctions may be initiated simultaneously to solve one problem.

Tools and techniques

Dozens of examples can be provided to illustrate the processes by which third parties are recruited and used by the police. Against the backdrop of a legal foundation to force a third-party to cooperate, the police operate on a continuum to engage third parties in their crime prevention or crime control activities. At the more benign end of the spectrum, the police can approach third parties and politely ask them to cooperate. The police might consult with members of the community as well as local property owners and ask them about ways that they see fit to control an existing crime problem or help them to alter underlying conditions that the police believe might lead to future crime problems. For these types of cases the ultimate sanctions that might be unleashed on third parties most likely go unnoticed. The police may themselves consciously utilize their persuasive powers, yet be unconscious about the alternative methods of coercion that they may resort to if the third-party target proves to be an unwilling participant. At the more coercive end of the spectrum the police engage third parties to participate in their crime control activities by threatening or actually initiating actions that compel the third party to cooperate. We point out that there are several stages in the forcible initiation of third parties in taking a crime control role: the first stage may involve a building services agency issuing citations to a property owner following building inspections of their property (see Green 1996). The latter stages of this most coercive practice involve the initiation of prosecutions against the non-compliant landowner and ultimately court-forced compliance by the third party.

Types of implementation

There are many different ways that the police implement third-party policing practices including third-party policing within the context of problem-oriented policing or situational crime prevention programs. Problem-oriented policing provides the management infrastructure (see Goldstein 1990) and step-wise approach to solving a crime problem (Eck and Spelman 1987) and situational crime prevention offers the police an appreciation for situational opportunities that might be exploited using third-party policing tactics (Clarke 1992; 1995). A review of the Goldstein awards from 1993 to 2003 reveals that about 50 percent of problem-oriented policing submissions incorporated third-party policing activities (see Mazerolle and Ransley 2005), yet just one third of third-party policing occurs within a situational crime prevention or problem-oriented policing framework.

The most common manifestation of third-party policing, however, is the *ad hoc* utilization of third-party principles initiated by patrol officers. These police are simply "flying by the seats of their pants," there is no script for them to follow, no police department policy that they are working within, and generally very little accountability for their actions.

Evaluation evidence

Measuring program performance and being able to say whether or not an intervention works is the bread and butter of sound policy decisionmaking. We use performance measurement for "evidenced-based policymaking" or making policies based on the outcomes of well-designed and executed evaluations. In the policing arena, Sherman and colleagues (1997) draw analogies with "evidence-based medicine" and defines evidenced-based policing as the use of the best available research on the outcomes of police work to implement guidelines and evaluate agencies, units, and

Table 10.1 *Summary of third-party policing evaluation evidence*

	All Studies		Studies where an effect size was calculated		Effect size outcomes (N = 23)	Most common third-party from all 77 studies	Most common type of legal lever
	N 77	percent 100	N 12	percent 100			
1. Drugs	21	27.3	8	66.7	13/18 (72 percent) outcomes were *desirable*	Residential and commercial property owners	Municipal ordinances (e.g., building & health & safety codes, nuisance abatement)
2. Violent crime	21	27.3	2	16.7	2/2 (100 percent) outcomes were *desirable*	Licenced premises owners	Code of practice with restrictions on serving of alcohol
3. Places	15	19.4	0	0	NA	Local councils	Municipal ordinances
4. Young people	11	14	1	8.3	1/1 (100 percent) outcome was *desirable*	Parents	Curfews
5. Property crime	9	12	1	8.3	2/2 (100 percent) outcomes were *undesirable*	Business owners	Theft prevention policies

Source: Mazerolle and Ransley (2005).

officers. In short, evidenced-based policing "uses the best evidence to shape the best practice" (Sherman *et al.* 1997: 4).

Mazerolle and Ransley (2005) conducted a search of the international literature to uncover evaluations of police tactics involving third-party policing. We categorized the studies into five groups: the use of third-party policing in controlling drugs, violent crimes, property crime, youth problems and crimes at criminogenic places. Our search strategies resulted in the identification of seventy-seven studies that included an evaluation component and also involved a third-party policing tactic. Of these, only twelve studies included sufficient data to calculate effect sizes (see Table 10.1). These twelve studies generated twenty-three effect sizes (odds ratios and standardized mean differences) across a variety of outcome measures (calls for service, arrests, field contacts, observations). The heterogeneous units of analysis and the variety of ways researchers had operationalized their outcome measures precluded calculation of mean effect sizes. As such, the individual outcomes were examined independently (see Mazerolle and Ransley 2005). Table 10.1 summarizes the evaluation evidence.

As the table shows, it appears that third-party policing is an effective mechanism to control drug problems. It is likely that it is an effective strategy for controlling violent crime and for dealing with young people. Whilst the number and quality of the reported outcomes limits our assessment of the effectiveness of third-party policing, Table 10.1 also indicates that third-party policing is somewhat ineffective at controlling property crime problems. Our review suggests that the majority of evidence collated about third-party policing involves property owners (commercial property owners in particular) as third parties. We were also able to uncover limited, yet important, evidence that identifies parents, local councils, housing authorities, and victims as third parties.

Despite our systematic attempts to uncover the evidence surrounding third-party policing tactics, limited evaluations of third-party policing initiatives exist in the research literature and very little systematic effort has been expended to document, collate, and consolidate the third-party policing research evidence. We suggest that there is a great need to continue to evaluate, document, and assess the effectiveness of third-party policing.

Conclusions

In this chapter we provided a synopsis of third-party policing and discussed the regulatory context of third-party policing. We described how third-party policing is part of a general transformation in contemporary society that has seen a movement from state sovereignty and control to networks of power. We argued that third-party policing is a manifestation of these broader societal trends. We have also discussed what we know about the effectiveness of third-party policing in preventing or responding to crime.

We argue that the future of the third-party policing approach is reinforced by a number of factors: first, third-party policing is not a bottom-up, grassroots innovation in the way that problem-oriented policing has been articulated and developed (see Goldstein 2003). Rather, third-party policing is part of a broader transformation in regulation. As such, the partnership approach is likely to be foisted upon the police in the future not from within, but rather from external forces. An example of this is Britain's Crime and Disorder Act 1998, which specifically mandates police networks. We are likely to see more of this type of top-down approach in the future. Second, the future of third-party policing is reinforced by early evidence that suggests it is a successful way of handling at least street level crime problems. Obviously, success breeds success and the more a strategy is found to reduce a problem, then the more likely it is to be used again.

But to examine the context, mechanics and effectiveness of third-party policing is to consider only half the equation – we also need to ask about the side effects of third-party policing, intentional and unintentional, positive and negative, on the partners who work with police, as well as on other groups in the community, on the proximate and ultimate targets, and even on the police organizations themselves (see Meares in this volume). Some of the questions raised in third-party policing include: How does third-party policing affect the community in which it is practiced? How equitably does it affect different communities, both internally and in comparison to other communities? Just as importantly, who is held accountable for the outcomes and impacts of third-party policing, and how? Are traditional police accountability mechanisms adaptable to take account of this new way of doing business, or is there a need for new mechanisms to be developed? In short, is third-party policing an ethical policing practice?

NOTE

Many of the arguments presented in this chapter are more fully developed in Mazerolle and Ransley (2006).

REFERENCES

Ayres, I. and Braithwaite, J. (1992). *Responsive regulation: Transcending the deregulation debate*. New York: Oxford University Press.

Braithwaite, J. (1999). Accountability and governance under the new regulatory state. *Australian Journal of Public Administration*, 58 (1), 90–97.

(2000). The new regulatory state and the transformation of criminology. *British Journal of Criminology*, 40, 222–238.

Braithwaite, J. and Drahos, P. (2000). *Global business regulation*. Melbourne: Cambridge University Press.

Buerger, M. E. and Mazerolle, L. G. (1998). Third-party policing: A theoretical analysis of an emerging trend. *Justice Quarterly*, 15 (2), 301–328.

Cheh, M. (1991). Constitutional limits on using civil remedies to achieve criminal law objectives: Understanding and transcending the criminal-civil law distinction. *Hastings Law Journal*, 42, 1325–1413.

(1998). Civil remedies to control crime: Legal issues and constitutional challenges. In L. G. Mazerolle and J. Roehl (eds.), *Civil remedies and crime prevention: Crime prevention studies*, 9 (pp. 45–66). New York: Criminal Justice Press.

Clarke, R. V. (1992). *Situational crime prevention: Successful case studies*. New York: Harrow and Heston.

(1995). Situational crime prevention. In M. Tonry and D. P. Farrington (eds.), *Building a safer society: Strategic approaches to crime prevention. Crime and justice*, 19 (pp. 91–150). Chicago: University of Chicago Press.

Eck, J. E. (1994). Drug places: Drug dealer choice and the spatial structure of illicit drug markets. Unpublished doctoral thesis, University of Maryland.

Eck, J. E. and Spelman, W. (1987). *Problem solving: Problem-oriented policing in Newport News*. Washington, DC: Police Executive Research Forum and National Institute of Justice.

Eck, J. E. and Wartell, J. (1998). Improving the management of rental properties with drug problems. In L. Green Mazerolle and J. Roehl (eds.), *Civil remedies and crime prevention: Crime prevention studies*, 9 (pp. 161–83). Monsey, NY: Criminal Justice Press.

Eck, J. E. and Weisburd, D. (1995). *Crime prevention studies: Crime and place*, 4. Monsey, NY: Criminal Justice Press.

Ericson, R. V. and Haggerty, K. D. (1997). *Policing the risk society*. Toronto: Toronto University Press.

Feeley, M. and Simon, J. (1994). Actuarial justice: The emerging new criminal law. In D. Nelken (ed.), *The futures of criminology* (pp. 173–201). London: Sage Publications.

Felson, M. (1994). *Crime and everyday life: Insights and implications for society*. Thousand Oaks, CA: Pine Forge Press.

Finn, P. and Hylton, M. O. (1994). *Using civil remedies for criminal behavior: Rational case studies and constitutional issues*. Washington, DC: National Institute of Justice, US Department of Justice.

Garland, D. (1996). The limits of the sovereign state. *British Journal of Criminology*, 36, 445–471.

(1997). "Governmentality" and the problem of crime: Foucault, criminology, sociology. *Theoretical Criminology*, 1 (2), 173–214.

Goldstein, H. (1990). *Problem-oriented policing*. New York: McGraw-Hill.

(2003). On further developing problem-oriented policing: The most critical need, the major impediments and a proposal. In J. Knutsson (ed.), *Crime prevention studies*, 15. Monsey, NY: Criminal Justice Press.

Green, L. (1996). *Policing places with drug problems*. Thousand Oaks, CA: Sage Publications.

Loader, I. (2000). Plural policing and democratic governance. *Social and legal studies*, 9 (3), 323–345.

Mazerolle, L. G. and Ransley, J. (2006). *Third-party policing*. Cambridge: Cambridge University Press.

Mazerolle, L. G. and Roehl, J. (1998). Civil remedies and crime prevention: An introduction. In L. Green Mazerolle and J. Roehl (eds.), *Civil remedies and crime prevention: Crime prevention studies*, 9 (pp. 1–20). Monsey, NY: Criminal Justice Press.

Mazerolle, L.G., Kadleck, C., and Roehl, J. (1998). Controlling drug and disorder problems: The role of place managers. *Criminology*, 36, 371–404.

National Crime Prevention Council. (1996). *New ways of working with local laws to prevent crime*. Washington, DC: National Crime Prevention Council.

O'Malley, P. (1992). Risk, power and crime prevention. *Economy and Society*, 21 (3), 252–275.

(2000). Risk, crime and prudentialism revisited. In K. Stenson and R. Sullivan (eds.), *Risk, crime and justice: The politics of crime control in liberal democracies* (ch. 5). London: Willan.

Scott, M. (2000). *Problem-oriented policing: Reflections on the first 20 years*. Washington, DC: Office of Community Oriented Policing Services, US Department of Justice.

Shearing, C. (1996). Reinventing policing: Policing as governance. In O. Marenin (ed.), *Policing change, changing police: International perspectives. Current Issues in Criminal Justice*, 4 (pp. 285–308). New York: Garland.

Shearing, C. and Stenning, P. (1987). *Private policing*. Thousand Oaks, CA: Sage Publications.

Sherman, L.W., Gottfredson, G., MacKenzie, D., Eck, J., Reuter, P., and Bushway, S. (1997). *Preventing crime: What works, what doesn't, what's promising: A report to the United State Congress*. College Park: Department of Criminology and Criminal Justice, University of Maryland.

Smith, M. (1998). Regulating opportunities: Multiple roles for civil remedies in situational crime prevention. In L. Green Mazerolle and J. Roehl (eds.), *Civil remedies and crime prevention: Crime prevention studies*, 9 (pp. 67–88). Monsey, NY: Criminal Justice Press.

Sparrow, M. (1994). *Imposing duties: Government's changing approach to compliance*. Westport: Praeger.

Sparrow, M. (2000). *The regulatory craft: Controlling risks, solving problems, and managing compliance*. Washington, DC: Brookings Press.

Weisburd D., Mastrofski, S. D., McNally, A. M., Greenspan, R., and Willis, J. J. (2003). Reforming to preserve: Compstat and strategic problem solving in American policing. *Criminology and Public Policy*, 2 (3), 421–456.

White, R. (1998). Curtailing youth: A critique of coercive crime prevention. In L. Green Mazerolle and J. Roehl (eds.), *Civil remedies and crime prevention: Crime prevention studies*, 9 (pp. 117–140). Monsey, NY: Criminal Justice Press.

11 *Critic*
Third-party policing: a critical view

Tracey L. Meares

According to Lorraine Mazerolle and Janet Ransley (2003), "third-party policing" describes police efforts to persuade or to coerce third parties, such as landlords, parents, local government regulators, and business owners to take on some responsibility for preventing crime or reducing crime problems. Obviously this definition seeks to distinguish policing directed at those who are and who might be criminal offenders from policing efforts directed at non-offending "others." Thus, the definition emphasizes the affinities that third-party policing has with other forms of civil regulation. Examples of such regulation abound. In an effort to ensure that corporations do not defraud stockholders, regulators place constraints, both civil and criminal, on accountants and lawyers. In an effort to make sure that employers do not violate civil rights laws, legislators have structured statutes so that violators pay plaintiffs' attorneys fees should the plaintiffs win. In this way, plaintiffs are persuaded to become "private attorneys general" helping public officials to enforce the law. In an effort to ensure that athletes do not take illegal drugs, the National Football League requires teams to complete random urine tests of players. The federal government is now pressuring the Major League Baseball to do the same. In this way, the sports leagues become third-party enforcers of laws prohibiting the use of certain drugs.

Given the pervasive forms of such regulation today, that such "third-party" efforts are becoming common in the enterprise of street crime control should hardly be surprising. In fact, we can redescribe even those efforts typically conceptualized as directed primarily at offenders in terms of third-party controls. One common consequence of criminal offending is a sanction in the form of a prison sentence or fine. However, it is silly to think that only the offender suffers the opprobrium that accompanies such sanctions. Families of the offender, as well as friends, can also suffer (e.g., Braman 2004). In a world in which the costs associated with formal punishment extend beyond the actual offender to non-offenders, we should expect such third parties to engage in efforts to persuade, or even informally coerce, potential offenders to refrain from crime. And,

207

social theorists have long explained how informal norms combine with formal sanctions to effect deterrence.[1] When informal social controls are supported by legal sanctions, social costs are made more salient so that behavior is better regulated.

Importantly, informal controls are not relevant simply when they support formal legal sanctions. Informal controls also involve the normative processes and ethics of social interaction that regulate everyday social life, as well as the mobilization of community that occurs in response to problem behaviors (Doyle and Luckenbill 1991). Thus, informal social controls are effective in several ways: inhibition of problem behaviors, facilitation of conformity, and restraint of social deviance once it appears. The key is to see that that evaluation of the deterrent effect of a policy cannot depend simply on the likely impact of formal punishment, but, rather, must also include some kind of assessment of the *reciprocity* between legal and social controls. It is not enough to ask whether a potential offender will be persuaded not to offend by assessing how he will compare the costs of potential punishment against the benefit of engaging in the crime. We also need to know about the potential offender's community context and social role to be able to begin to make assessments regarding the potential effectiveness of a planned formal legal sanction.

My task here is not to bring all policing efforts under the potentially commodious umbrella of third-party policing, however. While it should be clear that much of traditional criminal law enforcement and policing can be described as "third-party policing," in this volume the meaning of the term is more limited. Contributors to this volume have pinpointed third-party policing as those relatively recent efforts by many policing agencies that recognize that much social control is exercised by institutions other than the police and that crime can be managed through agencies besides those concerned primarily with dispensing criminal justice, such as the police. Specific examples include nuisance abatement, anti-gang loitering laws, and public housing eviction policies among others (Mazerolle and Ransley in this volume).

The primary purpose of this chapter is to review the arguments made by the critics of third-party policing efforts. Although the concerns of most of these critics are based in constitutional law, some critics make a special effort to explicate the potentially destructive racial dynamics of some third-party policing strategies. These arguments target the distributional effects of exactly which groups bear the burden of third-party law enforcement. After reviewing these arguments, this chapter will conclude by attempting to address the costs and benefits of third-party policing strategies with special emphasis on the race-based critiques of these approaches.

Civil libertarian critique

One basic criticism of government targeting of third-party non-offenders to persuade or informally coerce the so-called "real offenders" to refrain from lawbreaking is that by targeting third parties the government uses its power to restrict the liberty of those who "really aren't doing anything wrong." The essence of civil libertarianism is that coercive government power should be deployed only in those instances in which it is necessary to protect individuals from the use of force or fraud by others. Under this view, a threat to levy a civil fine against a landlord in order to persuade her to better scrutinize and identify potential drug-dealing renters is patently impermissible. According to libertarian beliefs, state power ought to be trained upon the drug dealer, not the landlord, as the dealers are the true wrongdoers.

Private groups, legislators, and other governmental officials have an answer to this foundational criticism. Criminal offenders are sometimes difficult to locate and bring to justice through the conventional criminal justice apparatus. In fact, criminal liability itself has, over time, expanded to address this problem. We punish offenders not only for the crime of robbery, but also for the offense of *attempted* robbery. Further, prosecutors often utilize offenses such as conspiracy and solicitation in order to ferret out and punish crime before it takes place. Neither the doctrine of conspiracy nor of solicitation actually requires that the prohibited act occur. The doctrines require simply that a person agrees with another to commit a criminal offense (conspiracy),[2] or request that another engage in conduct that constitutes a crime (solicitation).[3] Additionally, we punish those who assist others in criminal offending under the doctrine of accomplice liability even when the accomplice has not himself or herself committed any act that most would deem criminal. According to the doctrine of accomplice liability, individuals can be punished when they make a decision to further the criminal act of another and engage in an act that furthers the principal's criminal act. In addition to all of this, civil remedies have long been used to hold offenders to account outside of the traditional criminal justice context.

Prophylactic measures, combined with civil remedies, provide law enforcers with a wider range of alternatives to crime control that are less costly than traditional criminal justice approaches. Third-party policing, then, is simply a small extension of this trend. There is, however, one basic difference between third-party policing efforts and prophylactic criminal and civil remedies directed at wrongdoers: those co-opted into enforcement efforts are not themselves wrongdoers in the usual sense.

This basic difference is a key difference for critics of third-party policing concerned with civil liberties. Such critics might point to *Bennis* v. *Michigan* as a paradigmatic case of third-party policing gone awry. In *Bennis*, a car was seized from Mr. Bennis after he had been convicted of committing an indecent act with a prostitute while the two were in the car. Mrs. Bennis claimed that her interest in the car could not be forfeit to the State of Michigan because she was completely unaware of her husband's activities. The United States Supreme Court, in a plurality opinion, nonetheless ruled against her. As a result of the Court's decision, the State of Michigan was allowed to keep the Bennis family 1977 Pontiac, which was paid for primarily with money Mrs. Bennis earned from babysitting.

The *Bennis* plurality stated that there was a long history of permitting forfeiture against innocent owners in order to *prevent* further use of illicit property. The reasoning is obvious: if an innocent owner knows that there is a risk that her property might be forfeit if someone else uses the property for illegal purposes, she likely will take greater care than she otherwise would to ensure that her property is not so used. That is, she will become a third-party police officer.[4]

The problem with this reasoning, according to civil libertarians, is not whether the procedure works or not; rather, the problem is that the forfeiture process is fundamentally unfair under basic principles of due process of law. For one thing, the deterrence rationale that applies to Mrs. Bennis potentially implies that Michigan can punish Mrs. Bennis for her husband's crime. Such punishment is clearly inconsistent with due process. The Supreme Court has recognized the due process right of an innocent person to be free of punishment.[5] Mrs. Bennis was not tried and convicted before her punishment – the forfeiture of her interest in the family car – was meted out by the state. Indeed, she could not possibly have been convicted for the crime her husband committed. Mrs. Bennis had no awareness of her husband's activities, so she possessed no criminal intent to engage in the offense or to further it in any way. Moreover, Mrs. Bennis had engaged in no act that could be considered criminal. While her husband was involved with a prostitute, Mrs. Bennis was simply waiting for her husband to come home for dinner.

Even if one were convinced that Michigan's actions in this case were not punitive, but instead were merely regulatory,[6] one might still conclude that the state's action offended due process. Deterring an activity such as prostitution is, of course, a legitimate aim of a state's police powers; however, due process principles require that government respect the rights of property owners and afford them procedural protections under civil law as well as criminal law. The Constitution's text is clear: government may not deprive individuals of life, liberty, or property without providing due process of law. Unfortunately for Mrs. Bennis and for others similarly situated, the procedural protections required to satisfy constitutional minimums are minimal.[7] Still, the fact that a particular procedure meets the minimum requirements of procedural due process does not mean that critics are without recourse. Critics often contend that an enforcement operation like that in *Bennis* is inconsistent with substantive due process even when the operation meets the constitutional requirements of procedural due process. As Mary Cheh (1994: 25) has neatly summarized:

Substantive due process analysis ordinarily proceeds along two tracks. Almost all laws touching social and economic matters are judged under a lenient rational-basis test, while laws that interfere with certain intimate and personal rights, such as child rearing, marriage and divorce, and use of contraceptives, are judged under a vigorous strict-scrutiny test. The rational basis test is easily satisfied. Ordinary social and economic regulation is presumed constitutional, and so long as the law serves any permissible police power objective, it will be upheld. Legislatures are free to decide, without court interference, how they will tax, regulate, and control behavior.

Under these analyses a litigant must prove either that the forfeiture is so unreasonable as to fail rational basis, or that there is a protected interest at issue such that the more rigorous strict scrutiny test applies. Both of these types of arguments fail more often than they succeed.

This review of *Bennis* and related constitutional doctrines might suggest that it is futile for civil libertarians to adopt these constitutional arguments to block third-party policing efforts. Such a conclusion would be mistaken. Consider litigation against anti-gang loitering ordinances and curfews, which some consider third-party policing tools, and which have become increasingly popular in municipalities. Loitering and curfew ordinances are designed to keep teens from congregating at night to attract the ire of rival gang members and pick fights, or standing on corners to help friends hidden in alleys to sell drugs. By enforcing these laws, it is thought that police can help adults simply by acting as additional eyes and ears in the neighborhood. Some of these laws also are designed to make parents more accountable by penalizing parents whose children violate the ordinance. These laws have been met with resistance and constitutional challenge, and in many cases, the civil libertarian critics have been successful. Chicago's first anti-gang loitering law was deemed unconstitutionally vague, a fate shared by numerous "loitering with intent" statutes around the country. Curfews in Washington, DC (*Hutchins* v. *District of Columbia*), San Diego (*Numez* v. *City of San Diego*), and other cities (e.g., *City of Maquoketo* v. *Russell*) have likewise been deemed to abridge the due process rights of teens and their parents.

Ultimately the civil libertarian critique of government agencies involved in third-party policing boils down to one basic point: a concern with the scope of accountable government power. Civil libertarian critics believe, with some justification, that the greater the government's power, the more difficult it is to control; therefore, we all are better off if government power is limited as much as possible. One suspects that these critics would not be so concerned if they could be persuaded government power in these areas was utilized in a rational and transparent manner. Unfortunately, to the extent that preferred strategies utilize civil justice and political mechanisms as controls, as opposed to criminal justice mechanisms, it becomes that much more difficult to keep track of government activity and to limit it. Police discretion, always a powerful tool even when confined to criminal justice processing, potentially grows to almost unrecognizable proportions once let out of the criminal justice cage.

Racial equity critique

Some critics of third-party policing strategies have complained about a specific problem that could be considered a subset of the critique detailed above. Namely, these critics are worried that as third-party policing strategies loosen the reins on governmental discretion regarding whom to engage as the law is enforced, such discretion inevitably will be exercised more often against poor and minority-race citizens than against those who are not poor and/or of minority race.

Consider as an example Professor Dorothy Roberts's (1999) race-based critique of an anti-gang loitering law adopted by the City of Chicago in 1992. The ordinance exhibited unique third-party policing features. The Chicago City Council passed the ordinance to restrict gang-related congregations in public ways (Chicago, Il., Code § 8-4-015 1992). The ordinance was designed to respond to the grievances of citizens concerned about commonly occurring criminal street gang activity in their neighborhoods, such as drive-by shootings, fighting, and open-air drug dealing. By loitering in alleyway entrances and on street corners, drug dealers both solicited business and warned hidden compatriots of police patrols. The ordinance empowered designated police officers in specified areas to approach groups of three or more people loitering "with no apparent purpose" provided that those officers had reasonable cause to believe that *at least one member of the group* was a street gang member and ask the group to move along. If the group refused, then the officer was entitled to arrest the group. The third-party policing aspect is clear. Even those individuals whom the police had no reason to suspect were gang members, were potentially subject to arrest merely because of the company those individuals chose to keep (and where they chose to keep the company). By subjecting non-gang members to liability, municipal regulators incentivized them to help police constrain the behavior of their gang-involved compatriots.

Professor Roberts's (1999: 775) assessment of the law is blunt: "expansive and ambiguous allocations of police discretion are likely to unjustly burden members of unpopular or minority groups." In support of this claim, Roberts (1999: 785) points to the fact that in 1995 46.4 percent of people arrested for vagrancy across US cities were black even though blacks made up only 13 percent of the nation's population. No doubt a critic such as Roberts would also take data compiled by Justin Ready, Lorraine Green Mazerolle, and Elyse Revere (1998), demonstrating that 91 percent of the tenants evicted from public housing developments in Jersey City as part of a civil remedy program to achieve greater level of order in those developments were black, as evidence of the unjust burden suffered by minorities as third-party policing strategies are implemented (Ready, Mazerolle, and Revere 1998).

An assumption that minorities are unfairly burdened by third-party policing strategies that are designed to give law enforcers more flexibility to address crime and disorder is based upon a fundamental premise – the weak political power of minority groups. Consider a famous *Yale Law Journal* article written in 1960 by William O. Douglas. In the piece Douglas railed against the argument that anti-loitering laws were beyond constitutional reproach. It was naïve to trust contemporary communities to apply such laws evenhandedly, Douglas asserted, because those arrested under such laws typically came "from minority groups" with insufficient political clout "to protect themselves" and without "the prestige to prevent an easy laying-on of hands by the police" (Douglas 1960: 13). When the court did ultimately deem traditionally worded loitering laws unconstitutionally vague in *Papachristou* v. *City of Jacksonville*, Douglas wrote the court's opinion.

Unlike the more general strategy of civil libertarians, advocates of constitutional arguments designed to protect minority groups from overweening police power have achieved more success in the Supreme Court and lower courts. In the 1960s the prevailing sense of the court was that the coercive incidence of law enforcement, in both the North and South, was concentrated most heavily on minority citizens, who by virtue of their exclusion from the political process had no say about whether those policies were just. The result was the systematic devaluation of both the liberty of individual minority citizens and the well-being of minorities as a group. By insinuating courts deeply into the process of criminal-law enforcement, the federal constitutionalization of state police procedures was intended to correct this imbalance (Klarman 1991). Similarly, in the political context of the 1960s, law enforcement officials were accountable only to representatives of the white majority. Indeed, for precisely this reason, the police predictably used their discretion to harass and repress minorities. Insisting that law-enforcement authority be exercised according to hyper-precise rules was a device for *impeding* the responsiveness of law enforcers to the demands of racist white political establishments. Such rules also made it much easier for courts to detect and punish racially motivated abuses of authority.

Thus, by pointing to racial imbalances in the enforcement of loitering laws, curfews, public housing evictions, and nuisance abatement laws, modern critics intentionally draw upon the particularized racial history of such strategies – and the courts' pointed disfavor of them. But, one question is whether the costs of such strategies, even considering the specific race-based arguments offered by critics such as Dorothy Roberts, outweigh their benefits.

Costs and benefits

As noted above, police departments across the country have turned to third-party policing strategies as seemingly low-cost alternatives to traditional criminal justice apparatus to prevent crime. If such strategies are successful, the benefits are clear: reduced crime for (presumably) less money, as civil justice mechanisms typically are less costly than criminal justice ones. There is a dearth of available evaluations, but the initial studies are promising. For example, Jeffrey Grogger (2002) has found through an empirical analysis of civil injunctions designed to reduce gang violence that in the first year after the injunctions are imposed violent crime falls by 5 to 10 percent. Moreover, in a recent edited volume, Lorraine Mazerolle and her colleagues (Mazerolle and Roehl 1998) collect studies of various civil remedy programs designed to control drug problems. Most of the studies contained in the volume point to the effectiveness of such programs at reducing levels of targeted drug offenses.

The case for third-party policing, then, might be made on this evidence. Note, however, that many third-party policing strategies are place-based programs. And, if such place-based programs caused crime reduction in the targeted areas while simply diverting crime elsewhere, that would be an obvious cost. Geographic displacement of crime is a serious concern when place-oriented interventions are employed (Committee to Review Research 2004: 240). Interestingly, the small body of research pertaining directly to this issue with respect to third-party policing indicates the *opposite* – a diffusion of crime control *benefits* (e.g., Mazerolle and Roehl

1998) to areas contiguous to the places targeted for third-party policing interventions.

Still, the fact that a few studies indicate some benefit through reduction in crime does not resolve the accounting for costs and benefits in favor of the benefit side of the ledger. While promising, the available studies do not point to sizable results. Moreover, to be confident about a cost-benefit analysis, one must ask in this context whether such crime reduction benefits would be achieved through more traditional policing methods – methods that are less likely to raise the hackles of civil liberties proponents (Caulkins 1998). The results of such an analysis are difficult to attain to say the least, but without such results, police departments and other governmental entities ought to tread lightly before embarking on strategies that present the kinds of grave risks to civil liberties discussed earlier. Critics of third-party policing have a point when they assert that third-party policing interventions cannot be justified on crime reduction, even if substantial, alone.

Presumably the critics whose arguments are sound in racial equity concerns would agree with this assessment. Urban minority residents face more crime than other non-minority groups, so such residents would likely benefit in the form of reduced crime, nuisance, and the like in their communities. However, such residents may not believe that reductions in say, observable open-air drug selling[8] are worth the costs in terms of civil liberties incursions. The case for benefits needs more.

An additional argument that can be made on the benefits side is that third-party strategies potentially can help to change the social dynamics of neighborhoods in ways that promote crime-reducing norms. One way to do this is to point out that traditional criminal law enforcement methods potentially can *impede* a community's ability to resist and reduce crime. Traditional law enforcement methods rely on criminal justice processing and punishment – especially incarceration – to achieve crime reduction.

Scholars have articulated theories describing how mass incarceration concentrated at the community or neighborhood level could hamper institutions of informal social control (Nagin 1998; Rose and Clear 1998). Drawing on Shaw and McKay's (1969) foundational work on the relationship between the social disorganization of neighborhoods and the persistence of high crime rates at the community level, these scholars have focused on various social processes, including (1) the prevalence, strength, and interdependence of social networks; (2) the extent of collective supervision by neighborhood residents and the level of personal responsibility they assume for addressing neighborhood problems; and (3) the rate of resident participation in voluntary and formal organizations (Sampson and Wilson 1995; Wilson 1996; Rose and Clear 1998).

The hypothesis is straightforward: When the processes of community social organization are prevalent and strong, crime and delinquency should be less prevalent, and vice versa. Burgeoning research suggests that mass incarceration following from traditional law enforcement methods inhibits social processes that support crime reduction and prevention (Lynch and Sabol 2004); thus, law enforcement that does *not* rely heavily on incarcerative approaches, like third-party policing strategies, may be less harmful than traditional law enforcement approaches to fragile urban poor community structures and may indeed *support* those structures in ways that lead to less crime.

Specifically, civil remedies can be democratizing in a sense. Such remedies typically are not reactive; rather, they are proactive. Neighborhood residents who have been (or feel they have been) underserved by policing organizations historically often can turn to civil remedies as an alternative to traditional strategies. Indeed, an argument can be made that third-party strategies are especially *empowering* to residents of disadvantaged neighborhoods in a way that traditional policing often is not. That is, state-sponsored strategies that encourage individuals to work with one another can help to sustain a healthy social organization dynamic that can be harnessed in favor of crime reduction and resistance (Meares 2002). Such forces can in themselves be supportive of neighborhood collective efficacy, which itself is associated with lower crime at the neighborhood level (Sampson, Raudenbush, and Earls 1997).

Finally, there may be normative concerns that can be arrayed against the civil libertarians' own arguments, whether those arguments are grounded in individual libertarian concerns or take on a more group-based, race-specific character. It is important to pay attention to where the groundswell of support for many third-party policing strategies lies. In no small number of cases, the support for these strategies comes from the residents of high-crime neighborhoods who are themselves often members of minority groups – the very people who face a heightened risk of criminal victimization and who live with the destructive impact of crime on the economic and social life of their communities and who feel the pinch of these laws in a meaningful way.

There is often little room in either the general civil libertarian critique or the more specifically racialized critique for the voice of this group of people, but it should be clear that as a normative matter their voices and votes ought to count for something. Of course, deciding that one ought to listen to the people who are most affected by third-party policing strategies does not guarantee a "right answer" to balancing issues inherent in these debates. There is no perspective-free way to determine whether the general structure of third-party approaches violates the Constitution.

Some individual or set of individuals, judging the question in the light of her own experiences and values, must decide whether particular policies embody a reasonable balance between liberty and order. The question is who should decide.

To illustrate, consider an exchange from the City Council hearings on the Chicago gang-loitering ordinance. At the hearings, dozens of inner-city residents – from church leaders, to representatives of local neighborhood associations, to ordinary citizens – testified in favor of the proposed law. Harvey Grossman, Illinois director of the ACLU, testified against it:

> I am a lawyer, and I spend a great deal of time doing nothing more than reviewing ordinances and statutes, and it turns into a little bit of a long exam game. . . . We pick apart the statute. We focus on [a] word or [a] phrase, and we try to say why that phrase might or might not be constitutional. (Transcript of Meeting before Chicago City Council Committee on Police and Fire 107. May, 18, 1992)

He then proceeded to "pick apart" the gang-loitering ordinance, demonstrating the tension between it and various judicial precedents.

Alderman William Beavers, a council member who represented a poor and high-crime minority district on Chicago's south side, objected to this bookish conception of how to appraise the constitutionality of the law. "I don't know if you are attuned to what's going on in these neighborhoods," he told Grossman. "Maybe I need to take you out there and show you what's really going on" (ibid.: 119). Grossman replied that that wouldn't be necessary: "I think our ability to come together and to try to resolve issues [like this] really doesn't . . . depend on if I see what's happening in your neighborhood or you see what's happening in my neighborhood." Rather, what it does depend on is "empathy or ability to understand what's happening to other people and, two, some commitment, some intellectual integrity and some commitment to principle. And the principle that I am suggesting to you is inviolate. It doesn't change" (ibid.: 120).

The tough issues surrounding the new community policing obviously aren't an "exam game" for the median inner-city voter. The people who experience both law enforcement and crime are people who think empathy is motivated by "inviolate" "intellectual" "principles" and just "doesn't depend," "really," on "see[ing] what's happening in [inner-city] neighborhood[s]." The values at stake and the difficult tradeoffs that must be made are not abstractions. They are real. This perhaps is a place where critics and advocates can come together. Procedural justice scholars have suggested that a reliance on procedures is useful when correct outcomes are not obvious to disparate members of a group. Groups may not always decide on an outcome, but they can almost always decide on procedures that everyone finds satisfying (Lind and Tyler 1988). Thus, to the extent that we achieve very little agreement on constitutional substance, perhaps the best strategy to adopt as third-party policing goes forward is to insure that those most affected are insinuated into the political process and that their voices are heard.

Conclusion

As we progress into the twenty-first century, it is likely that non-traditional approaches to policing will continue to include strategies that appear to stray from criminal justice norms. This is to be expected in a world in which community policing, with its reliance on police and citizen inter-action, increasingly focuses upon problems that are not obviously con-nected to crime control such as garbage clean-up, neighborhood marches, and even community prayer vigils. The third-party policing strategies reviewed in this volume clearly are congenial to this brave new world of policing. But the question remains whether this new world adequately recognizes the values that American citizens have always held dear. Civil liberties proponents fear not, but perhaps such critics have not taken ade-quate account of the instrumental benefits to be obtained through the new policing. Instrumental benefits aside, both critics and proponents of third-party policing seem to have overlooked the potential for polit-ical engagement that the new policing strategies can offer to citizens – especially to crime-beleaguered citizens of poor urban communities. Whatever else may be said about these approaches in terms of crime reduction, the normative benefits of expanded political participation for those who have traditionally been shut out of governmental processes may be worth the cost of these controversial programs.

NOTES

1. Zimring and Hawkins (1997) explain this point by distinguishing the educa-tive and deterrent effects of punishment. Likewise, Williams and Hawkins (1992) explain the conceptual differences between the deterrent effect of legal sanctions and social control through informal mechanisms.
2. A person is guilty of conspiracy with another person to commit a crime if with the purpose of promoting or facilitating its commission he: (a) agrees with such other person or persons that they or one of them will engage in conduct which constitutes such crime or an attempt or solicitation to commit such crime; or (b) agrees to aid such other person or persons in the planning or commission of such crime (Model Penal Code, § 5.03).
3. A person is guilty of solicitation to commit a crime if with the purpose of pro-moting or facilitating its commission he commands, encourages, or requests another person to engage in specific conduct which would constitute such

crime or an attempt to commit such crime or which would establish his complicity in its commission or attempted commission (Model Penal Code, § 5.02).

4. Note that one dissenter in *Bennis*, Justice Stevens, clearly disagrees with this point (see *Bennis* at 1009, Stevens, J., dissenting). Justice Stevens declares that the goal of deterrence is not served by punishing "a person who has taken all reasonable steps to prevent an illegal act."

5. In fact, the court, relying on substantive due process principles, held that once a criminal is found "not guilty" of a crime, the State may not impose punishment" (*Foucha v. Louisiana*).

6. *Salerno* vs. *United States* describes preventive detention as regulatory rather than punitive and thus requiring more lenient procedural protection under the Due Process Clause.

7. For example, see *18 USC. 981* (1988 & Supp. V 1993) for a discussion of the government's civil money laundering forfeiture provision or *21 U.S.C. 881* (1988 & Supp. V 1993) which authorizes the civil forfeiture of property connected to narcotics activity. Forfeiture is authorized in more than 140 federal statutes and most states have one or more laws permitting forfeiture (Steven L. Kessler [1994]. Civil and Criminal Forfeiture: Federal and State Practice 2.01, at 2–1). Typically the government can effect its seizure without notice to the owner and without giving the owner a prior opportunity to object. See, for example, *19 USC. 1609*–1615 (1988 & Supp. V 1993), the US Customs Service's procedures for seizure, forfeiture, and recovery of seized property.

8. I should acknowledge here that the two noted aims do not necessary proceed in step. That is, it is certainly possible to imagine a world in which there is much less open-air drug selling and a simultaneous increase in consumption.

REFERENCES

Braman, D. (2004). *Doing time on the outside: The hidden effects on families and communities*. Ann Arbor: University of Michigan Press.

Caulkins, J. P. (1998). The cost effectiveness of civil remedies: The case of drug control interventions. In L. G. Mazerolle and J. Roehl (eds.), *Civil remedies and crime prevention*, 9. Monsey, NY: Criminal Justice Press.

Cheh, M. M. (1994). Can something this easy, quick, and profitable also be fair? Runaway civil forfeiture stumbles on the Constitution. *New York Law School Law Review*, 29, n1.

Committee to Review Research on Police Policy and Practices. (2004). *Fairness and effectiveness in policing: The evidence*. Washington, DC: National Academies Press.

Douglas, W. O. (1960). Vagrancy and arrest on suspicion. *Yale Law Journal*, 70, n1: 1–14.

Doyle, D. P. and Luckenbill, D. F. (1991). Mobilizing law in response to collective problems: A test of Black's Theory Of Law. *Law & Society Review*, 25, 103–116.

Grogger, J. (2002). The effects of civil gang injunctions on reported violent crime. *Journal of Law and Economics*, 45, 69.

Klarman, M. J. (1991). The puzzling resistance to political process theory. *Virginia Law Review, 77*, 747–766.

Lind, E. A. and Tyler, T. R. (1988). *The social psychology of procedural justice.* New York: Plenum Press.

Lynch, J. P. and Sabol, W. J. (2004). Assessing the effects of mass incarceration on informal social control in communities. *Criminology and Public Policy, 3*, 267–294.

Mazerolle, L. and Ransley, J. (2003). *Third-party policing: Prospects, challenges and implications for regulators.* Paper presented at the Current Issues In Regulations: Enforcement and Compliance Conference, Melbourne.

Mazerolle, L. G. and Roehl, J. (eds.). (1998). *Civil remedies and crime prevention.* Monsey, NY: Criminal Justice Press.

Meares, T. L. (2002). Praying for community policing. *California Law Review, 90*, 1593–1634.

Nagin, D. (1998). Criminal deterrence research at the outset of the twenty-first century. In M. Tonry (ed.), *Crime and justice: A review of research.* Chicago: University of Chicago Press.

Ready, J., Mazerolle, L. G., and Revere, E. (1998). Getting evicted from public housing: An analysis of the factors influencing eviction decisions in six public housing sites. In L. G. Mazerolle and J. Roehl (eds.), *Civil remedies and crime prevention.* Monsey, NY: Criminal Justice Press.

Roberts, D. (1999). Foreword: Race, vagueness, and the social meaning of order maintenance policing: Supreme court issue. *Journal of Criminology and Criminal Law, 89*, n3: 776–785.

Rose, D. and Clear, T. (1998). Incarceration, social capital and crime: Implications for social disorganization theory. *Criminology, 36*, 441–480.

Sampson, R. J. and Wilson, W. J. (1995). Toward a theory of race, crime and urban inequality. In J. Hagan and R. Peterson (eds.), *Crime and inequality.* Stanford: Stanford University Press.

Sampson, R. J., Raudenbush, S. W., and Earls, F. (1997). Neighborhoods and violent crime: a multilevel study of collective efficacy. *Science, 277*, 918–925.

Shaw, C. R. and McKay, H. D. (rev. ed. 1969). *Juvenile delinquency and urban areas: A study of rates of delinquency in relationship to differential characteristics of local communities in American cities.* Chicago: University of Chicago Press.

Transcript of Meeting before Chicago City Council Committee on Police and Fire 107 (1992, May 18).

Williams, R. and Hawkins, R. (1992). Wife assault, costs of arrest, and the deterrence process. *Journal of Research in Crime and Delinquency, 29*, n3: 292–294.

Wilson, W. J. (1996). *When work disappears: The world of the new urban poor.* New York: Knopf.

Zimring, F. E. and Hawkins, G. (1997). *Crime is not the problem: Lethal violence in America.* New York: Oxford University Press.

CASES CITED

Bennis v. *Michigan,* 116 S. Ct. 994 (1996).

City of Maquoketa v. *Russell,* 484 N.W.2d 179 Iowa (1992).

Foucha v. *Louisiana,* 504 US 71, 95–98. (1992).

Hutchins v. *District of Columbia,* 942 F. Supp. 665 D.D.C. (1996).

Nunez v. *City of San Diego*, 114 F.3d 935 9th Cir. (1997).
Salerno vs. *United States*, 481 US 739 (1987).

STATUTES CITED

18 USC. *981* (1988 & Supp. V 1993).
19 USC. *1609*–1615 (1988 & Supp. V 1993)
21 USC. *881* (1988 & Supp. V 1993)
Chicago, Il., Code § 8-4-015 (1992).

Part VI

Hot spots policing

12   *Advocate*
Hot spots policing as a model for police innovation

David Weisburd and Anthony A. Braga

Looking at the major police innovations of the last decade, what is most striking from a criminologist's perspective is the extent to which new programs and practices have been developed without reference to either criminological theory or research evidence. Some institutional theorists might argue that this is understandable given the limited ability of police agencies to reliably demonstrate their successes, and the political environments within which police agencies must operate (Meyer and Rowan 1977; Mastrofski and Ritti 2000; Willis, Mastrofski, and Weisburd 2004). However, this reality is very much at odds with a model of policing that would seek to draw new policies and practices from a solid research base (Sherman 1998), and suggests an approach to policing that is based more on intuition and luck than on research and experimentation. Recent studies of the adoption of police innovation reinforce this problematic portrait of American police innovation. Widely touted programs such as Community Policing or Compstat have been widely diffused across the landscape of American policing absent any reliable evidence that they accomplish the goals that they set out to achieve at the outset (Weisburd, Mastrofski, McNally *et al.* 2003; Weisburd and Eck 2004).

In this context, "hot spots policing" represents a particularly important innovation on the American police scene. Its origins can be traced to innovations in criminological theory, and it was subjected to careful empirical study before it was diffused widely across American police agencies. In the following pages we describe the origins of hot spots policing in theory and basic research, and the research evidence that has been developed to support hot spots policing practices. We will argue that there is strong theoretical justification for hot spots policing, and that evaluation evidence provides a solid empirical basis for continued experimentation and development of this approach.

From theory to practice: an evidence-based model

The idea of hot spots policing can be traced to recent critiques of traditional criminological theory. For most of the last century criminologists have focused their understanding of crime on individuals and communities (Nettler 1978; Sherman 1995). In the case of individuals, criminologists have sought to understand why certain people as opposed to others become criminals (e.g., see Hirschi 1969; Akers 1973; Gottfredson and Hirschi 1990; Raine 1993), or to explain why certain offenders become involved in criminal activity at different stages of the life course or cease involvement at other stages (e.g., see Moffitt 1993; Sampson and Laub 1993). In the case of communities, criminologists have often tried to explain why certain types of crime or different levels of criminality are found in some communities as contrasted with others (e.g., see Shaw and McKay 1972; Sampson and Groves 1989; Bursik and Grasmick 1993; Agnew 1999) or how community-level variables, such as relative deprivation, low socioeconomic status, or lack of economic opportunity may affect individual criminality (e.g., see Cloward and Ohlin 1960; Wolfgang and Ferracuti 1967; Merton 1968; Agnew 1992). In most cases, research on communities has focused on the "macro" level, often studying states (Loftin and Hill 1974), cities (Baumer, Lauritsen, Rosenfeld, and Wright 1998), and neighborhoods (Sampson 1985; Bursik and Grasmick 1993).

This is not to say that criminologists did not recognize that the opportunities found at more micro levels of place can impact upon the occurrence of crime. Edwin Sutherland, for example, whose main focus was upon the learning processes that bring offenders to participate in criminal behavior, noted in his classic criminology textbook that the immediate situation influences crime in many ways. For example, "a thief may steal from a fruit stand when the owner is not in sight but refrain when the owner is in sight; a bank burglar may attack a bank which is poorly protected but refrain from attacking a bank protected by watchmen and burglar alarms" (Sutherland 1947: 5). Nonetheless, Sutherland, as other criminologists, did not see micro crime places as a relevant focus of criminological study. This was the case, in part, because crime opportunities provided by such places were assumed to be so numerous as to make concentration on specific places of little utility for theory or policy. In turn, criminologists traditionally assumed that situational factors played a relatively minor role in explaining crime as compared with the "driving force of criminal dispositions" (Clarke and Felson 1993: 4; Trasler 1993). Combining an assumption of a wide array of criminal opportunities, and a view of offenders that saw them as highly motivated to commit crime, it is understandable that criminologists paid little attention to the problem of the development of crime at micro levels of place.

While the focus on individuals and communities has continued to play a central role in criminological theory and practice, traditional theories and approaches were subjected to substantial criticism beginning in the 1970s.

Starting with Robert Martinson's critique of rehabilitation programs in 1974, a series of studies documented the failures of traditional crime prevention initiatives (e.g., Sechrest, White, and Brown 1979; Whitehead and Lab 1989). In policing, as well, there was substantial criticism of traditional approaches. For example, there was no more visible approach to crime prevention in policing in the 1970s, or one that involved greater cost, than preventive patrol in cars. The idea that police presence spread widely across the urban landscape was an important method for preventing crime and increasing citizens' feelings of safety was a bedrock assumption of American policing. But in a major evaluation of preventive patrol in Kansas City, Missouri, the Police Foundation concluded that increasing or decreasing the intensity of preventive patrol did not affect either crime, service delivery to citizens, or citizens' feelings of security (Kelling, Pate, Dieckman, and Brown 1974). Similarly, rapid response to emergency calls to the police was considered to be a crucial component of police effectiveness. Yet in another large-scale study, Spelman and Brown (1984) concluded that improvement in police response times has no appreciable impact on the apprehension or arrest of offenders.

These and other studies in the 1970s and 1980s led scholars to challenge the fundamental premise of whether the police could have a significant impact on crime (see also Levine 1975; Greenwood, Petersilia, and Chaiken 1977). By 1994, the distinguished police scholar David Bayley was able to write:

The Police do not prevent crime. This is one of the best-kept secrets of modern life. Experts know it, the police know it, but the public does not know it. Yet the police pretend that they are society's best defence against crime . . . This is a myth. First, repeated analysis has consistently failed to find any connection between the number of police officers and crime rates. Secondly, the primary strategies adopted by modern police have been shown to have little or no effect on crime. (1994: 3)

A number of scholars argued that the failures of traditional crime prevention could be found in the inadequacies in program development and research design in prior studies (e.g., Farrington, Ohlin, and Wilson 1986; Goldstein 1990). Other reviews stressed that there are examples of successful offender-focused crime prevention efforts, which can provide guidance for the development of more effective prevention policies (Farrington 1983; Lipsey 1992). Nonetheless, even those scholars who looked to improve such policies, came to recognize the difficulties inherent in trying to do something about criminality (Visher and Weisburd 1998). Summarizing the overall standing of what they define as traditional "offender-centred" crime prevention, Patricia and Paul Brantingham wrote: "If traditional approaches worked well, of course, there would be little pressure to find new forms of crime prevention. If traditional approaches worked well, few people would possess criminal motivation and fewer still would actually commit crimes" (1990: 19).

One influential critique of traditional criminological approaches to understanding crime that had a strong influence on the development of hot spots policing was introduced by Cohen and Felson (1979). They argued that the emphasis placed on individual motivation in criminological theory failed to recognize the importance of other elements of the crime equation. They noted that for criminal events to occur there is need not only of a criminal, but also of a suitable target and the absence of a capable guardian. They showed that crime rates could be affected by changing the nature of targets or of guardianship, irrespective of the nature of criminal motivations. Cohen's and Felson's suggestion that crime could be affected without reference to the motivations of individual offenders was a truly radical idea in criminological circles in 1979. The routine activities perspective they presented established the context of crime as an important focus of study.

Drawing upon similar themes, British scholars led by Ronald Clarke began to explore the theoretical and practical possibilities of situational crime prevention (Clarke 1983; Cornish and Clarke 1986; Clarke 1992; 1995). Their focus was on criminal contexts and the possibilities for reducing the opportunities for crime in very specific situations. Their approach, like that of Cohen and Felson, turned traditional crime prevention theory on its head. At the center of their crime equation was opportunity. And they sought to change opportunity rather than reform offenders. In situational crime prevention, more often than not "opportunity made the thief" (Felson and Clarke 1998). This was in sharp contrast to the traditional view that the thief simply took advantage of a very large number of potential opportunities. Importantly, in a series of case studies situational crime prevention advocates showed that reducing criminal opportunities in very specific contexts can lead to crime reduction and prevention (Clarke 1992; 1995).

One natural outgrowth of these perspectives was that the specific places where crime occurs would become an important focus for crime prevention researchers (Eck and Weisburd 1995; Taylor 1997). While concern with the relationship between crime and place goes back to the founding generations of modern criminology (Guerry 1833; Quetelet 1842), the "micro" approach to places emerged only in the last few decades (e.g., see Brantingham and Brantingham 1975; Duffala 1976; Mayhew, Clarke, Sturman, and Hough 1976; Rengert 1980; Brantingham and Brantingham 1981; Rengert 1981; LeBeau 1987; Hunter 1988).[1] Places in this micro context are specific locations within the larger social environments of communities and neighborhoods (Eck and Weisburd 1995). They are sometimes defined as buildings or addresses (see Sherman, Gartin, and Buerger 1989a; Green 1996), sometimes as block faces, or street segments (see Sherman and Weisburd 1995; Taylor 1997), and sometimes as clusters of addresses, block faces, or street segments (see Block, Dabdoub, and Fregly 1995; Weisburd and Green 1995).

In the mid to late 1980s a group of criminologists began to examine the distribution of crime at micro places. Their findings were to radically alter the way many criminologists understood the crime equation, drawing them into a new area of inquiry that was to have important implications for police practice. Perhaps the most influential of these studies was conducted by Lawrence Sherman and his colleagues (Sherman *et al.* 1989b). Looking at crime addresses in the city of Minneapolis they found a concentration of crime at places that was startling. Only 3 percent of the addresses in Minneapolis accounted for 50 percent of the crime calls to the police. Similar results were reported in a series of other studies in different locations and using different methodologies, each suggesting a very high concentration of crime in micro places (e.g., see Pierce, Spaar, and Briggs 1986; Weisburd, Maher, and Sherman 1992; Weisburd and Green 1994; Weisburd, Bushway, Lum, and Yang 2004). A recent study by Weisburd *et al.* (2004) shows moreover that the concentration of crime in hot spots is fairly stable across time.

Importantly, such concentration of crime at discrete places does not necessarily follow traditional ideas about crime and communities. There were often discrete places free of crime in neighborhoods that were considered troubled, and crime hot spots in neighborhoods that were seen generally as advantaged and not crime prone (Weisburd and Green 1994). This empirical research thus reinforced theoretical perspectives that emphasized the importance of crime places, and suggested a focus upon small areas, often encompassing only one or a few city blocks that could be defined as hot spots of crime.

The emergence of hot spots policing

These emerging theoretical paradigms and empirical findings led Sherman and Weisburd (1995) to explore the practical implications of the hot spots approach for policing. With cooperation from the Minneapolis Police Department they developed a large experimental field study of "police patrol in crime hot spots." They sought to challenge the conclusions of the Kansas City Preventive Patrol Experiment noted earlier, then well established, that police patrol has little value in preventing or controlling crime. But they also sought to show that the focus of police efforts on crime hot spots presented a new and promising approach for police practice.

The idea of focusing police patrol on crime hot spots represented a direct application of the empirical findings regarding the concentration of crime in micro places. The Kansas City Preventive Patrol Experiment had looked at the effects of police patrol in large police beats. However, if "only 3 percent of the addresses in a city produce more than half of all the requests for police response, if no police are dispatched to 40 percent of the addresses and intersections in a city over one year, and, if among the 60 percent with any requests the majority register only one request a year (Sherman *et al.* 1989b), then concentrating police in a few locations makes more sense that spreading them evenly through a beat" (Sherman and Weisburd 1995: 629).

Nonetheless, the application of these findings to police practice raised significant questions about the overall crime control benefits of a hot spots approach. How would one know if crime prevention benefits gained at hot spots would not simply be displaced to other areas close by? Sherman and Weisburd noted that displacement was a potential but not necessarily certain occurrence. However, they argued that the first task for researchers was to establish that there would be any deterrent effect of police presence at the hot spots themselves:

The main argument against directing extra resources to the hot spots is that it would simply displace crime problems from one address to another without achieving any overall or lasting reduction in crime. The premise of this argument is that a fixed supply of criminals is seeking outlets for the fixed number of crimes they are predestined to commit. Although that argument may fit some public drug markets, it does not fit all crime or even all vice . . . In any case, displacement is merely a rival theory explaining *why* crime declines at a specific hot spot, if it declines. The first step is to see whether crime can be reduced at those spots at all, with a research design capable of giving a fair answer to that question. (1995: 629)

The results of the Minneapolis Experiment stood in sharp distinction to those of the earlier Kansas City study. The study used a rigorous experimental design including randomization of 110 crime hot spots of about a city block to treatment and control conditions. The treatment sites received on average between two and three times as much preventive patrol as the control sites. For the eight months in which the study was properly implemented, Sherman and Weisburd found a significant relative improvement in the experimental as compared to control hot spots both in terms of crime calls to the police and observations of disorder. Indeed, the effects of the program on crime, as measured by the difference

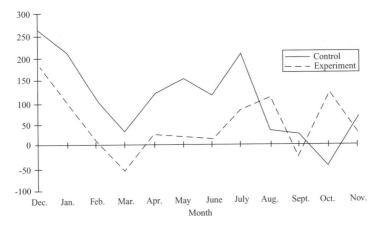

Figure 12.1 The Minneapolis hot spots experiment (Lines represent absolute differences between baseline and experimental years in total crime calls per month)
Source: Sherman and Weisburd, 1995

between crime calls in the pre-experimental and experimental years, was found to be stable across the eight-month period in which the program was properly implemented (see Figure 12.1). Crime, or at least crime calls and disorder, appeared to be prevented in the treatment as opposed to the control locations. Sherman and Weisburd (1995: 645) concluded that their results show "clear, if modest, general deterrent effects of substantial increases in police presence in crime hot spots." They noted that it was time for "criminologists to stop saying 'there is no evidence' that police patrol can affect crime" (1995: 647).

The empirical evidence for hot spots policing

The Minneapolis Hot Spots Experiment led to a series of federal government supported studies of hot spots policing. These findings in turn provided what is perhaps the strongest weight of empirical evidence for the introduction of any policing practice (see Committe to Review Research 2004; Weisburd and Eck 2004). Moreover, subsequent studies began to examine the displacement impacts of policing crime hot spots. For the most part this was in terms of immediate spatial displacement, or displacement to areas close to the targeted areas. Nonetheless, the findings reinforce the utility of hot spots approaches.

In a systematic review of the research evidence, Braga (2001) identified nine evaluations of focused police interventions at crime hot spots. The effects of problem-oriented policing initiatives, comprised mostly of traditional tactics with limited situational responses, were evaluated in the Minneapolis Repeat Call Address Policing (RECAP) Program (Sherman *et al.* 1989a), the Jersey City Drug Markets Analysis Program (Weisburd and Green 1995); the Jersey City Problem-Oriented Policing at Violent Places Study (Braga, Weisburd, Waring *et al.* 1999), the St. Louis Problem-Oriented Policing at Drug Market Locations Study (Hope 1994), and the Beenleigh (Australia) Calls for Service Project (Criminal Justice Commission 1998). The evaluation of the Houston Targeted Beat Program examined the effects of three types of treatments applied in different target areas. These interventions included high-visibility patrol, zero tolerance disorder policing, and enforcement problem-oriented policing (Caeti 1999). The Kansas City Gun Project examined the gun violence prevention effects of proactive patrol and intensive enforcement via safety frisks during traffic stops, plain view searches and seizures, and searches incident to arrests on other charges (Sherman and Rogan 1995a). The Minneapolis Hot Spots Patrol Program, as described earlier, evaluated the effects of increased levels of preventive patrol on crime. The Kansas City Crack House Police Raids Program (Sherman and Rogan 1995b) evaluated the effects of court-authorized raids on crack houses.

Noteworthy crime reductions were reported in seven of the nine selected studies. Five studies examined whether focused police efforts were associated with crime displacement or diffusion of crime control benefits. None of the five studies reported substantial immediate spatial displacement of crime into areas surrounding the targeted locations. Four studies suggested a possible "diffusion of crime control benefits" (Clarke and Weisburd 1994) effect associated with the focused police interventions. In these studies, areas near to the target sites, but which did not receive special police attention, also improved in terms of measures used in the studies. Table 12.1 summarizes the findings of that review.

Based on these studies, a recent review of police practices and policies by a National Academy of Sciences panel concluded that the strongest evidence presently available in support of any policing approach is found for hot spots policing:

(S)tudies that focused police resources on crime hot spots provide the strongest collective evidence of police effectiveness that is now available. On the basis of a series of randomized experimental studies, we conclude that the practice described as hot-spots policing is effective in reducing crime and disorder and can achieve these reductions without significant displacement of crime control

Table 12.1 *Results of hot spots policing evaluations*

Study	Crime Outcomes	Other Outcomes	Displacement / Diffusion
Minneapolis (MN) RECAP, Sherman *et al.* (1989a)	No Effect	None	Not measured
Minneapolis (MN) Hot Spots, Sherman and Weisburd (1995)	Reductions in total citizen calls for service	Observational data revealed reductions in crime and disorder	Not measured
Jersey City (NJ) DMAP, Weisburd and Green (1995)	Reductions in citizen calls for disorder offenses	None	Little evidence of displacement; analyses suggest modest diffusion of crime control benefits
Jersey City (NJ) POP at Violent Places, Braga *et al.* (1999)	Reductions in total calls for service and total crime incidents. All subcategories of crime experienced varying reductions	Observational data revealed reductions in social and physical disorder	Little evidence of immediate spatial displacement. Possible diffusion of crime control benefits
St. Louis (MO) POP in 3 Drug Areas, Hope (1994)	All 3 drug locations experienced varying reductions in total calls	None	One location experienced significant displacement
Kansas City (MO) Crack House Raids, Sherman and Rogan (1995a)	Modest decreases in citizen calls and offense reports that decayed in two weeks	None	Not measured
Kansas City (MO) Gun Project, Sherman and Rogan (1995b)	Increase in guns seized by the police followed by decrease in gun crimes	Community survey revealed favorable opinion of police efforts	No significant crime displacement Diffusion effects reported
Houston (TX) Targeted Beat Program, Caeti (1999)	Aggregated experimental beats experienced significant crime reductions. Specific beats reported mixed results	None	No evidence of displacement Diffusion effects reported

(*cont.*)

Table 12.1 (*cont.*)

Study	Crime Outcomes	Other Outcomes	Displacement / Diffusion
Beenleigh (AUS) *Calls for Service Project*, Criminal Justice Commission (1998)	No noteworthy differences in total number of calls between Beenleigh and Brown Plains areas. Noteworthy reductions in calls reported in majority of case studies	None	Not measured

Source: Adapted from Braga (2001).

benefits. Indeed, the research evidence suggests that the diffusion of crime control benefits to areas surrounding treated hot spots is stronger than any displacement outcome (Committee to Review Research 2004: 250).

Some caveats regarding the outcomes of hot spots policing

While the evidence for the effectiveness of hot spots policing is convincing, we think it important to note that there are still significant gaps in our knowledge about the effects of these interventions. For example, we know little of which specific hot spots strategies work best in which specific types of situations. While there is strong evidence that focusing on hot spots reduces crime and disorder, research has not yet distinguished the types of hot spots strategies that lead to the strongest crime prevention benefits (Braga 2001). The National Academy of Sciences review suggests that the most generalized strategies, for example, preventive patrol (Sherman and Weisburd 1995) and drug raids (Sherman and Rogan 1995a), are likely to have less impact than approaches that include more problem-solving elements, such as working with landlords (Eck and Wartell 1996; Green-Mazerole and Roehl 1998). However, our understanding of the effects of hot spots policing remains very general. If we are to maximize the crime prevention effects of hot spots approaches we need to examine carefully the interaction of different strategies with different hot spots settings. This effort would demand a large group of studies. But given the promise of hot spots policing, such an investment in research in this area seems appropriate.

Also, too little attention has been paid to the potential harmful effects of hot spots approaches. Police effectiveness studies have traditionally overlooked the effects of policing practices upon citizen perceptions of police legitimacy (Tyler 2000; 2001). Does the concentration of police enforcement in specific hot spots lead citizens to question the fairness of police practices? There is some evidence that residents of areas that are subject to hot spots policing welcome the concentration of police efforts in problem places (see Shaw 1995). Nonetheless, focused aggressive police enforcement strategies have been criticized as resulting in increased citizen complaints about police misconduct and abuse of force in New York City (Greene 1999). As in the case of understanding the effectiveness of police strategies, the potential impacts of hot spots policing on legitimacy may depend in good part on the types of strategies used and the context of the hot spots affected. But, whatever the impact, we need to know more about the effects of hot spots policing approaches on the communities that the police serve.

Finally, the research overall strongly supports the position that hot spots policing can have a meaningful effect on crime without simply displacing crime control benefits to areas nearby. However, a recent study which reinforces the findings that there is little immediate spatial displacement of crime as a result of hot spots policing approaches, identifies other displacement outcomes that may occur in focused policing efforts (Weisburd, Wyckoff, Ready et al. 2004). Offenders interviewed in the study described factors that inhibited spatial displacement, including the importance of familiar territory to offenders, and the social organization of illicit activities at hot spots which often precluded easy movement to other areas that offer crime opportunities. Prostitutes, for example, were found to work near to their homes, and described being uncomfortable moving to other areas where different types of people worked and different types of clients were found. Prostitutes and drug dealers in the study described the importance of the familiarity of a place to their clients, and some offenders talked of the dangers of encroaching on the territory of offenders in other hot spots.

Overall, a number of factors seemed to discourage spatial displacement in the study. Nonetheless, Weisburd et al. (2004) find that offenders will often try other modes of adaptation to police interventions, the most common being a change in the methods of committing illegal acts. For example, prostitutes and drug dealers may begin to make "appointments" with their customers, or move their activities indoors in order to avoid heightened police activity on the street. While the net gain in crime prevention may still be large for hot spots efforts, these findings suggest the importance of continued investigation of possible non-spatial displacement outcomes in hot spots policing.

The link between research and practice

We have so far shown that hot spots policing emerged from theoretical developments in criminology, and basic research indicating a very high concentration of crime at hot spots. Hot spots policing was also subjected to substantial experimental evaluation during the early 1990s that showed that it could be an effective policing strategy to prevent crime and disorder. Importantly, it is also the case that this approach had diffused widely in American policing by the turn of the last century. In a 2001 Police Foundation study more than seven in ten police departments with more than 100 sworn officers reported using crime mapping to identify "crime hot spots" (Weisburd, Mastrofski, McNally, and Greenspan 2001). But the fact that the research literature is supportive of hot spots policing and that police have implemented this approach widely, does not necessarily mean that research strongly impacted police practice. For example, it may be that the police adopted hot spots policing independently and later evidence simply confirmed that the strategy was useful.

While the Minneapolis Hot Spots Experiment is the first example we know of a successful program in which micro-level crime hot spots were systematically identified on a large scale for the purpose of police intervention, it is not the first example of police use of crime mapping to identify crime problems. Police officers have long recognized the importance of place in crime. Hand-developed pin maps have been widely used in police agencies for over half a century (Weisburd and McEwen 1997). And one can find isolated examples of what today we would define as hot spots policing in earlier periods (e.g., see Weiss 2001). Moreover, during the 1970s, crime analysts looked for patterns in crime by plotting the locations and times at which crimes were committed to direct patrol officers to the most likely targets (Reinier 1977), and cutting-edge crime analysts were experimenting with computerized crime mapping before the hot spots studies were well known (Weisburd and Lum 2005).

Nonetheless, a recent study by Weisburd and Lum (2005) suggests that the timing of the wide-scale implementation of hot spots policing follows very closely the basic and applied research we have reviewed. The study examined the diffusion of computerized crime mapping in police agencies using data from the National Institute of Justice Crime Mapping Laboratory (Mamalian, LaVigne, and Groff 1999), and a small pilot study of 92 police agencies of over 100 sworn officers conducted by the researchers. They found that computerized crime mapping in

Weisburd and Lum Pilot Study Cumulative Adoption Curve

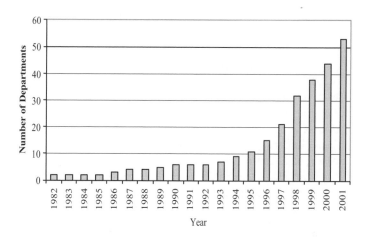

1997 CMRC Cumulative Adoption Curve

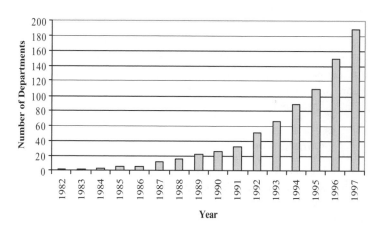

Figure 12.2 Cumulative distribution of computerized crime mapping adopted from the Weisburd *et al.* Pilot Study and the CMRC study
Source: Weisburd and Lum 2005

larger police agencies first began to emerge in policing in the late 1980s and early 1990s. Adoption began to grow steeply in the mid-1990s with the number of adopters increasing at a large rate after 1995 (see Figure 12.2).

Weisburd and Lum (2005) make a direct link in their survey between the diffusion of innovation in crime mapping and the adoption of hot spots policing. When they asked why departments developed a crime mapping capability, nearly half of those surveyed responded that crime mapping was adopted to facilitate hot spots policing. Of other categories of responses, many were likely related to hot spots approaches, though respondents gave more general replies such as "crime mapping was initially developed in response to a specific police strategy." Moreover, they found that 80 percent of the departments in their sample that have a computerized crime mapping capability conduct computerized hot spots analysis, and two thirds of departments that have computerized crime mapping capabilities use hot spots policing as a policing tactic.

If we can make the link between hot spots policing and computerized crime mapping suggested by Weisburd and Lum, then the data suggest that hot spots policing emerged as an important police strategy precisely during the period that evaluation findings were being widely disseminated. Results of the Minneapolis Hot Spots experiment, for example, though first published in an academic journal in 1995, were the focus of a plenary panel at the Academy of Criminal Justice Sciences in 1990 that was chaired by the then Director of the National Institute of Justice, James K. Stewart. Overall, the emergence of crime mapping and hot spots policing follow closely the development of strong research evidence regarding the hot spots approach. Of course, these data do not confirm with certainty a causal link between research and practice in the adoption of hot spots policing, but they suggest that hot spots policing approaches began to be widely implemented after research studies began to show their effectiveness.

Conclusion

In policing, most innovation has been developed using what might be termed a "clinical experience model." In such a model, research may play a role, but the adoption of innovation is determined primarily by the experiences of practitioners and often has little to do with research evidence. Such models often have a weak theoretical basis and it is not uncommon to discover that they have little crime prevention value once they are subjected to serious empirical investigation. Given the importance of policing for public safety, it seems unreasonable that policing should continue to rely on such a model for the development and diffusion of innovation.

Our discussion of hot spots policing suggests an alternative model for police innovation. Hot spots policing was consistent with developing theoretical insights in criminology and was supported by basic criminological research on crime and place. Accordingly, before hot spots policing was to emerge as a coherent strategic approach there was strong theoretical justification and empirical support for testing the value of this strategy. Hot spots policing was subjected to rigorous empirical investigation before it was widely diffused and adopted by American police agencies. In this sense, hot spots policing suggests that "evidence-based policing," as Lawrence Sherman (1998) has called it, can form the basis for important police innovation. We think, overall, that hot spots policing is an exception to the rule of how police innovation has developed in the United States. Nonetheless, it provides a model for how policing innovation might be developed even if, to date, it is the exception rather than the rule.

Hot spots policing is a model for the integration of research in the world of policing, and this integration has produced what is, according to empirical evidence, the most effective police innovation of the last decade. However, as we noted earlier, there is still much to be learned. For example, our knowledge is too general and must be focused more on how specific policing strategies affect specific types of hot spots. The research to date has also ignored many of the potential social consequences of hot spots policing. While it is clear that crime prevention benefits can be gained from hot spots approaches, we need to know more about how they affect the lives of people who live in areas that are targeted. Finally, we need to focus more carefully on problems of displacement and diffusion. Spatial displacement appears to be a much less serious threat to the gains of hot spots policing than had been originally thought, and indeed the evidence suggests that diffusion of crime control benefits to areas near targeted places is more common. Nonetheless, we don't know enough about how other forms of displacement, such as changes in methods of crime commission, affect the crime control benefits of hot spots approaches.

NOTE

1. It should be noted that a few early criminologists did examine the "micro" idea of place as discussed here (see Shaw and Myers 1929). However, interest in micro places was not sustained and did not lead to significant theoretical or empirical inquiry.

REFERENCES

Agnew, R. (1992). Foundation for a general strain theory of crime and delinquency. *Criminology, 30,* 47–84.

(1999). A general strain theory of community differences in crime rates. *Journal of Research in Crime and Delinquency, 36,* 123–155.

Akers, R. (1973). *Deviant behavior: A social learning approach.* Belmont, CA: Wadsworth Publishing.

Baumer, E., Lauritsen, J., Rosenfeld, R., and Wright, R. (1998). The influence of crack cocaine on robbery, burglary, and homicide rates: A cross-city, longitudinal analysis. *Journal of Research in Crime and Delinquency, 35* (3), 316–340.

Bayley, D. (1994). *Police for the future.* New York: Oxford University Press.

Block, C., Dabdoub, M., and Fregly, S. (eds.). (1995). *Crime analysis through computer mapping.* Washington, DC: Police Executive Research Forum.

Braga, A. (2001). The effects of hot spots policing on crime. *Annals of the American Academy of Political and Social Science, 578,* 104–125.

Braga, A., Weisburd, D., Waring, E., Mazerolle, L. G., Spelman, W., and Gajewski, F. (1999). Problem oriented policing in violent crime places: A randomized controlled experiment. *Criminology, 37* (3), 541–580.

Brantingham, P. J. and Brantingham, P. L. (1975). Residential burglary and urban form. *Urban Studies, 12* (3), 273–284.

    (1981). Notes on the geometry of crime. In P. J. Brantingham and P. L. Brantingham (eds.), *Environmental criminology.* Beverly Hills, CA: Sage Publications.

    (1990). Situational crime prevention in practice. *Canadian Journal of Criminology,* January, 17–40.

Bursik, R. J., Jr. and Grasmick, H. G. (1993). *Neighborhoods and crime.* San Francisco: Lexington.

Caeti, T. (1999). *Houston's targeted beat program: A quasi-experimental test of police patrol strategies.* Doctoral dissertation, Sam Houston State University. Ann Arbor, MI: UMI.

Clarke, R. V. (1983). Situational crime prevention: Its theoretical basis and practical scope. In M. Tonry and N. Morris (eds.), *Crime and justice: An annual review of research,* 4 (pp. 225–256). Chicago: University of Chicago Press.

    (1992). *Situational crime prevention: Successful case studies.* Albany, NY: Harrow and Heston.

    (1995). Situational crime prevention: Achievements and challenges. In M. Tonry and D. Farrington (eds.), *Building a safer society: Strategic approaches to crime prevention, crime and justice: A review of research,* 19 (pp. 91–150). Chicago: Chicago University Press.

Clarke, R. V. and Felson, M. (eds.). (1993). Routine activity and rational choice. *Advances in Criminological Theory, 5,* 1–14. New Brunswick, NJ: Transaction Press.

Clarke, R. V. and Weisburd, D. (1994). Diffusion of crime control benefits: Observations on the reverse of displacement. In R. V. Clarke (ed.), *Crime prevention studies,* 2 (pp. 165–183). Monsey, NY: Criminal Justice Press.

Cloward, R. and Ohlin, L. (1960). *Delinquency and opportunity.* Glencoe, IL: Free Press.

Cohen, L. E. and Felson, M. (1979). Social change and crime rate trends: A routine activity approach. *American Sociological Review, 44,* 588–605.

Committee to Review Research on Police Policy and Practices. (2004). *Fairness and effectiveness in policing: The evidence.* Washington, DC: National Academies Press.

Cornish, D. B. and Clarke, R. V. (1986). *The reasoning criminal: Rational choice perspectives on offending*. New York: Springer-Verlag.

Criminal Justice Commission. (1998). *Beenleigh calls for service project: Evaluation report*. Brisbane, Queensland: Criminal Justice Commission.

Duffala, D. C. (1976). Convenience stores, robbery, and physical environmental features. *American Behavioral Scientist*, 20, 227–246.

Eck, J. E. and Spelman, W. (1987). *Problem solving: Problem-oriented policing in Newport News*. Washington, DC: Police Executive Research Forum.

Eck, J. E. and Wartell, J. (1996). *Reducing crime and drug dealing by improving place management: A randomized experiment. Report to the San Diego Police Department*. Washington, DC: Crime Control Institute.

Eck, J. E. and Weisburd, D. (eds.). (1995). *Crime and place: Crime prevention studies*, 4. Monsey, NY: Criminal Justice Press.

Farrington, D. P. (1983). Offending from 10 to 25 years of age. In K. Van Dusen and S. A. Mednick (eds.), *Prospective studies of crime and delinquency* (pp. 17–38). Boston: Kluwer-Nijhoff.

Farrington, D. P., Ohlin, L., and Wilson, J. Q. (1986). *Understanding and controlling crime*. New York: Springer-Veriag.

Felson, M. and Clarke, R. V. (1998). Opportunity makes the thief: Practical theory for crime prevention. *Police Research Series: Policing and Reducing Crime Unit*, Paper 98. London: Home Office.

Franks, W. D. (1980). Montpelier, Vermont's directed patrol experiment. *Police Chief*, January, 24–26.

Gay, W. G., Beall, T. M., and Bowers, R. A. (1984). *A four-site assessment of the integrated criminal apprehension program*. Washington, DC: University City Science Center.

Gay, W. G., Schell, T., and Schack, S. (1977). *Prescriptive package: Improving patrol productivity, volume I – routine patrol*. Washington, DC: US Government Printing Office.

Goldstein, H. (1990). *Problem-oriented policing*. New York: McGraw-Hill.

Gottfredson, M. R and Hirschi, T. (1990). *A general theory of crime*. Stanford, CA: Stanford University Press.

Green, L. (1996). *Policing places with drug problems*. Thousand Oaks, CA: Sage Publications.

Green-Mazerolle, L. and Roehl, J. (1998). *Controlling drugs and social disorder using civil remedies: Final report of a randomized field experiment in Oakland, California*. Washington, DC: National Institute of Justice.

Greene, J. A. (1999). Zero tolerance: A case study of police practices and policies in New York City. *Crime and Delinquency*, 45, 171–181.

Greenwood, P. J., Petersilia, J., and Chaiken, J. (1977). *The criminal investigation process*. Lexington: D.C. Heath.

Guerry, A. M. (1833). *Essai sur la Statistique morale de la France*. Paris: Crochard.

Hirschi, T. (1969). *Causes of Delinquency*. Berkeley, CA: University of California Press.

Hope, T. (1994). Problem-oriented policing and drug market locations: Three case studies. In R. V. Clarke (eds.), *Crime prevention studies*, 2 (pp. 5–31). Monsey, NY: Criminal Justice Press.

Hunter, R. D. (1988). *Environmental characteristics of convenience store robberies in the state of Florida*. Paper presented at the annual meeting of the American Society of Criminology, Chicago.

Kelling, G., Pate, A. M., Dieckman, D., and Brown, C. E. (1974). *The Kansas City preventive patrol experiment: Summary report*. Washington, DC: The Police Foundation.

LeBeau, J. (1987). The methods and measures of centrography and the spatial dynamics of rape. *Journal of Quantitative Criminology*, *3*, 125–141.

Levine, J. P. (1975). Ineffectiveness of adding police to prevent crime. *Public Policy*, *23*, 523–545.

Lipsey, M. W. (1992). Juvenile delinquency treatment: A meta-analytic inquiry into the variability of effects. In T. D. Cook, H. Cooper, D. S. Cordray, H. Hartman, L. V. Hedges, R. J. Light, T. A. Louis, and F. Mosteller (eds.), *Meta-analysis for explanation: A casebook* (pp. 83–127). New York: Sage Publications.

Lipton, D., Martinson, R., and Wilks, J. (1975). *The effectiveness of correctional treatment: A survey of treatment evaluation studies*. New York: Praeger Publishers.

Loftin, C. and Hill, R. (1974). Regional subculture and homicide: An examination of the Gastil-Hackney thesis. *American Sociological Review*, *39*, 714–724.

Mamalian, C., LaVigne, N., and Groff, E. (1999). *The use of computerized crime mapping by law enforcement: Survey results. NIJ Research Preview*. Washington, DC: National Institute of Justice. Available online at http://www.ncjrs.org/pdffiles1/fs000237.

Martinson, R. (1974). What works? – Questions and answers about prison reform. *The Public Interest*, *35*, 22–54.

Mastrofski, S. and Ritti, R. (2000). Making sense of community policing: A theoretical perspective. *Police Practice and Research Journal*, *1* (2), 183–210.

Mayhew, P., Clarke, R. V., Sturman, A., and Hough, M. (1976). *Crime as opportunity*. (Home Office Research Study 34). London: H.M. Stationery Office.

Merton, R. K. (1968). Social structure and anomie. *American Sociological Review*, *3*, 672–682.

Meyer, J. and Rowan, B. (1977). Formal structure as myth. *American Journal of Sociology*, *83*, 340–363.

Moffitt, T. (1993). Adolescence-limited and life-course persistent antisocial behavior: A developmental taxonomy. *Psychological Review*, *4*, 674.

Nettler, G. (1978). *Explaining crime*. 2nd ed. New York: McGraw Hill.

Pierce, G. L., Spaar, S., and Briggs, L. R. (1986). *The character of police work: Strategic and tactical implications*. Boston, MA: Center for Applied Social Research, Northeastern University.

Quetelet, A. J. (1842). *A treatise of man*. Gainesville, FL: Scholar's Facsimiles and Reprints (1969 ed.).

Raine, A. (1993). The psychopathy of crime. New York: Academic Press.

Reinier, G. H. (1977). *Crime analysis in support of patrol*. National Evaluation Program: Phase I Report. Washington, DC: US Government Printing Office.

Rengert, G. F. (1980). Theory and practice in urban police response. In D. Georges-Abeyie and K. Harries (eds.), *Crime: A spatial perspective*. New York: Columbia University Press.

(1981). Burglary in Philadelphia: A critique of an opportunity structure model. In P. J. Brantingham and P. L. Brantingham (eds.), *Environmental criminology* (pp. 189–201). Beverly Hills, CA: Sage Publications.

Sampson, R. J. (1985). Neighborhood and crime: The structural determinants of personal victimization. *Journal of Research in Crime and Delinquency, 22* (1), 7–40.

Sampson, R. J. and Groves, W. B. (1989). Community structure and crime: Testing social disorganization theory. *American Journal of Sociology, 94,* 774–802.

Sampson, R. J. and Laub, J. H. (1993). *Crime in the making: Pathways and turning points through life.* Cambridge, MA: Harvard University Press.

Sechrest, L. B., White, S. O., and Brown, E. O. (1979). *The rehabilitation of criminal offenders: Problems and prospects.* Washington, DC: National Academy of Sciences.

Shaw, J. (1995). Community policing against guns: Public opinion of the Kansas City gun experiment. *Justice Quarterly, 12,* 695–710.

Shaw, C. R. and McKay, H. (1972). *Delinquency and urban areas.* Chicago: University of Chicago Press.

Shaw, C.R. and Myers, E. D. (1929). *The juvenile delinquent.* In Illinois Crime Survey. Chicago: Illinois Association for Criminal Justice.

Sherman, L. W. (1995). Hot spots of crime and criminal careers of places. In J. E. Eck and D. Weisburd (eds.), *Crime Prevention Studies,* 4 (pp. 35–52). Monsey, NY: Criminal Justice Press.

(1998). Evidence-based policing. *Ideas in American policing series.* Washington, DC: The Police Foundation.

Sherman, L. W. and Rogan, D. (1995a). Effects of gun seizures on gun violence: Hot spots patrol in Kansas City. *Justice Quarterly, 12,* 673–694.

(1995b). Deterrent effects of police raids on crack houses: A randomized controlled experiment. *Justice Quarterly, 12,* 755–782.

Sherman, L. W. and Weisburd, D. (1995). General deterrent effects of police patrol in crime "hot-spots": A randomized controlled trial. *Justice Quarterly, 12,* 626–648.

Sherman, L. W., Gartin, P. R., and Buerger, M. E. (1989a). *Repeat call address policing: The Minneapolis RECAP experiment.* Final report to the National Institute of Justice. Washington, DC: Crime Control Institute.

(1989b). Hot spots of predatory crime: Routine activities and the criminology of place. *Criminology, 27,* 27–56.

Spelman, W. and Brown, D. K. (1984). Calling the police: Citizen reporting of serious crime. Washington: US Government Printing Office.

Sutherland, E. (1947). *Principals of criminology.* Chicago: J. B. Lippincott Co.

Taylor, R. (1997). Social order and disorder of street blocks and neighborhoods: Ecology, microecology, and the systemic model of social disorganization. *Journal of Research in Crime and Delinquency, 34* (1), 113–155.

Trasler, G. (1993). Conscience, opportunity, rational choice, and crime. In R. V. Clarke and M. Felson (eds.), *Routine activity and rational choice: Advances in criminological theory,* 5 (pp. 305–322). New Brunswick, NJ: Transaction Publishers.

Tyler, T. (2000). Social justice: Outcomes and procedures. *International Journal of Psychology*, 35 (2), 117–125.

(2001). Public trust and confidence in legal authorities: What do majority and minority groups members want from the law and legal institutions? *Behavioral Sciences and the Law*, 19 (2), 215–235.

Visher, C. and Weisburd, D. (1998). Identifying what works: Recent trends in crime prevention strategies. *Crime, Law and Social Change*, 28, 223–242.

Weisburd, D. and Green, L. *(Green-Mazerolle)* (1994). Defining the drug market: The case of the Jersey City DMA system. In D. L., MacKenzie and C.D. Uchida (eds.), *Drugs and crime: Evaluating public policy initiatives*. Newbury Park, CA: Sage Publications.

(1995). Policing drug hot-spots: The Jersey City drug market analysis experiment. *Justice Quarterly*, 12, 711–735.

Weisburd, D. and McEwen, T. (eds.). (1997). *Crime mapping and crime prevention: Crime prevention studies*, 8. Monsey, NY: Criminal Justice Press.

Weisburd, D. and Eck, J. E. (2004). What can police do to reduce crime, disorder, and fear? *The Annals of the American Academy of Political and Social Science*, 593, 42–65.

Weisburd, D. and Lum, C. (2005). The diffusion of computerized crime mapping policing: Linking research and practice. In *Police Practice and Research*, 6 (5), 433–448.

Weisburd, D., Maher, L., and Sherman L.W. (1992). Contrasting crime general and crime specific theory: The case of hot-spots of crime. *Advances in criminological theory*, 4 (pp. 45–70). New Brunswick, NJ: Transaction Press.

Weisburd, D., Mastrofski, S., McNally, A. M., and Greenspan, R. (2001). *Compstat and organizational change: Findings from a national survey*. Washington DC: The Police Foundation.

Weisburd, D., Bushway, S., Lum, C., and Yang, S. M. (2004). Trajectories of crime at places: A longitudinal study of street segments in the city of Seattle. *Criminology*, 42 (2), 283–321.

Weisburd, D., Mastrofski, S. D., McNally, A. M., Greenspan, R., and Willis, J. J. (2003). Reforming to preserve: Compstat and strategic problem solving in American policing. *Criminology and Public Policy*, 2 (3), 421–456.

Weisburd, D., Wyckoff, L. A., Ready, J., Eck, J., Hinkle, J., and Gajewski, F. (2004). *Does crime just move around the corner? A study of displacement and diffusion in Jersey City, NJ*. Washington, DC: The Police Foundation.

Weiss, A. (2001). *The police and road safety*. Paper prepared for The National Research Council Committee to Review Research on Police Policy and Practice.

Whitehead, J. T. and Lab, S. P. (1989). A meta-analysis of juvenile correctional treatment. *Journal of Research in Crime and Delinquency*, 26, 276–295.

Willis, J. J., Mastrofski, S. D., and Weisburd, D. (2004). Compstat and bureaucracy: A case study of challenges and opportunities for change. *Justice Quarterly*, 21 (3), 463–496.

Wolfgang, M. E. and Ferracuti, F. (1967). *The subculture of violence: Toward an integrated theory in criminology*. New York: Tavistock.

13　Critic
The limits of hot spots policing

Dennis P. Rosenbaum

Introduction

This author is a strong advocate of using sophisticated information technology and the latest research findings to guide decisionmaking in police organizations. Hence, this article begins with a brief acknowledgment of the potential benefits of hot spot policing in theory, followed by a serious critique. The thesis of this chapter is that, while the concept of hot spots policing is attractive, we should be disappointed in how scholars have narrowly defined it in theory and research and how police organizations have narrowly practiced it. This approach has failed to embody the fundamental principles of either problem-oriented policing or community policing, which many scholars believe represent the basic pillars of "good policing" in the twenty-first century.

Acknowledging the benefits

The concept of hot spots is indisputable as a criminological phenomenon and suggests the need for focused responses. From the very beginning of criminological inquiries in nineteenth century France, scholars noted that criminal activity is not randomly distributed, but rather varies by geographic area such as regions, states, and communities (see Eck and Weisburd 1995). More recent micro-level analyses have focused on sizable variations between and within urban neighborhoods. Hence, a sensible policy implication is to recommend the concentration of more resources in these high-crime areas, including police resources (Sherman, Gottfredson, MacKenzie *et al.* 1997). The most important question, however, is not whether we should assign more resources to problem areas, but rather, what resources should be deployed and how should they be deployed?

Also, the concept of data-driven policing is difficult to dispute. Relying on information to make decisions about tactics, strategies, and programmatic interventions, assuming the data are accurate and complete, is preferred to "cursing the dark" or making decisions primarily on the basis of personal whim, personal experience, opinions of friends, or political pressure. On the basis of controlled evaluation research, hot spots researchers have encouraged the police to focus their attention on geographic areas smaller than police beats, including addresses, with a high concentration of activity or repeat calls for service (e.g., Sherman, Gartin, and Buerger 1989; Sherman and Weisburd 1995). Building on these studies and the revolution in information technology, including mapping programs (Mamalian and LaVigne 1999), the field has witnessed the strategic deployment of police personnel in response to geo-based patterns of crime incidents and calls for service. New York's Compstat program was a trendsetter in the 1990s and Chicago's CLEAR program epitomizes the IT capabilities of law enforcement for the next decade (Skogan, Steiner, Hartnett *et al.* 2002).

Short-term impact

Hot spots policing, when implemented under controlled experimental conditions with researchers involved, appears to have some effects on crime and disorder (for reviews, see Sherman 1997; Taylor 1998; Braga 2001; Weisburd and Eck 2004). But the qualifications on this conclusion are extremely important: first, the effects on crime are small and not as consistent as the effects on disorder. Second, and most importantly, the effects dissipate quickly. Sherman's (1990) review of the police crackdown literature indicates that any residual deterrence effect is weak and likely to decay rapidly. The conclusion regarding drug market crackdowns is that they are ineffective in controlling drug hot spots. In one of the stronger experimental tests, crime dropped on targeted blocks in Kansas City after raids of crack houses, but returned within seven days, leading the authors to conclude, "Like aspirin for arthritis, the painkiller does nothing to remedy the underlying condition" (Sherman and Rogan 1995a: 777). For directed patrols of high-crime locations, the best research in Minneapolis suggests a positive relationship between the length of patrol presence at a hot spot and the length of the deterrent effect, up to 15 minutes, after which time, the effect reverses (Koper 1995).

The implication of these findings are that (1) the enormous expense of concentrating police resources, especially for drug market crackdowns, is difficult to justify given the cost of sustaining the effect; (2) a more sophisticated understanding of deterrence is required before police are ready to implement high-impact "schedules of punishment"; and (3) the absence of larger and more sustained effects suggests the need for a more complete understanding of the criminogenic forces at work in hot spots. Much more evaluation research is needed in this area, especially using randomized longitudinal designs.

Problem definition

What follows is a critique of hot spots policing from a problem-oriented and community policing framework, beginning with the definition of the problem. Engaging in "good" hot spot policing is not feasible if the hot spot itself cannot be easily identified or well defined. The definitional problem is complex and involves both conceptual and operational issues. At the conceptual level, we need to ask, how does a particular place achieve the status of being a "hot spot"? And who decides – the police on the street, administrators or politicians, or the community? Generally, the police have decided that a hot spot is a place where there are too many violent crimes, drug deals, or gangs. But why is the definition of "the problem" so narrowly construed? Undoubtedly, urban neighborhoods have hot spots of public fear of crime, hot spots of public hostility toward the police, of slum landlords, of racial profiling, disorder, weak informal social control, institutional disinvestments, and weak interagency partnership, to name just a few. Yet these problems are not treated as hot spots because they are not police priorities, because they are not well measured or understood, and because they do not fit within the traditional definition of the police function.

The notion of hot spots, even if expanded, still limits the definition of the problem to geographically linked phenomena. This approach overlooks a number of serious crime-related problems that are not structured in this way. Terrorism, computer crime, economic and international crime, and even drug trafficking are examples of serious problems that stretch beyond small geographic or neighborhood boundaries. Even gang homicide, which is associated with geography, is best understood in terms of the social structure of the gang and social interactions rather than location (Papachristos 2003). In fact, the Boston Gun Project was a big success because it focused on disrupting conflicts between gangs rather than on the places where shots were fired (Braga, Kennedy, Piehl, and Waring 2001). Hence, place-based conceptions can sometimes restrict our ability to understand and respond effectively to serious crime problems, even those that cluster in space and time.

Even if we accept the traditional concept of hot spots, we still face serious problems trying to identify and operationally define them. First, the judgments of individual officers about hot spots can be inaccurate if not supported by computer analysis of larger samples. Second, when community input is sought, the police and local residents often disagree when evaluating and prioritizing neighborhood problems (Skogan *et al.* 2002). Third, when GIS mapping software is employed, the hot spot boundaries can be "fuzzy" (Taylor 1998). Circles can be imposed over data plots, but in reality, these are somewhat arbitrary cut-offs. Where does one hot spot end and another begin? In high-crime neighborhoods this can be a serious problem. If a hot spot is enlarged, then what is the benefit of a focused deployment scheme? If the hot spot is circumscribed to a small area, the risk of making a false positive identification has been increased. One can question whether small hot spots that come and go quickly are sufficiently stable to warrant this label.

Finally, the selection of places as hot spots on the basis of extreme scores (e.g., a spike in violence during the past month) can lead police managers and researchers to draw false conclusions about the effectiveness of hot spots policing. "Regression to the mean" – a statistical artifact that would show up as a decline in the crime rate regardless of policing efforts – is more likely under these circumstances, so a strong evaluation design is needed to avoid making false causal inferences about the effectiveness of intensive directed policing (see Shadish, Cook, and Campbell 2003).

Weak problem analysis

Identifying a hot spot is not the same as understanding it. The analysis phase of problem-oriented policing is often lacking in hot spots policing. Too often the data analysis team is satisfied with colorful crime maps as the final product. Rarely do we see a detailed analysis of the characteristics of the hot spot and the nature of the problem. How much can we really learn about the problem from the spatial distribution of calls about drug transactions, crime incidents, or arrests? A thorough and comprehensive analysis of the hot spot would require that these data be placed in the larger environmental context. Knowing the physical and social milieu is critical for understanding the factors that facilitate and constrain hot spot behaviors. Census, housing, and survey data can be used to triangulate police data. Interviews and observations of users of the hot spot environment are essential (see Rosenbaum and Lavrakas 1995). The real problems are hidden behind the calls for service or arrest data. The real story is more complex, more dynamic, and more difficult to summarize. Without digging deeper, the police responses will be standardized and superficial, thus resulting in either short-term impact or no impact at all.

For the modern high-tech police organization, the information managers believe that the most sophisticated type of hot spot analysis involves using real-time data to engage in "crime forecasting" and deployment.

Analyses of monthly or weekly data are used to identify emerging hot spots and deploy officers in a proactive, preventative manner. But statisticians will caution against making this type of prediction because the estimates are unstable within small geographic areas using small amounts of data (Spelman 1995). Yet police commanders today can be chided for a single shooting in a hot spot area.

Narrow and predictable response options

After the police (and hopefully, the community) identify and analyze the hot spot, they are still facing the problem of what to do about it. On this topic, only rarely have the police followed the guidance of Herman Goldstein (1990: 102), the father of problem-oriented policing: "This requires a process both broad and uninhibited – broad in that it breaks out of the rigid mindset of the past, and uninhibited in that it explores sensible responses without regard, at least initially, to potential impediments to adopting them." Instead, police departments have turned to what they have done for years: patrols, sweeps, stakeouts, buy and busts, reverse stings, etc. The responses are narrow and predictable – surveillance, stop and frisk, question, and arrest – regardless of the nature and causes of the problem. Goldstein (1990) encouraged a systematic inquiry into the nature of these problems and the creation of strategic responses that would likely be effective in reducing or eliminating them. Frankly, I do not see this happening in American law enforcement. Problem analysis tends to be superficial, non-existent, or based on a limited set of specific criteria. Responses tend to be prepackaged, cookie-cutter reactions rather than tailored, researched strategic plans for solving or eliminating the problem over the long haul.

The simple fact that crime is concentrated in identifiable locations does not justify the geographic concentration of limited police resources unless the police have a compelling plan for dealing with the problem. What is the plan? What is the theory of action behind the plan? Why should it work? How long will it work? What are the potential adverse effects of the plan? How is "success" defined and when is a problem "solved"? Arguably, short-term reductions in crime and disorder are overrated and give the false impression that the problem has been solved. This is a very expensive way to run an organization.

The deterrence model

One major reason that hot spots policing tactics are not likely to have a *sustained* impact on serious crime is because they are not based on a compelling understanding of criminality or the larger hot spot environment. The importance of place (hot spots) in crime causation and prevention can be viewed through the lenses of rational choice theory (Cornish and Clarke 1986), routine activity theory (Cohen and Felson 1979), crime pattern theory (Brantingham and Brantingham 1993), or social disorganization theory (Bursik and Grasmick 1993; Sampson 2002). But hot spots policing, in practice, is not so sophisticated and reflects a basic deterrence model. Directed patrols, undercover intelligence gathering, visible surveillance systems (such as cameras), and various types of aggressive enforcement in the target areas are hypothesized to deter offending by increasing the actual and perceived risk of detection, apprehension, and punishment. The preventative focus of hot spots policing tends to be the potential offender's fear of punishment and not the other elements of criminal opportunity in the environment (e.g., victims, witnesses, social control agents, physical features) that influence offender motivation. Repeat offenders often do not fear punishment and have become increasingly sophisticated in avoiding it. Also, police sanctioning of gang members can be viewed as a "badge of honor" (Klein 1999). Suffice it to say that subjective assessments of risk by potential offenders (the key element!) are based on a variety of factors, including the perceived certainty, severity, and speed of punishment (Tittle and Paternoster 2000). Unfortunately, the criminal justice system has failed to deliver on these threats in a consistent manner and has not demonstrated an understanding of the complexity of the deterrence processes.

Deterrence theories are based on the assumption that people are rational and accurate processors of information, but research suggests that we are not good at estimating probabilities of events, and we often ignore or misperceive information presented to us (e.g., Kahneman and Tversky 1973; Nisbett and Ross 1980; Kahneman, Slovic, and Tversky 1982). This is not to say that people are always irrational. In general, individuals have their own rationality and logic that is not always evident to those empowered to administer formal sanctions. Selling drugs or carrying a gun on the streets may seem "irrational" to the average person, but these behaviors can seem very sensible to the person who faces daily threats of bodily injury or theft of contraband, sees no good employment opportunities, and has nothing to lose from another arrest.

Community and problem-oriented theories

Hot spots policing, in practice, is like old wine in new bottles. Police continue to do what they do best – undercover and visible enforcement activities – but with greater efficiency and focus on specific locations.

Police administrators ask themselves: How can we deploy more police officers (and the right officers) to these locations to make more arrests and seize more contraband? The real question should be, What are the best strategies to combat crime, disorder, and quality of life in these hot spots given all that we know about these problems, these locations, and the many resources that can be leveraged (including non-police resources)?

Theories of community policing (e.g., Skogan 1990; Greene 2000; Skogan 2003), problem-oriented policing (Goldstein 1990), and community crime prevention (Tonry and Farrington 1995; Rosenbaum, Lurigio, and Davis 1998) have, to all intents and purposes, been ignored in hot spots policing, despite advocates' claims to the contrary. These models all suggest that police would be unwise to limit their focus to pictures of *where* crime is occurring, and should give more attention to *why* it is occurring. Hot spots policing somehow leaves the impression that our knowledge of hot spots is limited to GIS plots of crime incidents. In fact, we know a lot more about hot spots, and this knowledge could be exploited to develop lasting solutions to neighborhood problems. Criminologists have examined the role of the physical environment, families, peers, schools, neighborhood resources, housing policies, labor markets, social organization processes, public attitudes, gun markets, offender re-entry problems, and many other factors that contribute to crime, disorder, and deviance within specific geographies (see Tonry and Farrington 1995; Tittle and Paternoster 2000; Wilson and Petersilia 2002). Our knowledge of how to prevent crime is substantial! The only question here is whether the police have any role in converting this knowledge into practice. The argument here is that they do.

Police as experts on crime

Over the years, police organizations have acquired an image of "effective crime fighters" and "experts" on crime in general, thus receiving the lion's share of taxpayer dollars for public safety programs. To justify this reputation, law enforcement must demonstrate a deeper knowledge of the forces that contribute to crime and the quality of urban life. Educated people can disagree about whether the police have any responsibility to reach beyond short-term strategies to address the underlying, chronic causes of crime. (Most police officers would say, "that's not our job.") I would argue that law enforcement leaders can play an important role by (1) working with criminologists to educate policymakers and the public about what can, and should be, done to prevent crime; (2) creating and leading multiagency partnerships that have a higher probability of yielding a sustainable impact on crime; and (3) focusing on comprehensive strategies that attack crime at all levels (Rosenbaum 2002; Schuck and Rosenbaum forthcoming). Unfortunately, hot spots policing can reinforce the persistent public misperception that police can solve the crime problem alone, without the help of the communities they serve, other government agencies, or the private sector.

A close adherence to the principles of problem-oriented policing would, I believe, lead most police administrators to question current stand-alone hot spots practices. The urban problems of youth violence cannot be explained by simple statements such as, "kids make bad choices and they need to pay the price" or "our job is to take the scumbags and gang bangers off the street." The solutions are much more complex and, furthermore, most convicted offenders will return to the neighborhood within a year or two. The goal of problem-oriented policing is to eliminate the problem, not to increase the efficiency of the response. Furthermore, a major goal of community policing is to achieve fair and equitable policing through community input and feedback, not just to achieve efficient policing (Eck and Rosenbaum 1994). Hot spots policing, as currently practiced, may be at odds with these goals for reasons noted below.

Adverse effects of hot spots policing

Arguably, hot spots policing is not only ineffective at solving persistent problems, but is potentially harmful to both targeted and non-targeted communities. Some of the potential untoward effects of hot spots policing are discussed in this section.

Displacement effects

One of the big question marks surrounding hot spots policing is about possible displacement effects. If hot spots policing is simply altering criminal activity by location, time, modus operandi, or type of offense, rather than preventing it, then the collective benefits to the larger community are non-existent. The problem of displacement, if occurring, may indicate that non-targeted residents or locations are suffering *more* because additional criminal activity is being pushed into their environment.

Criminologists are divided on this issue and the evidence is mixed. Most evaluations do not define and measure displacement adequately if at all, and most research designs are biased in favor of the null hypothesis (Weisburd and Green 1995a). Some studies suggest there is evidence of diffusion of crime control benefits to nearby areas (see Sherman and Rogan 1995b; Weisburd and Green 1995b; Green-Mazerolle and Roehl 1998; Braga *et al.* 1999), but some of these effects may reflect a mis-specification of the target area boundaries. On the other side of the fence, there is considerable evidence of spatial displacement of calls or crime incidents as a result of police crackdowns, especially during drug enforcement (e.g., Kleiman 1988; Potter, Gaines, and Holbrook 1990; Smith, Sviridoff, Sadd *et al.* 1992; Uchida, Forst, and Annan 1992; Kennedy 1993; Hope 1994; Sherman and Rogan 1995a; Braga *et al.* 1999; Maher and Dixon 2001). A meta-analysis by Sherman (1997), however, suggests that displacement effects are not as large as crime prevention effects, but the research in this field is inconclusive. Clearly, there are many types of displacement that have not been measured.

Police–community relations

Hot spots policing, because it has been operationally defined as aggressive enforcement in specific areas, runs the risk of weakening police–community relations (see Kleiman 1988; Worden, Bynum, and Frank 1994; Sherman 1997; Rosenbaum et al. 1998). Hot spots policing can easily become zero tolerance policing and broken windows policing since these are models that police find easy to adopt. These tactics can drive a wedge between the police and the community, as the latter can begin to feel like targets rather than partners. Because the police have chosen to focus on removing the "bad element" and serving as the "thin blue line" between "good" and "bad" residents, these strategies can pit one segment of the community against another, as the "good" residents are asked to serve as the informants and the "eyes and ears" of police. Parents, siblings, and friends of gang members and drug dealers can feel a divided loyalty and be caught in the crossfire.

The success of police organizations depends largely on the cooperation of the citizenry, but the legitimacy of the institution is compromised when the public's trust and confidence in the police is undermined. The consequences are enormous, ranging from lawsuits to a declining willingness to obey the law (e.g., Tyler 1990; 2001). What determines public trust in the police? The answer is complex (see Weitzer and Tuch in press). Certainly, perceptions of police effectiveness in lowering crime rates is one factor that affects attitudes about the police, but research indicates that it is not as important as procedural justice during the exercise of authority (Skogan in press; Tyler in press). That is, positive attitudes about the police drop when citizens feel that they have been treated unfairly, disrespected, not listened to, or physically abused during encounters with the police. Minorities, who are much more likely than non-minorities to live in hot spot areas, express these sentiments at much higher rates than whites (Rosenbaum, Hawkins, Costello, Skogan *et al.* 2005; Skogan in press).

We must acknowledge that residents of high-crime areas are very ambivalent about aggressive enforcement. Many demand it and are pleased to see the police restore order. In fact, surveys indicate that many are willing to give up their civil liberties to achieve this sense of security, however fleeting (Rosenbaum 1993). Residents will insist on aggressive enforcement up to the point where it directly affects them, their family, or their friends, who frequently end up in jail and prison or report being mistreated by the police. How much of this policing they will tolerate remains to be seen. Like other Americans, however, hot spots residents should have the opportunity to experience both safety *and* liberty and not be required to choose one or the other. This topic demands much more careful policy deliberation and research.

Abusive policing

Hot spots policing, as practiced, runs the risk of becoming abusive and/or corrupt policing. When officers feel the pressure to make arrests, seize drugs, and seize guns, some will be inclined to cut corners and, as a result, every officer's credibility is compromised. Complaints about excessive force and police corruption are not uncommon in hot spots neighbor- hoods where police are sometimes viewed as an "occupying force." The issue of due process is critical to the criminal justice system. A twenty- year prosecutor recently summarized the problem for me in this way: "Winking at questionable stops and arrests may serve to get major waves of contraband off the streets for a while but it eventually begins to draw the ire of the judiciary and threatens the credibility of both the police and that of the prosecuting authorities" (Andreou, personal communication, 2003).

Stigma from labeling

There is a real risk that neighborhoods and smaller areas identified as hot spots will acquire a more negative image as a result of the labeling process. In some cases, the stigma of being a hot spot of crime may stimulate greater fear of crime among residents (both inside and outside the neighborhood) and eventually lower property values. Granted, some hot spots already have a bad reputation, but others on the margins could be further damaged by the labeling process. Yet police face a "Catch 22." The adverse effects of labeling could be minimized by keeping the identity of the location confidential and internal to the police, but that would prevent the department from soliciting community support for aggressive police interventions.

Policing bias by race and class

We cannot avoid the fact that policing tactics and strategies vary by race and social class. These differences are due, in part, to data-driven deployment of police officers on the basis of crime hot spots. Violence and illicit drug activity are most visible in low-income, minority communities and, therefore, these areas receive a disproportionate share of police attention in response to public demand. By definition, the pressure on the police to lower crime rates is greatest in these hot spot areas.

The problem is that civil liberties are more easily jeopardized in low-income and minority neighborhoods where residents feel disenfranchised and do not have easy access to legal remedies when feeling mistreated. Minority communities are the primary focus of not only drug and gun enforcement, but also minor disorders (e.g., hanging out, public drinking) and various types of traffic enforcement activities (e.g., road checks for seat belt usage and drinking). Following the lead of New York City and the "broken windows" model, a commonly employed strategy is to use these police-initiated contacts (often involving minor infractions) as a tool to identify weapons, drugs, guns, and persons with outstanding warrants. One problem is that the "hit rate" is extremely low, so the vast majority of persons who are inconvenienced (if not offended) by these stops are innocent persons of color and limited means.

Beyond inconvenience is the troubling question of police abuse, which, as it turns out, is not randomly distributed. Looking at twenty years of data in New York, one study concluded that police misconduct seems to be attracted to neighborhoods with structural disadvantage, population mobility, and increases in the Latino population, among other factors (Kane 2002). So, neighborhoods that suffer the most from crime are also areas where the police are more likely to violate the rules of conduct.

Finally, there is the macro-level question regarding the long-term consequences of applying greater enforcement resources to minority communities. The bottom line, after the criminal justice system has completed its work, is called "disproportionate minority confinement." Minorities are being confined and incarcerated at much higher rates than non-minorities (for a review, see Pope, Lovell, and Hsia 2003), which will continue to be a hotly debated political issue. This begs the question of whether we can solve these neighborhood problems differently.

In sum, the style and consequences of policing in low-income minority communities are often different than in middle-class neighborhoods and the application of enforcement tactics in specific locations is increasingly driven by hot spot analyses.

Direct and opportunity costs

Intensifying police resources in hot spots can be expensive in terms of added personnel costs and additional activity for the criminal justice system. The options are to increase the police budget, borrow resources from other neighborhoods, or discontinue the program after a short period. Intensive policing is simply not affordable in many cases and, therefore, not sustainable in the absence of careful planning about deployment.

A bigger concern is the opportunity costs associated with hot spots policing. In other words, what is the police department *not* doing because it is involved in hot spots policing? First, there is a tendency to reduce police resources in low and moderate crime neighborhoods by creating special teams, transferring personnel, or redrawing beat boundaries. Low crime communities may feel shortchanged, but moderate crime communities may experience crime increases. Second, there may be a tendency to reduce police resources for community policing and joint problem-solving activities.

Opportunity costs come in many sizes and shapes. One could argue that hot spots policing discourages an intelligent public policy debate about long-term solutions to our crime problems. As noted earlier, this type of policing is designed to leave the public with the impression that crime is under control, thus contributing to the image of law enforcement agencies as effective crime-fighting machines.

Unanticipated effects on crime

Arrest (and for some, conviction and incarceration) does not always have the desired deterrent effects, and may even produce boomerang effects. A couple of examples will suffice. First, there is some evidence that arresting inner-city youths can have a criminogenic effect of increasing, rather than reducing, the probability of recidivism (Klein 1986). Second, there is evidence that having a criminal record reduces one's probability of finding gainful employment (Bushway 1996). The plight of 600,000 ex-offenders who return from prison each year illustrates the many legal and social obstacles they face to successful reintegration (Travis, Solomon, and Waul 2001), thus explaining why most return to a life of crime. Also, the extent to which law enforcement agencies use technology to track and monitor ex-offenders by address is unprecedented.

In sum, our criminal justice system may be having criminogenic effects, making crime more probable for those who are targeted, arrested, and labeled (many for life) as "criminals." This is especially troubling for the large volume of incidents involving misdemeanor and non-violent drug offenses and raises the question of whether aggressive enforcement activity in high-crime neighborhoods is helping or hurting public safety in the long run. Someday, we will take the time to answer these questions.

Collective efficacy

Neighborhoods with high rates of violent crime that are typically the target of hot spots policing also suffer from social disorganization and a lack of collective efficacy in solving problems (Sampson, Raudenbush, and Earls 1997). "Get tough" policies run the risk of further undermining social control and a community's capacity for self-regulation. By strengthening the hand of the police to solve crime-related problems, the residents may feel less empowered to solve neighborhood problems. Policymakers may need to be reminded that community crime rates, in the final analysis, are influenced more by the social ecology of communities than by formal control mechanisms (Sampson 2002). Hence, within the community policing framework, a primary mission of police organizations should be to work with other organizations to design strategies that strengthen community capacity rather than to supplant or weaken the role of community. But in fairness to the police, restoring order would seem to be a necessary element in the process of restoring community capacity. The only question is about the means of restoring order, the timeframe, and the strategies that will accompany these police activities.

Rethinking hot spots policing

If police can rethink the concept of place, the notion of hot spots policing can be given new meaning. I would encourage police departments to adopt a more holistic approach to problems that cluster in space and time, including: (1) conducting an in-depth, comprehensive analysis of the hot spot environment and the many factors that are responsible for making the area "hot"; (2) exploring a wide range of alternative solutions that might reasonably be expected to have either a short-term or long-term impact on the problem (both are important!); (3) attempting to build real partnerships among government, private sector, and community organizations that have a stake in public safety; and (4) giving more attention to the prevention of crime at the individual, family, and community levels.

The Chicago Police Department (CPD) is an interesting case study that seeks to achieve some of these objectives. While investing in enforcement-oriented hot spots policing, the CPD is also pursuing a more holistic approach to hot spots. First, in selected hot spot locations, the CPD has sought to expand the responsibility for crime control to third parties, such as landlords and business owners, using both rewards and sanctions to clean up entire blocks. Second, the superintendent's office has also taken a leadership role in building a coalition of organizations to address hot spots of violence in selected areas of the city and to provide feedback on police performance. Third, Chicago has a nationally recognized community policing effort (CAPS) that allows community concerns to be aired in monthly beat meetings. As part of this process, the CPD is working with the University of Illinois at Chicago to develop a geo-based Internet survey that will "measure what matters" to the public, including indicators of hot spots of disorder, fear, and strained police–community relations, among other factors. These new data are expected to result in new definitions of local problems, a stronger community policing/problem-solving process, and greater accountability for all parties (Rosenbaum 2004). Thus, police departments can supplement traditional hot spots enforcement with community policing and/or problem-oriented policing approaches (for other examples, see Weisburd and Green 1995b; Eck and Wartell 1996; Green-Mazerolle and Roehl 1998; Braga *et al.* 1999).

In this chapter I have suggested that the concept of hot spots, despite its theoretical and empirical attractiveness, can create problems that were unintended. Police administrators and researchers need to exercise caution when labeling and responding to locations in a narrow manner, given the political and social sensitivities associated with hot spots. Aggressive enforcement has its place in the arsenal of urban policing and is essential for providing short-term relief to distressed areas, but it should not be used as a stand-alone strategy or as society's primary answer to crime. Also, it requires close supervision of police officers and regular feedback from the community members to prevent abuses. Most importantly, given the central role of urban law enforcement agencies in public policy analysis, the argument put forth here is that the majority of tax-based police resources should be devoted to strategies that (1) show promise for *long-term* impact on rates of community crime and the quality of community life; (2) reflect the equitable distribution of police resources based on human need; and (3) embody the police organization's commitment to the fair and impartial treatment of all segments of society.

In essence, hot spots policing, as currently practiced, does not adequately address the historical, economic, political, social, and cultural dimensions of these target areas, all of which contribute to crime rates. The solution is not as simple as getting local residents, under the threat of arrest, to make better choices or accept responsibility for their behavior. These assumptions are overly simplistic and do not acknowledge the loss of hope and despair among these residents, their disconnection from conventional institutions, the stigma and rejection that result from having a criminal record, the neighborhood's loss of public and private resources to support healthy families, and the fact that dozens of other social problems (beyond crime) cluster in these hot spots. Hence, real solutions in these hot spots will require sophisticated research and intelligence, strategic planning, and comprehensive prevention programs involving many entities working in concert. I believe that senior police officials are capable of meeting this challenge by playing a lead role in multiagency partnerships and accepting the full responsibility that comes with being "the crime experts."

NOTE

The author would like to thank the following individuals for reviewing and providing helpful comments on previous drafts of this manuscript: Anthony Braga, Susan Hartnett, Amie Schuck, Cody Stephens, and David Weisburd.

REFERENCES

Braga, A. A. (2001). The effects of hot spots policing on crime. *Annals of American Political and Social Science*, *578*, 104–125.

Braga, A. A., Kennedy, D. M., Piehl, A. M., and Waring, E. J. (2001). *Reducing gun violence: The Boston Gun Project's Operation Ceasefire*. Washington, DC: Department of Justice, National Institute of Justice.

Braga, A., Weisburd, D., Waring, E., Green Mazerolle, L., Spelman, W., and Gajewski, F. (1999). Problem-oriented policing in violent crime places: A randomized controlled experiment. *Criminology*, *37* (3), 541–580.

Brantingham, P. L. and Brantingham, P. J. (1993). Environment, routine, and situation: Toward a pattern theory of crime. In R. V. Clarke and M. Felson (eds.), *Routine activity and rational choice. Advances in Criminological Theory*, 5. New Brunswick, NJ: Transaction Publications.

Bursik, R. J., Jr. and Grasmick, H. G. (1993). *Neighborhoods and crime: The dimensions of effective community control*. New York: Lexington.

Bushway, S. (1996). The impact of a criminal history record on access to legitimate employment. Unpublished doctoral dissertation. H. John Heinz School of Public Policy and Management, Carnegie Mellon University.

Cohen, L. E. and Felson, M. (1979). Social change and crime rate trends: A routine activity approach. *American Sociological Review*, *44*, 588–605.

Cornish, D. and Clarke, R. V. (eds.) (1986). *The reasoning criminal: Rational choice perspectives on offending*. New York: Springer-Verlag.

Eck, J. E. and Rosenbaum, D. P. (1994). The new police order: Effectiveness, equity, and efficiency in community policing. In D. P. Rosenbaum (ed.), *The challenge of community policing: Testing the promises* (pp. 3–23). Newbury Park, CA: Sage Publications.

Eck, J. E. and Weisburd, D. (1995). Crime places in crime theory. In J. E. Eck and D. Weisburd (eds.), *Crime and place, crime prevention studies* 4 (pp. 1–33). Monsey, NY: Criminal Justice Press.

Eck, J. E. and Wartell, J. (1996). *Reducing crime and drug dealing by improving place management: A randomized experiment*. Report to the San Diego Police Department. Washington, DC: Crime Control Institute.

Goldstein, H. (1990). *Problem-oriented policing*. New York: McGraw-Hill.

Green, J. R. (2000). Community policing in America: Changing the nature, structure, and function of the police. In J. Horney, J. Martin, D. L. MacKenzie, R. Peterson, and D. P. Rosenbaum (eds.), *Policies, processes, and decisions of the criminal justice system*, 3, Criminal Justice 2000 series. Washington, DC: US Department of Justice, National Institute of Justice.

Green-Mazerolle, L. and Roehl, J. (1998). *Civil remedies and crime prevention*. Munsey, NJ: Criminal Justice Press.

Hope, T. (1994). Problem-oriented policing and drug market locations: Three case studies. In R. V. Clarke (ed.), *Crime prevention studies*, 2. Monsey, New York: Criminal Justice Press.

Kahneman, D., Slovic, P., and Tversky, A. (1982). *Judgment under uncertainty: Heuristics and biases*. Cambridge: Cambridge University Press.

Kahneman, D. and Tversky, A. (1973). On the psychology of prediction. *Psychological Review*, *80*, 237–251.

Kane, R. J. (2002). The social ecology of police misconduct. *Criminology*, *40* (4), 867–896.

Kennedy, D. (1993). *Closing the market: Controlling the drug trade in Tampa, Florida*. NIJ Program Focus. Washington, DC: National Institute of Justice, US Department of Justice.

Kleiman, M. (1988). *Street-level drug enforcement: Examining the issues*. Washington, DC: National Institute of Justice, US Department of Justice.

Klein, M. W. (1986). Labeling theory and delinquency policy: An empirical test. *Criminal Justice and Behavior*, *13*, 47–79.

    (1999). Attempting gang control by suppression: The misuse of deterrence principles. In L. K. Gaines and W. Cordner (eds.), *Policing perspectives: An anthology* (ch. 18, pp. 269–282). Los Angeles, CA: Roxbury.

Koper, C. (1995). Just enough police presence: Reducing crime and disorderly behavior by optimizing patrol time in crime hot spots. Unpublished paper.

Maher, L. and Dixon, D. (2001). The cost of crackdowns: Policing Cabramatta's heroin market. *Current Issues in Criminal Justice*, *13* (1), 5–22.

Mamalian, C. A. and LaVigne, N. G. (1999). *The use of computerized mapping by law enforcement*. Washington, DC: National Institute of Justice, Office of Justice Programs, US Department of Justice.

Nisbett, R. E. and Ross, L. (1980). *Human inference: Strategies and shortcomings of social judgment*. Englewood Cliffs, NJ: Prentice-Hall.

Papachristos, A. V. (2003). The social structure of gang homicide in Chicago. Paper presented at the Annual Conference of the American Society of Criminology, November 21, Denver, Colorado.

Pope, C., Lovell, R., and Hsia, H. M. (2003). *Disproportionate minority confinement: A review of research literature from 1989 to 2001*. Washington,

DC: Office of Juvenile Justice and Delinquency Prevention, Office of Justice Programs, US Department of Justice.

Potter, G., Gaines, L., and Holbrook, B. (1990). Blowing smoke: An evaluation of marijuana eradication in Kentucky. *American Journal of Police, 9* (1), 97–116.

Rosenbaum, D. P. (1993). Civil liberties and aggressive enforcement: Balancing the rights of individuals and society in the drug war. In R. C. Davis, A. J. Lurigio, and D. P. Rosenbaum (eds.). *Drugs and the community* (pp. 55–82). Springfield, IL: Charles C. Thomas.

(2002). Evaluating multi-agency anti-crime partnerships: Theory, design and measurement issues. *Crime Prevention Studies, 14*, 171–225.

(2004). Community policing and web-based communication: Addressing the new information imperative. In L. A. Fridell and M. A. Wycoff (eds.), *Community policing: The past, present and future*. Washington, DC: Police Executive Research Forum.

Rosenbaum, D. P. and Lavrakas, P. J. (1995). Self-reports about place: The application of survey and interview methods to the study of small areas. In J. E. Eck and D. Weisburd (eds.), *Crime and place: Crime prevention studies* 4 (pp. 285–314). Monsey, NY: Criminal Justice Press.

Rosenbaum, D. P., Lurigio, A. J., and Davis, R. C. (1998). *The prevention of crime: Social and situational strategies*. Belmont, CA: Wadsworth.

Rosenbaum, D. P., Hawkins, D. F., Costello, S. K., Skogan, W. G., Roman Rivera, L., Vera, C., Rokita, R., Ring, M. K., Larson, T., and Munansangu, M. (2005). *Race and police: A matter of public trust*. Report to the National Institute of Justice, Office of Justice Programs, US Department of Justice.

Sampson, R. J. (2002). The community. In J. Q. Wilson and J. Petersilia (eds.), *Crime: Public policies for crime control* (pp. 225–252). Oakland, CA: Institute for Contemporary Studies Press.

Sampson, R. J., Raudenbush, S. W., and Earls, F. (1997). Neighborhoods and violent crime: A multilevel study of collective efficacy. *Science, 277*, 918–924.

Schuck, A. M. and Rosenbaum, D. P. (forthcoming). Promoting safe and healthy neighborhoods: What research tells us about intervention. In K. Fulbright-Anderson (ed.), *Community change: Theories, practices and evidence*. Washington, DC: The Aspen Institute.

Shadish, W. R., Cook, T. D., and Campbell, D. T. (2002). *Experimental and quasi-experimental designs for generalized causal inference*. Boston: Houghton Mifflin.

Sherman, L.W. (1990). Police crackdowns: Initial and residual deterrence. In M. Tonry and N. Morris (eds.), *Crime and justice: A review of research,* 12. Chicago: University of Chicago Press.

(1997). Policing for crime prevention. In L. W. Sherman, D. Gottfredson, D. MacKenzie, J. E. Eck, P. Reuter, and S. Bushway. *Preventing crime: What works, what doesn't, what's promising* (ch. 8). Report to the National Institute of Justice, Office of Justice Programs, US Department of Justice (NCJ 165366).

Sherman, L. W. and Rogan, D. P. (1995a). Deterrent effects of police raids on crackdowns: A randomized, controlled experiment. *Justice Quarterly 12* (4), 755–781.

(1995b). Effects of gun seizures on gun violence: "Hot spots" patrol in Kansas City. *Justice Quarterly 12* (4), 673–693.

Sherman, L. W. and Weisburd, D. (1995). General deterrent effects of police patrol in crime "Hot spots": A randomized, controlled trial. *Justice Quarterly 12* (4), 625–648.

Sherman, L. W., Gartin, P. R., and Buerger, M. E. (1989). Hot spots of predatory crime: Routine activities and the criminology of place. *Criminology*, 27, 27–55.

Sherman, L. W., Gottfredson, D., MacKenzie, D., Eck, J., Reuter, P., and Bushway, S. (1997). *Preventing crime: What works, what doesn't, what's promising.* Report to the National Institute of Justice, Office of Justice Programs, US Department of Justice. (NCJ 165366).

Skogan, W. G. (1990). *Disorder and decline: Crime and the spiral of decay in American neighborhoods.* New York: Free Press.

(ed.). (2003). *Community policing: Can it work?* Belmont, CA: Wadsworth.

(In press). Citizen satisfaction with police encounters. *Police Quarterly.*

Skogan, W. G., Steiner, L., Hartnett, S. M., DuBois, J., Bennis, J., Rottinghaus, B., Young Kim, S., Van, K., and Rosenbaum, D. P. (2002). *Community policing in Chicago, years eight and nine: An evaluation of Chicago's Alternative Policing Strategy and information technology initiative.* Final report to the Illinois Criminal Justice Information Authority. Evanston, IL: Northwestern University, Institute for Policy Research. December.

Smith, M., Sviridoff, M., Sadd, S., Curtis, R., and Grinc, R. (1992). *The neighborhood effects of street-level drug enforcement. Tactical Narcotics Teams in New York: An evaluation of TNT.* New York: Vera Institute of Justice.

Spelman, W. (1995). Criminal careers of public places. In J. E. Eck and D. Weisburd (eds.) *Crime and place: Crime prevention studies*, 4 (pp. 115–144). Monsey, NY: Criminal Justice Press.

Taylor, R. B. (1998). Crime and small-scale places: What we know, what we can prevent, and what else we need to know. *Crime and place: Plenary papers of the 1997 conference on criminal justice research and evaluation.* Washington, DC: National Institute of Justice, Office of Justice Programs, US Department of Justice. (NIJ 168618).

Tittle, C. R. and Paternoster, R. (2000). *Social deviance and crime: An organizational and theoretical approach.* Los Angeles, CA: Roxbury.

Tonry, M. and Farrington, D. P. (eds.). (1995). Building a safer society: Strategic approaches to crime prevention. *Crime and Justice: A Review of Research*, 19.

Travis, J., Solomon, A. L., and Waul, M. (2001). *From prison to home: The dimensions and consequences of prisoner reentry.* Washington, DC: The Urban Institute.

Tyler, T. R. (1990). *Why people obey the law.* New Haven: Yale University Press.

(2001). Trust and law-abiding behavior: Building better relationships between the police, the courts, and the minority community. *Boston University Law Review 81*, 361–406.

(In press). Policing in black and white: Ethnic group differences in trust and confidence in the police. *Police Quarterly.*

Uchida, C., Forst, B., and Annan, S. (1992). *Modern policing and the control of illegal drugs: Testing new strategies in two American cities.* Washington, DC:

National Institute of Justice, Office of Justice Programs, US Department of Justice.

Weisburd, D. and Eck, J. E. (2004). What can police do to reduce crime, disorder, and fear? *Annals of the American Academy of Political and Social Science, 593*, 42–65.

Weisburd, D. and Green, L. (1995a). Measuring immediate spatial displacement: Methodological issues and problems. In J. E. Eck and D. Weisburd (eds.), *Crime and place: Crime prevention studies*, 4 (pp. 349–361). Monsey, NY: Criminal Justice Press.

(1995b). Policing drug hot spots: The Jersey City Drug Market Analysis Experiment. *Justice Quarterly, 12* (4), 711–735.

Weitzer, R. and Tuch, S. A. (In press). Determinants of public satisfaction with the police. *Police Quarterly*.

Wilson, J. Q. and Petersilia, J. (eds.). (2002). *Crime: Public policies for crime control*. Oakland, CA: Institute for Contemporary Studies Press.

Worden, R., Bynum, T., and Frank, J. (1994). Police crackdowns on drug abuse and trafficking. In D. McKenzie and C. Uchida (eds.), *Drugs and crime: Evaluating public policy initiatives*. Thousand Oaks, CA: Sage.

Part VII

Compstat

14   *Advocate*
Compstat's innovation

Eli B. Silverman

Introduction

Compstat tributes are extensive. Compstat has been described as "perhaps the single most important organizational/administrative innovation in policing during the latter half of the 20th century" (Kelling and Sousa 2001: 6). A *Criminology and Public Policy Journal* editor recently termed Compstat "arguably one of the most significant strategic innovations in policing in the last couple of decades" (*Criminology and Public Policy* 2003: 419). The authors of a major study note that Compstat "has already been recognized as a major innovation in American policing" (Weisburd, Mastrofski, McNally *et al.* 2003: 422). In 1996, Compstat was awarded the prestigious Innovations in American Government Award from the Ford Foundation and the John F. Kennedy School of Government at Harvard University. Former Mayor Giuliani proclaims Compstat as his administration's "crown jewel" (Giuliani 2002: 7).

Why the praise, what are they specifically praising and is this praise warranted? These questions constitute the core of this chapter which maintains that Compstat praise, criticism, and replication are frequently based on a superficial understanding of its proper development, implementation, and many dimensions. The literature inadequately reflects how Compstat's successful implementation and maintenance is often incomplete when it lacks substantial organizational revamping and proper managerial preparation. This contributes to an insufficient appreciation of Compstat's array of attributes. In addition, there is often a lack of understanding of how any particular Compstat may reflect the organizational and managerial arrangements of an individual law enforcement agency at any specific time.

Exploration of these points will center on: Compstat's many facets, its origins, the reasons for and the nature of its replication in numerous versions and venues, and its very positive strengths as well as its prospective drawbacks.

Understanding Compstat

Compstat is most frequently understood by its most visible elements today. These include: up-to-date computerized crime data, crime analysis, and advanced crime mapping as the bases for regularized, interactive crime strategy meetings which hold managers accountable for specific crime strategies and solutions in their areas.

Familiar explanations

It is fair to say that the widespread diffusion of Compstat refers to these most noticeable elements. Since Compstat was first unveiled by the New York City Police Department (NYPD) in 1994, a Police Foundation 1999 survey for the National Institute of Justice (NIJ) revealed that a third of the nation's 515 largest police departments had implemented a Compstat-like program by 2001 and 20 percent were planning to do so. The same survey found that about 70 percent of police departments with Compstat programs reported attending a NYPD Compstat meeting (Weisburd, Mastrofski, McNally, and Greenspan 2001). My own research indicates that very few of the over 250 outsiders who attended Compstat meetings between 1994 and September 1997 were exposed to any Compstat elements other than the meetings (with the exception of a NYPD booklet on Compstat). It is unlikely that the Police Foundation's 70 percent differed much in their exposure to Compstat. (There may, in fact, be some overlap between the two groups.)

This process is continuing. Gootman reported that 219 police agency representatives visited NYPD Compstat meetings in 1998, 221 in 1999, and 235 in the first ten months of 2000 (Gootman 2000: B1). *Attendance at a Compstat meeting, while a useful introduction, does not provide adequate preparation for introducing and establishing Compstat.* In fact, it may be misleading because attendees often become mesmerized by the flashy overhead display of multiple crime maps synchronized with technologically advanced portrayals of computerized crime statistics.

The lure of Compstat

The first three years of the NYPD's Compstat corresponded with dramatic declines in the city's crime rate. According to the FBI's Unified Crime Reports, the city's 12 percent decline in index crime in1994 (compared to a national drop of less than 2 percent) grew to 16 percent in 1995 and yielded another 16 percent in 1996. These decreases accounted for more than 60 percent of the national decline during this period.

While these figures, of course, do not prove a causal relationship, they received extraordinary law enforcement and national attention. The New York Model (Compstat) was offered as the road to rapid crime reduction (Gootman 2000: B1). A *Time* magazine 1996 observation is still applicable today. "Compstat has become the Lourdes of policing, drawing pilgrim cops from around the world . . . for a taste of New York's magic" (Pooley 1996: 55–56).

Too often, therefore, Compstat has been interpreted as primarily a meeting with a statistical computer program which, when it generates accurate and timely crime statistics, transforms a traditional bureaucracy into a flexible, adaptable police agency geared to effective crime control strategies. In the vernacular, it is only necessary to display computer-generated crime maps and pressure commanders in order "to make the dots go away" (Maple 1999: 38). This superficial approach is emblematic of the quick managerial fix approach, thus contributing to the misunderstanding and misapplication of Compstat.

This Compstat allure of crime reduction through technological advancement is reflected in the in-depth study of the Lowell Police Department Compstat:

What police department, however, would not want to adopt a program whose clear purpose is to reduce crime through the implementation of a well-defined set of technologies and procedures? The appeal of Compstat's crime fighting goal to the police increases the likelihood that it will endure. (Willis, Mastrofski, Weisburd, and Greenspan 2003: 11)

The full Compstat

Compstat, however, is a far more complex product of changes in managerial and organizational arrangements, including flattening, decentralization, greater personnel authority, discretion and autonomy, geographic managerial accountably, and enhanced problem solving. Based on the New York experience, it is my view that Compstat cannot be a fully viable entity if the above administrative, managerial, and operational activities do not precede it.

It is worthwhile noting that the Police Foundation study's "six key elements" essential to Compstat contain similar components. They are "mission clarification, internal accountability, geographic organization of operational command, organizational flexibility, data driven problem identification and assessment and innovative problem solving tactics, and external information exchange" (Weisburd *et al.* 2003: 427).

It is equally noteworthy that the Police Foundation study found many of these key elements lacking in many police Compstat programs. In their comparison of Compstat and non-Compstat agencies, the study concludes that the Compstat agencies "have opted for a model much heavier on control than on empowerment" (Weisburd *et al.* 2003: 448). Moreover, despite its virtues, the authors found that:

Compstat agencies were largely indistinguishable from non-Compstat agencies on measures that gauged geographic organization of command, organizational flexibility, the time availability of data, and the selection and implementation of innovative strategies and tactics . . . Compstat departments are more reluctant to relinquish power that would decentralize some key elements of decisionmaking geographically . . . enhance flexibility, and risk going outside of the standard tool kit of police tactics and strategies. The combined effect overall, whether or not intended, is to reinforce a traditional bureaucratic model of command and control. (Weisburd *et al.* 2003: 448)

But I find this conclusion less than surprising. The study's Compstat programs are self-designated. There is no evidence that these police agencies underwent the self-diagnosis, reengineering, and organizational and managerial overhaul processes that preceded the New York Compstat experience.

Thus a more complete understanding of Compstat may be gained through a review of the context and origins of New York's Compstat in order to fully appreciate its positive qualities for modern day policing. Failure to grasp the differences between popular accounts and Compstat's actual origins can deflect attention away from Compstat's merits while activating undesirable features.

Immediate origins

In the immediate sense, contrary to a widely held view, Compstat was not a preordained planned system of managerial supervision, accountability, and strategic policing. Its first meeting, as a matter of fact, was almost serendipitous. Upon taking office in 1994, Commissioner Bratton called for a weekly, one-on-one, current events briefing with a representative from each of the NYPD's eight bureaus during the early months of his administration. Deputy Commissioner Maple authorized the head of the Patrol Bureau to discuss crime statistics with the commissioner. A disturbing reality surfaced: the NYPD did not know its current crime statistics; there was a reporting time lag of three to six months.

Maple, in conjunction with other key people pressed the precincts to generate crime activity statistics on a weekly basis. During the second week of February 1994, all precincts provided a hand count of the seven major crimes for the first six weeks of 1993 compared to the same period in 1994. The Patrol Bureau's staff computerized this crime activity and assembled it into a document referred to as the "Compstat book." The first Compstat book included current data on a year-to-date basis for crime complaints and arrests for every major felony category, as well as gun arrests, compiled on citywide, patrol borough, and precinct levels.

Contrary to most accounts, the acronym Compstat is not short for "computer statistics." Compstat actually arose from a computer file, "compare stats," in which the data was originally stored. Compstat, then, was simply short for "compare stats." This distinction is not trivial since the "computer statistics" interpretation frequently suggests that an advanced statistical computer program is synonymous with effective crime control, further contributing to Compstat's misapplication.

In fact, at the outset, Compstat was based on an elementary database, created in a set of desktop office software called Smart Ware, from Informix. This was later replaced, for a considerable period, by Microsoft's very basic FoxPro database for businesses to enter all the statistics into files.

In New York, regularized Compstat meetings grew out of a need for a mechanism to ensure precinct COs' accountability and to improve performance. In April 1994, the leadership was searching for ways to sharpen the NYPD's crime-fighting focus. At that time, for example, boroughs held monthly field robbery meetings in which precinct COs and robbery and anti-crime sergeants met with the borough staffs (to whom they reported) to discuss robbery trends.

Top-level executives requested that the Brooklyn North patrol borough hold its monthly robbery meeting at headquarters – One Police Plaza. After the Brooklyn borough CO's overview of special conditions, several precinct COs were called to the front of the room. Their presentations, although suitable for public community council meetings, lacked in-depth analyses of complex crime problems. Dissatisfied, the chief abruptly terminated the meeting and announced monthly headquarters meetings for each borough. The Compstat process was launched; there was no turning back.

Late in April 1994 the NYPD leadership decided to use these headquarters meetings to link the newly released drug and gun strategies with the Compstat books. Tenacity was essential. The meetings, held twice weekly, became mandatory. They began promptly at 7:00 a.m., a time when there are likely to be few distractions.

Organization and managerial foundations

Compstat's roots, however, are far deeper than the scenario described above. Many managerial and organizational interventions laid the foundation for Compstat. The groundwork for Compstat centered on early developments prior to the Bratton administration (Silverman 1999: 21–66). Even during the Bratton administration which began in 1994, *all interventions took place before Compstat's introduction.* Early in 1994, the NYPD began to redesign its organizational structure, employing management strategies designed to re-engineer its business processes and create a "flatter" organizational structure based on geographic decentralization, teamwork, information sharing, and managerial accountability (Silverman and O'Connell 1999).

Information flow, for example, was eased by the elimination of the level of division which, prior to 1994, was interposed between the precincts and the boroughs. Each of the twenty-three divisions was responsible for from two to four precincts. Since the divisions' responsibilities were primarily administrative, the new organizational arrangement smoothed relationships between newly beefed up precinct and borough responsibilities and capabilities.

The rapid redesign of the department's organizational architecture was based upon the concept of continuous performance improvement characterized by clearly delineated objective standards, benchmarking, sharing of "best practice," and the development and analysis of timely and accurate information to manage change.

Modern management provided the orchestral score; "reengineering" was its name. Contemporary management literature explains that reengineering requires "radical change," a "starting over" throughout the entire organization, nothing less than a "reinvention of how organizations work." Commissioner Bratton insisted: "We reengineered the NYPD into an organization capable of supporting our goals" (Bratton 1996: 1).

Reengineering acted like a booster cable to the NYPD's battery, providing the cranking power needed to activate decentralization and command accountability. Relinquishing control of daily ground operations was the most fundamental yet difficult challenge facing the new administration. Traditionally, the person at the apex of the NYPD pyramid would retain control through standardized procedures and policies. But in order to hold precinct commanders accountable for crime prevention, the new leadership knew the organization must grant them more discretion. Rather than allow headquarters to determine staffing and deployment on a citywide basis, it was decided that reducing crime, fear of crime, and disorder would flow from patrol borough and precinct coordination of selected enforcement efforts.

In essence, the NYPD was able to achieve what Peters and Waterman label "simultaneous loose-tight properties," meaning the "co-existence of firm central direction and maximum individual autonomy" (Peters and Waterman 1982: 318). So while the top NYPD levels were now fortified with greater detail, this knowledge extends beyond activities such as arrest particulars to more informative data such as the characteristics, times, and locations of precinct-selected enforcement strategies and their relationship to crime reduction.

These reengineering structural, operational, and strategic reconfigurations stemmed from a so-called "cultural diagnostic" which rested on deliberations emanating from multirank and functional NYPD focus groups. These groups examined various dimensions of NYPD missions and strategies and the obstacles which hindered strategy effectiveness and goal achievement.

Consequently, the reengineering reports questioned the NYPD's operating procedures. What current policy yields, they claimed, was inadequate. The precinct organization report, for example, noted:

2 or 3 percent reduction in crime is not good enough. We need to change the organization to do more. The need to reengineer precincts is not immediately apparent. City-wide crime continues to decline year after year. Every annual precinct state of command report, without exception, includes evidence of neighborhood improvements. Bureau and Special Unit Commanders to a man, or a woman, will vigorously defend the effectiveness of the present system. Why fix what's not broken?

The answer is in the new mission of the department to dramatically reduce crime, fear, and disorder. Slow, continuous improvement doesn't cut it, and that is all the present system can deliver . . . [R]eengineering in its simplest forms means starting all over, starting from scratch. (New York City Police Department 1994: v)

Selling Compstat

What started out as a computer file and a book to satisfy crime informational needs has evolved and been reconstructed into a multifaceted forum for coordinated, reenergized, and accountable organizational crime-fighting strategies. Its strength lies in its adaptability and compliance mechanisms. It is vitally important to recognize that Compstat's initial and prime *raison d'être* was and is to measure and hold managers accountable for performance. In Moore's words:

It becomes a powerful managerial system in part because the technical capacity of the system allows it to produce accurate information on important dimensions of performance at a level that coincides with a particular manager's domain of responsibility . . . [Compstat] is, in the end, primarily a performance measurement system. (Moore 2003: 470, 472; see also Walsh 2001)

All these characteristics have contributed to its widespread replication in various formats in numerous locations. The claims and counterclaims are numerous and often difficult to evaluate since Compstat has frequently been associated with and introduced at the same time as other law enforcement and societal changes.

The boldest claims assert that Compstat plays a significant role in crime reduction due to its accountability and decentralized components. Kelling and Sousa include Compstat in their analysis of NYPD effective crime reduction policing in six precincts. They conclude that

> Both the problem-solving strategy and the notion of accountability came to fruition in weekly NYPD headquarters meetings known as Compstat . . . But the true effectiveness of Compstat lies in its ability to drive the development of crime reduction tactics at the precinct level. By making precinct commanders accountable, centralized Compstat allows the problem solving strategy to operate in a decentralized manner. (Kelling and Sousa 2001: 17)

Compstat crime reduction efficacy is also frequently advocated by police administrators, several of whom moved from the NYPD to head other city police departments. Compstat's introduction in New Orleans, for example, corresponded with a decline in murders from 421 in 1994, diving 55 percent in 1999 to 162. Minneapolis' Compstat's version, CODEFOR (Computer Optimized Deployment-Focus on Results) has been credited for a double digit decrease in homicides, aggravated assaults, robberies, burglaries, and auto thefts between 1998 and 1999 (Anderson 2001: 4). In 2000 Compstat was introduced in Baltimore by its new chief, a former NYPD deputy police commissioner. By the end of the year, the city experienced its first below 300 homicides in 20 years accompanied by an overall crime drop of 25 percent (Anderson 2001: 4; Clines 2001: 15; Weissenstein 2003: 27). Between 1999 and 2001, Baltimore's overall violent crime declined 24 percent, homicides dropped 15 percent, shootings fell 34 percent, robberies dropped 28 percent, rapes 20 percent, and assaults 21 percent (Henry and Bratton 2002: 307). Philadelphia's former police commissioner, another former NYPD deputy police commissioner, attributed a decline in the city's crime to Compstat-driven policing. "Social conditions in the city have not changed radically in the two years and we have the same police department, the same number of officers. Nothing has changed but how we deploy them and utilize them" (Anderson 2001: 3).

Similar crime reduction assertions have been made for police agencies around the world. Two Australian scholars, for example, recently published an evaluation of the New South Wales Compstat-modeled Operation and Crime Review (OCM). The authors found that this process was effective in reducing three of the four offence categories studied (Chilvers and Weatherburn 2004).

Although these claims are repeated elsewhere, some scholars are not convinced. While Eck and Maguire acknowledge that "homicide rates have declined significantly from 1994 to 1997, following the implementation of Compstat" in the United States, they raise serious reservations (Eck and Maguire 2000: 231). First, they correctly assert that "Compstat was implemented along with a number of changes in the NYPD . . . Consequently it is difficult to attribute any reductions in crime to specific police changes" (Eck and Maguire 2000: 230).

Beyond this valid point, the relationships are even more complicated. A full Compstat program, as discussed earlier, rests upon and ultimately encompasses many changes including police deployment driven by more accurate Compstat crime mapping. The efficacy of these strategies depends on the extent to which Compstat can permeate the agency's entire operations. So some Compstats may be viewed as "Compstat Lite" while others may be more fully developed, embracing many dimensions of Compstat's crime strategy management. Compstat's prime architect, the late Jack Maple, referred to the pale Compstat imitations as the "knock off versions" whereby administrators "just sit in a circle and chat about the intelligence" (Maple 1999: 47). This vivid Compstat contrast explains why, in my view, Eck and Maguire are compelled to maintain:

We do not know, however, whether this [homicide] reduction is produced through general deterrence of all those who frequent hot spots, through specific deterrence of hot-spot offenders who come under closer scrutiny of the police, or through incapacitation of repeat offenders following their arrest at these hot spots. So, there is an array of possible mechanisms through which directed patrol can reduce crime at hot spots. (Eck and Maguire 2000: 231)

Finally, Eck and Maguire find that the rate of homicide reductions in other cities does not lend credence to the independent impact of Compstat on homicide rates. Yet they acknowledge that these findings are tenuous:

Our analysis does not find that Compstat is ineffective. These explorations can not be interpreted as a rigorous exploration of Compstat . . . It is possible, given the complexity of homicide patterns, that the Compstat process had a subtle and even meaningful but difficult to detect effect on crime in New York. (Eck and Maguire 2000: 235)

Less controversial, however, is Compstat's surging popularity and adoption by numerous agencies and jurisdictions seeking to more effectively administer their operations and hold managers accountable. Omaha's year-old Compstat is credited with improving cooperation among all units. "Instead of one unit tackling a problem, everyone gets involved . . . The entire culture has changed now" (*Law Enforcement News*, March 2004: 11).

In 1996, New York City's Corrections Department modeled its TEAMS (Total Efficiency Accountability Management System) program on Compstat with an examination of the department's "most fundamental practices and procedures" (O'Connell 2001: 17). Again, accountability is a major theme which, when fused with more accurate and timely statistical reporting and analysis and interunit cooperation, has been credited with a dramatic reduction in inmate violence. Between 1995 and 1999, stabbings and slashing declined from 1093 to 70 (Anderson 2001: 3).

TEAMS has evolved and now addresses more than just jail violence. Its accountability system has been continually expanded to retrieve and assess almost 600 performance indicators addressing such issues as religious service attendance, maintenance work orders, health care, overtime, compliance with food service regulations, completed searches conducted, and the performance of personnel who have been the subject of the department's civility tests (O'Connell and Straub 1999a; 1999b; 1999c).

Since TEAMS is oriented to system-wide innovation, its impact has contributed to a "shift in organizational culture and philosophy" (O'Connell 2001: 19). A former commissioner observed:

> The key is really the way that it assists us in using proactive and creative management. It expands possibilities and get more people involved in the decisionmaking process. Our people don't just think of themselves as corrections officers anymore. Now they see themselves as managers. (O'Connell 2001: 19)

Compstat accountability mechanisms, long a staple of the private sector, have also become increasingly attractive to non-law-enforcement public agencies. There are numerous examples. The New York City Department of Parks and Recreation, for instance, developed its own version of Compstat, calling it Parkstat. When Parks officials visited NYPD Compstat meetings in 1997, they realized that they could utilize this system to develop and refine their Parks Inspection Program (PIP) which oversees the maintenance and operation of over 28,000 acres of property throughout New York City. Now parks department data analysis and managerial accountability are combined with monthly meetings to assess overall conditions, cleanliness of structural features such as benches, fences, sidewalks, play equipment, and landscape features such as trees, athletic fields, and water bodies (O'Connell 2001: 20). The percentage of parks rated acceptably clean and safe increased from 47 percent in 1993 to 86 percent in 2001 (Webber and Robinson 2003: 3). One observer's assessment of Parkstat ranks it comparable to Compstat's high rating:

As with Compstat and TEAMS, an emphasis is placed on pattern or trend identification. All performance data are viewed through three lenses, which look for district wide trends, borough wide comparison and trends, and citywide comparison and trends. . .
    Parkstat serves many functions, not the least of which is the fostering of organizational learning. Senior administrators learn about what is occurring in the field at the same time that districts are learning from one another. Effective practices are openly shared and disseminated throughout the entire organization.
    The Parkstat program is continually developing. Indeed, the department recently renamed it Parkstat Plus and has expanded it to include a broader range of performance measures . . . relating to personnel, vehicle maintenance, resource allocation and enforcement activity to ensure superior service delivery. Parkstat stands as an excellent example of how the Compstat model can be adopted and successfully implemented outside the field of criminal justice. (O'Connell 2001: 21, 22)

Perhaps the most ambitious extension of Compstat's managerial accountability and informational exchange processes began in the City of Baltimore in mid 2000 when its mayor was delighted with the results of the Baltimore Police Department's first year with Compstat. Baltimore's program, called Citistat (first developed by Compstat architect, the late Jack Maple) is an attempt to evaluate and coordinate performance on a citywide basis whereby supervisors report every two weeks (as opposed to the previous quarterly basis) on their departments' performance. Citistat's timely data permits the assessment and coordination of diverse social services dealing with graffiti, abandoned vehicles, vacant housing, lead paint abatement, urban blight, drugs, and drug treatment. Discussions are based on up-to-date information. Citistat meetings are similar to those of Compstat whereby data, graphs, and maps are projected to track and display department performance.

    So far, the city is pleased with Citistat's development. There has been a 40 percent reduction in payroll overtime with savings of over $15 million over two years. Its director of operations maintains that "The charts, maps and pictures tell a story of performance, and those managers are held accountable" (Webber and Robinson 2003: 4). The fact that the prestigious Innovations in American Government Award was awarded to Baltimore's Citistat ten years after NYPD's Compstat received the same award speaks to the enduring concepts embedded in this managerial and organizational approach. Speaking for Harvard University's Kennedy School, Stephen Goldsmith stated: "Citistat is a management tool for public officials that translates into real, tangible results for citizens. Government leaders across the country and around the world are taking notice of its success – and for good reason" (July 28, 2004).

Citistat, like most Compstat-type programs, seeks to lower the informational barriers that generally hinder intra and interagency collaboration. Baltimore is constantly expanding the number of agencies included in the data analyses and its Citistat meetings. It appears that Citistat is the ultimate test of Compstat's ability to serve as the informational cement of reform, the central mechanism that provides communication links to traditionally isolated specialized units. Fragmentation plagues many organizations. Harvard management expert Rosabeth Kanter calls it "segmentalism" and notes, "The failure of many organization-change efforts has more to do with the lack . . . of an integrating, institutionalizing mechanism than with inherent problems in an innovation itself" (Kanter 1983: 301). Without Compstat, fragmentation would continue to rule supreme. Compstat's confrontation of informational splintering can be indispensable to organizational well-being. Compstat can serve as the organizational glue that bonds many changes together.

Maintaining Compstat

Like any administrative-managerial-technological innovation, Compstat is not an unalloyed asset when either of two conditions is not met. The first pertains to the proper and full fundamental organizational and managerial reforms necessary to establish Compstat as an innovation. The absence of these reforms yields a Compstat that is more in name than in substance. The second refers to the obligation to maintain these structural and managerial underpinnings.

Since the first condition was previously discussed (see pp. 271–273), I now turn to the second condition of Compstat maintenance. Just as it is mistaken to assume that all Compstats are the same, it is equally erroneous to suppose that all Compstats will receive steady attention to their reform underpinnings. The vitality of a well-functioning Compstat rests on its connections to, indeed its centrality to, a reenergized, restructured, and adaptable problem-solving law enforcement organization.

Compstat's proper introduction should not be confused with long-term preservation. As a study of Compstat and organizational change in one law enforcement agency observed: "police organizations are notoriously resistant to change and any subsequent changes usually require many years to take effect" (Willis *et al.* 2003: 58). Properly installing and maintaining Compstat, therefore, requires vigilance.

There are serious liabilities when Compstat is not properly implemented or sustained. Compstat can be easily engulfed by a culture of top-down directives dominated by numbers reflecting the predominant control system of the particular agency.

When Compstat performance and accountability measurement becomes excessively supervised, whether within a highly centralized organization or from external hierarchical organizations, the consequences can be alarming. Subordinate units will naturally concentrate on those items being measured. Or, as the saying goes, what gets measured gets done. This can lead to crime statistics manipulation and/or downgrading which has been recently reported in numerous locales including Philadelphia, Atlanta (Hart, 2004: 6), New Orleans (Ritea, 2003a: 1; Ritea, 2003b: 1), New York (Parascandola and Levitt, 2004: 5; Gardiner and Levitt, 2003: 8) and Broward County, Florida (Hernandez, O'Boye, and O'Neill, 2004: 9). Any performance measurement instrument, including Compstat, has the capacity to aggravate this condition, posing serious problems for law enforcement's statistical accuracy (Manning 2001: 331–333; Willis *et al.* 2003: 13).

Thus it is crucial to recognize that Compstat is not some distinct identity isolated from the law enforcement agency in which it functions. Measurement of its success cannot be divorced from the structure in which it operates since it often reflects the prevailing organizational and political climate. To view Compstat in any other way is to reify it and endow it with elements beyond its control.

Compstat's evolving role in department priorities can be observed even in the police departments where it gained the greatest notice. Over the years, the NYPD's Compstat has become increasingly centralized with specialized units more likely directed from above:

In effect a centralization thrust has been superimposed on decentralized reforms. But centralization now has a powerful weapon in its arsenal – Compstat.

Compstat, in many senses, has been turned on its head. Instead of a tool to reevaluate objectives and tactics and scan the environment for future trends, the information from computer-generated comparative statistics is becoming known for only its most visible aspects – crime mapping and deployment activity. Greater information now is used to bear down on the management of many street operations. Numbers, sometimes any numbers, rule the day.

The original technocratic components of Compstat have been reified and duplicated, while its analytical underpinnings dwindle. In this mix, organizational learning often gets lost in the shuffle. . .

And what happens when painstaking and constant lessons of implementation are neglected for the quick fix? The short-haul dominates. (Silverman 2001: 206–213)

Conclusion: Compstat as an innovation

Despite its liabilities in specific circumstances, Compstat constitutes a significant law enforcement innovation. At its best, Compstat is a unique blending of performance measurement, computer technology, crime mapping, data analysis, information sharing, managerial accountability, interactive strategy meetings, and organizational cohesiveness and learning. It is easy to forget the freshness of Commissioner Bratton's approach over ten years ago when entrance to his higher echelon was restricted to commanders committed to double-digit crime reduction. Establishing a specific objective – a 10 percent reduction in crime for 1994 – was the initial propellant for change. While target-setting is the norm for the private sector, usually it is anathema for public organizations because it offers a yardstick against which performance can be more accurately measured and, if deficient, condemned.

The need to instill and recognize good performance in public policing is a vital managerial imperative. Certainly, the call for improved police performance grew out of felt necessities. For both real and/or imagined reasons, there was wide discontent with the effectiveness and management of police performance.

For Compstat, the question, then, is not should performance be measured. The questions are: what performance should be measured (Jones and Silverman 1984); how should performance measurement be implemented, assessed, and maintained; and by whom; and, more importantly, in what type of organizational and political context.

In New York, as in many other jurisdictions, Compstat originally focused on crime statistics and police arrest and quality of life enforcement activities. But Compstat, *per se*, is not inherently restricted to these measurements. Compstat's beauty lies in its versatility and adaptability. In New York, for example, Compstat, at various times, has included citizen satisfaction survey statistics, precinct commander community meeting activities, citizen complaints, and domestic violence issues and data.

Furthermore, as previously discussed (see pp. 276–278) Compstat lends itself to a variety of law enforcement and non-law-enforcement contexts. Numerous additional agencies are currently adopting their own versions of Compstat. These include New York's Office of Health Insurance with its Healthstat designed to assist uninsured New Yorkers enroll in a publicly funded health insurance program. "In the first 18 months, participating agencies enrolled about 340,000 eligible New Yorkers" (Webber and Robinson, 2003: 4). The Department of Transportation instituted MOVE, an accountability and performance management system that meets twice a month to assess operational performance. The cities of Miami and Pittsburgh are pursuing comprehensive Compstat-like systems similar to Baltimore's Citistat.

Societal needs for information sharing, data analysis, and effective organizational-managerial performance will only continue to proliferate and even expand Compstat's rapid diffusion. Two and a half years before the 9/11 terrorist attacks on the United States, Compstat's architect, the late Jack Maple, was asked about the future of Compstat. He replied:

This should not be limited to the police department. It should involve every city agency, the fire department, the building department, the transportation department; everybody should be contributing and coordinating. And other law enforcement agencies need to participate fully. The FBI, DEA and ATF offices in a city should be running their own numbers and then bring those to Compstat meetings at the police department. (Dussault 1999: 2)

Now in this post 9/11 era, there are numerous calls to overcome institutional barriers by federalizing the Compstat process in order to combat terrorism.

The intelligence and accountability mechanism known as Compstat is tailor made for combating terrorism. Applying this to America's new war, however, requires solving one of the most enduring problems in policing: turf jealousy, especially between the FBI and local law enforcement agencies.

The FBI's anti-terrorism efforts should be Compstated in every city where the bureau operates. Where a Joint Terrorism Task Force exists, the commanders of the agencies should meet on a biweekly basis to interrogate task force members about the progress of their investigations. Where JTTFs don't exist, the FBI should assemble comparable meetings with all relevant agency heads. The new Fedstat meetings would have two purposes: to ensure that each ongoing investigation is being relentlessly and competently pursued, and to share intelligence. (MacDonald 2001: 27)

Compstat has provided significant advances in policing and organizational performance. It enables key decisionmakers to engage in face-to-face discussions of issues and proactive practices that draw upon the collective expertise of the entire organization. It has developed as an interactive management device that enables the organization to learn, teach, supervise, and evaluate personnel in one central forum. Compstat's multifaceted possibilities embrace an array of positive outcomes. It is incumbent upon effective leadership to seize upon this potential.

REFERENCES

Anderson, D. C. (2001). Crime control by the numbers: Compstat yields new lessons for the police and the replication of a good idea. *Ford Foundation Report*. New York.

Bowerman, M. and Ball, A. (2000). Great expectations: Benchmarking for best value. *Public Money and Management*, 20 (2), 21–26.

Bratton, W. (1996, August 1). Management secrets of a crime-fighter extraordinaire. *Bottom Line*.

Chilvers, M. and Weatherburn, D. (2004). The New South Wales Compstat process: Its impact on crime. *Australian and New Zealand Journal of Criminology*.

Clines, F. X. (2001, January 3). Baltimore gladly breaks 10 year homicide streak. *New York Times*, A11.

Dussault, R. (1999). Jack Maple: Betting on intelligence. *Internet, govtech.net/publications*, April.

Eck, J. E. and Maguire, E. R. (2000). Have changes in policing reduced violent crime? An assessment of the evidence. In A. Blumstein and J. Wallman (eds.), *The crime drop in America* (pp. 207–65). Cambridge: Cambridge University Press.

Gardiner, S. and Levitt, L. (2003, June 21). NYPD: Some crime stats misclassified. *New York Newsday*, 11.

Giuliani, R. W. (2002). *Leadership*. New York: Hyperion.

Goldsmith, S. (2004). *The innovations in American government awards*. Cambridge, MA: John F. Kennedy School of Government, Harvard University.

Gootman, E. (2000, October 24). A police department's growing allure: Crime fighters from around world visit for tips. *New York Times*, B1.

Hart, A. (2004, February 21). Report finds Atlanta police cut figures on crimes. *The New York Times*, 26.

Henry, V. E. and Bratton, W. J. (2002). *The Compstat paradigm: Management accountability in policing, business and the public sector*. New York: Looseleaf Law Publications.

Hernandez, J., O'Boye, S., and O'Neill, A. W. (2004, February 25). Sheriff's office scrutinizes its crime data bonuses tied to performance under review. *Sun-Sentinel*, A1, 6.

Jones, S. and Silverman, E. (1984). What price efficiency. *Policing*, 1 (1), 31–48.

Kanter, R. M. (1983). *The change masters*. New York: Simon and Schuster.

Kelling, G. L. and Sousa, W. H. (2001). *Do police matter? An analysis of the impact of New York City's police reforms*. Civic Report No. 22. New York: Manhattan Institute.

Law Enforcement News. (2004). Compstat is doing more than just driving down Omaha's rate. March.

MacDonald, H. (2001). Keeping New York safe from terrorism. *City Journal*. Autumn.

Manning, P. K. (2001). Theorizing policing: The drama and myth of crime control in the NYPD. *Theoretical Criminology*, 5 (3), 315–344.

Maple, J. (1999). *Crime fighter*. New York: Broadway.

Moore, M. (2003). Sizing up Compstat: An important administrative innovation in policing. *Criminology and Public Policy*, 2 (3), 469–494.

New York City Police Department. (1994). Re-engineering team. *Precinct Organization*. New York.

O'Connell, P. E. (2001). *Using performance data for accountability*. Arlington, VA: Price Waterhouse Coopers.

O'Connell, P. E. and Straub, F. (1999a). Why the jails didn't explode. *City Journal*, 2, Spring, 28–37.

(1999b). Managing jails with T.E.A.M.S. *American Jail*, March/April, 48–54.

(1999c). For jail management, Compstat's a keeper. *Law Enforcement News*, 9.

Parascandola, R. and Levitt, L. (2004, March 22). Police statistics: Numbers scrutinized. *New York Newsday*, 14.

Peters, T. and Waterman, R. H. (1982). *In search of excellence*. New York: Warner.

Pooley, E. (1996). One good apple. *Time*, January, 55–56.

Ritea, S. (2003a, October 24). Five N.O. officers fired over altered crime stats. *The Times Picayune*, 1.

(2003b, October 25). Crime, coercion and cover-up. *The Times-Picayune*, 1.

Silverman, E. B. (1999). *NYPD battles crime: Innovative strategies in policing*. Boston: Northeastern University Press.

(2001). *Epilogue. NYPD battles crime: Innovative strategies in policing*. Boston: Northeastern University Press.

Silverman, E. B. and O'Connell, P. (1999). Organizational change and decision-making in the New York City Police Department. *International Journal of Public Administration*, 22 (2).

Walsh, W. F. (2001). Compstat: An analysis of an emerging police managerial paradigm. *Policing: An International Journal of Police Strategies and Management*, 24(3), 347–362.

Webber, R. and Robinson, G. (2003). Compstamania. *Gotham Gazette*. New York: Citizens Union, July 7.

Weisburd, D., Mastrofski, S. D., McNally, A. M., and Greenspan, R. (2001). *Compstat and organizational change: Findings from a national survey*. Report submitted to the National Institute of Justice by the Police Foundation.

Weisburd, D., Mastrofski, S. D., McNally, A. M., Greenspan, R., and Willis, J. J. (2003). Reforming to preserve: Compstat and strategic problem solving in American policing. *Criminology and Public Policy*, 2 (3), 421–456.

Weissenstein, M. (2003). Call on NY's top cops: NYPD brass recruited by other cities to lower crime rates. *Newsday*, January 2.

Willis, J. J., Mastrofski, S. D., Weisburd, D., and Greenspan, R. (2003). *Compstat and organizational change in the Lowell police department: Challenges and opportunities*. Washington, DC: Police Foundation.

15 Critic
Changing everything so that everything can remain the same: Compstat and American policing

David Weisburd, Stephen D. Mastrofski, James J. Willis, and Rosann Greenspan

Compstat has come to be seen as a major innovation in American policing. It has received national awards from Harvard University and former Vice President Gore, and has been featured prominently along with William Bratton (the police administrator who created the program) in the national news media. Its originators and proponents have given Compstat credit for impressive reductions in crime and improvements in neighborhood quality of life in a number of cities that have adopted the program (Silverman 1996; Remnick 1997; Gurwitt 1998; Bratton 1999). And while introduced only in 1994 in New York City, police departments around the country have begun to adopt Compstat or variations of it (Law Enforcement News 1997; Maas 1998; McDonald 1998; Weisburd, Mastrofski, McNally *et al.* 2003). Indeed, a Police Foundation survey suggests that Compstat had literally burst onto the American police scene. Only six years after Compstat emerged in New York City, more than a third of American police agencies with 100 or more sworn officers claimed to have implemented a Compstat-like program (Weisburd, Mastrofski, McNally, and Greenspan 2001).

Drawing from a series of studies we conducted at the Police Foundation (Weisburd *et al.* 2001; Greenspan, Mastrofski, and Weisburd 2003; Weisburd *et al.* 2003; Willis, Mastrofski, Weisburd, and Greenspan 2004; Willis, Mastrofski, and Weisburd 2004a, 2004b), we will argue in this chapter that there is a wide gap between the promise of Compstat and its implementation in American policing. While Compstat promises to reinvigorate police organizations and to empower them to solve crime problems in America's cities, it appears to be more focused on maintaining and reinforcing the "bureaucratic" or "paramilitary" model of police organization (see Goldstein 1977; Bittner 1980; Punch 1983). In turn, we argue that there is little substantive evidence of the much touted crime control benefits of Compstat, and indeed that the Compstat model

284

in many ways inhibits the problem-solving capabilities of police agencies that it is in theory meant to foster. This leads us to question whether Compstat is more of a reaction than a reform in policing – a program that enables police agencies to claim that much has changed, but in fact allows the police to return to traditional models of police organization.

We begin our chapter by describing the promise of the Compstat model as an innovation in American policing. We then illustrate how specific elements of Compstat that reinforce traditional models of policing have been dominant in its diffusion onto the American police scene, and argue that the Compstat model includes a fundamental tension that undermines Compstat's promise of innovation in police strategies and tactics. Before concluding, we speculate on the evidence regarding Compstat's crime control effectiveness.

The promise of Compstat

In a ground-breaking article written in 1979, Herman Goldstein described an underlying pathology in police agencies that he viewed as a fundamental cause of the malaise that surrounded policing at the time. Police agencies, Goldstein argued, were more concerned with the means of policing than its ends. The police as an institution had in Goldstein's view lost its way, and was in need of fundamental change. He began his article with a quote from an English newspaper suggesting just how serious he thought the problem in policing had become.

Complaints from passengers wishing to use the Bagnall to Greenfields bus service that "the drivers were speeding past queues of up to 30 people with a smile and a wave of a hand" have been met by a statement pointing out that "it is impossible for the drivers to keep their timetable if they have to stop for passengers." (Goldstein 1979: 236)

Just as bus drivers in this English town had in the pursuit of meeting schedules forgotten that the purpose of having a bus route was to pick up passengers, so too Goldstein argued, American police in their efforts to efficiently manage police organization had forgotten that the primary task of policing was to solve community problems.

Though Goldstein's article is often cited for its description of how police strategies could become more "problem oriented," he called more generally for broad organizational and cultural change in policing that would lead to police organizations that could be focused on solving problems. His article was the first step in a wider movement toward problem-oriented policing practices in the United States. However, Goldstein gave little guidance in his article on the fundamental question that he had raised about the reorganization of policing, and this question received little attention in the vast problem-oriented policing literature that was to develop in subsequent years. For scholars, including Goldstein, problem-oriented policing was to become primarily a tactical innovation concerned with how police solve problems and not how the police organization should be managed.

Compstat is a systematic attempt to answer Goldstein's original question about how police organization could be redefined to focus on problem solving, and in this sense represents an important attempt to reform American police agencies. Compstat is a policing model that seeks to focus police organization on specific problems and to empower police organizations to identify and solve those problems. For this reason we have defined Compstat elsewhere as a type of "strategic problem solving" (Weisburd *et al.* 2003). Compstat, as opposed to problem-oriented policing as it has been traditionally discussed and implemented, takes a "big picture approach," focusing not so much on the specific strategies that police use as the ways in which police agencies can be organized as problem-solving institutions.

But how does Compstat achieve this goal? The impetus behind Compstat's development in New York was Commissioner Bratton's intention to make America's largest police agency, legendary for its resistance to change, responsive to his leadership – a leadership that had clearly staked out crime reduction and improving the quality of life in the neighborhoods of New York City as its top priorities (Bratton 1999). Strictly speaking, Compstat in New York City referred to a "strategic control system" developed to gather and disseminate information on crime problems and track efforts to deal with them. It has, however, become shorthand for a full range of strategic problem-solving approaches. These elements are most visibly displayed in Compstat meetings during which precinct commanders appear before the department's top brass to report on crime problems in their precincts and what they are doing about them.

Drawing from what those who developed Compstat have written (see Bratton 1996; 1998; 1999; Maple 1999) as well as what those who have studied Compstat have observed (see Kelling and Coles 1996; Silverman 1999; McDonald, Greenberg, and Bratton 2001), we identify six key elements that have emerged as central to the development of Compstat as a form of strategic problem solving: mission clarification; internal accountability; geographic organization of command; organizational flexibility; data-driven problem identification and assessment; and innovative problem solving. Together they form a comprehensive approach for mobilizing police agencies to identify, analyze, and solve public safety problems.

Mission clarification

Compstat assumes that police agencies, like military organizations, must have a clearly defined organizational mission in order to function effectively. Top management is responsible for clarifying and exalting the core features of the department's mission that serve as the overarching reasons for the organization's existence. Mission clarification includes a demonstration of management's commitment to specific goals for which the organization and its leaders can be held accountable – such as reducing crime by 10 percent in a year (Bratton 1998).

Internal accountability

Internal accountability must be established so that people in the organization are held directly responsible for carrying out organizational goals. Compstat meetings in which operational commanders are held accountable for knowing their commands, being well acquainted with the problems in the command, and accomplishing measurable results in reducing those problems – or at least demonstrating a diligent effort to learn from the experience – form the most visible component of this accountability system. However, while such meetings are the visual embodiment of Compstat, they are part of a more general approach in which police managers are held accountable and can expect consequences if they are not knowledgeable about or have not responded to problems that fit within the mission of the department. As Jack Maple, one of the program's founders in New York, remarked: "Nobody ever got in trouble because crime numbers on their watch went up. I designed the process knowing that an organization as large as the NYPD never gets to Nirvana. Trouble arose only if the commanders didn't know why the numbers were up or didn't have a plan to address the problems" (Maple 1999: 33). Internal accountability in Compstat establishes middle managers as the central actors in carrying out the organizational mission, and holds them accountable for the actions of their subordinates.

Geographic organization of operational command

While Compstat holds police managers to a high level of accountability, it also gives commanders the authority to carry out the agency's mission. Organizational power is shifted to the commanders of geographic units. Operational command is focused on the policing of territories, so central decisionmaking authority in police operations is delegated to commanders with territorial responsibility (e.g., precincts). Functionally differentiated units and specialists (e.g., patrol, community police officers, detectives, narcotics, vice, juvenile, traffic, etc.) are placed under the command of the precinct commander, or arrangements are made to facilitate their responsiveness to the commander's needs. Silverman notes that, in New York, "Rather than allow headquarters to determine staffing and deployment on a citywide basis, it was decided that reducing crime, fear of crime, and disorder would flow from patrol borough and precinct coordination of selected enforcement efforts" (1999: 85).

Organizational flexibility

Middle managers are not only empowered with the authority to make decisions in responding to problems, they are also provided with the resources necessary to be successful in their efforts. Compstat requires that the organization develop the capacity and the habit of changing established routines to mobilize resources when and where they are needed for strategic application. For example, in New York City, "Commanding officers (COs) were authorized to allow their anticrime units to perform decoy operations, a function that had previously been left to the City-wide Street Crime Unit. Precinct personnel were permitted to execute felony arrests warrants, and COs could use plainclothes officers for vice enforcement activities. Patrol cops were encouraged to make drug arrests and to enforce quality-of-life laws" (Silverman 1999: 85).

Data-driven problem identification and assessment

Compstat requires that data are made available to identify and analyze problems and to track and assess the department's response. Data are expected to be available to all relevant personnel on a timely basis and in a readily usable format. According to Maple, "We needed to gather crime numbers for every precinct daily, not once every six months, to spot problems early. We needed to map the crimes daily too, so we could identify hot spots, patterns, and trends and analyze their underlying causes" (1999: 32).

Innovative problem-solving tactics

The five elements of Compstat described above would have little substance if Compstat did not encourage innovative problem-solving tactics. Such tactics have been the core concern of problem-oriented policing and they are central to the Compstat model (Bratton 1998). Middle managers are expected to select responses because they offer the best prospects of success, not because they are "what we have always done." Innovation and experimentation are encouraged; use of "best available knowledge" about practices is expected. In this context, police are expected to look beyond their own department by drawing upon knowledge gained in other departments and from innovations in theory and research about crime prevention.

Compstat and the bureaucratic paramilitary model of control

Compstat promises a model of policing that is focused on solving problems. Indeed, in the model of Compstat we have just described policing is not only focused on specific problems, it is organized around the problem-solving process. But what does Compstat actually deliver in police agencies that have implemented Compstat programs?

In a national survey we conducted at the Police Foundation we tried to assess to what extent agencies that claimed to have implemented Compstat or "Compstat-like" programs carried out the elements of Compstat that we have described above (Weisburd et al. 2001). Surveying all US police agencies with over 100 sworn police officers and with municipal policing responsibilities, we examined the extent of implementation of these core elements of Compstat in agencies that claimed to implement a Compstat program, and compared this to that found in agencies that did not claim to implement a Compstat program. The findings of the Police Foundation study are instructive in understanding how police agencies have used the Compstat model.

When the department goals of those who had recently developed a Compstat program were compared with the goals of those who were not intending to develop a Compstat program, the most significant differences were in the areas of crime control, increased control of managers over field operations, improving rank-and-file policing skills, and improving police morale. Importantly, departments that had claimed to have recently adopted Compstat were more concerned with reducing crime and increasing internal accountability than departments that reported neither having nor planning to develop a Compstat-like program. At the same time, agencies that had adopted Compstat programs were much less likely to focus on improving the skills and morale of street-level officers. This suggests that Compstat represents a departure from the priorities of "bubble-up" community and problem-oriented policing programs that had been predominant in police innovation until Compstat's arrival on the scene and had focused attention on the empowerment and training of street-level police officers. Indeed, Compstat appears in this sense to be modeled more closely on the traditional "bureaucratic" or "paramilitary" form of police organization (e.g., see Goldstein 1977; Melnicoe and Menig 1978; Bittner 1980; Davis 1981; Punch 1983; Weisburd, McElroy, and Hardyman 1988).

Police departments have traditionally relied on a highly articulated set of rules defining what officers should and should not do in various situations to ensure internal control. This supervisory system is strongly hierarchical and essentially negative, relying primarily on sanctions for non-compliance with police rules and regulations. Importantly, this bureaucratic, military model of organization has increasingly come under attack (Greene and Mastrofski 1988; Goldstein 1990; Bayley 1994; Mastrofski 1998). Innovations such as community-oriented policing and problem-oriented policing (as it was developed outside the Compstat model) included a strong current of dissatisfaction with traditional bureaucratic, top-down command-and-control management (Weisburd *et al.* 1988; Mastrofski 1998). They promoted the professionalization of the rank-and-file, who – equipped with the necessary training, education, and motivation to solve problems – are supposed to use their best judgment to make important decisions about how to solve problems and to serve the neighborhoods to which they are assigned. Some scholars have called this a movement toward "decentralization of command" or "debureaucratization" (Skolnick and Bayley 1987; Mastrofski 1998).

The Police Foundation study suggests that Compstat works to preserve and reinforce the traditional hierarchical structure of the military model of policing. While fairly strong on elements of mission clarification and internal accountability, Compstat agencies were found to be largely indistinguishable from non-Compstat agencies on measures that gauged geographic organization of command, organizational flexibility, the timely availability of data, and the selection and implementation of innovative strategies and tactics. More generally, the Police Foundation data present a picture of Compstat departments that have embraced control of middle managers, tending to rely more heavily on punitive than positive consequences. At the same time, Compstat departments are more reluctant to relinquish power that would decentralize some key elements of decisionmaking geographically (e.g., letting precinct commanders determine beat boundaries and staffing levels), enhance flexibility, and risk going outside of the standard tool kit of police tactics and strategies.

But does Compstat empower police organization more generally to solve problems through its emphasis on the accountability of police managers? In theory, the original developers of Compstat did not dispute the community policing view that giving "cops more individual power to make decisions is a good idea" (Bratton 1998: 198). However, they believed that in the real world of police organization street-level police officers "were never going to be empowered to follow through" (Bratton 1998: 199). Moreover, Compstat offered a more efficient approach for large organizations to encourage problem solving. Middle managers were expected to spearhead the Compstat approach, bringing the Compstat message to the line officers who served under them.

Our intensive field observations in three police agencies that were seen as model Compstat programs, suggest, however, that the rank and file remain largely oblivious to Compstat and that it intrudes little, if at all, into their daily work (Willis et al. 2004b). As one patrol officer put it when asked about Compstat, "If you don't go [to Compstat meetings], you don't know." In that department, in contrast to almost the entire command staff, only two or three patrol officers are present at any given Compstat meeting. They may answer a question or two, and they may give a brief presentation, but they play a peripheral role. A high-ranking officer we interviewed remarked that "patrol officers can hide in the meeting and get away without saying anything."

Whereas members of the command staff in Compstat departments we observed, in particular the sector captains, are expected to respond to the chief's questions, line officers are rarely called upon to explain a particular decision. It is true that a sector captain who has been "roasted" in Compstat for an inadequate strategy may return to his sector and rebuke his line officers, but the force of the message is considerably weakened for three reasons. First, Compstat ultimately holds middle managers, not line officers, accountable. Second, the message that is received by street-level police officers (as opposed to middle managers) is not being delivered by the highest-ranking official in the police department. And third, failure to innovate at the street level does not result in public censure on the same scale as that experienced by middle managers in Compstat meetings (Willis et al. 2004).

These field observations suggest that in Compstat agencies the problem-solving processes are principally the work of precinct commanders, their administrative assistants, and crime analysis staff (sometimes available at the precinct level, as well as at headquarters). The pressures on these people can be quite profound. One precinct commander noted that Compstat was "very stressful." Another told us: "We're under constant pressure. It's the toughest job in this department. We're held a little closer to the fire . . . I'll go home at night after ten hours at work and keep working – 50–60 hours per week on average." His lieutenant reinforced this. "A precinct commander has no life [outside Compstat]." While this level of intense accountability was commonly expressed by middle managers in Compstat departments, nothing remotely resembling this was found at lower levels in the organization, except on the rare occasion when a line officer was required to make a substantial presentation at a department Compstat meeting.

In sum, specific components of Compstat that reinforce traditional hierarchical structures of police organization have taken a predominant role in Compstat programs nationally. The predominance of these components, moreover, does not appear to empower police organization more generally toward the goal of problem solving.

Internal contradictions in the Compstat model

· The fact that police agencies that have adopted the Compstat model have emphasized elements of command and control over other components of Compstat does not in itself challenge Compstat as a programmatic entity. The problem we have identified so far is one of implementation of Compstat as it has diffused across the United States. The fact that many departments emphasize specific elements of Compstat does not mean that the program is not capable of being implemented more fully. But our research at the Police Foundation suggests that the Compstat model suffers from a more basic contradiction that hampers the ability of the model to achieve its goal of solving crime problems.

We conducted in-depth field observations in three "model" Compstat programs, chosen because they scored high on elements of Compstat implementation in our survey and followed closely the New York Police Department Compstat model (Willis *et al.* 2004; 2004a; 2004b). Again, as in our survey, we found in these "model" departments that Compstat's implementation placed the greatest stress on mission clarification and internal accountability. But perhaps more notably, when we assessed the strength of problem-solving efforts in these agencies we found that Compstat had done very little to change existing crime-fighting strategies.

We did witness some innovation, such as the successful use of a comprehensive and coordinated problem-oriented approach to shutting down a dilapidated, crime-ridden rooming house in one jurisdiction, but this was the exception not the norm. The vast majority of problem-solving approaches identified in these model Compstat agencies relied on traditional police strategies that had been used before – in particular, asking patrol officers to identify suspects and keep an eye on things, area saturation, stepping up traffic enforcement, "knock-and-talks," and increasing arrests. For example, in response to two unrelated incidents in a particular location (an increase in prostitution and the constant use of a specific pay-phone by suspected drug dealers), one district commander put "extra cruisers" in the area. During another Compstat meeting showing that the street-side windows of several parked cars had been smashed, the chief asked, "What kinds of things have we done in the past?" His deputy suggested that in the past they clamped down on motor vehicle violations: "You know, chief, sometimes you just get lucky. You catch a kid and they just talk. We need to get people in to talk to them." Similarly, when we asked a district commander what he had done regarding a spate of violent crimes within an area of the city, he told us, "good old police work" that included putting extra people in the area, increasing police visibility, sending in the drug unit, etc.

One area where there was greater innovation was in the use of geographic models of policing in which police activities were concentrated on specific locales identified by the Compstat process. While concentrating on "hot spots" represents an important innovation in policing that has been supported by strong research evidence (Sherman and Weisburd 1995; Braga 2001; Weisburd and Braga 2003), there was little innovation once hot spots were identified. In this sense, there was often innovation in the focusing of police resources, but relatively little innovation in what the police did once they had identified problems.

There did appear to be some very small, but observable differences in each organization's capacity to facilitate innovative problem-solving. For example, one chief strongly encouraged his command staff to share ideas on crime strategies, and in another jurisdiction task forces provided a similar forum. However, we found that innovative thinking was generally not encouraged at Compstat meetings, in good part because of time constraints. Questions and discussion were generally put off until the end of the meeting. In fact, even when one of the top managers in one agency advocated the creation of a poster delineating the most effective problem-solving strategies at the department's annual command meeting to assess Compstat, his suggestion was opposed; the district commanders responded that they already knew the answers to the problems in their districts.

Our ethnographic field observations suggest that the failure to achieve more in-depth problem solving in Compstat departments develops in part from a fundamental tension in Compstat's implementation. The pressure of internal accountability strengthened the existing command hierarchy, but appeared to work against two of Compstat's other key elements – innovative problem solving and geographic organization of operational command. For example, officers were reluctant to brainstorm problem-solving approaches during Compstat meetings for fear of undermining the authority of more senior officers. Thus the reinforcement of the hierarchy in Compstat has the unintended consequence of stifling the kind of creative and open discussion that is essential to creative problem solving. Since it is the rank hierarchy within the bureaucratic organization that legitimates superior power by providing the foundation for authority relations, any actions that would jeopardize the legitimacy of command are likely to be avoided. Consequently, lower or same ranking officers are reluctant to question their superiors during Compstat meetings.

In addition, the danger of "looking bad" in front of superior officers discouraged district commanders from pursuing more creative crime strategies with a higher risk of failure. Similarly, the decisionmaking authority of middle managers was limited by top management's willingness to question their judgment and to intervene in deployment decisions. And in this regard, actions that reinforce the legitimacy of the command hierarchy, such as top leadership's involvement in the decisions of their subordinates, are difficult to change. Thus, paradoxically, the strengthening of the command hierarchy under Compstat not only undermines innovative problem solving, but it also interferes with the decentralization of decisionmaking authority to middle managers.

There may be no silver bullet for resolving the tension between traditional bureaucratic features and Compstat's core elements; that is, it is zero sum. The arrangement of certain bureaucratic structures and routines, such as hierarchical authority, is necessary for the successful operation of a large administrative apparatus. It is the overdevelopment or underdevelopment of these features that hinders the functioning of the organization (Merton, Gray, Hockey, and Selvin 1952). For example, too much control from top leadership stifles innovation, but too little exposes the organization to excessive risk due to the reckless actions of its employees (Simons 1995). With this in mind, the challenge for any department that chooses to implement Compstat is picking the compromise that most suits its needs and those of its constituencies. Since there will always be friction between those Compstat elements that conflict with existing bureaucratic features, implementing Compstat resembles driving down the road with one foot on the accelerator and the other on the brake: there is going to be a lot of friction at the wheel.

The proponents of Compstat have seen the reinforcement of traditional hierarchical models of policing as a key component of Compstat's efforts to focus police organization on problem solving. Our observations suggest that the reality of Compstat in the nation as well as in model Compstat programs departs markedly from this promise. Indeed, the emphasis on the hierarchy has led to internal inconsistencies in the Compstat model, which work against successful innovation. Compstat's reinforcement of the bureaucratic hierarchy of policing stifles rather than enhances creative problem-solving approaches.

Does Compstat enhance crime prevention?

Whatever the internal contradictions of Compstat, from the outset it has been seen by its originators and proponents as an effective approach to reducing crime in America's cities (e.g., see Bratton 1998; Henry 2002). As early as 1995 an impressive set of statistics had been marshaled to tout the program's effectiveness in New York. Homicide rates were down almost 31 percent from the same period the year before, and crime generally was down 18.4 percent (Bratton 1998: 289). Henry (2002: 1) reports that by the year 2000, major crimes had declined 57.26 percent from their level in 1993, and murder had declined 65.18 percent. Other cities also attributed crime declines to Compstat (Anderson 2001), though to date there is not a single systematic review of the impacts of the implementation of Compstat programs.

One problem in evaluating Compstat as a crime prevention approach is that it includes many individual elements that may in themselves be successful in reducing crime. For example, Compstat has become associated with a focused geographic approach to crime problems. Crime mapping has become an integral part of many Compstat programs and, according to our Police Foundation survey, Compstat departments are much more likely to utilize crime mapping and try to identify crime hot spots than are agencies that do not have Compstat programs (Weisburd *et al.* 2001). This highly focused geographic approach, often termed hot spots policing (Sherman and Weisburd 1995; Weisburd and Braga 2003), has been found to have significant effects on crime and disorder at the places that are targeted by the police (Braga 2001; Weisburd and Eck 2004). But clearly police agencies can implement hot spots policing both in the context of Compstat and without a Compstat approach.

Similarly, Compstat in New York has been strongly linked to what has been called disorder or broken windows policing (Wilson and Kelling 1982; Kelling and Coles 1996; Bratton 1998; Kelling and Sousa 2001). Disorder policing assumes that if the police focus aggressively on less serious crimes that affect the look and feel of neighborhoods they will in the long run impact more serious offenses. This is because a developmental sequence is assumed that begins with disorder on the street and ends with serious criminal predators taking control of the urban environment (Wilson and Kelling 1982). The effectiveness of disorder policing is much debated and the research evidence supporting this approach is mixed (Kelling and Sousa 2001; Taylor 2001; Weisburd and Eck 2004). But again, Compstat has been implemented in some police agencies without an emphasis on disorder policing, and disorder policing has been implemented in police agencies without a Compstat program.

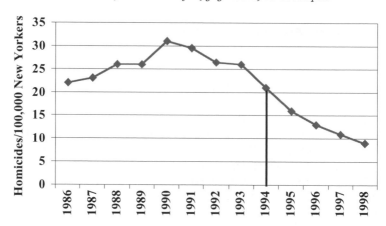

Figure 15.1 New York City homicide rate per 100,000 population, 1986–1998
Note: Vertical line shows year that Compstat was implemented.
Source: Eck and Maguire 2000

What this means is that any evaluation of the effectiveness of Compstat will be confounded with crime control strategies that are not necessarily part of Compstat. And, unfortunately, the police agencies that have so strongly advocated Compstat as an approach have had little interest in disentangling the complex network of effects that surround this program's impact. This is perhaps not surprising, when so much "good news" emerged from the simple reporting of official crime rates.

But is there reason to be more sober about the impact of Compstat even when relying upon such simple descriptive analyses? John Eck and Edward Maguire (2000) suggest this in their analysis of the crime drop in New York. One of the most important pieces of evidence brought by Compstat advocates is the extremely large decline in homicides in New York after Compstat was initiated. But Eck and Maguire show that the trend toward lower homicide rates after 1994, when Compstat was established in New York, follows a similar pattern to that found between 1990 and 1994 (see Figure 15.1). While it is still noteworthy that the homicide rate declined in New York for such a long period of time, the decline began much before the Compstat program was initiated.

Eck and Maguire also examine whether the decline in homicides in New York could have been accelerated by Compstat, even if it did not begin with the program. They do note that homicide rates fell more quickly in New York after than before 1994, when Compstat began.

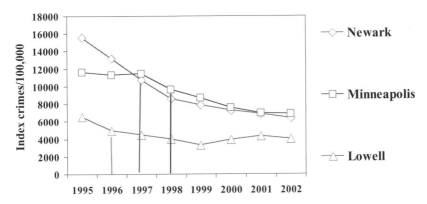

Figure 15.2 Crime rates before and after Compstat implementation in three model Compstat departments
Note: Vertical lines show year that Compstat was implemented.

However, they also show that states surrounding New York also evidenced more rapid declines in homicide in the latter period. Moreover, in comparing the homicide decline in New York to a series of large cities that did not implement Compstat during the early to mid-1990s, they find that the New York trend is "almost indistinguishable" from that in a number of other cities that they examined.

While our Police Foundation studies did not focus on the crime outcomes associated with Compstat's implementation, we did examine crime trends before and after the implementation of Compstat in the three model Compstat program cities in which we conducted intensive field observations. As can be seen in Figure 15.2, our observations follow closely those of Eck and Maguire in New York. Despite the fact that in each of these cities Compstat was given credit in one form or another for the declining crime trends observed, we can see an overall decline in index crimes even before Compstat began as a program.

While these analyses do not disprove Compstat's alleged impact upon crime rates in New York or other cities, they suggest the complexity of making a claim of Compstat's effectiveness without a systematic analysis of Compstat's crime control effects. Compstat is yet to be proven as an effective crime control strategy in New York or in other cities that have adopted the Compstat approach. It is a sobering thought that Compstat has spread so widely across American police agencies absent strong empirical evidence that it actually does something about the crime problem.

Conclusion

In a classic Italian novel, *The Leopard* (Di Lampedusa 1991), about the reunification of Italy in the nineteenth century, we are told about a meeting between the Prince of Salina and his nephew in which the nephew has just told the Prince of his decision to join the republican forces against the King of Salina. The Prince responds: "You're crazy, my son. To go and put yourself with those people . . . a Falconeri must be with us, for the King." The nephew, Tancredi Falconeri, responds: "For the King, certainly, but which King? If we're not there with them, that bunch is going to make a republic on us. *If we want everything to remain the same, then everything is going to have to change*" (Di Lampedusa 1991: 40, emphasis added).

In some sense Compstat in American policing appears to follow Tancredi Falconeri's strategy for retaining the existing order in Italy in the nineteenth century. Compstat promises to enhance police effectiveness by capitalizing on recent police innovations, especially those that have been associated with problem-oriented approaches to policing. Indeed, Compstat, in theory, provides the first real attempt to implement problem-oriented policing at the organizational level, an idea proposed by Herman Goldstein more than a quarter of a century ago, but seemingly forgotten by police scholars including Goldstein, who focused more on the practice of problem-oriented policing than the nature of police organization.

We have argued that Compstat as it has actually been implemented by American police agencies has been focused more on reinforcing and legitimating the traditional bureaucratic military model of police organization than on innovation in the practices of policing. In contrast to reforms such as community policing which emphasize the importance of challenging the traditional policing models of command and control, Compstat works to reinforce them. In this sense, Compstat can be seen more as a reaction than as a reform in American police organization. It is a return to what is comfortable for American police agencies, and provides a justification for traditional models of police organization that have been under attack by scholars for the last three decades. In this sense, Compstat is indeed a method of changing everything so that everything can remain the same. It is a reform in American policing that allows police agencies to return to what is familiar and comfortable.

If in doing so Compstat can reinvigorate conventional police organization for solving problems, then such a reform can of course still be seen as innovative in the most positive sense. But we have also shown that Compstat is plagued with a type of internal inconsistency which leads to what might be termed bureaucratic dysfunction. By strengthening the bureaucratic hierarchical model of policing, Compstat agencies impede the ability of police agencies to develop innovative problem-solving approaches. In this sense, the emphasis on command and control found in Compstat departments has the ironic consequence of making it difficult for these agencies to achieve what Compstat is designed to do in the first place.

In the end, the success of Compstat as an innovation will of course be judged on whether its claims of crime control effectiveness are confirmed. The problems we raise about Compstat do not mean that Compstat programs that are thoughtfully and fully implemented will not be successful in preventing crime. However, as we have illustrated, the data to date do not provide a solid basis for the claims of Compstat's proponents. This, combined with the trends in the implementation in Compstat we have described, should dampen the present enthusiasm for Compstat models.

REFERENCES

Anderson, D. C. (2001). Crime control by the numbers: Compstat yields new lessons for the police and the replication of a good idea. *Ford Foundation Report*: 5. New York.
Bayley, D. (1994). *Police for the future*. New York: Oxford University Press.
Bittner, E. (1980). *The functions of the police in modern society*. Cambridge, MA: Oelgeschlager, Gunn and Hain.
Braga, A. (2001). The effects of hot spots policing on crime. *The Annals of American Political and Social Science*, 578, 104–125.
Bratton, W. J. (1996). Cutting crime and restoring order: What America can learn from New York's finest. Heritage Foundation *Lectures and Educational Programs*, Heritage Lecture #573. Retrieved from: www.nationalsecurity.org/heritage/library/categories/crimelaw/lect573.html.
  (1998). *Turnaround: How America's top cop reversed the crime epidemic*. New York: Random House.
  (1999). Great expectations: How higher expectations for police departments can lead to a decrease in crime. In R. H. Langworthy (ed.), *Measuring what matters: Proceedings from the Policing Research Institute meetings* (pp. 11–26). Washington, DC: National Institute of Justice.
Davis, E. M. (1981). Professional police principles. In H. W. More, Jr. (ed.), *Critical issues in policing*. Cincinnati, OH: Anderson Publishing Company.
Di Lampedusa, G. (1991). *The leopard*. (Translated by Archibald Colquhoun). New York: Pantheon Books [1960].
Eck, J. E. and Maguire, E. R. (2000). Have changes in policing reduced violent crime? An assessment of the evidence. In A. Blumstein and J. Wallman (eds.), *The crime drop in America* (pp. 207–65). Cambridge: Cambridge University Press.
Goldstein, H. (1977). Toward a community-oriented policing: Potential, basic requirements, and threshold questions. *Crime and Delinquency*, 33 (1), 6–30.

(1979). Improving policing: A problem oriented approach. *Crime and Delinquency, 24,* 236–258.

(1990). *Problem-oriented policing.* New York: McGraw-Hill.

Greene, J. R. and Mastrofski, S. D. (1988). *Community policing: Rhetoric or reality.* New York: Praeger.

Greenspan, R., Mastrofski, S. D., and Weisburd, D. (2003). *Compstat and organizational change: Short site visit report.* Washington, DC: Police Foundation.

Gurwitt, R. (1998). The comeback of the cops. *Governing,* January, 14–19.

Henry, V. E. (2002). *The COMPSTAT paradigm: Management accountability in policing, business, and the public sector.* New York: Looseleaf Publications.

Kelling, G. L. and Coles, C. M. (1996). *Fixing broken windows: Restoring order and reducing crime in our communities.* New York: Free Press.

Kelling, G. L. and Sousa, W. H., Jr. (2001). Do police matter? An analysis of the impact of New York City's police reforms. Retrieved from: http://www.manhattan-institute.org/cr_22.pdf

Law Enforcement News. (1997). NYC's compstat continues to win admirers. October 13.

Maas, P. (1998). What we're learning from New York City. *Parade,* May 10, 4–6.

Maple, J. (1999). *The crime fighter: Putting the bad guys out of business.* New York: Doubleday.

Mastrofski, S. D. (1998). Community policing and police organization structure. In J. P., Brodeur (ed.), *How to recognize good policing: Problems and issues* (pp. 161–189). Thousand Oaks, CA: Sage Publications.

McDonald, P. P. (1998). The New York City crime control model: A guide to implementation. Unpublished manuscript. Washington, DC.

McDonald, P. P., Greenberg, S., and Bratton, W. J. (2001). *Managing police operations: Implementing the NYPD crime control model using COMPSTAT.* Belmont, CA: Wadsworth Publishing Co.

Melnicoe, W. B. and Menig, J. (1978). *Elements of police supervision.* Encino, CA: Glencoe Publishing Company.

Merton, R. K., Gray, A. P., Hockey, B., and Selvin, H. G. (eds.). (1952). *Reader in bureaucracy.* New York: Free Press.

Punch, M. (1983). Management, supervision and control. In M. Punch (ed.), *Control in the police organization.* Cambridge, MA: MIT Press.

Remnick, D. (1997). The crime buster. *The New Yorker,* February 24 & March 3, 94–109.

Sherman, L. and Weisburd, D. (1995). General deterrent effects of police patrol in crime 'hot spots': A randomized controlled trial. *Justice Quarterly, 12* (4), 625–648.

Silverman, E. B. (1996). Mapping change: How the New York City police department re-engineered itself to drive down crime. *Law Enforcement News,* December.

(1999). *NYPD battles crime: Innovative strategies in policing.* Boston, MA: Northeastern University Press.

Simons, R. (1995). Control in an age of empowerment. *Harvard Business Review, 73,* 1–7.

Skolnick, J. H. and Bayley, D. H. (1987). Theme and variation in community policing. *Crime and Justice.* Washington, DC: National Institute of Justice.

Taylor, R. B. (2001). *Breaking away from broken windows: Baltimore neighborhoods and the nationwide fight against crime, grime, fear, and decline.* Boulder, CO: Westview Press.

Weisburd, D. and Braga, A. (2003). Hot-spots policing. In H. Kury and J. Obergfell-Fuchs (eds.), *Crime prevention: New approaches* (pp. 337–355). Mainz, Germany: Weisser-Ring.

Weisburd, D. and Eck, J. (2004). What can police do to reduce crime, disorder, and fear. *Annals of American Political and Social Science, 593,* 42–65.

Weisburd, D., McElroy, J., and Hardyman, P. (1988). Challenges to supervision in community policing: observations on a pilot project. *American Journal of Police 7* (2), 29–50.

Weisburd, D., Mastrofski, S. D., McNally, A. M., and Greenspan, R. (2001). *Compstat and organizational change: Findings from a national survey.* Report submitted to the National Institute of Justice by the Police Foundation.

Willis, J. J., Mastrofski, S. D., Weisburd, D., and Greenspan, R. (2004). Compstat and organizational change in the Lowell police department: Challenges and opportunities. Washington, DC: Police Foundation. Also available from: http://www.policefoundation.org/pdf/compstat.pdf

Weisburd, D., Mastrofski, S. D., McNally, A. M., Greenspan, R., and Willis, J. J. (2003). Reforming to preserve: Compstat and strategic problem solving in American policing. *Criminology and Public Policy, 2* (3), 421–456.

Willis, J. J., Mastrofski, S. D., and Weisburd, D. (2004a). COMPSTAT and bureaucracy: A case study of challenges and opportunities for change. *Justice Quarterly, 21* (3), 463–496.

(2004b). *Compstat in practice: An in-depth analysis of three cities.* Washington DC: The Police Foundation.

Wilson, J. Q. and Kelling, G. L. (1982). Broken windows: The police and neighborhood safety. *The Atlantic Monthly,* March, 29–38.

Part VIII

Evidence-based policing

16 *Advocate*
Evidence-based policing for crime prevention

Brandon C. Welsh

Introduction

In recent weeks Big City has experienced an increase in young people selling drugs on the street. The police chief directs one of his managers to
organize a small group of officers to look into the matter and report back
with a plan of action. One of these officers is tasked with researching
what works to address the problem of street-level drug sales. The officer carries out literature searches, contacts other police departments and
police research organizations such as the Police Foundation, and follows
up with some of the researchers involved in evaluation studies. The most
rigorous evaluations are coded according to the outcomes of interest,
results are analyzed, and a report is prepared that shows what type of
intervention works best. Detailed observational and other information
on the problem gathered by the other officers is used to assess the appli-
cability of the "best practice" to the local context and conditions. On the
basis of this information, the chief authorizes the needed resources for a
program to be implemented to address street-level drug sales, and intro-
duces a monitoring and evaluation scheme to aid in-house policy and for
dissemination purposes.

This fictitious scenario, while brief on details, is an example of
evidence-based policing in action. Evidence-based policing involves the
police using the highest quality available research evidence on what works
best to reduce a specific crime problem and tailoring the intervention to
the local context and conditions. This approach likely holds wide appeal.
To local government and policymakers the police may be seen as being
efficient in their use of monetary and other resources. To police scholars
the police may be seen as acting like scientists: targeting crime problems
with accumulated scientific evidence of the highest quality on what works
best; here the police are seen as not reinventing the wheel. Evidence-
based policing could be another example of, in Bayley's (1998: 174)
words, "smarter law enforcement." To citizens, evidence-based policing
may also hold appeal because of its commitment to the use of what works

best and its clear intent to bring about positive change. But for some citizens, especially those who reside in high-crime neighborhoods, how the police interact with residents and suspected offenders may ultimately influence their feelings toward evidence-based policing. Arguably, these residents may reserve judgment on all police practices.

This chapter argues that there is strong scientific merit in the police adopting a formalized evidence-based approach to preventing crime and that a great deal of public good can come about from this. This chapter also argues that evidence-based policing holds much promise in making a difference – indeed where other police innovations in recent years have been unsuccessful – in those very neighborhoods where crime and violence are most intractable and public confidence in the police is lowest. The latter may come about not just because police are using scientific evidence about what works best, but also because police are targeting crime-risk factors and tailoring what works to local context and conditions.

This chapter is not the first piece on evidence-based policing. Sherman's (1998) seminal piece, *Evidence-Based Policing*, and his earlier works dating back to his *Crime and Justice* essay, "Attacking crime: policing and crime control" (Sherman 1992), spelled out the arguments in support of the police using accumulated scientific evidence on what works best to prevent crime, and set the stage for this approach being acknowledged by police scholars (the editors of the present volume included) as one of the important police innovations of the last two decades. Importantly though, evidence-based policing is but one part of a larger evidence-based movement, from which it draws institutional and intellectual support. This may be one feature that distinguishes evidence-based policing from other police innovations.

The chapter is organized as follows. The first part describes the evidence-based model with special reference to evidence-based policing, and overviews the movement that has given rise to its use in the social sciences. It then reviews the state of evidence-based research on policing with a specific focus on the prevention of crime. One of the aims of this part is to address the pressing question: Is there enough evidence to develop evidence-based policing? This is followed by a discussion of whether we can expect the police to use or perhaps institutionalize the evidence-based model to prevent crime. The chapter concludes with a discussion on why the police should adopt an evidence-based approach to prevent crime.

The evidence-based model and policing

In characterizing the evidence-based model and policing it is important to first define what is meant by the term "evidence." Throughout this chapter evidence is taken to mean scientific, not criminal evidence (see Sherman 1998: 2, note 1). Evidence introduced in criminal court proceedings, while bound by laws and procedures, is altogether different from scientific evidence. The latter "refers to its common usage in science to distinguish data from theory, where evidence is defined as 'facts . . . in support of a conclusion, statement or belief'" (*Shorter Oxford English Dictionary* 2002, as cited in Sherman 2003: 7).

At the heart of the evidence-based model is the notion that "we are all entitled to our own opinions, but not to our own facts" (Sherman 1998: 4). Many may be of the opinion that hiring more police officers will yield a reduction in crime rates. However, an examination of the empirical research evidence on the subject reveals that this is not the case (see below). Use of opinions instead of facts to guide crime policy has a greater chance to result in harmful or iatrogenic effects (McCord 2003) or to not work at all, waste scarce public resources (Welsh and Farrington 2000), and divert policy attention from the real priorities of the day. Moreover, within the evidence-based paradigm, drawing conclusions based on facts calls attention to a number of fundamental issues: the validity of the evidence; the methods used to locate, appraise, and synthesize the evidence; and implementation.

In an evidence-based model, the source of scientific evidence is empirical research in the form of evaluations of programs, practices, and policies. But not all evaluations are made equal. Some are more scientifically valid than others. The randomized controlled experiment is the most convincing method of evaluating crime prevention programs (Farrington 1983; Weisburd, Lum, and Petrosino 2001). This type of evaluation design involves the random allocation of subjects to treatment (the condition that receives the intervention) and control conditions. Through the process of random assignment, treatment and control groups are equated (prior to intervention) on all possible extraneous variables (e.g., age, gender, social class, school performance) that may be related to the outcome of interest, which for the present purposes is crime. Hence, any subsequent differences between them must be attributable to the intervention. Technically, randomized experiments have the highest possible internal validity in unambiguously attributing an effect to a cause (Shadish, Cook, and Campbell 2002).

Other things being equal, a program evaluation in which experimental and control units are matched or statistically equated prior to intervention – what is called a non-randomized experiment – has less internal validity than a randomized experiment. A program evaluation with no control group has even less internal validity, since it fails to address many threats to internal validity, such as history (an event occurring at the same time as the intervention), maturation (a continuation of preexisting trends, for example, in normal human development), and instrumentation (a change in the method of measuring the outcome) effects (Cook and Campbell 1979).

Just as it is crucial to use the highest-quality evaluation designs to investigate the effects of police practices, it is also important that the most rigorous methods be used to locate, appraise, and synthesize the available research evidence. The main types of review methods include the single study, narrative, vote-count, systematic, and meta-analytic (Welsh and Farrington 2001; see below for details on these review methods). Single study and narrative reviews are less rigorous than the others, and are not recommended in carrying out evidence-based research. Comprehensiveness, adherence to scientific rules and conventions, and transparency are at the heart of the rigorous review methods.

The question, What does the evidence say?, is in direct reference to existing evaluation studies. Rather than the self-selection of individual studies to substantiate one's position, evidence refers to the accumulated body of studies (published and unpublished) on the subject of interest. This degree of comprehensiveness is one way that the evidence-based model attempts to address researcher or institutional bias. Adherence to scientific rules and conventions is most germane to the use of appropriate quantitative techniques in analyzing results, as well as the presentation of these results. The transparency of search methods, criteria used to include (and exclude) studies, quantitative techniques, and so on is also important in allowing the reviews to be replicated by other researchers.

The importance of implementation to the evidence-based model is best captured by the following: "Evidence-based policing assumes that experiments alone are not enough. Putting research into practice requires just as much attention to implementation as it does to controlled evaluations" (Sherman 1998: 7).

Successful implementation calls for taking account of local context and conditions. Some critics of the evidence-based paradigm (Lab 2003) claim that it fails to adequately account for local context and conditions in reaching conclusions about what works. The main thrust of this argument is that unless local context and conditions are investigated undue weight may be ascribed to any effects of the intervention on the outcome of interest. Evidence-based policing has in place the capacity to take account of these features. For example, those tasked with investigating the research evidence on the effectiveness of police practices to deal with a particular crime problem can question the original researchers or solicit unpublished reports to learn about how local context and conditions may have influenced the observed results. This information can then be integrated into the existing profile of the program.

Evidence-based policing also has the capacity to appropriately tailor proven strategies or practices to the local setting. While perhaps obvious and supported in research on diffusion of knowledge and replication studies (see Ekblom 2002; Liddle, Rowe, Quille *et al.* 2002), not paying attention to this (and using the "one-size-fits-all" approach) can severely impact upon implementation as well as the overall effectiveness of the intervention. Hough and Tilley (1998: 28) make this point clear:

> Routinely used techniques often cannot be taken off the shelf and applied mechanically with much real prospect of success. Standard, broad-brush, block-buster approaches to problems tend to produce disappointing results. Where new approaches are adopted it is likely that adjustments will be needed in the light of early experience. All crime prevention measures work (or fail to do so) according to their appropriateness to the particular problem and its setting.

Detailed observational and other information on the crime problem that is the focus of attention, as well as the setting (e.g., urban density, unemployment rates), can be matched with the proven practice and modifications can then be made as needed.

Another important feature of the evidence-based model is the outcome of interest. While it is acknowledged that evidence-based policing can serve other useful purposes (e.g., improving police training standards, improving police–community relations), the main outcome of interest or "bottom line" is crime prevention (see Welsh 2002). The parallel is with evidence-based medicine's primary focus on saving lives or improving the quality of life of those suffering from terminal or chronic illnesses. For evidence-based policing or evidence-based crime prevention in general, the prevention of crime is a first tier or primary outcome. This is the focus throughout this chapter.

Part of a larger movement

Evidence-based policing is a part of a larger and increasingly expanding evidence-based movement. In general terms, this movement is dedicated to the betterment of society through the utilization of the highest quality scientific evidence on what works best. The evidence-based movement first began in medicine (Millenson 1997) and has, more recently, been embraced by the social sciences (Mosteller and Boruch 2002; Sherman, Farrington, Welsh, and MacKenzie 2002; Sherman 2003).

In 1993, the Cochrane Collaboration was established to prepare, maintain, and make accessible systematic reviews (see below for details on this review methodology) of research on the effects of health care and medical interventions. The Cochrane Collaboration established collaborative review groups (CRGs) across the world to oversee the preparation and maintenance of systematic reviews in specific areas, such as heart disease, infectious diseases, and breast cancer. All reviews produced by Cochrane CRGs follow a uniform structure. The same level of detail and consistency of reporting is found in each, and each review is made accessible through the *Cochrane Library*, a quarterly electronic publication.

The success of the Cochrane Collaboration in reviewing health care interventions stimulated international interest in establishing a similar infrastructure for conducting systematic reviews of research on the effects of interventions in the social sciences, including education, social work and social welfare, and crime and justice. In 2000, the Campbell Collaboration was established. It is named after the influential experimental psychologist Donald T. Campbell (see Campbell 1969). The Collaboration's Crime and Justice Group aims to prepare and maintain systematic reviews of criminological interventions and to make them accessible electronically to practitioners, policymakers, scholars, and the general public.

The state of evidence-based research on policing for crime prevention

It is not known to what extent police departments across the country or even big city police departments for that matter undertake evidence-based research to aid in the development and implementation of programs and practices to prevent crime. In the absence of being able to report on the state of evidence-based policing in real-world settings, this section brings together leading reviews on the effectiveness of policing for crime prevention. This serves two main purposes: (a) to take stock of what we know (and do not know) about what works best in policing for crime prevention; and (b) to assess if there is sufficient research evidence to develop evidence-based policing.

Sherman and Eck (2002)

As part of a larger project to assess the scientific evidence on the effectiveness of preventing crime in seven major institutional settings in which crime prevention efforts take place (families, communities, schools, labor markets, places, police agencies, and courts and corrections) in the United States and internationally, Sherman and Eck (2002) undertook a review of police practices. This piece updates Sherman's (1997) chapter in the widely cited report prepared for the US Congress, *Preventing crime: What works, what doesn't, what's promising* (Sherman, Gottfredson, MacKenzie *et al.* 1997).

Table 16.1 *Sherman and Eck's (2002) conclusions on the effectiveness of police practices to prevent crime*

What Works
Increased directed patrols in street-corner hot spots of crime
Proactive arrests of serious repeat offenders
Proactive drunk driving arrests
Arrests of employed suspects for domestic assault
Problem-oriented policing

What Does Not Work
Neighborhood block watch
Arrests of some juveniles for minor offenses
Arrests of unemployed suspects for domestic assault
Drug-market arrests
Community policing with no clear crime-risk factor focus
Adding extra police to cities, regardless of assignment or activity

What Is Promising
Police traffic enforcement patrols against illegally carried handguns
Community policing with community participation in priority setting
Community policing focused on improving police legitimacy
Warrants for arrest of suspect absent when police respond to domestic
    violence

Source: Adapted from Sherman and Eck (2002: 321–322).

As shown in Table 16.1, the authors, on the basis of the highest-quality available scientific evidence, identified five police practices that are effective in reducing crime. Most of these practices are highly specific, such as increased directed patrols in street-corner hot spots of crime and arrests of employed suspects for domestic assault. Also important to police managers and other consumers of this evidence-based research is that this review draws conclusions about what does not work, what is promising, and what is unknown (the latter is not shown in Table 16.1). Some of the police practices of unknown effectiveness include police recreation activities with juveniles (e.g., Police Athletic Leagues) and in-car computer terminals (Sherman and Eck 2002: 322).

One of the first questions that may be asked of these conclusions is: How much confidence can one have in them? This is a critical question in any evidence-based research, and one that goes to the heart of the underlying methodology employed (e.g., type of evaluation studies included, method used to aggregate results). The saying, "garbage in, garbage out," needs to be kept in mind in judging the results of any single study or review. As noted above, the evidence-based model is committed to the use of the highest-quality available scientific evidence and the most rigorous methods.

Sherman and Eck's (2002) review used what is known as a vote-count methodology. The vote-count method adds a quantitative element to the narrative review,[1] by considering statistical significance (the probability of obtaining the observed effect if the null hypothesis of no relationship were true). In essence, this method tallies-up the "number of studies with statistically significant findings in favor of the hypothesis and the number contrary to the hypothesis (null findings)" (Wilson 2001: 73). The main problem with using statistical significance is that it depends partly on sample size and partly on effect size. For example, a significant result may reflect a small effect in a large sample or a large effect in a small sample (Farrington, Gottfredson, Sherman, and Welsh 2002).

However, Sherman and Eck's (2002) review adopted a more comprehensive vote-count methodology, first developed by Sherman *et al.* (1997) and revised by Farrington *et al.* (2002). In addition to statistical significance, this vote-count method integrates a "scientific methods scale" (SMS) that is largely based on the work of Cook and Campbell (1979), and describes research designs that are most effective in eliminating threats to internal validity. The scale ranges from level 1 (correlation between a prevention program and a measure of crime at one point in time) to level 5 (random assignment of program and control conditions to units), with level 5 being the highest. Only studies with a minimum of a level 3 evaluation design (presence of before and after measures of crime in experimental and comparable control conditions) were included in the review. This was considered to be the minimum interpretable design by Cook and Campbell (1979). (For more details on the SMS, see Farrington *et al.* 2002; Welsh, Farrington, Sherman, and MacKenzie 2002.) Importantly, external validity (the generalizability of internally valid results) was addressed to some extent by establishing rules for accumulating evidence.[2]

Eck and McGuire (2000) and Weisburd and Eck (2004)

As part of a larger project to characterize and explain the decline in crime rates in the United States during the 1990s (Blumstein and Wallman 2000), Eck and Maguire (2000) examined whether the contributions of seven major policing strategies (increase in number of police officers, community policing, zero tolerance policing, directed patrols in hot spots, firearms enforcement, retail drug-market enforcement, and problem-oriented policing) during this period of time reduced violent crime. Their work is relevant here because in order to do this Eck and Maguire reviewed the scientific evidence on the effectiveness of these policing strategies. The authors found that some of the policing strategies hold sufficient empirical support to reduce violent crime. These included directed patrols in hot spots, firearms enforcement, retail drug market enforcement (especially when combined with the threat of civil action against property owners), and problem-oriented policing. For the other three strategies the authors found that the evidence was mixed for increasing the number of police officers, weak for community policing, and non-existent for zero tolerance policing.

Weisburd and Eck's (2004) review was carried out as part of a larger National Academy of Sciences panel investigating police policy and practices (Committee to Review Research 2004). In reviewing the extant research evidence about what works in policing, the authors set out to address a number of critical questions facing American policing, including "Does the research evidence support the view that standard models of policing are ineffective in combating crime and disorder?" and "Do recent police innovations hold greater promise of increasing community safety, or does the research evidence suggest that they are popular but actually ineffective?" (Weisburd and Eck 2004: 43).

As shown in Table 16.2, Weisburd and Eck (2004) found that focused (or targeted) police strategies are more likely to yield crime reduction benefits than unfocused (or uniformly applied) strategies. The authors found moderate to strong evidence of effectiveness for recent innovations of problem-oriented policing, problem solving in hot spots, focused intensive enforcement, and hot spots patrols. Also revealing was the finding that the standard model of policing (e.g., adding more police, general patrol), which is both unfocused and relies almost exclusively on law enforcement sanctions, is not supported by solid empirical study. On the latter, the authors observe, "While this approach remains in many police agencies the dominant model for combating crime and disorder, we find little empirical evidence for the position that generally applied tactics that are based primarily on the law enforcement powers of the police are effective" (Weisburd and Eck 2004: 57).

While somewhat different in scope, these two reviews have been grouped together because each reviewed only the most methodologically rigorous studies. As in the Sherman and Eck (2002) review, these reviews sought to separate out the wheat from the chaff, the former serving as the empirical evidence upon which conclusions are drawn about effectiveness or ineffectiveness.

Braga (2001)

Under the auspices of the Campbell Collaboration's Crime and Justice Group, Braga (2001) carried out a review of the effects of hot spots

Table 16.2 *Weisburd and Eck's (2004) summary of findings on police effectiveness research*

Police Strategies that . . .	Are Unfocused	Are Focused
Apply a diverse array of approaches, including law enforcement sanctions	Inconsistent or weak evidence of effectiveness: – impersonal community policing (e.g., newsletters)	Moderate evidence of effectiveness: – problem-oriented policing
	Weak to moderate evidence of effectiveness: – personal contacts in community policing – respectful police-citizen contacts (improving police legitimacy, foot patrols (fear reduction))	Strong evidence of effectiveness: – problem solving in hot spots
Rely almost exclusively on law enforcement sanctions	Inconsistent or weak evidence of effectiveness: – adding more police – general patrol – rapid response – follow-up investigations – undifferentiated arrest for domestic violence	Inconsistent or weak evidence of effectiveness: – repeat offender investigations Moderate to strong evidence of effectiveness: – focused intensive enforcement – hot spots patrols

Source: Adapted from Weisburd and Eck (2004: 57; table 1).

policing on crime and disorder. This form of policing involves the targeting of police enforcement measures on high-risk crime places. Also examined were the effects on the displacement of crime (an unintended increase in crime, for example, in a different location) and the diffusion of crime control benefits (an unintended decrease in crime in an adjacent location).

Nine studies were identified that met the inclusion criteria for the review. The nine studies involved a range of enforcement strategies (e.g., problem-oriented policing interventions involving both traditional enforcement tactics and situational crime prevention responses, uniformed police patrol) targeted at a range of crime problems (e.g., illegal gun carrying, street-level drug sales, assaults and robberies) in high-risk places. Braga (2001) found evidence that targeted police actions can prevent crime and disorder in hot spots, displacement of crime is rare, and some enforcement actions produce unintended crime prevention benefits in adjacent locations.[3]

Unlike the above reviews this one is focused on investigating the effectiveness of one particular police practice or strategy. This narrow focus is purposeful. Among other reasons, it is meant to enable the researcher to carry out a comprehensive search for relevant studies. Through this it is hoped that the researcher will uncover all available studies on the subject. This narrow focus is also meant to allow the researcher to look in depth at each study on multiple dimensions (and code them) to assess any potential influence on the observed outcomes.

Braga's (2001) review is known as a systematic review, which is the most rigorous method for assessing the effectiveness of criminological interventions (Chalmers 2003). Systematic reviews use rigorous methods for locating, appraising, and synthesizing evidence from prior evaluation studies, and they are reported with the same level of detail that characterizes high-quality reports of original research. Systematic reviews, according to Johnson and his colleagues (2000: 35), "essentially take an epidemiological look at the methodology and results sections of a specific population of studies to reach a research-based consensus on a given topic." They have explicit objectives, explicit criteria for including or excluding studies, extensive searches for eligible evaluation studies from across the world, careful extraction and coding of key features of studies, and a structured and detailed report of the methods and conclusions of the review.

Toward evidence-based policing?

Overall, these reviews, using different high-quality methods, demonstrate (with a high degree of concordance) that there are a number of policing practices with robust empirical evidence of effectiveness in preventing crime. These reviews also show (also with a high degree of concordance) that there are some promising practices that police currently employ, and many more that police should consider abandoning or perhaps modifying. (It is of course recognized that all crime prevention programs, policing included, that become institutionalized and take on brand-name appeal, think of DARE (Drug Abuse and Resistance Education) can be terribly difficult to do away with or even change.)

These reviews of the empirical evidence on policing for crime prevention also suggest that there is sufficient capacity to develop evidence-based policing. Critics may charge that a handful of effective practices is hardly sufficient grounds for the development of evidence-based policing. But underlying this aggregate number of effective policing practices are a few important points that speak to the capacity for the development of evidence-based policing. One is that the effective practices represent a diverse range of policing practices. This is important because different communities have different policing needs. A second and related point is that the effective practices are by no means obscure or relegated to one region or another. Instead, they are used by police departments across the country.

Another reason to believe there is sufficient capacity to develop evidence-based policing is that there are even more promising practices, or those with moderate evidence of effectiveness, that, with some modest resources directed to replication studies, could conceivably become effective practices. This is by no means a long shot. Notwithstanding the concern that "knowledge of many of the core practices of American policing remains uncertain" (Weisburd and Eck 2004: 59), few if any areas of research in criminal justice or crime prevention more generally, can boast the level and high-quality nature of experimental evaluation in policing. In the words of Sherman and Eck (2002: 321), "It is no small achievement that police crime prevention research has developed to the point of having some conclusions to discard."

Can we expect the police to use the evidence-based model?

If history is any indication the answer to this question may be mixed. On the one hand, we can look to the widespread adoption of some police innovations in the absence of a link to research evidence, such as community policing. On the other hand, we can find a connection to the evidence-based paradigm – although perhaps not necessarily conceived of in this form – in the adoption of problem-oriented policing and other targeted police practices that go beyond a reliance on police powers.

Sherman (1998) has critiqued community policing as not being linked to research evidence on what works best in preventing crime. Community policing "is much more about how to do police work – a set of outputs – than it is about desired results, or outcomes" (Sherman 1998: 5). As noted above, Sherman and Eck (2002) found community policing with no clear focus on crime-risk factors to be ineffective in preventing crime. Critics may charge that community policing was never intended just to prevent crime. This is true. But returning to a point made earlier, within an evidence-based model, crime prevention is the chief concern of policing.

In contrast to community policing, "[p]roblem-oriented policing is clearly the major source of evidence-based policing" (Sherman 1998: 5–6). Sherman (1998) notes that this comes from problem-oriented policing emphasizing systematic problem-solving responses. What may be missing more often though is a commitment to the use of the scientific evidence on what works best. That is, once the underlying problems of the crime or disorder incidents have been identified, are the police using practices with proven effectiveness? In the case of problem-oriented policing, with its focused or targeted nature and its use of a diverse array of law enforcement sanctions and alternative crime control measures (Weisburd and Eck 2004), proven practices need not always come from the policing community. Indeed, the evaluation research on situational crime prevention or place-based crime prevention (Clarke 1997; Eck 2002) and, to a lesser extent, community crime prevention (Welsh 2003) offer police many more efficacious options.

There will always exist barriers to getting the police to use research evidence on what works best in preventing crime. Some of these have already been addressed; others include administrative constraints (e.g., too few resources, need for training of personnel), philosophical differences, and institutional resistance to change. Overcoming the disconnect between research evidence and practice may best be achieved through the employment of what Sherman (1998) refers to as an "evidence cop." This individual, ideally working within a police department (for smaller police departments it may be necessary to pool resources), would serve as both a research scientist and manager. In the capacity of a research scientist the evidence cop would be responsible for keeping up to date on the latest police research findings and coming up with recommendations based on the accumulated research evidence. In the capacity of a manager the evidence cop's role would be to monitor policing practices in the field to ensure they are adhering to recommendations based on research evidence. Importantly, his/her role would also be to "redirect practice through compliance rather than punishment" (Sherman 1998: 3). The police community could learn from similar initiatives that have shown promise in the medical profession (Millenson 1997) and in agriculture (MacKenzie 1998).

Why the police should adopt an evidence-based approach

Evidence-based policing brings scientific evidence to center stage in decisions about which police practices should be used to deal with certain crime problems. It also brings to policing a greater focus on the prevention of crime. Improved effectiveness in the prevention of crime, greater efficiency in the use of scarce public resources, and improved relations with the public may be some of the outcomes of police adopting an evidence-based approach. Of course, the police have achieved and continue to achieve various degrees of success in these areas through a number of

318   *Brandon C. Welsh*

diverse practices. So what are some of the key reasons for why the police should adopt an evidence-based approach?

Returning to the scenario that opened this chapter, one of the most important reasons for the police to use an evidence-based approach is that it brings yet another innovative tool to a field of criminal justice that is a leader in innovation. More importantly perhaps, evidence-based policing may serve as a catalyst in focusing limited resources on identifiable risks, further developing a knowledge base on what works best, and, in continuing to develop new approaches to crime problems, encouraging police departments to keep an eye on the bottom line of crime prevention effectiveness.

In fact, at a time of police experimentation with new technologies like Compstat and 3-1-1 non-emergency call systems to aid in the more efficient use of police resources (see Mazerolle, Rogan, Frank, Famega *et al.* 2002; Weisburd, Mastrofski, McNally, Greenspan *et al.* 2003) and new deterrence-based problem-solving strategies to reduce serious crimes (see Kennedy 1997; Tita, Riley, and Greenwood 2003), the adoption of an evidence-based approach in policing may not be such a great departure from the current state of policing. While this is hardly a reason for the police to adopt an evidence-based approach, it may go some way toward selling the idea. And this cannot hurt.

NOTES

I wish to thank David Weisburd and Anthony Braga for helpful comments and suggestions on an earlier draft of this chapter.

1. Narrative reviews of the literature quite often include many studies and may be very comprehensive. The main drawback of the narrative method is researcher bias. This bias, whether intentional or not, typically starts right from the beginning with a less than rigorous methodology for searching for studies. More often than not, the researcher will limit his or her search to published sources or even self-select studies to be included, based on the researcher's familiarity with them, quite possibly leaving many studies out of the review. This can sometimes lead to an incorrect interpretation of the particular intervention's effect on crime; for example, what should have been presented as a desirable effect is instead reported as an uncertain effect (i.e., unclear evidence of an effect). The one main advantage to the narrative review is that the reader can usually glean a great deal more information about individual studies than would otherwise be possible in the more rigorous methods of vote-count and systematic reviews.

2. The aim was to classify all police practices into one of four categories: what works, what does not work, what is promising, and what is unknown. *What works*: These are programs that prevent crime. Programs coded as working must have at least two level 3 to level 5 evaluations showing statistically significant and desirable results and the preponderance of all available evidence showing effectiveness. *What does not work*: These are programs that fail to

prevent crime. Programs coded as not working must have at least two level 3 to level 5 evaluations with statistical significance tests showing ineffectiveness and the preponderance of all available evidence supporting the same conclusion. *What is promising*: These are programs wherein the level of certainty from available evidence is too low to support generalizable conclusions, but wherein there is some empirical basis for predicting that further research could support such conclusions. Programs are coded as promising if they were found to be effective in significance tests in one level 3 to level 5 evaluation and in the preponderance of the remaining evidence. *What is unknown*: Any program not classified in one of the three above categories is defined as having unknown effects.

3. Braga (2005) has since revised this piece to include only randomized controlled studies. This had the effect of decreasing the sample size from nine to five studies, but the findings did not change from the earlier systematic review. Furthermore, Braga (2003) reported that a meta-analysis involving these five studies supported the main finding that targeted police actions can prevent crime and disorder in hot spots. A meta-analysis involves the statistical or quantitative analysis of the results of prior research studies (Lipsey and Wilson 2001).

REFERENCES

Bayley, D. H. (1998). Introduction: Effective law enforcement. In D. H. Bayley (ed.), *What works in policing* (pp. 174–177). New York: Oxford University Press.

Blumstein, A. and Wallman, J. (eds.). (2000). *The crime drop in America*. New York: Cambridge University Press.

Braga, A. A. (2001). The effects of hot spots policing on crime. *Annals of the American Academy of Political and Social Science, 578*, 104–125.

(2003). Personal communication, November 19, 2003.

(2005). Policing crime hot spots. In B. C. Welsh and D. P. Farrington (eds.), *Preventing crime: What works for children, offenders, victims, and places*. New York: Springer, in press.

Campbell, D. T. (1969). Reforms as experiments. *American Psychologist, 24*, 409–429.

Chalmers, I. (2003). Trying to do more good than harm in policy and practice: The role of rigorous, transparent, up-to-date evaluations. *Annals of the American Academy of Political and Social Science, 589*, 22–44.

Clarke, R. V. (ed.). (1997). *Situational crime prevention: Successful case studies*, 2nd ed. Guilderland, NY: Harrow and Heston.

Committee to Review Research on Police Policy and Practices. (2004). *Fairness and effectiveness in policing: The evidence*. Washington, DC: National Academies Press.

Cook, T. D. and Campbell, D. T. (1979). *Quasi-experimentation: Design and analysis issues for field settings*. Chicago: Rand McNally.

Eck, J. E. (2002). Preventing crime at places. In L. W. Sherman, D. P. Farrington, B. C. Welsh, and D. L. MacKenzie (eds.), *Evidence-based crime prevention* (pp. 241–294). New York: Routledge.

Eck, J. E. and Maguire, E. R. (2000). Have changes in policing reduced violent crime? An assessment of the evidence. In A. Blumstein and J. Wallman (eds.), *The crime drop in America* (pp. 207–265). New York: Cambridge University Press.

Ekblom, P. (2002). From the source to the mainstream is uphill: The challenge of transferring knowledge of crime prevention through replication, innovation and anticipation. In N. Tilley (ed.), *Analysis for crime prevention: Crime prevention studies,* 13 (pp. 131–203). Monsey, NY: Criminal Justice Press.

Farrington, D. P. (1983). Randomized experiments on crime and justice. In M. Tonry and N. Morris (eds.), *Crime and justice: Annual review of research,* 4 (pp. 257–308). Chicago: University of Chicago Press.

Farrington, D. P., Gottfredson, D. C., Sherman, L. W., and Welsh, B. C. (2002). The Maryland scientific methods scale. In L. W. Sherman, D. P. Farrington, B. C. Welsh, and D. L. MacKenzie (eds.), *Evidence-based crime prevention* (pp. 13–21). New York: Routledge.

Hough, M. and Tilley, N. (1998). *Getting the grease to the squeak: Research lessons for crime prevention.* Crime Detection and Prevention Series Paper 85. London: Home Office Police Research Group.

Johnson, B. R., De Li, S., Larson, D. B., and McCullough, M. (2000). A systematic review of the religiosity and delinquency literature: A research note. *Journal of Contemporary Criminal Justice,* 16, 32–52.

Kennedy, D. M. (1997). Pulling levers: Chronic offenders, high-crime settings, and a theory of prevention. *Valparaiso University Law Review,* 31, 449–484.

Lab, S. P. (2003). Let's put it in context. *Criminology and Public Policy,* 3, 39–44.

Liddle, H. A., Rowe, C. L., Quille, T. J., Dakof, G. A., Mills, D. S., Sakran, E., and Biaggi, H. (2002). Transporting a research-based adolescent drug treatment into practice. *Journal of Substance Abuse Treatment,* 22, 231–243.

Lipsey, M. W. and Wilson, D. B. (2001). *Practical meta-analysis.* Thousand Oaks, CA: Sage Publications.

MacKenzie, D. L. (1998). Using the US land-grant university system as a model to attack this nation's crime problem. *The Criminologist,* 23 (2), 1, 3–4.

Mazerolle, L., Rogan, D., Frank, J., Famega, C., and Eck, J. E. (2002). Managing citizen calls to the police: The impact of Baltimore's 3-1-1 call system. *Criminology and Public Policy,* 2, 97–124.

McCord, J. (2003). Cures that harm: Unanticipated outcomes of crime prevention programs. *Annals of the American Academy of Political and Social Science,* 587, 16–30.

Millenson, M. L. (1997). *Demanding medical excellence: Doctors and accountability in the information age.* Chicago: University of Chicago Press.

Mosteller, F. and Boruch, R. (eds.). (2002). *Evidence matters: Randomized trials in education research.* Washington, DC: Brookings Institution Press.

Shadish, W. R., Cook, T. D., and Campbell, D. T. (2002). *Experimental and quasi-experimental designs for generalized causal inference.* Boston: Houghton Mifflin.

Sherman, L.W. (1992). Attacking crime: Policing and crime control. In M. Tonry and N. Morris (eds.), *Modern policing. Crime and justice: A review of research,* 15 (pp. 159–230). Chicago: University of Chicago Press.

(1997). Policing for crime prevention. In L. W. Sherman, D. C. Gottfredson, D. L. MacKenzie, J. E. Eck, P. Reuter, and S. D. Bushway, *Preventing crime: What works, what doesn't, what's promising* (ch. 8). Washington, DC: National Institute of Justice, US Department of Justice.

(1998). *Evidence-based policing. Ideas in American policing series.* Washington, DC: Police Foundation.

(2003). Misleading evidence and evidence-led policy: Making social science more experimental. *Annals of the American Academy of Political and Social Science*, 589, 6–19.

Sherman, L. W. and Eck, J. E. (2002). Policing for crime prevention. In L. W. Sherman, D. P. Farrington, B. C. Welsh, and D. L. MacKenzie (eds.), *Evidence-based crime prevention* (pp. 295–329). New York: Routledge.

Sherman, L. W., Farrington, D. P., Welsh, B. C., and MacKenzie, D. L. (eds.). (2002). *Evidence-based crime prevention.* New York: Routledge.

Sherman, L. W., Gottfredson, D. C., MacKenzie, D. L., Eck, J. E., Reuter, P., and Bushway, S. D. (1997). *Preventing crime: What works, what doesn't, what's promising.* Washington, DC: National Institute of Justice, US Department of Justice.

Tita, G., Riley, K. J., and Greenwood, P. W. (2003). From Boston to Boyle Heights: The process and prospects of a "pulling levers" strategy in a Los Angeles bario. In S. H. Decker (ed.), *Policing gangs and youth violence* (pp. 102–130). Belmont, CA: Wadsworth.

Weisburd, D. and Eck, J. E. (2004). What can police do to reduce crime, disorder, and fear? *Annals of the American Academy of Political and Social Science*, 593, 42–65.

Weisburd, D., Lum, C. M., and Petrosino, A. (2001). Does research design affect study outcomes in criminal justice? *Annals of the American Academy of Political and Social Science*, 578, 50–70.

Weisburd, D., Mastrofski, S. D., McNally, A. M., Greenspan, R., and Willis, J. J. (2003). Reforming to preserve: Compstat and strategic problem solving in American policing. *Criminology and Public Policy*, 3, 421–456.

Welsh, B. C. (2002). Technological innovations for policing: Crime prevention as the bottom line. *Criminology and Public Policy*, 2, 129–132.

(2003). Community-based approaches to preventing delinquency and crime: Promising results and future directions. *Japanese Journal of Sociological Criminology*, 28, 7–24.

Welsh, B. C. and Farrington, D. P. (2000). Monetary costs and benefits of crime prevention programs. In M. Tonry (ed.), *Crime and justice: A review of research*, 27 (pp. 305–361). Chicago: University of Chicago Press.

(2001). Toward an evidence-based approach to preventing crime. *Annals of the American Academy of Political and Social Science*, 578, 158–173.

Welsh, B. C., Farrington, D. P., Sherman, L. W., and MacKenzie, D. L. (2002). What do we know about crime prevention? *International Annals of Criminology*, 40 (1 and 2), 11–31.

Wilson, D. B. (2001). Meta-analytic methods for criminology. *Annals of the American Academy of Political and Social Science*, 578, 71–89.

17 *Critic*
Improving police through expertise, experience, and experiments

Mark H. Moore

The words "expertise," "experience," and "experiment" all come from the same Latin root: *ex per*, and it means *from danger*. The common root suggests that at one time in human history, these ideas were closely connected with one another. Interpreting unforgivably, we might conclude that human beings have long been aware of the danger of acting with uncertain knowledge of consequences; further, that an important way to reduce this danger was to rely on the *expertise* that was rooted in *experience* of which one important type was an *experiment*.

The commitment to "evidence-based policing" is today's effort to reduce the danger associated with relying on police practices and methods whose consequences are, in an important sense, unknown, or at least uncertain. The proposed solution lies in the careful accumulation of actual concrete experience with particular police methods to discover which methods seem to work to produce desired results. But the focus on *evidence-based*, rather than *experience-based* knowledge suggests that it is not just any old experience that can be used in developing a more solid base for action. It is not, for example, the kind of experience we recognize as commonsense. Nor is it the kind that accumulates as police lore. It is not even the kind of experience captured in detailed case studies. It is instead the kind of experience that is captured in observational studies that reduce experience to numbers that can be systematically analyzed to discover the generality and reliability with which a particular intervention produces desired results. It may be even more particularly the kind of experience generated by carefully designed, randomized experiments.

As a social scientist, and as a person who longs to put police work on a more solid empirical basis, it is impossible to be against a movement that supports "evidence-based policing." I think it is important to find out what works in policing. I think social science methods provide the most powerful methods available to us to determine what works in policing as well as in other fields. My only concern is that by focusing too much on the experience that can be captured in quantitative observational studies and controlled experiments – by assuming that these methods can stand alone, and that they are the only ones that can provide a relatively firm basis for action – we will end up, paradoxically, both reducing the amount of experience that is available to us, and slowing the rate at which the field as a whole can learn about what works in policing.

I set out this argument below in the form of a skeptical commentary on evidence-based policing. For clarity and concreteness, I use Lawrence Sherman's (1998) paper on evidence-based policing as the point of departure. I understand that the idea of evidence-based policing is broader than the approach suggested by Sherman, and that there are many others who propose different ideas. But Sherman's paper provides such a convenient foil for my arguments, and is so clearly an exemplar of the commitments that lie behind a larger movement for evidence-base medicine, evidence-based education and evidence-based policing that it is irresistible to use it as a target. I hope both Larry and others working on evidence-based policing will forgive the distortion that this focus gives to my discussion. I only hope that my arguments will have merit even when considered against a wider and more nuanced idea of evidence-based policing.

"Scientific evidence"

Let's begin where Sherman does: with the apparently incontrovertible claim that "police practices should be based on scientific evidence about what works best." Anyone who believes in science as an important driver of human progress has to accept this idea. Since that includes virtually all police researchers, and no small number of police practitioners, Sherman starts off with a large and sympathetic audience. The difficulties arise when we begin to think hard about what we mean by "scientific evidence," by "police practices," and by "works best."

Take, first, the issue of what constitutes "scientific evidence." In Sherman's view, too much current police practice is based on nothing more than "local custom, opinions, theories, and subjective impressions" (1998: 6). Current practices of policing are viewed as "unsystematic 'experience'" that provides the raw material for, but not the true essence of the kind of "scientific evidence" that would put policing on a stronger intellectual footing (Sherman 1998: 4). What lies between this "unsystematic experience" guided by "local custom, opinions, etc." is the rigorous examination of those practices through scientific methods – ideally, randomized trials of particular methods used in dealing with "repetitive circumstances." Thus, Sherman sets up a simple dichotomy: mere "custom, opinion and theory" versus "scientific facts."

The problem is that this is a false dichotomy. The options that Sherman describes anchor the ends of a continuum of scientific methods that can be used to test the efficacy of police methods; not a stark choice between superstitious tradition on one hand, and scientific certainty on the other. Science, as a human disposition and as a method, has never been strictly limited to randomized experiments; it has always included many more different types of investigations to acquire and use knowledge.

Science begins with curiosity about the size and character of some phenomenon in the world (for example, different kinds of crime). It continues with the development of some (as yet untested) ideas about the causal factors that are shaping the size and character of the phenomenon of interest (such as levels of poverty, or the development of a culture of violence). It proceeds with measurements made through particular instruments specially designed to make the link between a theoretical concept, and an empirical reality. It continues with the use of statistical techniques designed to discover the relationship, if any, between changes in the phenomenon being observed and changes in the variables that are thought to be causing the change.

It is worth noting that this basic method of science (interest in a phenomenon, speculation about causes, observation and measurement, analysis of differences) can be used not only to discover the "natural causes" of a phenomenon as it exists in nature, but also to investigate the consequences of a specifically imagined human intervention designed to alter the phenomenon that is observed. Thus, scientific methods can, in principle, be used to discover not only the causes of crime, but also the crime control effectiveness of particular interventions made by police departments. The search for causes is often described as basic research, while the search for remedies and cures is described as applied research.

But the distinction between basic and applied research should not blind one to the fact that both basic and applied sciences depend on exploring relationships between so-called "dependent variables" on one hand, and "independent variables" on the other.[1] The major difference is that when we are trying to explain the causes of crime, the independent variables are social structural and population characteristics that we hypothesize generate a certain amount of crime. When we are trying to explore the impact of a crime control intervention, the independent variable of particular interest is the intervention to be evaluated.[2]

It is also worth noting that the general form of "observational studies" described above (in which a phenomenon is observed in nature being affected both by natural cases and certain kinds of policy interventions) are generally only capable of showing a *correlation* between changes in the independent variables on one hand, and the dependent variables on the other (Winship and Morgan 1999). They cannot demonstrate *causation* with any high degree of reliability. To show *causation*, nature has to be manipulated a bit more carefully (Heckman 1997).

Specifically, to demonstrate that a particular hypothesized factor actually caused an effect to occur; or to show convincingly that a particular effect was the result of a particular policy intervention, we have to be able to compare two situations that are identical in all respects except for the fact that one situation was affected by a cause, or received a particular intervention, and the other did not so that any observed difference in results can be attributed to that causal variable, or that particular intervention. Repeated enough times, if we find that the treated situation produces a different result than the untreated situation, we can conclude with a high degree of confidence that the intervention produced the result we observed. It is this simple fact that makes randomized trials the "gold standard" for reliably inferring causation whether looking for natural causes or estimating the impact of an intervention, since randomization of conditions is the best method of ensuring that the two situations that are being compared are similar (Campbell 1969).

While everyone agrees that randomized trials are the best way of creating confident knowledge about the existence and size of an effect of police practices on levels of crime, an important question remains about how much we should rely on randomized trials, and how much on other, lesser means. This would not be an important question if we thought we could produce randomized trials to test every police practice. But there are many things that stand in the way realizing this particular dream – including the cost of such experiments, the technical difficulty of executing them, and various ethical cautions that arise when we experiment with the fates of human beings (Cook and Campbell 1979).

If, realistically, we cannot expect to test every police practice through randomized trials, then the issue of whether it makes sense to use some of the lesser methods of science (simple inquiry, logical thought, direct observation of actions and apparent results, program evaluations carried out through statistical analyses rather than randomized trials) becomes important. Put somewhat differently, both the research and the practice field in policing face the important question of how far down the path of scientific sophistication they should go in their combined efforts to establish a firm experiential and empirical basis for policing. More provocatively put, they have to decide what to do with the knowledge that lies between mere opinion on one hand, and results established through randomized trials on the other.[3]

In my preferred vision of "evidence-based policing," the standards of what constituted "research," or "evidence," or "scientific knowledge" would be more open and flexible than in Sherman's conception.

Obviously, one would want to get to the "gold standard" with as many important police practices as we could. But the central aim of a movement for "evidence-based policing" wouldn't be simply to push some arbitrarily selected police practices to the promised land of randomized trials, it would be to subject as many police practices as possible to increasingly stringent tests of their efficacy through methods that seemed appropriate and feasible.

In this conception of evidence-based policing, it would be counted as a gain if one simply laid out the common sense logic that lay behind a particular police practice, and subjected it to what I would describe as "the giggle test" that measured the common-sense plausibility of a claim of efficacy.[4] It would also count if one gathered facts about particular kinds of crimes and problems that police face that could suggest innovative ideas about how that sort of crime, or that kind of problem might best be addressed. It would be counted as a bigger gain if one actually went ahead and captured the experience a police department produced by recording and measuring what the department did, and what happened later, possibly but not necessarily as a consequence of the department's actions. These ideas are key elements in the problem-oriented policing model proposed by Herman Goldstein (1990). It would be counted as an even bigger gain if the experience produced in one domain was checked with naturally occurring experiences in other domains that could be used as "quasi-control groups" (i.e., rough equivalents to the kind of planned variation that one would introduce in the design of randomized experiments). And so on.

The point is to recognize that different pieces of evidence about efficacy come with different degrees of weight and credibility. The task is not only to produce evidence that has the particularly heavy weight associated with randomized trials; it is also to produce and responsibly use evidence that is less strong than that produced by randomized trials.

Widening the range of acceptable methods, and learning how to calibrate their differential weight in policymaking is important for at least three different reasons. First, sometimes the lesser methods produce important knowledge. This occurs when the effect of an intervention is so large, and so obvious that one doesn't really need a fine-grained statistical analysis to "tease out" the effect. Second, sometimes the lesser methods are the only practicable methods to use. There is not enough time to wait for the result, or not enough money to pay for the experiments, or not enough capacity to structure the world into the form demanded by randomized experiments. Third, many more people can get involved in the effort to learn what works if we work hard on the cruder parts of science such as developing "thick descriptions" of the phenomenon of interest, reasoning about interventions that might make sense, and remembering to look as closely as one can at what happened when one tried a particular intervention. Developing these basic scientific orientations among a mass audience can provide not only a valuable base for learning, but also help to create a strong base of support for the use of more sophisticated methods. The alternative approach – allowing only a few elite folks to carry out these investigations – raises doubts and generates resistance among those for whom the research is ostensibly being conducted (Hartley, Bennington, and Binns 1997; Hartley and Bennington 2000).

Police practices

Take next the question of what constitutes a "police practice" that could be evaluated through scientific means. Again, the scientific method works best (most reliably, most simply, most inexpensively) when the phenomenon being examined is causally simple, easy to observe, and occurs often. Such conditions often occur in manufacturing processes where physical inputs are converted to physical outputs through a well-defined technological process engineered to produce a specific result. That is the reason that statistical control systems work as well as they do in manufacturing operations.

In principle, one can always characterize some specific police practice as a kind of manufacturing technology that takes inputs (human labor, professional skill, assistance from victims and witnesses, forensic support, etc.) and produces a potentially valuable output (e.g., arrest of a murder suspect with enough evidence to support an effective prosecution). All one has to do is draw a "black box" around the inputs and the outputs, and carry out a statistical analysis of the relationship between the inputs and the outputs to identify the relevant "production function" (see e.g., Pindyck and Rubenfeld 2001). Look at enough homicide investigations and burglaries in this way, and one can identify the factors that contribute to the solution of the case (Greenwood, Chaiken, and Petersilia 1977). Similarly, one can imagine that we have particular approaches to particular crimes – such as arresting offenders for domestic violence – and experiment with the use of this technique to see whether it reduces the recurrence of these events, and thereby results in a reduction in these kinds of crimes.

In principal, at one higher level of abstraction, one can also think of a police department as a whole as the cumulative sum of these particular practices, brought out by the personnel of the department at the right time when triggered by an external demand for performance. Thus, one can conceptualize a police department as a kind of manufacturing or service facility designed to prevent crime in a particular jurisdiction, draw a box around the police department as a whole, and ask about the degree to which it is effective in reducing crime throughout its particular jurisdiction.

While this is fine in principle, when one begins to try to scientifically design and evaluate police practices, some important difficulties emerge. The first comes in defining a particular "police practice" that is worth scientifically evaluating.

At the outset of modern police research, this was not a particularly difficult problem. The "professional model" of policing relied on only a few large "practices" that were thought to be just and effective in dealing with all kinds of crime. The "logic model" of professional policing hypothesized (reasonably, I think) that all kinds of crime could be prevented and controlled through a few general methods of policing: namely, patrol, rapid response to crime calls, and retrospective investigations (Moore 2002). By threatening offenders with arrest, such methods could be expected to prevent and control crime through general deterrence. By producing arrests that led to convictions, such tactics could prevent and control crime through the additional mechanisms of specific deterrence, incapacitation, and (sometimes) rehabilitation.[5]

These police practices – patrol rapid response, retrospective investigation – represented large, significant targets for evaluative research (including both observational studies and randomized experiments) since they encompassed a great deal of what police departments actually did to control crime. What that research showed, however, was that these methods had much smaller effects on levels of crime and fear in the community than we initially thought (Kelling, Pate, Dieckman, and Brown 1974; Greenwood *et al.* 1977; Spelman and Brown 1984). Nor did they result in the apprehension of offenders as often as we thought desirable (Greenwood *et al.* 1977). And they were not able to cope very well with crimes that were invisible to the police because they did not necessarily happen in public, or produce a victim or witness who could alert the police (Moore 1983).

One of the most important effects of these studies was to encourage the police to search for more specialized practices designed to deal with particular kinds of crime. And it is this approach to dealing with crime that recently won the endorsement of the National Academy of Science's Panel on Policing (Committee to Review Research 2004). But an important consequence of this development for those who would like police methods to be carefully evaluated is that the more specialized focus on particular kinds of crime implied a dramatic increase in the number of specific police practices that had to be developed and evaluated. Instead of evaluating a few police practices that used most police resources and were considered robust in dealing with all manner of crime, the research task now became the evaluation of a much larger number of more specialized practices designed to deal with more particular kinds of crimes. We can, and have, looked at how the police respond to domestic violence, to serial killers, to robberies, to street-level drug dealing, to vandalism and vagrancy, and to mentally ill individuals who are creating disturbances, or threatening to commit suicide, and so on (Sherman 1992; Plotkin and Narr 1993; Rossmo 1995).

Once we begin to think that it is wrong to look at a general method for dealing with a homogenous problem called crime, and to rely instead on a wide array of more particular methods for dealing with a highly heterogeneous set of crimes, the challenge of evaluating police practices begins to resemble the problem of investigating the huge variety of medical practices used to cope with different kinds of illnesses. In medicine, instead of imagining that there is a general cure for all disease, and that hospitals are the organizations that do only that general thing to protect us from disease, we have begun to distinguish many different kinds of diseases, each with their own proper response, specially tailored to the unique circumstances of an individual. We have also come to view the practice of medicine in hospitals as bundles of these particular practices that are hauled out by doctors and nurses when particular cases require them. Perhaps police departments should be seen as collections of professional police officers organized in a particular organization that brings out particular treatments for particular cases as needed. Ideally, then, the knowledge base of policing would consist of the knowledge of what particular interventions work with what particular diseases, and the adaptation of those particular interventions to the particular condition of a given circumstance – just what the idea of problem-oriented policing prescribed for the field.

Unfortunately, just as in medicine, only a portion of what is now thought to constitute the "best practices" in policing with respect to particular kinds of crime have actually been tested in randomized trials. That means that the police are still operating in the dangerous situation of relying on untested best practices. On the other hand, it also suggests that all we have to do is to increase the rate of experimentation so science can catch up to our current practices. That is what Sherman seems to believe. But I think there is a deeper problem here, and the difficulties that medicine faces in evaluating its own practices should provide a cautionary tale to policing as it seeks a firmer basis for its professional practice.

One part of the difficulty has to do with knowing how to divide up the world of crime problems into meaningful categories for which particular best practices can be developed. So far, much of that work seems to be guided by common sense – not some deductive logic. For example, we started out distinguishing domestic violence from other kinds of aggravated assault because we thought it was a "different" kind of problem in at least the following ways: (1) we were less likely to hear about it from victims; (2) the victims would be less cooperative in supporting arrests and prosecutions; (3) there were often repeat offenses, so that each offense could be used as an occasion to do something that would make the next offense more or less likely to occur, and more or less serious; (4) we had to be worried about the effect of the intervention we made not only on the likelihood of future violence against the victim, but also on the impact that the intervention had on children living in close proximity to and dependent on the victims, and so on. All these features of domestic violence seemed to make it a special category of crime that deserved it own diagnosis and its own treatment (Chalk and King 1998).

Yet, as we have gone deeper into the exploration of methods for dealing with domestic violence, two surprises have occurred that raise doubts about categorizing domestic violence as a unique kind of crime. On one hand, we have found that other kinds of violence share some important characteristics with domestic violence. For example, we have discovered that many homicides and aggravated assaults among young men occur in the context of continuing relationships that are as criminogenic as those between domestic partners (Kennedy, Piehl, and Braga 1996). They are rivals for turf, for the leadership of a gang, or for the affections of a young woman. Violence they commit on one another will create another round of violence as families and friends of the victims seek revenge. In short, gang murders are similar to domestic violence in that it is a continuing relationship among individuals that seems to stimulate and focus the violence.

On the other hand, we have learned that there are many different kinds of domestic violence cases that seem to respond differently to different kinds of interventions. Indeed, Sherman (1992) illustrates this phenomenon in his own account of what happened with the experiments in policing domestic violence. We began with the idea that there was a relatively homogenous problem called "domestic violence," and the challenge was to determine whether a particular method – mandatory arrest – was successful in dealing with this general problem. What we learned (after more than $10 million in experimental studies) was: (1) that arrest reduces domestic violence in some cities but increases it in others; (2) that arrest reduces domestic violence among employed people but increases it among unemployed people; (3) that arrest reduces domestic violence in the short run but can increase it in the long run; and (4) that the police can predict which couples are most likely to suffer future violence, but our society seems to value privacy too highly to allow effective preventive action.

These observations suggest that the search for effective crime control methods may not go on as systematically or as scientifically as we might wish. While we could follow the approach of differentiating different kinds of crime, and looking for the best method of dealing with each particular kind of crime, it is not at all clear how such categories of crime should be constructed, nor how many will have to be investigated. The more particular our characterization of crimes, the more experiments we will have to run. On the other hand, we could start with a generalized idea of crime, and find a method that would be effective in dealing with all kinds of crime. Unfortunately, we tried that, and produced only mixed results. Perhaps our best chance is the method suggested by Goldstein (1990): namely, to learn as much as we can about the likely causes and potential points of intervention in dealing with particular crime problems through the development of a thick description of a certain class of crimes, and then use common sense to imagine and test interventions to see if they work. That clinical (as opposed to scientific) approach might be both necessary and sufficient to help us develop the knowledge we need to deal with a highly differentiated crime problem, just as it was necessary and sufficient to give us most of the means we now rely on in medicine.

If it is hard to evaluate any particular police operation focused on a particular problem, imagine how much harder it is to evaluate the performance of a police department as a whole. Of course, one could rule out the evaluation of a whole department's performance as not the kind of "practice" Sherman had in mind. But Sherman seems inclined to think that the overall performance of an entire department could be viewed as a kind of "macro-practice" that could be evaluated scientifically as well as the kind of "micro-practices" we associate with the "best practices" that exist for dealing with particular kinds of crime.[6] He suggests this inclination by explicitly introducing the analogy to manufacturing organizations on one hand, and by claiming that departments as a whole could be evaluated, motivated, and guided by scientific evidence of what works in policing, on the other. In both moves, he changes the definition of the police practice to be evaluated from a specific operational program designed to deal with a specific kind of crime to the operations of the police department as a whole.

When we focus on the "scientific evaluation" of the performance of a police department as a whole rather than the efficacy of a particular procedure in dealing with a particular kind of crime, many things change.

One key difference is that the kinds of police practices that need to be evaluated change. Police practices observed at the organizational level of the police would include all the specific *operational* practices used by the department to deal with particular crimes as defined above. But police practices observed at the organizational level would include the *administrative* practices that the police use to manage themselves; the methods they use to recruit and train personnel, the methods they use to motivate their line commanders and individual officers to achieve organizational goals, the methods they use to minimize corruption and abuses of force, and so on. These administrative practices might even include the arrangements the department made to evaluate their own operational practices (Moore, Sparrow, and Spelman 1997; Moore 2003).

A second key issue, however, is that while effective crime control is certainly one thing that citizens want from police organizations, it is also quite clear that citizens want other things from their police as well (Moore 2002). They want to have a subjective sense of security in their streets that may be somewhat independent of the objective risks of victimization. They want certain kinds of services from the police that make their individual and collective life better.

But the problem continues. Often specific police activities and operations produce results that register on many different objectives of policing – not just one. The DARE Program, for example, has long been evaluated as though its most important justification is the impact such a program would have on future levels of drug use by students exposed to the program (Esbensen, Frend, Taylor, Peterson *et al.* 2002). But the most important practical effect of the DARE Program might be to build relationships between the police on one hand, and parents and youth on the other, that will allow them to be more effective in dealing with all kinds of problems both encountered and created by these individuals in the future.

There may also be synergies (positive or negative) in the activities of police viewed across the department as a whole. For example, the strong work of an officer who was focused on building community relations in a particular neighborhood could be undermined in an instant by a drug raid carried out by a centralized unit that ended up in the wrong apartment arresting the wrong person in a way that terrorized rather than reassured the neighborhood about the competence and intentions of the police. In short, policing may simply be too complex an endeavor to ever be sorted out – just as it would be too complex to sort out the operations of a public health system that included not only emergency rooms, but also long-stay hospitals, neighborhood clinics, and public health immunization and well-baby programs.

"What works?"

Take, finally, the question of what we mean when we say that a particular police practice "works." The obvious next question is: "Works to do what?" A question that follows closely after that is: "Works at what cost, and with what unintended and unexpected side effects?" In answering these questions, one is gradually constructing an analytic framework that one could use normatively to decide whether a given police practice was worth continuing.

This is importantly an empirical question, of course. To determine whether a practice is a good one or not, we have to be able to describe the effects it produces in the world. And that is a profoundly empirical issue.

But the construction of an analytic framework for *evaluating* a given police practice also requires a *normative* stance. To identify an effect of a program as something that would be worth noticing in any attempt to evaluate its value to the wider society is inherently a normative enterprise. The effects that we consider when evaluating a program are important precisely because they have normative significance to the world.

For example, we could observe that police crackdowns on gang members could reduce gun violence and fatalities in a city. That alone might seem to make a strong case for engaging in more police crackdowns on gang members. But suppose those police crackdowns produced other effects as well such as increased resentment and fear of the police in the neighborhoods in which the crackdowns occurred. There would be an empirical question to be answered about whether this was a real effect of the police crackdown. There would be a normative question about whether such an effect should be counted when we were considering the overall value of the crackdowns as a police response to a social problem. If we thought this effect was a plausible one, and that it was normatively significant, then the analytic framework for measuring the impact of the crackdown would have to look at the effect it had on local residents' attitudes toward the police as well as on the level of gun violence. A new dependent variable would have to be introduced into the analysis. This is an example of an important conclusion drawn by the National Academy of Sciences Panel on Policing. They concluded that police practices had to be evaluated in terms of their impact on the legitimacy of the police as well as their crime control cost effectiveness (Committe to Review Research 2004).

Often, we do not feel obliged to say what we mean by a police practice that works, because we assume that we know what the point of police practices should be: namely, to control and reduce crime. We assume that all police practices should be evaluated only in terms of this single dimension of performance. But I think it is clear that both micro police practices and the overall operations of macro police institutions need to be evaluated in more dimensions than their crime control efficacy. Some of these added dimensions focus on the output or value side of police operations. For example, we might be as interested in the capacity of a given police practice to reduce fear, and reduce the burden of self-defense as well as on their capacity to control a particular crime. We might also be interested in the capacity of a given police practice to produce the kind of justice we associate with both calling offenders to account, and protecting the rights of citizens as well as efficacy in dealing with crime. We might even be interested in the impact that the police practice has on perceptions of police responsiveness and fairness as well as effectiveness in dealing with particular crime problems (see e.g., Moore 2002).

Other dimensions of evaluation focus not on the value of the outputs, but on the costs of mounting the operation. That includes monetary costs for sure. But it also could include costs associated with abridging individual rights, or exacerbating a sense of unfairness in the way that the police do their business. These costs could show up as monetary costs (when the police were successfully sued for wrongful conduct); or they could show up in terms of reduced effectiveness as disillusioned citizens stopped cooperating with the police in the production of justice and security; or they could show up in nothing more than the continued disgust and disappointment that citizens feel when they think their tax dollars and liberty are being abused by an organization they would like to be able to trust.

To say that a police practice, or a police organization, works, then, is to make a set of claims about not only what effects a police department produces, but also what a political community that authorizes the police department does or should want. This means that we have to admit both values and politics into the construction of the analytic framework we use to evaluate police practices and police departments as a whole. What effects of a police practice should be considered important for evaluation purposes is not, strictly speaking, a value-free scientific enterprise. A fact taken by itself may be value neutral. And in trying to develop a fact it may be important to push one's values to the side as best one can. But to develop a fact that is useful in *evaluating* police practices, one has to construct a value framework that makes the fact interpretable as an evaluation of whether something is good or bad. And that is inevitably a value question.

How does policing improve?

In the end, both police researchers and police practitioners have to concern themselves with the way in which policing can be improved. An important part of that effort depends on developing more reliable knowledge about what works. And that, in turn, depends on deploying the methods of science to help us separate false claims of efficacy from true claims, or to gradually increase our confidence in the methods we are using to accomplish the goals of policing. Thus, science, and particularly the use of science in carrying out randomized trials of police practices, could be the "rate determining step" in determining the rate of police improvement.

If this is true, then the principal responsibility for improving policing seems to lie primarily in the research community. It is there that police practitioners must look to find out what is known to work. It is there that police practitioners must turn to develop the guidelines they use to instruct their officers to do their work. And it is from that source that any new doubts about the efficacy of old methods, or any new ideas about the proven efficacy of new methods must come.

That, at least, seems to be the core of the vision of how to improve policing that is contained in the idea of evidence-based policing: improvement through science, and the work of scientists.

I hope I can be forgiven if I suggest that this puts a bit too much of the load on science and scientists, and that it uses the commitment and knowledge of the police profession a bit too little. Science cannot become useful in the practical world of policing unless the practitioners embrace some aspects of science as an important part of the way they do their work. We have to create the equivalent in the profession not only of academic researchers and clinicians, but also of clinical professors, and reflective practitioners; and they have to learn to work together in a kind of intellectual and practical partnership to solve concrete problems as best they can – not compete with each other over whose knowledge is more authoritative.

Science alone cannot answer important questions that are central to the development of effective clinical practice. Science, by itself, cannot tell us how to divide up the world of practical problems we see in front of us in a way that is most amenable to their solution. Science, by itself, cannot necessarily suggest the particular intervention that should be tried to deal with a given problem. Science, by itself, cannot tell us in what terms we ought to evaluate the interventions we make. For all this work, we need the experience of practitioners as well as the experiments of science.

If our vision of evidence-based policing going forward is one that embraces these aspects of science, I am all for it. If our vision is one that seeks to privilege a certain kind of science and a particular kind of scientist, I am against it. The world of crime and policing is far too important, far too complex, and far too urgent to leave entirely in the hands of scientists. We need a great deal of practical wisdom as well as a rigorous and responsive science to move the field forward.

NOTES

1. Karl Popper describes what is here called the dependent variable, the *explanandum* – the thing to be explained, and the independent variables, the *explanans* – or the thing that explains the *explanandum* (Popper, 1902).

2. James Q. Wilson (1985) has made some important observations about the difference between criminology on one hand, and the effort to find important means for controlling crime on the other.

3. Howard Raiffa (1924) has developed some systematic ways of thinking about using imperfect information in practical decisions. He recommends a Bayesian approach in which the decisionmaker begins with more or less strong prior probability estimates of the likely effects of a given policy. He then updates those prior probability estimates as new information comes in through observation and experimentation. Since each piece of information has a different weight, each piece of information can be brought in to improve the estimate. We don't have to discard imperfect information; only discount its weight.

4. This is often accomplished as a necessary part of any program evaluation. Wes Skogan (1990) has demonstrated the importance of developing the "logic model" that connects a planned intervention to a desired effect as an important step in carrying on a program evaluation. Often, once one goes through this particular discipline, one can see errors in thought and planning even before one gets into the field. That is what I mean by the "giggle test" – the use of logic, common sense, and a sense of proportion to test the very plausibility of an idea before one goes to the trouble of trying it out and carefully evaluating it. In my experience, many police practices would be improved by taking this very first step in science.

5. These basic ideas remain strong in policing because they align both with common sense, and with certain ideas of justice; namely that it would be just, as well as practically useful, to call offenders to account for their crimes, and to put them in prison. They show up these days in police tactics that encourage aggressive preventive patrol focusing on disorder offenses.

6. Note that thinking about the idea of a police department as a macro practice could include two quite different ideas. One is that the department had a general approach to dealing with crime that worked. That could be located in a particular robust operational procedure such as aggressive preventive patrol. Or it could be located in a particular administrative approach such as Compstat. Or it could be located in a particular organizational strategy such as community-oriented or problem-oriented policing. Or, it could be in some combination of the police department having in its repertoire a wide variety

of responses that it uses, along with some principles that help it decide which particular procedures to use.

REFERENCES

Campbell, D. (1969). Reforms as experiments. *American Psychologist* 24, 409–429.

Chalk, R. and King, P. (eds.). 1998. *Violence in families: assessing prevention and treatment programs.* Washington, DC: National Academy Press.

Committee to Review Research on Police Policy and Practices. (2004). *Fairness and effectiveness in policing: The evidence.* Washington, DC: The National Academies Press.

Cook, T. and Campbell, D. (1979). *Quasi-experimentation: Design and analysis issues for field settings.* Boston: Houghton Mifflin Company.

Esbensen, F., Freng, A., Taylor, T., Peterson, D., and Osgood, D. (2002). National evaluation of the gang resistance education and training (G.R.E.A.T.) program. In W. Reed and S. Decker (eds.), *Responding to gangs: Evaluation and research.* Washington, DC: National Institute of Justice, US Department of Justice.

Goldstein, H. (1990). *Problem-oriented policing.* Philadelphia, PA: Temple University Press.

Greenwood, P., Chaiken, J., and Petersilia, J. (1977). *The investigative process.* Lexington, MA: Lexington Books.

Hartley, J. and Bennington, J. (2000). Co-research: A new methodology for new times. *European Journal of Work and Organizational Psychology*, 7, 1–16.

Hartley, J., Bennington, J., and Binns, P. (1997). Researching the role of internal change agents in the management of organizational change. *British Journal of Management*, 8, 61–73.

Heckman, J. (1997). Instrumental variables: A study of implicit assumptions used in making program evaluations. *Journal of Human Resources*, 33, 441–462.

Kelling, G., Pate, T., Dieckman, D., and Brown, C. (1974). *The Kansas City preventive patrol experiment: A technical report.* Washington, DC: Police Foundation.

Kennedy, D., Piehl, A., and Braga, A. (1996). Youth violence in Boston: Gun markets, serious offenders, and a use-reduction strategy. *Law and Contemporary Problems*, 59, 147–196.

Moore, M. H. (1983). Invisible offenses: A challenge to minimally intrusive law enforcement. In G. Kaplan (ed.), *ABSCAM ethics: Moral issues and deception in law enforcement.* Washington, DC: Police Foundation.

(2002). *Recognizing value in policing.* Washington, DC: Police Executive Research Forum.

(2003). Sizing up compstat: An important administrative innovation in policing. *Criminology and Public Policy*, 2, 469–494.

Moore, M. H., Sparrow, M., and Spelman, W. (1997). Innovation in policing: From production lines to jobs shops. In A. Altshuler and R. Behn (eds.), *Innovation in American government.* Washington, DC: Brookings Institution Press.

Pindyck, R. S. and Rubenfeld, D. (2001). *Microeconomics* (5th ed.). Upper Saddle River, NJ: Prentice-Hall.

Plotkin, M. and Narr, T. (1993). *The police response to the homeless*. Washington, DC: Police Executive Research Forum.

Popper, K. (1902). *The poverty of historicism*. Boston: Beacon Press [1957].

Raiffa, H. (1924). *Decision analysis*. New York: McGraw-Hill [1997].

Rossmo, D. K. (1995). Place, space, and police investigations: Hunting serial violent criminals. In J. Eck and D. Weisburd (eds.), *Crime and place*. New York: Criminal Justice Press.

Sherman, L. W. (1992). *Policing domestic violence*. New York: The Free Press.

(1998). *Evidence-based policing: Ideas in American policing series*. Washington, DC: Police Foundation.

Skogan, W. (1990). *Disorder and decline*. New York: The Free Press.

Spelman, W. and Brown, D. (1984). *Calling the police: Citizen reporting of serious crime*. Washington, DC: US Government Printing Office.

Wilson, J. Q. (1985). *Thinking about crime*. Revised edition. New York: Vintage Books.

Winship, C. and Morgan, S. (1999). The estimation of causal effects from observational data. *Annual Review of Sociology*, 25, 659–706.

18   Conclusion: Police innovation and the future of policing

Anthony A. Braga and David Weisburd

In this volume, a group of leading scholars presented contrasting perspectives on eight major innovations in American policing developed over the course of the 1980s and 1990s. Police departments needed to improve their performance and innovation provided the opportunity to make these improvements. These innovations represent fundamental changes to the business of policing. However, as many of our authors point out, improving police performance through innovation is often not straightforward. Police departments are highly resistant to change and police officers often experience difficulty in implementing new programs (Sparrow, Moore, and Kennedy 1990; Capowich and Roehl 1994; Sadd and Grinc 1994). The available evidence on key dimensions of police performance associated with these eight innovations, such as crime control effectiveness and community satisfaction with services provided, is also surprisingly limited. These observations are not unique to the policing field. For example, as Elmore (1997) suggests, the field of education was awash in innovation during the 1990s, but there is little evidence examining whether those innovations advanced the performance of schools, students, or graduates.

While our knowledge about the effects of these innovations on police performance is still developing, we think there is much reason for optimism about the future of policing. This period of innovation has demonstrated that police can prevent crime and can improve their relationships with the communities they serve. In the near future, we don't anticipate the dramatic strategic innovations that characterized the last two decades. Rather, we expect further refinement of our knowledge of "what works" in policing, under what circumstances particular strategies may work, and why these strategies are effective in improving police performance. The challenge for the future of policing is to continue making progress in further developing and implementing promising strategies while addressing the new problems of public safety that have been created by 9/11 and the concerns that it has raised about the threat of terrorism and the need for police commitment to homeland security.

Categorizing recent police innovations

Moore, Sparrow, and Spelman (1997) suggest four distinct categories of police innovation: programmatic, administrative, technological, and strategic. These categories are not clearly separated from each other and, as Moore and his colleagues admit (1997), assigning any one innovation to one category over another is often a judgment call. Programmatic innovations establish new operational methods of using the resources of an organization to achieve particular results. These programs can include arresting fences as a way to discourage burglary, using police officers to provide drug education in the schools, and offering victim-resistance training to women. Administrative innovations are changes in how police organizations prepare themselves to conduct operations or account for their achievements. These include new ways of measuring the performance of an individual officer or the overall department as well as changes in personnel policies and practices such as new recruiting techniques, new training approaches, and new supervisory relations. Technological innovations depend on the acquisition or use of some new piece of capital equipment such as non-lethal weapons, DNA typing, or crime mapping software.

Strategic innovations represent a fundamental change in the overall philosophy and orientation of the organization (Moore *et al.* 1997). These changes involve important redefinitions of the primary objectives of policing, the range of services and activities supplied by police departments, the means through which police officers achieve their goals, and the key internal and external relationships that are developed and maintained by the police. Strategic innovations include shifting from "law enforcement" to "problem solving" as a means of resolving incidents, forming working relationships with community groups as a tactic in dealing with drug markets, and recognizing citizen satisfaction as an important performance measure. These innovations are strategic because they involve changing some of the basic understandings about the ends or means of policing or the key structures of accountability that shaped overall police efforts under the standard model of policing (Moore *et al.* 1997). We feel that the eight innovations described in this volume represent related attempts to change the ends and means of policing and, therefore, should be regarded as strategic innovations.

Weisburd and Eck (2004) suggest that recent strategic innovations expand policing beyond standard practices along two dimensions: *diversity of approaches* and *level of focus* (see Figure 18.1). The "diversity of approaches" dimension represents the content of the practices employed or tools used by the police. As represented by the vertical axis,

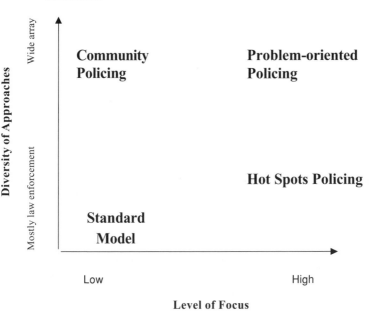

Figure 18.1 Dimensions of policing strategies
Source: Adapted from Weisburd and Eck 2004

tools can range from mostly traditional law enforcement to a wide array of approaches. The horizontal axis represents the extent to which police practices are focused or targeted. Weisburd and Eck (2004) contrast standard police practices with hot spots policing, problem-oriented policing, and community policing. The standard model of policing, with its emphasis on enforcing the law and its generalized application of law enforcement powers, scores low on both dimensions. Hot spots policing scores high on focus, but low on the diversity of tools used to control hot spot locations. Problem-oriented policing rates high on diversity of tools and focus as the approach challenges police officers to implement strategies designed to deal with the underlying conditions that give rise to discrete crime problems. Community policing, where police draw on a wider array of resources to prevent crime and engage the community in defining and dealing with problems, scores high on diversity of approaches. However, when implemented without problem-oriented policing, the approach is not well focused on crime problems and provides a common set of services throughout a jurisdiction.

Another dimension that could be added to Weisburd and Eck's (2004) classification of police practices is the degree to which the innovations change the goals of policing. Under the standard model, police departments were mostly focused on preventing serious crime by deterring and apprehending criminal offenders, serving justice by holding offenders accountable for their crimes, rendering immediate aid to people in crisis, and providing non-emergency services such as controlling traffic (Eck and Rosenbaum 1994). While the eight innovations described in this book do not remove any of these goals from the tasks of policing, the new strategies rearrange the priorities among the goals and add new ones. Non-criminal and non-emergency quality of life problems receive much more attention from the new police strategies. Community and problem-oriented policing represent the most radical departures from standard police work. Community policing, in its various manifestations, challenges police officers to work with citizens to deal with a broader range of concerns, most notably fear of crime and social and physical disorder (Skogan, in this volume). Problem-oriented policing similarly adds new goals to policing, but it also reorganizes police actions from focusing on incidents as units of work to focusing on classes of problems to be addressed by responses that can be quite different from routine police activities (Eck in this volume). Other innovations represent less dramatic changes to standard police goals. For example, disorder policing, if engaged without community and problem-oriented policing, expands the police mandate to include social and physical disorder but does not radically change the tactics engaged by the police to deal with these problems (Sousa and Kelling in this volume; Taylor in this volume).

Crime and disorder control effectiveness

When police departments focus their efforts on identifiable risks, such as crime hot spots, repeat victims, and serious offenders, they are able to prevent crime and disorder (Braga 2002; Eck 2003). The strongest evidence comes from evaluations of hot spots policing initiatives (Weisburd and Braga 2003; Weisburd and Braga, in this volume). Braga (2001) presents evidence from five randomized controlled experiments and four quasi-experimental designs to show that hot spots policing programs generate crime control gains without significantly displacing crime to other locations. Instead, in the five evaluations that examined immediate spatial displacement, hot spots policing initiatives were more likely to generate a "diffusion of crime control benefits" to areas immediately surrounding the targeted hot spots (Clarke and Weisburd 1994). While the rigor of evaluation designs varies from simple before-after comparisons without control groups to randomized experiments, problem-oriented policing, when appropriately focused on specific crime problems, has been found to be effective in preventing crime (Sherman and Eck 2002; Weisburd and Eck 2004; Eck in this volume). The available scientific evidence on third-party policing is derived from a similar mix of studies with varying degrees of rigor. Nonetheless, Mazerolle and Ransley (in this volume) report that third-party policing is effective in dealing with drug problems, violent crime problems, and problems involving young people. Pulling levers strategies also seem to be promising in controlling the violent behavior of groups of chronic offenders (Braga et al. 2001; Kennedy in this volume). However, the research base for this approach is very limited (Braga and Winship in this volume; Wellford, Pepper, and Petrie 2005).

As a general strategy, community policing has not been found to be effective in preventing crime (Mastrofski in this volume). The available research shows that unfocused community-oriented tactics such as foot patrol, storefront offices, newsletters, and community meetings do not reduce crime and disorder (Committee to Review Research 2004; Weisburd and Eck 2004). However, as will be discussed below, there is strong evidence to suggest that community policing tactics reduce fear of crime (Committee to Review Research 2004; Weisburd and Eck 2004). The available empirical evidence on the crime control effectiveness of broken windows policing is mixed (Sousa and Kelling in this volume; Taylor in this volume). It remains unclear whether police departments that engage a broad-based broken windows policing strategy actually reduce crime. Simple analyses of crime trend data suggest that cities experience decreases in crime after their police departments adopt Compstat (Silverman in this volume). However, since Compstat programs are often implemented in conjunction with other crime prevention initiatives such as broken windows and hot spots policing, it is very difficult to untangle the influence of Compstat on any observed crime control gains (Weisburd, Mastrofski, Willis, and Greenspan in this volume). Moreover, in New York City and three other cities, further analysis revealed the observed decreases in crime began before the implementation of Compstat (Eck and Maguire 2000; Weisburd, Mastrofski, McNally et al. 2003; Weisburd et al. in this volume). Compstat has yet to be proven as an effective crime control strategy in cities that have adopted the approach.

Evidence-based policing has not been empirically tested as an overall model of policing (Welsh in this volume). However, evidence-based police departments would draw policies and practices from a solid research base of strategies that have proven to be effective in controlling crime (Sherman 1998). While an evidence-based approach to policing may have the unintended effect of limiting the ability of police to innovate by privileging evidence over experience (Moore in this volume), we do not believe that engaging an evidence-based approach would undermine the crime and disorder control effectiveness of police departments.

Community reaction to innovative police strategies

In addition to concerns over the crime control effectiveness of the standard model of policing, police innovation in the 1980s and 1990s was also driven by high levels of community dissatisfaction with police services and a growing recognition that citizens had other concerns that required police action, such as fear of crime. Since citizen involvement in policing is a core element of community policing programs (Skogan in this volume), it is not surprising that we know most about citizen reaction to these types of programs. In general, broad-based community policing initiatives have been found to reduce fear of crime and improve the relationships between the police and the communities they serve (Committee to Review Research 2004; Weisburd and Eck 2004). Community policing strategies that entail direct involvement of citizens and police, such as police community stations, citizen contract patrol, and coordinated community policing, have been found to reduce fear of crime among individuals and decrease individual concern about crime in neighborhoods (Pate and Skogan 1985; Wycoff and Skogan 1986; Brown and Wycoff 1987).

Community policing also enhances police legitimacy. Citizen support and cooperation are closely linked to judgments about the legitimacy of the police (Tyler 2004). When citizens view the police as legitimate legal authorities, they are more likely to cooperate and obey the law (Tyler 1990). Public judgments about the legitimacy of the police are influenced by their assessments of the manner in which the police exercise their authority (Tyler 1990; 2004). The available evidence suggests that the police generally obey the laws that limit their power (Skogan and Meares 2004). However, minorities consistently express significantly lower confidence in the police when compared to whites (Tyler 2004). Community policing improves citizens' judgments of police actions (Skogan in this volume). For example, over an eight-year period of community policing, Chicago residents' views of their police improved on measures of their effectiveness, responsiveness, and demeanor (Skogan and Steiner 2004). Importantly, these improvements were shared among Latinos, African-Americans, and whites (Skogan and Steiner 2004). Clearly, community policing has been a strategic innovation that has helped bridge the police confidence gap in minority communities.

While there is a growing body of systematic research on the effects of community policing on citizen satisfaction with the police, there is a noteworthy lack of research assessing the effects of other police innovations on police–community relations. This gap in knowledge is noteworthy as many of the contributions to this volume suggest a tension between the crime prevention effectiveness of focused police efforts and their potential harmful effects on police–community relations (Braga and Winship; Mazerolle and Ransley; Meares; Rosenbaum; Taylor; Weisburd and Braga, all in this volume). Certainly, legitimacy is linked to the ability of the police to prevent crime and keep neighborhoods safe. However, the police also need public support and cooperation to be effective in preventing crime. While residents in neighborhoods suffering from high levels of crime often demand higher levels of enforcement, they still want the police to be respectful and lawful in their crime control efforts (Skogan and Meares 2004; Tyler 2004). Residents don't want family members, friends, and neighbors to be targeted unfairly by enforcement efforts or treated poorly by overaggressive police officers. If the public's trust and confidence in the police is undermined, the ability of the police to prevent crime will be weakened by lawsuits, declining willingness to obey the law, and withdrawal from existing partnerships (Tyler 1990; 2001). The political fallout from illegitimate police actions can seriously impede the ability of police departments to engage innovative crime control tactics.

This dilemma has been described elsewhere as "the trust dilemma" (Altshuler and Behn 1997). Innovation may be necessary for establishing public faith in the ability of government agencies to perform. But before the public grants government agencies a license to be truly innovative, it needs to be convinced that these same agencies have the ability to perform (Altshuler and Behn 1997). Police departments should be encouraged to pursue effective strategies that aggressively focus on identifiable risks such as hot spots, repeat victims, and high-rate offenders. However, police departments must be careful in their application of these approaches to crime prevention. For example, anecdotal evidence suggests that broken windows policing strategies enjoy broad community support as a legitimate way to reduce crime and disorder (Sousa and Kelling in this volume). However, when the broken windows approach is distorted into so-called zero-tolerance policing, indiscriminate and aggressive law enforcement can negatively affect police–community relations (Taylor in this volume). To avoid engaging tactics that will generate strong negative community reaction, police departments should encourage and embrace community involvement in their crime prevention efforts. In Boston, the involvement of black ministers in the police-led pulling levers violence prevention strategy allowed law enforcement agencies to pursue more intrusive and aggressive tactics that would not have been possible without community involvement (Braga and Winship in this volume).

Police reaction to innovative strategies

The eight innovations differed in their degree of departure from the standard model of policing. The police most easily adopt innovations that require the least radical departures from their hierarchical paramilitary organizational structures, continue incident-driven and reactive strategies, and maintain police sovereignty over crime issues. In its most basic form, hot spots policing simply concentrates traditional enforcement activity at high crime places. The familiarity of the approach to police is straightforward as they have a long history of temporarily heightening enforcement levels in problem areas. While law enforcement tools are deployed in a new way, the pulling levers deterrence strategy focuses existing criminal justice activities on groups of chronic offenders. Broken windows policing involves making arrests of minor offenders to control disorder and, as an end product, reduce more serious crime. As Kennedy (in this volume) observes, "law enforcement likes enforcing the law." Strategies such as hot spots, broken windows, pulling levers policing appeal to law enforcement practitioners primarily because they allow mostly traditional tactics to be deployed in new ways with the promise of considerably greater results. Compstat, as implemented by most American police agencies, has been focused more on reinforcing and legitimating the traditional bureaucratic military model of police organization than on innovation in the practices of policing (Weisburd *et al.* 2003; Weisburd *et al.* in this volume).

While all major American police agencies report some form of community policing as an important component of their operations (Bureau of Justice Statistics 2003), the police have been generally resistant to its adoption. This is not surprising since community policing involves the most radical change to existing police organizations. Skogan (in this volume) and Mastrofski (in this volume) report many shortcomings in the practical application of its three core elements: citizen involvement, problem solving, and decentralization. Citizens are generally used as information sources rather than engaged as partners in producing public safety. Officers prefer law enforcement strategies to developing and implementing alternative problem-oriented responses. Most "community-oriented" police agencies haven't made the organizational changes necessary to decentralize decisionmaking authority to the neighborhood level. Similarly, the available research on problem-oriented policing suggests that police officers experience difficulty during all stages of the problem-oriented process (Braga and Weisburd in this volume). Problem analysis is generally weak and implemented responses largely consist of traditional enforcement activities. Problem-oriented policing as practiced in the field is but a shallow version of the process recommended by Herman Goldstein (1990). Given its close relationship to community and problem-oriented policing, it seems likely that police departments engaging third-party policing will encounter similar practical problems.

It is not remarkable that the strategies that require the most radical changes to existing police practices and structures report the greatest difficulties in implementation. Nonetheless, the available evidence indicates a gradual transformation in police attitudes toward adopting these new strategies. In addition to the widespread reporting of innovative police practices across the United States, police officers' views toward the community and problem-oriented policing philosophy are becoming more positive. As summarized by Skogan (in this volume), studies point to positive changes in officers' views once they are involved in community policing, positive findings with respect to job satisfaction and views of the community, and growing support for community policing in districts that engage the strategy compared to districts that maintain traditional activities. Police history shows that it takes a long time for new models of policing to fully develop. The standard model of policing was itself a reform in reaction to corrupt and brutal police practices during the so-called "political era" of policing (Walker 1992). Initially, the reform movement progressed very slowly; in 1920, only a few departments could be labeled "professional" or engaging in the basic tenets of the standard model. It wasn't until the 1950s that virtually all American police departments were organized around the principles set forth by O. W. Wilson, August Vollmer, and other reformers (Walker 1992).

The future of policing

What will the future bring? Will the police continue to innovate at a rapid pace? We don't anticipate a new wave of strategic police innovation in the near future. The current context of policing suggests that future innovation will be incremental in nature. The conditions in the 1980s and 1990s that created the pressure for innovation simply no longer exist. Indeed, the atmosphere is precisely the opposite of earlier decades. Crime is down and federal funds available for demonstration projects to spur innovation are very limited. While the available research evidence is not as strong as some police executives believe, there is a general sense that these police innovations work in preventing crime and satisfying community concerns.

This perspective on the crime control effectiveness of new police practices is reinforced by the modest research evidence described in this volume and by a cursory examination of crime trends over the past decade (see Figure 18.2). The Federal Bureau of Investigation's Uniform Crime Reports reveals a 29 per cent decrease in the Index crime rate from 5820 per 100,000 residents in 1990 to 4118 per 100,000 residents in 2002 (www.bjsdata.ojp.usdoj.gov). While no single factor, including innovative policing, can be invoked as the cause of the crime decline of the 1990s (Blumstein and Wallman 2000), the "nothing works" view of policing in the 1970s and 1980s described in our introduction is no longer a topic of discussion in most policing circles.

Many of these innovative changes to policing appear positive and have shown crime control and community benefits. However, this volume reveals the need for greater research and knowledge about the effects of these innovations on police departments and the communities they serve. Relative to other criminal justice institutions, the police are very open to research and evaluation activities with universities and other research institutions (Committee to Review Research 2004). We believe that the police will continue to work with researchers to better understand crime problems, community concerns, police behavior, and structural issues in their organizations. These collaborations will support the police in further refining their practices to become even more effective, fair, efficient, and accountable agencies in the twenty-first century (Committee to Review Research 2004).

Over the next couple of decades, we anticipate that individual police departments will continue to institutionalize innovative practices by making administrative adjustments to their organizations and by developing a set of supporting strategies that fit the nature of their crime problems in the neighborhoods they police. Administrative arrangements and portfolios of crime prevention interventions will necessarily vary across departments as the police become more specialized in dealing with local crime problems. In essence, we believe police departments will continue their evolution from "production lines" that engage a static set of processes that are used over and over again to produce the same result to "job shops" where each police assignment is treated as a new challenge that might require a new solution (Moore *et al.* 1997).

We also anticipate some modest innovation in the development of systems to measure the performance of police departments. As police departments engage a broader set of tactics to deal with a wide range of community problems and concerns, there will be a need for sensible performance measurement that captures the value created by police along a number of dimensions such as reducing criminal victimization;

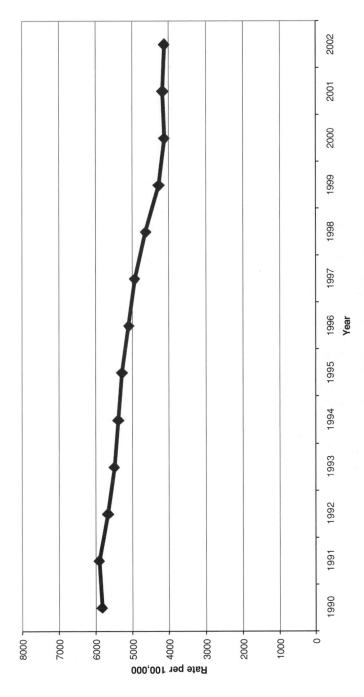

Figure 18.2 Index crime rates per 100,000 residents in the United States, 1990–2002
Source: Federal Bureau of Investigation, Uniform Crime Reports

calling offenders to account; reducing fear and enhancing personal security; guaranteeing safety in public spaces; using financial resources fairly, efficiently, and effectively; using force and authority fairly, efficiently, and effectively; and satisfying customer demands/ achieving legitimacy with those policed (Moore 2002). Appropriate measurement plays a vital role in transforming police departments into the learning laboratories they are now positioned to become in the future (Maguire 2004).

American police departments, however, will be challenged to maintain their current trajectory by the new set of homeland security demands created in the wake of the 9/11 tragedy. In many ways, this is a new crisis for police departments, as their goals will be further expanded by a new focus on preventing future terrorist attacks and dealing with potentially catastrophic events. On the one hand, this new set of demands, with its emphasis on collecting intelligence on terrorist networks, apprehending terror operatives, and protecting likely targets, may push policing back to a more professional model that is distant from the community. Indeed, there is real potential for a backward shift as federal financial support and attention has been directed toward enhancing local law enforcement's role in maintaining homeland security while, at the same time, funding for community crime prevention efforts has been drastically reduced. On the other hand, this crisis may create a new source for innovation as police departments will strive to continue their recent success in dealing with crime and community concerns. The US Department of Justice Community Oriented Policing Services office has already sponsored working group sessions and conferences on using community policing strategies to respond to the challenge of homeland security (US Department of Justice 2004).

Over the last two decades, the police industry has undergone radical changes in the ends and means of policing. This period of innovation has yielded a set of very promising strategies that can improve the ability of the police to prevent crime and enhance their relationships with the communities they serve. Police departments will be challenged to continue developing these new approaches while meeting the homeland security demands of the post-9/11 world. Nonetheless, we believe that the future is promising for police agencies, as they will continue to evolve into more effective and legitimate governmental institutions.

REFERENCES

Altshuler, A. and Behn, R. (1997). The dilemmas of innovation in American government. In A. Altshuler and R. Behn (eds.), *Innovations in American government: Challenges, opportunities, and dilemmas*. Washington, DC: Brookings Institution Press.

Blumstein, A. and Wallman, J. (2000). The recent rise and fall of American violence. In A. Blumstein and J. Wallman (eds.), *The crime drop in America*. New York: Cambridge University Press.

Braga, A. (2001). The effects of hot spots policing on crime. *Annals of the American Academy of Political and Social Science, 578,* 104–125.

(2002). *Problem-oriented policing and crime prevention.* Monsey, NY: Criminal Justice Press.

Braga, A., Kennedy, D., Waring, E., and Piehl, A. (2001). Problem-oriented policing, deterrence, and youth violence: An evaluation of Boston's operation ceasefire. *Journal of Research in Crime and Delinquency, 38,* 195–225.

Brown, L. and Wycoff, M. (1987). Policing Houston: Reducing fear and improving service. *Crime and Delinquency, 33,* 71–89.

Bureau of Justice Statistics. (2003). *Local police departments 2000.* Washington, DC: Bureau of Justice Statistics, US Department of Justice.

Capowich, G. and Roehl, J. (1994). Problem-oriented policing: Actions and effectiveness in San Diego. In D. Rosenbaum (ed.), *The Challenge of Community Policing: Testing the Promises*. Thousand Oaks, CA: Sage Publications.

Clarke, R.V. and Weisburd, D. (1994). Diffusion of crime control benefits: Observations on the reverse of displacement. *Crime prevention studies, 2,* 165–183.

Committee to Review Research on Police Policy and Practices. (2004). *Fairness and effectiveness in policing: The evidence.* Washington, DC: National Academies Press.

Eck, J. (2003). Police problems: The complexity of problem theory, research and evaluation. In J. Knutsson (ed.), *Problem-oriented policing: From innovation to mainstream.* Monsey, NY: Criminal Justice Press.

Eck, J. and Maguire, E. (2000). Have changes in policing reduced violent crime? An assessment of the evidence. In A. Blumstein and J. Wallman (eds.), *The crime drop in America.* New York: Cambridge University Press.

Eck, J. and Rosenbaum, D. (1994). The new police order: Effectiveness, equity, and efficiency in community policing. In D. Rosenbaum (ed.), *The challenge of community policing: Testing the promises.* Thousand Oaks, CA: Sage Publications.

Elmore, R. (1997). The paradox of innovation in education: Cycles of reform and the resilience of teaching. In A. Altshuler and R. Behn (eds.), *Innovations in American government: Challenges, opportunities, and dilemmas.* Washington, DC: Brookings Institution Press.

Goldstein, H. (1990). *Problem-oriented policing.* Philadelphia, PA: Temple University Press.

Maguire, E. (2004). *Police departments as learning laboratories: Ideas in American policing series.* Washington, DC: Police Foundation.

Moore, M. (2002). *Recognizing value in policing.* Washington, DC: Police Executive Research Forum.

Moore, M., Sparrow, M., and Spelman, W. (1997). Innovations in policing: From production lines to job shops. In A. Altshuler and R. Behn (eds.), *Innovations in American government: Challenges, opportunities, and dilemmas.* Washington, DC: Brookings Institution Press.

Pate, T. and Skogan, W. (1985). *Coordinated community policing: The Newark experience.* Technical Report. Washington, DC: Police Foundation.

Sadd, S. and Grinc, R. (1994). Innovative neighborhood oriented policing: An evaluation of community policing programs in eight cities. In D. Rosenbaum (ed.), *The challenge of community policing: Testing the promises*. Thousand Oaks, CA: Sage Publications.

Sherman, L.W. (1998). *Evidence-based policing: Ideas in American policing series*. Washington, DC: Police Foundation.

Sherman, L.W. and Eck, J. (2002). Policing for prevention. In L. Sherman, D. Farrington, B. Welsh, and D. MacKenzie (eds.), *Evidence-based crime prevention*. New York: Routledge.

Skogan, W. G. and Meares, T. (2004). Lawful policing. *Annals of the American Academy of Political and Social Science*, *593*, 66–83.

Skogan, W.G. and Steiner, L. (2004). *Community policing in Chicago, year ten*. Chicago: Illinois Criminal Justice Information Authority.

Sparrow, M., Moore, M., and Kennedy, D. (1990). *Beyond 911: A new era for policing*. New York: Basic Books.

Tyler, T. (1990). *Why people obey the law*. New Haven, CT: Yale University Press.
    (2001). Public trust and confidence in legal authorities: What do majority and minority group members want from legal authorities? *Behavioral Sciences and the Law*, *19*, 215–235.
    (2004). Enhancing police legitimacy. *Annals of the American Academy of Political and Social Science*, *593*, 84–99.

US Department of Justice. (2004). *Applying community policing principles post 9/11: Homeland security working session*. Washington, DC: US Department of Justice, Office of Community Oriented Policing Services.

Walker, S. (1992). *The police in America: An introduction*. (2nd ed.). New York: McGraw-Hill.

Weisburd, D. and Braga, A. (2003). Hot spots policing. In H. Kury and O. Fuchs (eds.), *Crime Prevention: New Approaches*. Mainz, Germany: Weisser Ring.

Weisburd, D. and Eck, J. (2004). What can police do to reduce crime, disorder, and fear? *Annals of the American Academy of Political and Social Science*, *593*, 42–65.

Weisburd, D., Mastrofski, S., McNally, A.M., Greenspan, R., and Willis, J. (2003). Reforming to preserve: Compstat and strategic problem solving in American policing. *Criminology and Public Policy*, *2*, 421–456.

Wellford, C., Pepper, J., and Petrie, C. (eds.). (2005). *Firearms and violence: A critical review*. Committee to Improve Research Information and Data on Firearms. Committee on Law and Justice, Division of Behavioral and Social Sciences and Education. Washington, DC: The National Academies Press.

Wycoff, M. and Skogan, W. (1986). Storefront police offices: The Houston field test. In D. Rosenbaum (ed.), *Community crime prevention: Does it work?* Thousand Oaks, CA: Sage Publications.

Index